TRANSNATIONAL SHIA POLITICS

SERIES IN COMPARATIVE POLITICS AND INTERNATIONAL STUDIES

This series consists of translations of noteworthy manuscripts and publications in the social sciences emanating from the foremost French researchers, from Sciences Po, Paris.

The focus of the series is the transformation of politics and society by transnational and domestic factors – globalisation, migration and the postbipolar balance of power on the one hand, and ethnicity and religion on the other. States are more permeable to external influence than ever before and this phenomenon is accelerating processes of social and political change the world over. In seeking to understand and interpret these transformations, this series gives priority to social trends from below as much as to the interventions of state and non-state actors.

LAURENCE LOUËR

Transnational Shia Politics

Religious and Political Networks in the Gulf

Columbia University Press
New York

*in association with the Centre d'Etudes et de
Recherches Internationales, Paris*

Columbia University Press
Publishers Since 1893
New York

Copyright © 2008, Laurence Louër
All rights reserved

Library of Congress Cataloging-in-Publication Data

Louër, Laurence.
 Transnational Shia politics : religious and political networks in the Gulf / Laurence Louër.
    p. cm.
 Includes bibliographical references and index.
 ISBN 978-0-231-70040-5 (cloth : alk. paper)
 1. Shi'ah—Political aspects. 2. Islam and state—Persian Gulf Region. I. Title.
 BP194.185.L68 2008
 320.5'57—dc22
                        2008028875

Columbia University Press books are printed on permanent and durable acid-free paper.
This book is printed on paper with recycled content.
Printed in India

c 10 9 8 7 6 5 4 3 2 1

References to Internet Web sites (URLs) were accurate at the time of writing. Neither
the author nor Columbia University Press is responsible for URLs that may have expired
or changed since the manuscript was prepared.

CONTENTS

ACKNOWLEDGEMENTS

This book is largely based on interviews with Shia Islamic activists as well as with other social and political actors. Many of them were collected in the three countries under scrutiny here, namely Kuwait, Bahrain and Saudi Arabia, at the occasion of fieldwork conducted between 2002 and 2007. While doing research about Shia political Islam in the Gulf monarchies has become much easier over the past years, the subject remains sensitive.

Hence, I am very much indebted to the many informants who accepted to share their knowledge with me, and without whom I would have been unable to achieve this book. Many of them not only accepted to speak about their life experience but also helped me to organize my sojourns and sometimes even hosted me in their homes. I wish here to thank them all, as well as to apologize for the possible divergence of opinions on some particular points.

Some of them have wished to remain anonymous. Among those who agreed to be explicitly mentioned, I would like to give a special thank to Ahmed Shehab, S. Mahmud al-Ghurayfi, Jasem Redha Husein, Dr Sami Naser al-Khalifa, S. Yusra al-Musawi, Sh. Rajab Ali Rajab, Mahdi al-Salman, Sh. 'Abd al-Shahid al-Sitrawi, Ja'far al-Shayeb.

I would also like to thank those who agreed to read the first version of the manuscript and whose comments helped me to improve it. The remaining inadequacies are of course not of their responsibility. Hence a special thank to Claire Beaugrand, Fatiha Dazi-Héni, Philippe Droz-Vincent, Jasem Redha Husein, Mahdi al-Salman and Ja'far al-Shayeb.

The Shia World

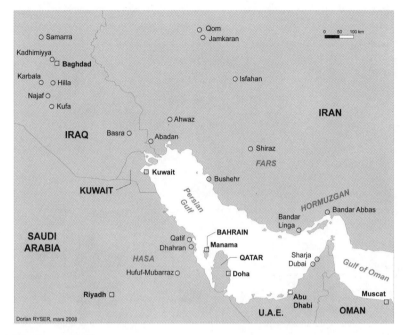

The Persian Gulf

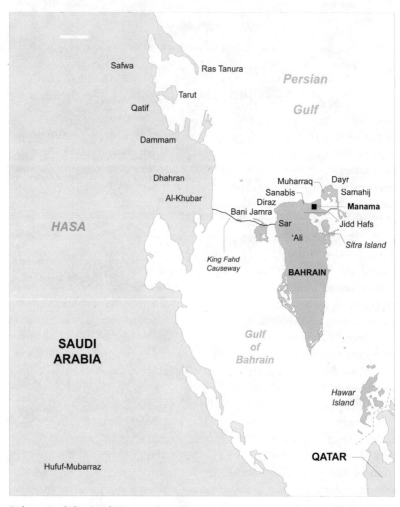

Bahrain and the Saudi Eastern Province

INTRODUCTION

When I began the empirical research that led to this book, my aim was to draw an overview of the evolution of the Shia Islamic movements in three Gulf states where Shia politics has been of central importance in the contemporary period: Bahrain, Saudi Arabia and Kuwait. What I rapidly realized however, was that I could not consider them without taking account of a much broader geographical environment than the Arabian side of the Gulf, a much larger geopolitical context than the domestic arenas and even a much older historical perspective than the mere contemporary period. Indeed, all the movements I had singled out as noteworthy were essentially emanations of Iraqi organizations. Moreover, these movements had been, and some of them still were, directly linked to religious dignitaries residing either in Iraq or Iran. What I quickly realized, was that the Shia Islamic movements of Saudi Arabia, Bahrain and Kuwait formed a field[1] together with their counterparts in Iraq and Iran. In this field, political identities often follow the factional quarrels structuring the clerical milieu of the Iraqi and Iranian shrine cities, so that important domestic political issues and social cleavages were often over-determined by distant ones.

On the one hand therefore, the Shia Islamic political field in the Gulf monarchies seemed profoundly heteronymous. On the other hand however, domestic stakes were far from being absent, sometimes taking the form of very parochial issues. Of course, each of the movements under scrutiny was the product of the particular socio-historical context in which it was inserted. But, much more than that, the Shia Islamic movements appeared, by some critical aspects of their political action, to be in a process of relative autonomization from the religious transnational chains they were born in a few decades before, taking more and more the form of rather traditional national – and even nationalist – political parties. While the tie

---

1   "Field" in the sense that Pierre Bourdieu gave to this word ("*champ*" in French), that is a relatively autonomous social space constituted around a specific social activity and, more specifically, on the conflictual relations between the actors who practice this activity.

to the transnational religious authority was still often asserted as a central element of political identity and legitimacy, the activists were at the same time very eager to affirm their independence, in political matters, from non-local influences. Assertion of national feelings and identities were even a conspicuous feature of the Shia Islamic political language.

Understanding this process of autonomization is the main aim of this book. As I shall show, this implies a twofold questioning. The first is about the concrete practice of politics in the transnational space. How do movements diffuse across national borders? What is the specificity of the Shia Islamic movements' transnationalization process? How do they articulate their transnational pledge with their domestic anchorage at various historical periods? The second part of the questioning concerns the relation between religion and politics. Indeed, since the peculiar relation of the Shia Islamic movements to the central religious institution is at the heart of their structuration into transnational networks, any inquiry about the transnational practices of these movements implies an examination of their relation to religious authority. What is the nature of the tie binding them to the *marja'iyya*, the supreme religious authority based in Iraq and Iran? How is this tie influencing their concrete political practices, in particular their internal decision-making process?

The Intertwining of Religious and Political Networks

In the Gulf, the Shia Islamic movements are by no means the only cases of political organizations that are basically the offspring of non-local groups. The region is even a particularly interesting area for scholars interested in the transnational diffusion of political movements since virtually all those active there, be they of secular or religious calling, are the result of the diffusion of mainly Egyptian, Iraqi or Syrian organizations. The secular movements like the communist party, the Ba'th party or the Nasserist groups spread to the Gulf through the massive displacement of people in search for job opportunities in the Gulf monarchies, where the discovery of oil in the 1930s and 1940s created a huge need for skilled and non-skilled manpower that the locals could not fill. The transnationalization of the religious movements operated in a different way. Exile was often the main incentive leading dozens of activists from the Muslim Brotherhood to relocate in the Gulf, in particular Saudi Arabia where they influenced the local religious tradition, marked by the teachings of Mohammed ibn 'Abd al-Wahhab, to create new types of religious ideologies and movements.[2]

---

2   As shown by Gilles Kepel, *The War for Muslim Minds: Islam and the West,*

Exile did play a central role in the transnationalization of the Shia Islamic movements born in the shrine cities of Iraq in the late 1950s and 1960s. Activists fled Iraq in the context of the massive repression of the religious seminaries in the 1970s, with many of them establishing themselves in the Gulf countries. Much before Iran became the sanctuary of Shia Islamic activism in the 1980s, Kuwait was the haven of those dreaming of establishing a state ruled by Islamic law in its Shia version. But the story of Shia transnational politics began much before and exile only gave a further impulse to a process that, although in different forms, had been under way for decades. Indeed, a distinct characteristic of the transnational diffusion of the Shia movements is the latter's ability to use the transnational networks established by the clerics of Najaf from the second half of the nineteenth century on, in their effort to impose their religious authority throughout the entire Shia world. Therefore, in contrast to the secular groups, but also to the Sunni groups that could not benefit from the existence of a centralized clerical authority, the Shia Islamic movements did not have to create a transnational infrastructure of circulation *ex nihilo* and followed in the footsteps of the religious networks.

In this, the case of the Shia Islamic movements offers a perfect empirical illustration to some key findings of the sociology of transnational social movements, and in particular the theoretical hypothesis drawn by Doug MacAdam, Dieter Rucht and Sydney Tarrow.[3] Challenging a widespread *doxa* that tends to misunderstand the effects of new means of communication like satellite TV channels and Internet in the transnational diffusion of ideas and organizations, they pointed out that relational diffusion – that is direct face-to-face ties – remains the most effective mode of diffusion, be it at a local or a transnational level. The implication is that in the transnational space, the physical travels of people remain the most effective way to spread ideas and movements, and eventually to co-ordinate political action cross-nationally. But, they further showed, the diffusion is even more rapid and lasting if it is channelled through previously established networks as well as long existing patterns of interaction. More than the secular movements studied by the sociologists of transnational movements, moreover

---

Cambridge Mass.: The Belknap Press of Harvard University Press, 2004, pp. 171-7.

3   Doug MacAdam and Dieter Rucht, "The Cross-National Diffusion of Movement Ideas", *Annals of the American Academy of Political and Social Sciences*, vol. 258, July 1993; Sydney Tarrow, *The New Transnational Activism*, Cambridge: Cambridge University Press, 2005; Sydney Tarrow and Donatella della Porta (eds), *Transnational Protest and Global Activism*, Lanham: Rowman & Littlefield Publishers, 2005.

mainly in the West, the religious political movements may exemplify this type of logic since their ability to spread cross-nationally is directly linked to their reliance on old transnational religious traditions.[4]

Their intimacy with the old clerical institution, being a central element of the Shia Islamic movements' power of diffusion, is an important source of concern among the rulers of the Middle East, who often question the loyalty of the Shia Islamic activists, and, by extension, the Shias overall. Shortly before I completed this book, I had an interesting conversation about this issue with a senior official of the United Arab Emirates. While we were discussing the general developments in the region, he expressed concern about the rising popularity of the Lebanese Hezbollah in the Middle East. I asked him why he was so concerned. Was it because Hezbollah was a tool of Iranian rising influence in the region? To this he answered that the problem with the Shias overall was that "they all believe in the *wilayat al-faqih*". He referred here to the doctrine systematized by S. Ruhollah Khomeini in 1970, according to which the clerics must rule the state. He went on by explaining that the Shias believed in a religious authority higher than that of their political rulers and, hence, could not be loyal to them. This was especially so since the Shia religious authorities were residing either in Iraq or, worse, in Iran. In brief, in his view, the Shias were intrinsically subservient to foreign powers.

Far from being isolated, this opinion reflects a widespread conception among the Sunni rulers of the Middle East. It was expressed publicly by King 'Abdallah II of Jordan and by Egyptian President Hosni Mubarak when commenting on the situation in Iraq since the regime change in 2003 and its possible spill-over effects.[5] Both pointed to the fact that Shias were unreliable citizens since they had an inherent leaning towards Iran, to date the sole state where Shiism is the state religion and the country where, in the city of Qom, lie the main religious seminaries and some of the most revered religious scholars worldwide. Implicit in this commonly held opinion is an assessment of the relation to religious authority of the Shias: that they would vow blind obedience to a handful of charismatic figures who are not

---

4   The ability of religious movements to use the clerical networks to diffuse world-wide has recently been underlined in the case of Christian NGOs. See the various contributions to the book of Bruno Duriez, François Mabille and Kathy Rousselet (eds), *Les ONG confessionnelles. Religions et action internationale*, Paris: L'Harmattan, 2007.

5   Robin Wright and Peter Baker, "Iraq, Jordan See Threat to Elections from Iran" *Washington Post*, 8 December 2004; Edward Wong, "Top Iraqis Assail Egyptian Leader's Talk of Civil War", *New York* Times, 9 April 2006.

content with issuing religious rulings but also have the regrettable habit of mixing in political affairs.

The Islamic revolution in Iran, with its images of mobs howling the name of Ruhollah Khomeini, greatly contributed to substantiate this representation in the contemporary period. As a matter of fact, if he did revolutionize Shia political thought, Ruhollah Khomeini was also in many respects the worthy representative of the traditional Shia clerical worldview for which religious authority had no frontier, and should certainly not be bounded by the borders of the nation-states. His attempt at exporting the Islamic revolution worldwide was the modern expression of this old conception. More recently, the emergence of S. 'Ali al-Sistani as a major power broker in post-2003 Iraq further added to the worries of some. Indeed, 'Ali al-Sistani did not only intervene in Iraqi political affairs. In the name of his religious magisterium, he felt entitled for example to become involved in Bahraini local affairs. In 2006, while the debate raged between partisans and opponents to the boycott of the legislative elections, he enjoined Bahrainis to go to the polls. In that case, it was just what Bahraini rulers wished, but it could have been otherwise.

Who Are the Shias?

The idea that the Shias are politically subservient to their religious authorities does not come from nowhere and there are actually many things in Shia doctrine that can appear somehow disturbing from the perspective of someone in charge of a state's government. Contrary to the Sunni conception, Shiism affirms the merging of religious and political authority. It was initially a legitimist movement born from a quarrel over the succession of Prophet Mohammed in the seventh century. Contrary to the Sunnis, the Shias believe that Mohammed explicitly designated his successors in the lineage of 'Ali, his cousin and the husband of his daughter Fatima, who became the fourth caliph of the history of Islam. For mainstream Shias who are the focus of this book, also called the Twelver or Imami Shias, 'Ali is considered as the first of a line of twelve Imams. For the Shias, they are not only the successors of Mohammed as the temporal leader of the *umma*, the community of the believers. They are also considered as religiously infallible because they have access to the hidden meaning of the Quranic message. The legitimacy of their temporal powers rests in their capacity to provide religious guidance to the Muslims.

If we except the caliphate of 'Ali (656-661), the Imams never exercised effective political power and were *de facto* reduced to religious leaders, who often died assassinated. The most famous of the twelve Shia Imams is probably the third one, Husein, who used military means to make his right to rule prevail and, in 680, died in dramatic circumstances near the city of Karbala in present-day southern Iraq. Betrayed by his allies who left him alone with a handful of his relatives in front of the caliph's army, he chose to die for a just cause rather than submit to an unjust and illegitimate ruler. His martyrdom is since celebrated every year on the tenth day of the month of Muharram – 'Ashura – by processions of mourners sometimes practising bloody rituals as well as by theatre plays recounting the details of the story. In the contemporary period, the 'Ashura rituals have become a powerful moment in the political mobilization orchestrated by the Shia Islamic movements, for which Imam Husein is the symbol of resistance to oppression.

In 874 however, the last Imam mysteriously disappeared in his palace of Samarra, in present-day northern Iraq. The Shias were hence left without a guide and their doctrine took its distinctive messianic character. The twelfth Imam is believed to have been occulted by God to men's eyes, and is hence known as the Hidden Imam or the Awaited Imam. The Shias believe he will return at the End of the Ages to restore truth and justice. While turning messianic, Shiism entered a new phase in which the religious scholars began to play an increasingly important role in the management of the Shias' daily affairs, claiming to be entitled to assume the powers of the Imam. The scope of their power as the Imams' delegates has since been an object of constant debate, the peak of which was attained when Ruhollah Khomeini formulated the famous doctrine of *wilayat al-faqih*, affirming that, in the absence of the Imam, the clerics should assume the latter's political power. A doctrinal upheaval, the *wilayat al-faqih* entailed a regional political turmoil when Ruhollah Khomeini became head of the Islamic Republic of Iran. The Gulf states were among the many targets of Shia Islamic groups claiming to act in the framework of religious authority exercised by the Iranian Supreme Guide.

The Shias in the Gulf

The Persian Gulf is a region of old Shia settlement. Today, 70 per cent of its population profess the Shia creed, of which the bulk resides on the Iranian shore. Since the census does not take into account membership of the various currents of Islam and includes the Shias in the broad category of "Muslims", it is impossible to give precise figures for the Shia populations on the Arabian side. One only has estimates coming from various sources that sometimes greatly differ in their assessment. Recently in 2006, a Riyadh-based think tank, the Saudi National Security Assessment Project (SNSAP), gave a general overview of the Shia and Sunni population in the Middle East.[6] Concerning the Gulf countries, the study mentioned that the Shias constituted 70 per cent of the Bahraini population, 7 per cent of the Saudi population and 35 per cent of the Kuwaiti population. It mentioned also that the Shias constituted a third of the population of the Saudi Eastern Province where lay the vast majority of the kingdom's oil reserves. The Saudi general figure included the Ismaili population of the region of Najran, whose religious and political dynamics differ widely from those of the Shia Twelvers. It contradicts the figures given by the Shias themselves, who often say that they represent as high as 20 per cent of the population. As for Bahrain, Bahraini Shias themselves agree with the 70 per cent figure. Among Kuwaiti Shias, the consensus is that Shias represent 25 per cent of the Kuwaiti national population.

The difficulty of assessing the real demographical weight of the Shias in Eastern Arabia is only one aspect of the scarcity of the sources on these populations. While several studies of Iranian, Iraqi and Lebanese Shiism have given us a fairly good picture of the historical, social and political situation in these countries, the Gulf monarchies have been neglected. In the aftermath of the Islamic revolution, some articles and chapters in collective books tried to fill the gap. Most of them focused on the destabilization brought about by the revolution. Some gave details about the domestic socio-economic reasons why Iranian developments had had such a huge impact. Few, however, were built on consistent fieldwork so that much false information circulated about the Shia Islamic movements, their ideology, their recruitment and, above all, their transnational connections. It is true that the field was then difficult to access, that most of the Shia activists had left for Iran where it would have been difficult to meet them and, if so, difficult to get from them accurate detailed information. The situation is largely different today where the Shia movements have become, if not all institutionalized political parties, at least legitimate components of the domestic political spaces in each of the three countries under scrutiny.

Understanding why and how this has happened is one of the major stakes of this book, since what has rendered the field accessible for direct observation is also a socio-political phenomenon that needs to be analyzed. Shia Islamic movements do not frighten the established regimes anymore or at least much less than in the 1980s. No longer clandestine cells of revo-

---

6   SNSAP, *A Shia Crescent and the Shia Revival: Myths and Realities*, Riyadh, 27 September 2006, Phase A Iran Project, Nawaf Obaid managing director.

lutionary avant-garde, they participate in elections and their activists gladly agree to discuss with those inquiring minds who take interest in them. Even in Saudi Arabia, the cradle of Sunni orthodoxy where the presence of a Shia minority was long a taboo, Shia repentant revolutionaries no longer hide and dare to complain overtly about their lot. They were also ready to reflect on their lives and choices. Engaged in their teens in political activism, many of them were still chief political actors at the time of writing. Hence their life stories offer useful material from which to draw the outline of the evolution, over almost four decades, of the Shia Islamic movements.

PART I

THE SHIAS AND THE STATE IN THE GULF

A widespread "spontaneous sociology"[1] of the Shias tends to portray them as oppressed people facing hostility from established powers as well as from their Sunni fellow citizens. The Shias themselves widely contributed to the spreading of this image by making victimization a central element of their religious identity, well embodied by the constant recalling of Imam Husein's martyrdom. The Shias' cruel repression by the Iraqi Ba'thist regime, the regular killing of Shias by Sunni Islamic radicals in Pakistan, the long socio-political marginalization of Lebanese Shias in front of the strong Maronite and Sunni communities, all added further to the conviction that Shias were in an intrinsic confrontational position in relation to the rulers, as well as the designated victims of religious intolerance in the Middle East.

In the Gulf, the example of Saudi Arabia has tended to obscure the debate on Shiism. It is true that, because of the Sunni orthodox rationale on which it is based, the Saudi regime has practiced widespread discrimination against its Shia population. From this sprung a well anchored *doxa* that, everywhere in the Gulf, Shias are second class citizens facing hostility from conservative rulers, generally reputed to display little tolerance for religious difference. But Saudi Arabia is the exception rather than the rule among the Gulf countries. First, although the Shias are most often not among the dominant segments of the Gulf's social fabric, they are not always in a conflictual relation with the rulers. Neither do they suffer systematic religious discrimination, and even less sectarian violence, which has been extremely rare not to say non-existent outside of Saudi Arabia. Second, the religious identity of the rulers is not a determining factor in accounting for the Shias' overall conditions. For example, the Al-Thani ruling dynasty of Qatar em-

---

1   To borrow Pierre Bourdieu's expression in *Le métier de sociologue*, Paris: Mouton, 1973 (second revised edition).

braced Wahhabi tenets, which generally pervade Qatari society. However, Qatari Shias were never among the rulers' opponents, they have participated in government institutions and have enjoyed religious freedom. On the other hand, the Al-Khalifa ruling family of Bahrain, despite its Sunni religious identity, has never legitimized its right to rule over the Shia majority by any kind of religious rationale. Bahraini Shias are nonetheless excluded from sensitive public positions and have engaged in regular violent confrontations with their rulers.

As shown by these examples, the Shias' situation in the Gulf is heterogeneous from one country to another and even from one group to another inside a single state. In order to understand why, one needs to shift from an explanation in terms of religious antagonism to present the main threads of a historical sociology of the Shia populations in Eastern Arabia. This will enable us to distinguish two patterns of relation to the state. They are apparent when one compares the case of Bahrain and Saudi Arabia on the one hand, and Kuwait on the other hand. In the first case, one is faced with old Shia societies whose identity has largely been built on a claim of prior settlement on the territory they inhabit. Hence for Bahraini and Saudi Shias, the modern states were imposed by alien Sunni conquerors. The memory of pre-invasion times, magnified by the work of activist intellectuals, has been the source of a fundamentally hostile vision of the established dynastic rules. The case of Kuwait offers a totally different picture. There the Shias, a relatively recent community made up of a collection of loosely integrated diasporas, display a sincere commitment to the state and its actual rulers. They feel part of the state's history and have a vested interest in its survival. Far from being isolated – although this will not be developed in detail in this book – what I would call the "Kuwaiti model" is valid to analyze the Shias' situation in Qatar, the United Arab Emirates and Oman, which are only variants of a single mode of participation in the state formation process.

1

IMPOSED STATES

A young Bahraini Shia I interviewed at the beginning of my fieldwork formulated the position of his co-religionists in the Bahraini social fabric in illuminating words, showing that the roots of his co-religionists' conflictual relations with their rulers had little to do with sectarian antagonism: "Here in Bahrain, discrimination is not against the Shias: it is against the Baharna. There is a difference between Shias and Baharna... 'Abd al-Nabi al-'Akri for example, he is Bahrani but he is not Shia: he is communist. Dr 'Abd al-Hadi Khalaf[1], he is communist, but he is also Bahrani. There are religious and ideological divisions between Sunnis and Shias, Christians, Jews, communists... And then you have divides according to the origin (*'irq*): Huwala,[2] 'Ajam,[3] Baharna, Sunni Arab Bedouins or Sunni Huwala. For the Baharna, it's different than for the others: they are the oppressed ones. Really. It's a matter of fact. But it has nothing to do with the fact that they are Shias. It's because they are Baharna. There is a difference between the two."[4]

In contemporary Bahrain, the name "Bahrani" (pl. Baharna) designates the Arab Shias who consider themselves as the original inhabitants of the country by contrast with those who came later on, in particular the Sunni Arab Bedouin from Central Arabia who have ruled the country since the

---

1   'Abd al-Nabi al-'Akri and 'Abd al-Hadi Khalaf are two well known leftist opponents to the Bahraini regime.

2   The Huwala (sing. Huli), whose name literally means "those who cross, who come and go", are Sunnis who claim an old Arab tribal descent. They settled on the Iranian side of the Gulf at various moments in time, and came back to the Arabian shore in the late 19th and early 20th century.

3   The 'Ajam (sing. 'Ijmi) are the Shias of Iranian descent who, for the most part, came to the Arabian shore of the Gulf in the late 19th and early 20th century.

4   Personal interview, Bahrain, August 2002.

eighteenth century and are also referred to as the "'Arab". The name "Bahrani" is also used by Saudi Shias, in particular some activist intellectuals close to the Shia Islamic movements, to designate the Shias living in the Eastern Province of the kingdom. In both Bahrain and Saudi Arabia, Shias like to point out that, under the name of Ancient Bahrain (*al-Bahrain al-qadim*) or Greater Bahrain (*al-Bahrain al-kubra*), present-day Bahrain and the Eastern Province of Saudi Arabia used to be one. At the time of writing, this common history was still felt in the fact that Arab Shias in Bahrain and their Saudi coreligionists still spoke the same form of colloquial Arabic, clearly distinct from that spoken by the Sunnis in both countries. This difference relates not to a different religious creed but to a different place of origin. Sunnis speak a typically Bedouin dialect which is to be found among other Sunni populations of the Gulf, while the Arab Shias speak a form common to other sedentary populations of the Arabian peninsula, namely the agriculturalists of Oman and Southern Yemen.[5]

The issues at stake behind these basic facts of the Bahraini and Saudi social fabric go far beyond mere ethnographic description. Indeed, the Shias' conflictual relation to the state in Bahrain and Saudi Arabia has deep roots in the history of Ancient Bahrain and its contemporary usages by Shia Islamic movements.

ANCIENT BAHRAIN: OUTLINES OF A HISTORY

The scarcity of accurate sources on the history of Ancient Bahrain renders very difficult the task of any researcher aiming to distinguish between history itself and the way people have integrated it in their representation of self and use it to substantiate political positions. This is all the more difficult since some who did write as historians are also political activists in whose works ideological commitments rise to the surface.[6] Moreover, contradictory accounts of history are made by both the Shias and their rulers.[7] The following, therefore, does not aim to recount the details of a history on which we still lack a comprehensive academic work, but to give the main

---

5   Clive Holes, *Dialect, Culture and Society in Eastern Arabia, vol. 1 Glossary*, Leiden: Brill, 2001, p. XXII.

6   Hamza al-Hasan, *The Shias in the Arab Kingdom of Saudi Arabia. Vol. I: The Turkish Period 1871-1913*, and *Vol. II: The Saudi Period 1913-1991* (in Arabic), Mu'assasat al-Baqi' li Ihya al-Turath, 1993; Fouad Ibrahim, *The Shi'is of Saudi Arabia*, London: Saqi Books, 2006. Both authors are activists of the Saudi Shia Islamic opposition.

7   Yitzhak Nakash, *Reaching for Power. The Shi'a in the Modern Arab World*, Princeton, New Jersey: Princeton University Press, 2006, p. 16.

historical threads of Shia history in Ancient Bahrain that can shed light on the Shias' relation with the Bahraini and Saudi states.

The Roots of Shiism in Ancient Bahrain

In the old historical accounts, the name Bahrain designates the Gulf coast comprised between Basra in present-day south Iraq and the peninsula of Qatar.[8] The heart of this territory was the archipelago of modern Bahrain together with the oases of Qatif and Hasa, today located in the Eastern province of Saudi Arabia and which constitute the main area of Shia settlement in the kingdom.[9] There are other places of Twelver Shia settlement in Saudi Arabia, mainly in the city of Medina in the Hijaz, which hosts the tombs of four Imams, including that of Imam Ja'far al-Sadiq who codified the Shia religious law – which, for this reason, is named the *"ja'fari* code".[10] Contrary to a widespread idea that tends to see the Shia presence there as the result of Iranian influence, its populations embraced Shiism from the beginning of the quarrel over Mohammed's succession when several Eastern Arabian tribes, among whom the 'Abd al-Qays of which the Baharna claim descent, espoused 'Ali's cause. This explains why the region soon became a refuge for various opponents to the caliphs justifying their revolt by resorting to the legitimist discourse of 'Ali's partisans.[11] In the second half of the ninth century, Ancient Bahrain was hit by the Zanj revolt, an insurgency by black slaves working in particularly harsh conditions in the Tigris-Euphrates delta around Basra and whose charismatic chief, 'Ali bin Mohammed, claimed descent from 'Ali and his grandson Zayd ibn 'Ali,

---

8   In his history of the Carmathian movement, May Mohammed Al-Khalifa made a detailed account of the various usages of the name "Bahrain" by historians. See May Mohammed Al-Khalifa, *From the Surroundings of Kufa to Bahrain. The Carmathians, from an Idea to a State* (in Arabic), Beirut, Al-Mu'assasa al-'Arabiyya lil-Dirasat wal-Nashr, 1999, pp. 226-38.

9   The Eastern Province is often referred to as "Hasa" but this is a rather recent usage. At the time of writing, the Shias of the region themselves made a clear distinction between Qatif and Hasa. As we shall see, the two oases bear fairly different social characteristics. On the various names used to designate the area and their evolution, *cf.* F. S. Vidal, *The Oasis of al-Hasa*, Dhahran: Aramco, 1955, pp. 6-11.

10   The Shias of Medina are even less known than the Shias of the Eastern Province. On the history of the Shia presence in the city, see Werner Ende, "The Nakhawila, a Shiite Community in Medina. Past and Present", *Die Welt des Islams*, vol. 37, n° 3, 1997. See also al-Hasan, Vol. I (1993), p. 65.

11   Yousef Ja'far Sa'ada, *The Political Force in the Hasa Fortress and its Role in the Events of the Gulf* (in Arabic), Kuwait: Matabi' al-Majmu'a al-Duwaliyya, 1997, pp. 59-60.

the eponym of the Zaydi Shias.[12] Only a few years after the final quelling of the Zanj in 883, the Carmathians succeeded in establishing a state in Ancient Bahrain, the capital of which was based in Hasa. This polity, which – according to the tradition – was based on an egalitarian social system and developed a rich intellectual life centred on the exegesis of the Ismaili doctrine, was destroyed around 1075.[13] The Carmathians were a radical movement derived from Ismailism, itself a movement born from a succession quarrel after the death of the sixth Imam Ja'far al-Sadiq in 765: while the bulk recognized Musa al-Kazem as his successor, the Imailis considered the legitimate Imam as being Mohammed bin Isma'il, the son of Ja'far al-Sadiq's deceased son.

According to Juan Cole, Ancient Bahrain remained an Ismaili stronghold long after the fall of the Carmathian state, up to the fifteenth century.[14] But this did not prevent the emergence of a community of religious scholars professing Twelver Shiism, who lived in symbiosis with the Ismaili powers. In the course of the thirteenth century, Ancient Bahrain even became an important Shia learning centre under the leadership of several Twelver scholars of important stature. In the fourteenth century, the Twelver scholars established good relations with the Banu Jarwan, who ruled Ancient Bahrain up to the next century and granted them important functions as head of justice and of market police. This first experience of institutionalization of religious authority in relation to a state apparatus is important to bear in mind if one wishes to understand the specificity of Bahraini and Saudi Shiism today. Contrary to the other states of the Arabian coast of the Gulf, the two countries witnessed the early formation of a Shia clerical class so that beyond mere folk religion, Shiism was embodied in religious and judicial institutions as well as in a vivid community of learning which has managed to survive the vicissitudes of history to this day.

In the mid-fifteenth century, Ancient Bahrain's Ismaili rulers were overthrown by Sunni tribes who put an end to the privileges of the Shia scholars, pushing some of them to expatriate, in particular to the Mesopo-

---

12   On the Zanj revolt, see Alexandre Popovic, *La révolte des esclaves en Iraq au IIIème/IXème siècle*, Paris: Geuthner, 1976 (translated into English by Léon King, *The Revolt of the African Slaves in Iraq in the 3rd/9th Century*, Princeton, New Jersey: Markus Wiener Publishers, 1999).

13   On the Carmathians in Bahrain, see Al-Khalifa (1999), pp. 239-322 ; Michael Johan de Goeje, *Mémoire sur les Carmathes du Bahrain et les Fatimides*, Onasbrück: Biblio Verlag, 1978.

14   Juan R. I. Cole, *Sacred Space and Holy War. The Politics, Culture and History of Shia Islam*, London: I. B. Tauris, 2002, chapter 3 "Rival Empires of Trade and Shi'ism in Eastern Arabia", pp. 32-5; Nakash, (2006), p. 22.

tamian shrine cities.[15] In 1521, the arrival of the Portuguese in the Gulf further weakened the Shias by cutting the territorial continuity of Ancient Bahrain: Awal archipelago (present day Bahrain) fell under the control of the Portuguese and their Sunni allies from Hormuz and south Iran, while mainland Qatif and Hasa (present day Eastern Province of Saudi Arabia) voluntarily surrendered to Ottoman rule (around 1550) to escape Portuguese domination.[16] The partition was confirmed in the seventeenth century when the islands became an Iranian dominion (1602). At the time, Shiism had already been the state religion in Iran since 1501 and the accession to power of the Safavid dynasty. This explains why Bahrain under Iranian rule developed again as an important Shia learning centre. In the meantime, the inland Shias, subjected to Sunni Ottoman rule, were marginalized, producing few scholars of calibre who for the most part chose to leave for Awal or directly to Iran. The difficult conditions facing the mainland Shias were largely due to Qatif and Hasa's situation as a frontier area between the Ottoman and the Persian empires, whose rivalry regularly took a religious undertone. After the transformation of Shiism into Iran's state religion, the Ottomans indeed reacted by accentuating their Sunni credentials and stressing their status as the upholders of Sunni orthodoxy combating the Safavid Shia heresy.[17] As Shiism became identified with the Iranian state, the Shias of the neighbouring countries were no longer only considered as religious deviants. They were also suspected of being the Trojan horse of Iranian interests.

The Shiaization of Iran had other important implications for the Shias of Bahrain, now a province of the Iranian Empire. Under the Safavid dynasty, Shia scholars developed into a hierocracy, a corps of religious professionals legitimizing the power of the sovereign.[18] In Bahrain therefore, the *'ulama* who had retreated during the period of Sunni government regained their status as a powerful body. Not only did they grow in number, but

15   *Ibid.*, pp. 36-7.

16   On the Portuguese penetration in the Gulf, see Fawziyya al-Jib, *The Portuguese Power in Bahrain (1521-1602)* (in Arabic), Beirut: Al-Mu'assasa al-'Arabiyya lil-Dirasat wal-Nashr, 2003, pp. 143-51. On the Ottomans in Qatif and Hasa, see Jon Mandaville, "The Ottoman Province of al-Hasa in the Sixteenth and Seventeenth Centuries", *Journal of the American Oriental Society*, vol. 90, n° 3, 1970, p. 488; al-Hassan Vol. I (1993), p. 18.

17   Adel Allouche, *The Origins and Development of the Ottoman-Safavid Conflict (906-962/1500-1555)*, Berlin: Klaus Schwarz, 1983.

18   Said Amir Arjomand, *The Shadow of God and the Hidden Imam. Religion, Political Order, and Societal Change in Shi'ite Iran from the Beginning to 1890*, Chicago: The University of Chicago Press, 1984, pp.122-59.

they exercised important functions in the new administration, thus tending more and more to constitute a fully-fledged clergy, a body of religious professionals distinct from the mere literati notables.[19] A lot of Bahrani scholars went to Iran, where they trained with some of the most prestigious scholars and also exercised important functions in the administration. They seem to have been particularly influential in south Iran, in the vicinity of Shiraz. By the beginning of the eighteenth century, scholars from Bahrain even became predominant among the major scholars in Iran.[20] Apart from creating new institutions like the congressional Friday prayer and the office of chief of the judiciary (Sheikh al-Islam), the Safavid influence also led to important doctrinal changes among the Bahrani Shia population. According to Juan Cole's demonstration, it is during the Safavid period that the bulk of the Baharna shifted from Ismailism to Twelver Shiism, to the point that today, there are no more Ismailis, neither in Bahrain nor in the Eastern Province of Saudi Arabia.[21]

While Bahrain regained its status as an important Shia learning centre under Safavid rule, the Shias of Qatif and Hasa faced harsher conditions under an intermittent Ottoman rule interrupted by periods of local Sunni domination. Despite the Ottoman-Safavid rivalry, the Shias do not seem to have been systematically persecuted by the Ottomans, although some documents show that the latter were concerned with the danger of Safavid agents acting through the local Shia population and taking the occasion of the pilgrimage to Mecca to infiltrate the Arabian Peninsula. For these reasons, Shia pilgrims were regularly harassed on their way to the holy city.[22] But more disturbing for the daily life of local Shias were the recurrent tribal revolts against Ottoman rule, which were keeping the region in a state of instability unfavourable to the development of learning activities. Indeed, having prevented the Portuguese from establishing themselves in Ancient Bahrain's mainland, the Ottomans never really succeeded in securing full control over the tribesmen of Eastern Arabia. In particular, they had to face revolts from the Bani Khaled who where ruling before their arrival and succeeded in regaining full control of a great part of the territory of Ancient Bahrain by the end of the seventeenth century (1670).[23]

---

19   Cole (2002), p. 45.

20   Arjomand (1984), p. 129.

21   In Saudi Arabia, Ismailis live in the vicinity of Najran close to the border with Yemen.

22   Mandaville (1970), p. 498.

23   *Ibid.*, p. 501.

The situation of the Shias under the Bani Khaled dominion is little documented. Several historians share the view that although initially professing the Sunni creed, many Bani Khalid clans embraced Shiism.[24] As in the case of the tribes of south Iraq in the nineteenth century,[25] there might have been a link between the sedentarization process and conversion to Shiism, which was perceived as the creed of the sedentary society. This is the hypothesis defended by Hamza al-Hasan.[26] The majority of the Bani Khaled nonetheless remained Sunni, especially the ruling branches of the tribe, so that one can also surmise that maintaining their religious specificity was also a way for them to assert their power through solidifying the symbolic boundary with the society they ruled. Be that as it may, the Bani Khaled never undertook to suppress Shiism and it is during their rule that Hasa hosted one of its most important religious thinkers: Sh. Ahmed al-Ahsa'i (1753-1826). The latter gave birth to a mystic Shia current which came to be known as Sheikhism after his death. Centred on the idea that religious authority should include elements of both legal reasoning and mystical illumination, his teachings spread to Iran where Ahmed al-Ahsa'i resided during the last twenty years of his life.[27]

The Conquests

A salient characteristic of the history of the Arabian Peninsula is the periodic migration of Bedouin tribes from the central areas to the more hospitable coastal regions. While many stayed on the Arabian shores of the Gulf, others – the Huwala – crossed the sea up to Iran where they established little sheikhdoms virtually independent from the central state which lacked a fleet to control the Gulf.[28] During the eighteenth century, the Safavids were severely weakened in Iran and were finally overthrown in 1722 by Sunni Afghan tribes who plunged the country into chaos. As no strong central power succeeded in imposing itself in the Gulf, the coastal sheikh-

---

24   Al-Hasan Vol. I (1993), p. 18; Sa'ada (1997), pp. 234-5.

25   Yitzhak Nakash, *The Shi'is of Iraq*, Princeton, New Jersey: Princeton University Press, 2003 (second paperback edition, first hardcover edition in 1994), pp. 32-42.

26   Al-Hasan Vol. I (1993), p. 27.

27   Juan R. I. Cole, "Shaykh Ahmad al-Ahsa'i on the Sources of Religious Authority", in Linda S. Walbridge (ed.), *The Most Learned of the Shi'a. The Institution of the Marja' Taqlid*, Oxford: Oxford University Press, 2001, pp. 82-93.

28   Ahmad Mustafa Abu Hakima, *History of Eastern Arabia 1750-1800. The Rise and Development of Bahrain and Kuwait*, Beirut: Khayats, 1965, pp. 34-5, pp. 10-11.

doms of Iran and Arabia took the upper hand in the area. Mutual raids were frequent and it is in the context of this quasi-permanent warfare that, in the mid-eighteenth century, Bahrain fell under the control of a Huwala clan – the al-Madhkur – based in Bushehr on the Iranian coast. The latter were formally vassals of the Iranian ruler to whom they paid tribute, but had actually considerable room for manoeuvre vis-à-vis the central state.[29]

The Al-Khalifa, the current rulers of Bahrain, were a section of the Bani 'Utub tribe from Najd in central Arabia. Explanation for their migration to Bahrain varies, with historians explaining that they were forced out of Najd following a period of severe drought[30] and others reckoning that they were caught in a tribal conflict.[31] Be that as it may, several clans of the Bani 'Utub migrated to the Gulf in the course of the seventeenth century where they founded several chieftaincies, the economy of which was centred on long distance trade and pearling. The bulk of the Bani 'Utub arrived in Kuwait in the first half of the eighteenth century, maybe after a short stay in the Peninsula of Qatar. One of their branches, the Al-Sabah, still rules Kuwait today. Following yet unclear circumstances, one of the three main clans of the Bani 'Utub, the Al-Khalifa, left Kuwait for Zubara (1766) in present day Qatar, where they founded a prosperous port which attracted much of the regional sea trade. Rapidly growing and attracting many newcomers from Kuwait and Najd, the new sheikhdom soon coveted the Bahraini islands located only a few miles north and at that time still some of the wealthiest territories of the Arabian coast with their dynamic pearl fisheries and extensive palm groves. The Al-Khalifa attacked and conquered Bahrain in 1783.[32] Despite attempts by the Iranians to regain Bahrain via the Huwala tribes, the conquest by the Al-Khalifa marked the definitive end of formal Iranian rule over Bahrain.

For the Shias of Bahrain, the Al-Khalifa conquest aroused dramatic changes that are still felt today. On the religious level, it entailed the virtual disappearance of the Usuli school of thought as the bulk of the Bahrani clerical establishment shifted to the Akhbari current.[33] Usuli scholars dominated the Safavid administration. Their central idea was that the *mujtahid* had the ability and the legitimacy to elaborate Islamic law during the period

---

29   Ahmad Mustafa Abu Hakima, *The Modern History of Kuwait 1750-1965*, London: Luzac and Company Limited, 1983, p. 20.

30   Abu Hakima (1965), p. 50.

31   Jacqueline S. Ismael, *Kuwait. Social Change in Historical Perspective*, New York: Syracuse University Press, 1982, p. 20.

32   Abu Hakima (1965), pp. 109-16.

33   Cole (2002), pp. 53-6.

of Occultation of the Imam by using four sources: the Quran, the oral reports from the Prophet and the Imams (*akhbar*), the deductive reasoning (*'aql*) and the consensus (*ijma'*) of the most learned of the *'ulama*. Akhbari scholars, on the contrary, considered that deductive reasoning and consensus were a source of distortion of the genuine Islamic doctrine as transmitted by the Imams and that the Quran and the reports were sufficient sources to elaborate Islamic law.[34] While the Usuli school dominated Iran under the Safavids, Akhbari scholars took the upper hand after the fall of the dynasty. Baharna played a leading role in this renewal and the most famous of the eighteenth century Akhbari scholars was Sh. Yusuf al-Bahrani (1695-1772), a native from Diraz in Bahrain who settled in Iran and then Karbala to escape the chaos created by the fall of the Safavid state. The dominance of Akhbarism, however, short-lived and by the end of the eighteenth century, Usulism had succeeded in re-imposing its views to the point that Akhbarism soon became a residual reality in the Shia world. Bahrain is one of the few places, if not the only one, where Akhbarism has maintained a strong presence to this day, becoming the distinctive attribute of Bahrani Shiism. This is also true with regards to Saudi Arabia, where Akhbarism was only residual at the time of writing. How do we explain that?

People often consider that Akhbarism is by nature a more quietist doctrine than Usulism. Indeed, because they do not think that the clerics can appropriate the prerogatives of the Imams, Akhbari scholars tend to be more compromising towards the established orders. In the absence of the Imam, no ruler can be legitimate but, conversely, none is more illegitimate than another provided that the ruler enforces the minimum Islamic ethic. One can venture that at times of uncertainty under hostile Sunni rule, Akhbarism must therefore have appeared as a much more suitable credo than Usulism for Baharna. This could also have been because Usulism was deeply associated with Safavid Iran so that its proponents could be easily suspected of being a vector of Iranian influence. Finally, in a context where the Bahrani clerics strove to preserve Shia traditions in the face of

34   On the Akhbari-Usuli debate, see Juan R. I. Cole, "Shi'i Clerics in Iraq and Iran, 1722-1780: The Akhbari-Usuli Conflict Reconsidered", *Iranian Studies*, vol. 18, n° 1, winter 1985, pp. 3-34; Andrew J. Newman, "The Nature of the Akhbari-Usuli Conflict in Late Safawid Iran, Part 1: 'Abdallah al-Samahiji's *'Munyat al-Mumarisin'*", *Bulletin of the School of Oriental and African Studies*, vol. 55, n° 1, 1992 and "The Nature of the Akhbari-Usuli Conflict in Late Safawid Iran, Part 2: The Conflict Reassessed", *Bulletin of the School of Oriental and African Studies*, vol. 55, n° 2, 1992; Etan Kohlberg, "Aspects of Akhbari Thought in the Seventeenth and Eighteenth Centuries", in Nehemia Levtzion and John O. Voll (eds), *Eighteenth Century Renewal and Reform in Islam*, Syracuse, New York: Syracuse University Press, 1987.

Sunni encroachment, Akhbarism could also have been a way to maintain the boundary with the Sunni invaders. Indeed, an important aspect of Akhbari thought as compared with Usulism is the tendency to refuse and even abhor any assimilation of Sunni scholarship into Shia legal thought. Speculative reasoning, in particular, was considered as an importation from the Sunni school of law.[35]

Having imposed *manu militari* on the Bahrani populations, the Al-Khalifa progressively established a new form of rulership over Bahrain, which Fuad Khuri has characterized as a "feudal estate system".[36] The territory was divided into several fiefdoms belonging to members of the Al-Khalifa family or one of the Sunni tribes who had participated in the conquest. Some Bahrani families who had sworn allegiance to the new rulers were able to retain their properties but this was in return for a heavy land tax. Thanks to the presence of fresh water springs, agriculture was the main occupation of the Bahrani population together with fishery and pearling. The majority of cultivation consisted in the exploitation of palm trees serving for a wide range of purposes: dates and palm heart were a basic element of the Bahrani diet, palm branches were used to build houses and furniture. Upon the arrival of the Al-Khalifa, the Baharna continued to live from palm cultivation but as the conquerors had appropriated most of the arable lands, the Baharna had to rent their plots from them under iniquitous terms. The rent consisted of a fixed number of boxes of dates calculated on the basis of the expected harvest for a particular palm grove. As the climatic conditions were greatly variable, the renter often failed to deliver the agreed amount and had no other choice than to become indebted in order to retain his garden.[37]

For their part, the Sunnis – the Bedouin conquerors – largely behaved as absentee lords and did not mix with the Bahrani population. They were rarely living on the land they owned and acted through Bahrani local intermediaries who were actually the true managers of the estates, being in charge of the collection of rents and taxes. While some Baharna were able to continue to engage in the pearl trade, this activity, which was by far the

---

35   Devin Stewart, "The Genesis of the Akhbari Revival", in Michel Mazzaoui (ed.), *Safavid Iran and Her Neighbors*, Salt Lake City: The University of Utah Press, 2003, p. 169.

36   Fuad I. Khuri, *Tribe and State in Bahrain. The Transformation of Social and Political Authority in an Arab State*, Chicago: The University of Chicago Press, 1980, p. 35.

37   Mohammed Ghanem Rumaihi, *Bahrain. Social and Political Change since the First World War*, London: Bowker, 1976, p. 51.

most fruitful, tended to be monopolized by the Sunnis. In contrast to the Baharna who were subjected to tight control in their cultivation activities, the pearling tribes enjoyed extensive freedom of action in the management of their pearling enterprises. As underlined by Fuad Khuri, this choice was not made out of sectarian discrimination but out of a pure economic calculus. Indeed, land tenure was only profitable for the Al-Khalifa as long as the cultivators were tied to them by taxes and rental fees. On the other hand, the pearling tribes, if not granted maximum freedom of organization, would have left for other pearling centres like Qatar or Dubai, which would have been damaging for the Al-Khalifa as they would lack a source of tax revenue. Besides the tax on arable lands, the ruling dynasty extracted its revenues from taxes on import and export, of which gems constituted the bulk.[38]

In Qatif and Hasa, the Bani Khalid dominions were also brought to an end by powers coming from Central Arabia, namely the Al-Sa'ud and their Wahhabi allies. At that time still no more than one of the many small local powers of Arabia, the Al-Sa'ud had established an emirate in Dar'iyya. In 1744, they agreed to host the Islamic Sunni reformer Mohammed bin 'Abd al-Wahhab (1703-1792) and to become the armed champions of his teachings. These mainly consisted in an appeal for the purification of Islam by a return to strict monotheism. The alliance between the Al-Sa'ud and the followers of Mohammed 'Abd al-Wahhab marked the transformation of the Dar'iyya emirate into a fully-fledged state and Wahhabism into an "ideology of conquest".[39] The Saudi emirate expanded its territory by unifying Central Arabia and conquering parts of Eastern Arabia (1792), Hijaz and even Bahrain which they controlled for a few years (1810-11). The smaller coastal emirates succeeded in avoiding absorption by the Saudi entity by establishing protectorate agreements with the British.

Either in the East or in the Hijaz, the Shias were one of the privileged targets of Wahhabi zeal. In the name of strict monotheism, the latter condemned some Shia rituals like the visitation of the tombs of the Imams and other revered members of the Prophet's family. Stigmatized as "worshippers of tombs", Shias were considered as closer to polytheists than Muslims. Their whole creed was viewed as misleading and the Shias were commonly referred to as "Rawafidh", the ones who refuse the legitimacy of the Sunni caliphs. Chroniclers report that Wahhabis destroyed Shia holy places in

---

38   *Ibid.*, p. 67.

39   Ibrahim (2006), p. 18.

the Eastern region and sent preachers to put the Shias back on the straight and narrow.[40]

The first period of Saudi-Wahhabi rule in Qatif and Hasa ended with the campaign of Mohammed Ali, the semi-independent Ottoman ruler of Egypt, who destroyed the first Saudi state in 1818. Although the Shias of Qatif and Hasa were temporally relieved from Wahhabi zealots, they suffered from the general instability of the period which was characterized by atomization and tribal warfare. In any case, the Al-Sa'ud succeeded in restoring their state only a few years later (1843) and re-established themselves on the shores of the Gulf. They were again defeated by another semi-independent Ottoman ruler, Midhat Pasha, who was then governor of Baghdad and brought back Ottoman rule in 1871. But the Al-Sa'ud succeeded once again in returning to power and 'Abd al-'Aziz ibn Sa'ud re-captured the region in 1913. It has since become an integral part of the Arab Kingdom of Saudi Arabia officially created in 1932 by the unification of Najd, Hijaz, Qatif-Hasa and Asir.[41] While some Shia notables of Qatif, arguing the suffering under previous Wahhabi rules, favoured resistance to Al-Sa'ud's army, they proved incapable of convincing the majority of the population who sided with those stressing that, after all, the Al-Sa'ud would bring security by putting an end to Bedouin raids. The notables of both Qatif and Hasa therefore surrendered peacefully to Ibn Sa'ud, who agreed to let the Shias continue to practice their faith freely.[42] However, he imposed heavy taxes on them and was eventually unable to prevent the Wahhabi zealots from implementing a repressive religious policy. The Ikhwan, a corps of Bedouin warriors of the faith which had been constituted as a result of Ibn Sa'ud's effort to pacify the nomads, forced the conversion of Shias to "true Islam" and destroyed many of their holy places, including the tombs of the Imams in the Baqi' cemetery in Medina (1925). Only by 1930, when Ibn Sa'ud suppressed the Ikhwan, were the Shias granted autonomy in the management of their religious affairs, although they have been seriously constrained in several matters like the construction of mosques and *huseini-*

---

40   Alexei Vassiliev, *The History of Saudi Arabia*, London: Saqi Books, 2000, p. 89.

41   For the details of the period between 1818 and 1913 in Hasa, see Mohammed 'Urabi Nakhleh, *The Political History of al-Hasa (1818-1913)* (in Arabic), Kuwait: Dhat al Salasil, 1980.

42   Guido Steinberg, "The Shiites in the Eastern Province of Saudi Arabia (al-Ahsa), 1913-1953", in Rainer Bruner and Werner Ende (eds), *The Twelver Shia in Modern Times. Religious Culture and Political History*, Köln: Brill, 2001, p. 245.

yya, the practices of 'Ashura and other rituals, the teaching of their creed, and the management of their personal status law.

FROM HISTORY TO MYTH

A Bahrani Nativism

In present day Bahrain and Saudi Arabia, popular consciousness aided by activist intellectuals selected elements of the above mentioned history to construct a mighty narrative that tends to constitute Ancient Bahrain's past into a myth of golden age.[43] It could be summed up as follows:

There was a time when the Shias of Eastern Arabia were united in one single country called Bahrain extending from Basra to Oman.[44] Its inhabitants were called the Baharna and had embraced Shiism since the beginning of Islam. Bahrain was a wealthy country blessed by several natural resources: fresh water springs, arable lands and pearls. People were living a simple but fully satisfactory peasant life in accordance with the prescriptions of the Imams. It was a time of social harmony and order. Everything changed when the Sunni tribes – the Al-Khalifa and the Al-Saʿud – took over the region, appropriated the natural resources for their own use and imposed their brutal and autocratic manners on the native population. They not only oppressed the Shias but cut their unity by breaking the organic ties between the islands and the inland. Since then, marginalized Shias have fought to recover their legitimate rights as the native inhabitants of Ancient Bahrain.

Significantly, reference to the Portuguese presence, which marked the beginning of the fracture between Ancient Bahrain's islands and mainland, is totally absent. So is the Iranian past of the archipelago. The whole discourse is focused on the conquest by the Al-Khalifa as if it were the real beginning of the breaking down of the Baharna's organic unity. This is not surprising since the function of this discourse is precisely the objectivization of the relations between the rulers and Shia society and not the accurate description of Ancient Bahrain's history. Totally de-historicized, the period before the conquest is idealized in order to affirm the Shias' privileged relation to the land of Ancient Bahrain and their status as the native population of the country by contrast with the alien Bedouins. Saying that before the conquest the Baharna were a happy people living according to the Imams' precepts not only gives a magnified representation of self but legitimates the fight

---

43   Nakash (2006), p. 24.

44   For many Bahrainis, Oman is still often understood in its old meaning as referring to present day Oman and present day United Arab Emirates.

against the oppressive rulers. In that respect, the myth of Ancient Bahrain is typical of the tales that sustain ideologies of national liberation.[45] Although the religious dimension is an important element of the discourse, it is only secondary by comparison to the omnipresence of the nativist element.

It is significant that this narrative was among the very first material I collected upon the beginning of my fieldwork in Bahrain in 2002. When I explained that I was doing research on Shias in Bahrain and the Gulf, Shias would almost systematically undertake to explain to me that the Shias were the original inhabitants of Bahrain and that they were called the Baharna in reference to Ancient Bahrain. It was the tale of Ancient Bahrain I was told upon my first encounter with a well-known cleric and Shia Islamic activist. He had been eighteen years in prison for participation in an attempted overthrow of the Al-Khalifa regime in 1981 and had been set free following a general amnesty by the new ruler in 2001. Even though he was himself a cleric and headed an association dedicated to the propagation of Islam, his first move was not, as was often the case with 'ulama, to outline the main tenets of the Shia version of Islam, but to tell the story of Ancient Bahrain before the conquest by the tribes. Only afterwards was he concerned to know how informed I was on Shia doctrine. Clearly for him, understanding the Shia predicament in Bahrain demanded first that I get historical information. Religion as such came second.

From this one understands that, far from being a mere religious divide, the Sunni/Shia split overlaps with older and maybe more significant ones: the divide opposing the society of conquerors to the conquered, the aliens to the natives and, in some respects also, the Bedouins to the peasants. This is all the more relevant in Bahrain where, contrary to Saudi Arabia, the Shias have never been submitted to specific religious persecution. While the conquerors probably despised the creed of the subjugated population, they were not Sunni zealots willing to spread their worldview. Contrary to the Al-Sa'ud, their military enterprise was not legitimized by any kind of religious ideology. What mattered was the maximization of their economic profits: Shias could continue to cry over Imam Husein's death. After all, Sunnism had always been the faith of the victors and Shiism of the vanquished so that the maintenance of the religious difference was a perfect way to remind everybody of their social position. Consequently, the Shias' religious freedom was never curbed and when the first constitution was voted in 1973, it granted the Shias two days off for 'Ashura, the ninth and

---

45   Anthony D. Smith, "The 'Golden Age' and National Renewal", in Geoffrey A. Hosking and George Schöpflin (eds), *Myths and Nationhood*, London: Hurst, 1997, p. 59.

tenth days of the month of Muharram, a concession no other state with a Shia population ever made. By the same token, in the contemporary period, the Emir of Bahrain always takes the precaution of marking his respect for the Shia faith by offering big meals and other generous gifts upon the commemoration of Husein's martyrdom. He assists in numerous opening ceremonies of *huseiniyya*.

A further proof that the Bahraini ruling dynasty has no problem with the Shias as a religious group is the overall excellent relations they have traditionally enjoyed with the Shia Iranian merchant class who established themselves in Bahrain between the second half of the nineteenth century and the beginning of the twentieth. The Al-Khalifa welcomed them with open arms as they stimulated the archipelago's economy and constituted a new source of revenues for them.[46] One of the most affluent and famous of these merchants, Mohammed Rahim Safar, entirely refunded the rulers' treasury after a civil war that opposed two Al-Khalifa contenders for rulership in 1869.[47]

Not so much a sign of religious broad-mindedness than a way of reasserting the boundaries between dominants and dominated, Bahraini rulers' apparent religious tolerance has therefore not prevented the persistence of a particularly rigid form of social hierarchy. Although Sunnis have become a demographic minority and today account for no more than 30 per cent of the Bahraini population, they still have the upper hand over key political and economic positions. This discrepancy of power positions is expressed in more subtle ways in everyday social life. The ethnologist Clive Holes has showed that the characters in the serials produced by the state-owned Bahraini media and painting an idealized past of Bahraini society speak a distinctive Sunni dialect and almost totally ignore the Bahrani vernacular, clearly showing that Shias, both Baharna and 'Ajam (Arab and Iranian), are not part of the representation of Bahraini collective self the rulers endeavour to promote.[48] The same can be said of the National Museum, which aims to recount Bahrain's social history but totally ignores the kind of agricultural activities practiced by the Baharna and focuses instead on the pearling

46   Nelida Fuccaro, "Mapping the Transnational Community. Persians and the Space of the City in Bahrain, *c.* 1869-1937", in Madawi al-Rasheed (ed.), *Transnational Connections and the Arab Gulf*, London: Routledge, 2005.

47   James Onley, "Transnational Merchants in the Nineteenth Century Gulf. The Case of the Safar Family", in Madawi al-Rasheed (2005), p. 72.

48   Clive Holes, "Dialect and National Identity. The Cultural Politics of Self-Representation in Bahraini *Musalsalat*", in Paul Dresch and James Piscatori (eds), *Monarchies and Nations. Globalization and Identity in the Arab States of the Gulf*, London: I. B. Tauris, 2005, p. 60.

activities, which were mainly practiced by the Sunnis after the Al-Khalifa conquest. In this context, it is no surprise to note that many Baharna tend to feel deep resentment towards the Sunni population and that, more than two hundred years after the settlement of the Sunni Najdi tribes, they keep alive the memory of the conquest. The failure to build a common sense of the past between Sunnis and Shias is well expressed by the significance Baharna attribute to the word "Bahraini". While it refers to the official status of citizen of the modern state of Bahrain, they have turned it into an ethnonym specially naming the Sunnis. The true people of Bahrain, they often say, are the Baharna, pointing out that the name "Bahraini" is a pure creation of the Sunni Bedouin conquerors in their attempt at pretending to belong to a country they have stolen from their owners.

The myth of Ancient Bahrain is to be found with hardly any variations among Saudi Shias. Although they have been subjected to a specific religious discrimination their co-religionists in Bahrain never experienced, their hostility towards the Saudi regime is as often expressed in terms of alien oppression as in terms of religious illegitimacy. Even among devoted Shias, discourses on the absence of religious freedom are intertwined with considerations on the predatory nature of the Al-Sa'ud, who still behave like conquerors. Totally disregarding the well-being of the native inhabitants of the Eastern Province, they are only preoccupied with exploiting local natural resources for the benefit of the central regions: oil is sold to the West to profit the Najdi clique that runs the country, the dates of Hasa's famous palm groves are sent to Riyadh, and so are the spring waters which flow to the capital by way of pipelines while the locals are reduced to drinking desalinated sea water. Sunnis are said to have the brutal and crude manners of desert dwellers while Shias display the gentleness and refinement of coastal dwellers, long habituated to living in a cosmopolitan and open environment of which hospitality and tolerance are key features. The Arabic term "*khaliji*", which can be translated as "of the Gulf" and refers to the inhabitants of the Arabian side of the Gulf, is said to apply only to the Saudis originating from the coastal province who share a common culture with Kuwaiti or Bahraini nationals.

Pervading Shia society, the Bahrani narrative has been taken up in a more sophisticated version by activist intellectuals belonging to the Shia Islamic movements that emerged in the 1970s. They produced various types of historical publications recounting the history of the Shias in Ancient Bahrain. The book by the Saudi opponent Hamza al-Hasan, *The Shias in the Arab Kingdom of Saudi Arabia*, is a typical example. A valuable contribution to the historiography of both Saudi and Bahraini Shia populations in the context of a quasi-total absence of other such attempts, it contains many pages dedicated to the demonstration that "the Shias of Hasa and Qatif are Arabs and are the native inhabitants (*sukkan asliyin*) of the region for a lot of centuries",[49] that they constitute an old civilization which is threatened in its very existence by the Sa'udi-Wahhabi quest for religious and cultural hegemony. For al-Hasan as indeed for many other Shia activist intellectuals, the military subjugation of the Shia native populations has been accompanied by a cultural endeavour to erase what, behind the particular religious credo, creates the very specificity of Bahraini and Saudi Shias: they are *hadhar*, a long settled population living in urban centres and villages, while the rulers are *badu*, Bedouin nomadic desert dwellers. According to al-Hasan, from these two different ways of life stem two radically different worldviews and, in particular, two relations to genealogy and to religion. Contrary to Bedouins, settled people do not consider pure Arab descent as a central value. Rather than descent, it is religion that is the yardstick of social pride:

"There is no doubt that this difficulty in defining the descent (*nasab*) of the Shias is linked, as we have stressed, to the rules of the civilization process (*tahadhdhur*) and sedentarization (*istiqrar*). Indeed, this region [Eastern Arabia] has an old history of civilization (*hadhara*) and civilized societies usually forget their descent and their origins. This is particularly true in religious societies that do not get any sense of pride from their descent. [...] What distinguishes the region [of Ancient Bahrain] and other areas in Oman from Najd and the sheikhdoms of the Gulf is that it has been civilized for hundreds – if not thousands – of years. These sheikdoms are no more than nomadic tribes that have settled for only a few years and have transformed into emirates... Tribes keep the memory of their descent because they do not have other values. Religion does not unite them strongly as descent does. Fraternity and Islam do not reinforce them as tribal solidarity (*'asabiyyat al-qabila*) does".[50]

In its various publications, the Islamic Bahrain Freedom Movement (*Harakat Ahrar al-Bahrayn al-Islamiyya*) has developed a strikingly similar vision. Here is, for example, how its web site, which contains a whole section dedicated to the history of Bahrain, describes the relation between the Al-Khalifa and the Shias:

"Bahrain, the ancient civil society, suffers from an alien culture that attempts to impose a tribal mentality against the will of the people. The tribal system in the

---

49   Al-Hasan (1993), Vol. I, p. 28.

50   *Ibid.*, p. 31. For a more detailed analysis of the *bedu/hadhar* scheme of interpretation in the Saudi Shia activist literature, see Madawi Al-Rasheed, "The Shi'a of Saudi Arabia: A Minority in Search of Cultural Authenticity", *British Journal of Middle Eastern Studies*, vol. 25, n° 1, May 1998.

Arabian Peninsula predates Islam. Prophet Mohammed reformed many of its ugly features. But, history is witness to the fact that the tribal system returned whenever it managed to take control."[51]

The paragraph is preceded by several pages on the history of Bahrain where the author essentially focuses on the idea that Bahrain was once a prosperous country that always attracted the lust of foreign powers and was definitively ruined by the successive razzias of the 'Utub tribes from 1700 onward, a period he calls "the ruin of Bahrain" (*kharab al-Bahrain*). Then follows an edifying description of the backward and cruel habits of tribesmen, people for whom blood ties are the prevalent value, who enslave the people they defeat, bury women alive, do not accept any form of debate and glorify their chief. In another text also included in the IBFM's web site, Mansur al-Jamri, once one of the main figures of the movement and since 2002 the editor of the only independent newspaper in Bahrain (*Al-Wasat*, the Center) goes further by explaining that not only does tribalism contradict true Islam (i.e. Shiism) but that "historically, it has been persistently demonstrated that tribal tradition denies people their constitutional rights".[52]

For the Shia Islamic activists, the political usefulness of this discourse describing the Shias as the native civilized inhabitants of Ancient Bahrain is twofold. First, it permits them to dismiss the Islamic credentials of the regimes they fight by reducing them to the expression of a distorted Bedouin version of Islam. But, second, it also allows them to set their action within the framework of the dominant register of political legitimacy of the contemporary world, which stresses the value of populating anteriority and of democratic rule. Indeed, in the IBFM's excerpts quoted above, the authors have operated a subtle shift in meaning which permits them to suggest that, roughly speaking, tribalism equates with autocracy and Shiism equates with democracy. Playing on the polysemy of the Arabic word "*hadhar*" which means to be sedentary but also to be civilized, they have chosen to translate it by the English word "civil". Shias are therefore presented as a "civil society", a term familiar to Western academics and promoters of democracy for whom the texts are meant and whose support Shia Bahraini

---

[51]   Bahrain Freedom Movement's web site (www.vob.org/english/information-db/ data.htm). The text is in English and has no corresponding version in the Arabic section of the web site.

[52]   Mansur al-Jamri, "Prospect of a Moderate Islamist Discourse. The Case of Bahrain" (www.vob.org/english/information-db/mesa.htm). The text is also in English with no corresponding version in Arabic. It was presented by its author at the 1997 annual meeting of the Middle East Studies Association (MESA).

and Saudi Islamic activists have sought. This Shia civil society is in conflict with savage tribesmen who are presented as intrinsically despotic.

One must add that the vision defended by Islamic activists is served by the Western scientific literature, which often tends to depict the states of the Gulf as mere emanations of archaic tribal Bedouin organization and values. The idea that the tribal ethos is a major impediment to democratization is indeed a commonplace of Western work on the Gulf. Yet, the reality is far more complex. Those who are familiar with the history of Saudi Arabia, for example, know that the Al-Sa'ud were a long-settled clan when they undertook to build a state in the mid-eighteenth century. Moreover, "the Saudi state is a *Hadhari* project that aimed [...] to end the Bedouin hegemony throughout pre-modern Arabia".[53] The Al-Sa'ud were even profoundly distrustful of the Bedouins to the point that although they appointed Shia local governors in the Eastern Province, they certainly never hired a Bedouin one.[54] As we shall see with the case of Kuwait, in the other Gulf states the Sunni ruling families together also consider themselves as *hadhar* in contradistinction with the recently sedentarized tribes who settled in the course of the first half of the twentieth century. Explaining the relation between Sunnis and Shias in terms of the old *hadhar/badu* paradigm does not grasp the actual reality of social practices in societies where nomadism is a residual phenomenon.

Last, but not least, one should note that although Ancient Bahrain and Bahrani identity are a central theme in both Saudi and Bahraini Shia activist literature, this appears to be less obsessive among ordinary Saudi Shias than among Bahraini ones. While the overall idea that the Shias are the native inhabitants of the Eastern Province of the kingdom was a recurring theme of the conversations I had with Saudi Shias, I had to provoke the discussion on Ancient Bahrain and Baharna. People would of course tell me the same story as their Bahraini co-religionists, but they were clearly less emotionally involved in it than Bahrainis and the recalling of the golden age of Ancient Bahrain was not a systematic prerequisite for explaining the current situation as was so often the case in Bahrain. Moreover, Saudi Shias, although they agree to the existence of something like a Bahrani people who used to populate Eastern Arabia before the conquest, do not spontaneously define themselves as "Baharna". People from Qatif and its outskirts speak about

53   Abdulaziz H. Al-Fahad, "The 'Imama vs. the 'Iqal: Hadari-Bedouin Conflict and the Formation of the Saudi State", in Madawi Al-Rasheed and Robert Vitalis (eds), *Counter-Narratives. History, Contemporary Society and Politics in Saudi Arabia and Yemen*, New York: Palgrave, 2004, p. 36.

54   *Ibid.*, p. 45.

29

themselves as "Qatifiyyin", while people from Hasa use the name "Hasawiyyin". While there are many family relations between Baharna and Shias from the Eastern Province in Saudi Arabia, especially in the region of Qatif which is just opposite to Bahrain and has moreover been linked to Bahrain by a bridge since 1986, this has not permitted the preservation of a common collective identity expressed in a shared ethnonym. In Saudi Arabia, the tale of Ancient Bahrain and the Bahrani people is more the business of the intellectual activists of Shia Islamic movements than the basis for a sense of collective identity.

One can put forward several hypotheses to explain this situation. First, the physical dissociation between Bahrain and what is now the Eastern Province of Saudi Arabia dates back five centuries so that it seems rather unsurprising that the inhabitants integrated this situation symbolically by adopting different ethnonyms. Second, it is likely that the importance of religious legitimation for the Saudi regime has in turn fostered a sense of essentially religious shared identity among Saudi Shias. Following the rule according to which discriminated groups tend to adopt the concepts and worldview of the dominants to express their grievances against them,[55] one can surmise that Bahrani identity, which is so meaningful in Bahrain where the regime has no religious pretension, has been overwhelmed by the religious discourse in the case of Saudi Shias. The latter are by the way much stricter in their religious practice than their Bahraini co-religionists. In Bahrain, it is rare to see a Shia woman with her face totally covered by a black veil (*niqab*), especially among the younger generation. While in Bahrain the *niqab* is considered as a typically Sunni dress code, it is common to both Sunni and Shia women in Saudi Arabia. For a woman, venturing out with the face uncovered in a Saudi Shia village exposes her to forceful reprehension from passers-by.

Is there a Bahrani Irredentism?

A third element likely to explain the relative indifference of the average Saudi Shia for the Bahrani identity could well be the fact that Bahraini Shias have a vested interest in enhancing Bahrain's shared destiny with the Saudi Eastern Province which their Saudi co-religionists do not have: at the time of writing, Bahrain had almost exhausted its own oil wells while the Saudi Eastern Province, which hosts the vast majority of the kingdom's hydrocarbon resources, still has the world's largest proven resources. Many

---

55   Erving Goffman, *Stigma. Notes on the Management of Spoiled Identity*, New York: Touchstone Book, 1986, p. 114.

Bahraini Shias, both Baharna and 'Ajam,[56] find it difficult to accept this state of affairs so that it is not uncommon to hear them say that Bahrain still has huge oil reserves. When asked about where these wells lie, people will point at offshore fields actually located in Saudi territorial waters. People do not go to the point of saying that Saudi onshore fields belong to Bahrain, but Saudi encroachment on what is considered as Bahraini soil is the object of fierce resentment among the Shia population, showing that, to say the least, many people do not accept the idea that Bahrain is only a tiny archipelago with no natural resources.

This naturally leads us to the issue of irredentism. Does the affirmation of a shared identity amounts to an irredentist claim by Bahraini Shias over Shia-populated and oil-rich Saudi territories? On the eve of the October 2002 parliamentary elections in Bahrain, which were marked by a massive boycott orchestrated by the Shia Islamic opposition, I had the opportunity to witness a tense conversation between one Shia Islamic activist and a Shia member of the Consultative Council, an assembly of independent non-oppositionist notables first appointed by the Emir in 1993. The notable was trying to convince the activist that the boycott was a foolish and unproductive option. As his interlocutor was sticking to his conviction that the elections were no more than a masquerade, the notable blew up and shouted at him: "what do you want ultimately? To restore the ancient kingdom of Bahrain?!" He only got a dismayed and phlegmatic silence signalling that the activist was unwilling to engage on such an uncertain ground. This actually brought the discussion to an end but the whole incident was a clear indicator that the myth of Ancient Bahrain does not only operate as a symbol of oppressed native identity but also nourishes what can be called Bahrani pan-nationalist feelings among a significant part of Bahraini Shias, especially the activists of the Islamic movements among whom, for example, the reference to Hasa as "the ancient capital of Bahrain" is not unusual.

However, one should immediately stress that while Bahrani pan-nationalist feelings do exist and are quite widespread in Bahrain, they have not materialized as a fully-fledged pan-nationalist ideology, even less as an articulated political programme. The reaction to the scenarios drawn by some American strategists was typical in that respect. In the aftermath of the attacks of 11 September 2001 in New York, as the alliance between the United States and Saudi Arabia was put into question, a debate was opened in Washington about the fate of the kingdom in the overall plan to redraw the Middle East articulated by George W. Bush's advisers. During a meeting held in July 2002 at the Pentagon, the scenario of a partition of

---

56   I lack empirical datas to analyse the position of the Sunnis on this matter.

Saudi Arabia was suggested.[57] The Eastern Province and its oil wells would be separated from the rest of the country and joined with Bahrain to constitute a Shia emirate under an American protectorate. The operation would put the Saudi oil resources out of reach of the no longer reliable Al-Sa'ud family or any hostile power likely to overthrow it. As the new entity would more or less correspond to the territory of Ancient Bahrain, it would have a solid historical legitimacy.[58] During a stay in Bahrain in September 2003, I had the occasion to broach the subject with some of my Shia informants, asking them directly: "After all, is it not what you always dreamt of?" Their reaction was quite embarrassed, as if the scenario was totally at odds with the real local context. They answered evasively that nobody was really taking the Americans seriously and, that, in the end, this project would bring more bad than good.

A few days later, I crossed the causeway to Qatif, where I was confronted with the same scepticism. A young Shia there told me clearly: "I am a Bahrani if this means belonging to an old civilization that used to live there, but not if it means commitment to a political entity that does not exist anymore and will never come back". He however acknowledged that the partition scenario had provoked huge debates among the Shias, among whom it became common to hear that the notables who had decided to surrender peacefully to the Al-Sa'ud's army in 1913 had made a historic mistake and should instead have accepted the British proposal to create an autonomous emirate in Qatif and Hasa.[59] For my informant as for many others, these discussions were however no more than nostalgic tales and not the sign of any sustainable political agenda. As in Bahrain, Saudi Shias were overall distrustful of Americans and few really believed they were serious about recreating Ancient Bahrain. On the other hand, some considered that it was possible to use the partition scenario tactically to pressure the Saudi government to do more to recognize its Shia citizens' rights.[60]

---

57   Thomas E. Ricks, "Briefing Depicted Saudis as Enemies", *Washington Post*, 6 August 2002.

58   For this kind of scenario, see Ralph Peters, "Blood Borders. How a Better Middle East Would Look", *Armed Forces Journal*, June 2006 (www.armedforces-journal.com/2006/06/1833899).

59   See also the article by Khaled al-Rashid in the Shia oppositionist journal *Saudi Affairs* published from London: "Political, Economic and Demographic Aspects and Roots. The Road to Separatism in the Arab Kingdom of Saudi Arabia" (in Arabic), *Saudi Affairs*, n° 18, July 2004.

60   This is, for example, clearly the perspective of someone like Mohammed Mahfuz, a renowned Saudi Shia religious intellectual and Islamic activist, who was interviewed in February 2003 by the *Wall Street Journal* in an article that caused

In conclusion, Bahrani pan-nationalism exists as a feeling but does not support a real pan-nationalist ideology and even less a pan-nationalist movement. However, Shia Islamic mobilization in Bahrain and Saudi Arabia definitely has a nativist dimension that distinguishes it from its counterparts in Kuwait and the other Gulf monarchies where the socio-history of the Shia population offers a very different picture than the one presented here.

PATTERNS OF SHIA POLITICAL MOBILIZATION
IN BAHRAIN AND SAUDI ARABIA

Before the discovery of oil, political opposition in Bahrain and Saudi Arabia tended to be restricted to factional quarrels inside the ruling families. It was only with the establishment of the oil industry and the progressive modification of the social fabric it entailed that the two countries witnessed the development of political movements involving larger segments of society, in which the Shias played an important role.

The Shias and the Reform Movement in Bahrain

Despite their difficult socio-economic conditions under the Al-Khalifa rule, the Baharna were remarkably absent from the main political contentions. At times of conflict, they often preferred exile to neighbouring countries than organizing to fight on one side or another in order to improve their own lot. The first shift in this pattern occurred in the 1920s when the Baharna began to take a more proactive stance towards important political issues. The move occurred thanks to the new policy of the British who, because of its convenient geographical location and its port facilities, had chosen Bahrain as the centre of their commercial activities after 1869. Great Britain had begun to interfere directly in Gulf affairs a few decades before in order to preserve its commercial interests in the East. One major objective was the pacification of the trade roads to India which had been rendered dangerous by the constant ransoming of British vessels by the coastal Arab tribes. The latter were quelled by 1820 with the signature of a treaty which forbade warfare and piracy in the Gulf waters. Bahrain was pacified in 1869 when the British intervened to put an end to strife between two Al-Khalifa contenders for rulership that had greatly impoverished the

---

quite a stir in Saudi Arabia. He stated that "if separation means that we will get our rights, then of course we'd want it. If the Shias become partners, our problem can be resolved locally – without waiting changes imposed from the outside." *Wall Street Journal*, article by Yaroslav Trofimov, "Saudi Shias May See Gains from U.S. Invasion of Iraq", 3 February 2003.

country. In the 1920s, in order to facilitate commerce, and particularly to better arbitrate commercial conflicts, the British undertook to set up an embryonic bureaucracy aimed at judging according to clear and fair laws. Furthermore they felt that in order to gain the sympathy of at least part of the local population, they should improve the overall judiciary system and make it more equitable, in particular towards the Baharna.[61]

The attempt was quite successful in that respect as the administrative reforms of the 1920s won over many Baharna. When the opponents to the reforms, who felt threatened in their privileges as feudal landlords or as pearl traders, began to organize to oppose them, the bulk of the Baharna sided with the reformers so that the conflict eventually came to follow the sectarian cleavages of Bahraini society: most of the partisans of the reforms were composed of Baharna allied with one faction of the Al-Khalifa led by the heir apparent, while the opponents were mainly Sunni clans backed by another section of the ruling family clustered around the Emir.[62] Everything degenerated into open violence in 1923 when riots opposed Sunnis and Shias in both Manama and the villages, leading to the death of a dozen persons. The British reacted by forcing the ruler to abdicate in favour of his heir apparent. Significantly, the crisis emboldened the Baharna who felt for the first time they had a chance to articulate their grievances to a benevolent power. They began regularly to launch protest movements to demand more reforms. This was the case, for example, in 1934 when they undertook to denounce publicly the arbitrary character of justice and demanded a more equitable representation of the Baharna in the new administration.[63]

Another step in the politicization of the Baharna was taken with the establishment of the oil industry in the 1930s. Bahrain hosts the oldest oil industry of Eastern Arabia, being the first Arabian emirate in which oil was discovered, in 1932. Commercialization began one year later by the Bahrain Petroleum Company (BAPCO), then the property of the American Standard Oil Company of California (SOCAL). The first refinery was built in 1936. The development of the oil industry took place in a context of deep economic crisis after the local economy had been severely hit by the worldwide Great Depression (1929) as well as by the launching of the Japanese cultured pearl, which virtually destroyed Bahraini pearling activity. With agriculture and *entrepôt* trade, pearling had been the backbone of the Bahraini economy and a major source of employment for the local

---

61   Khuri (1980), p. 88.

62   *Ibid.*, p. 92.

63   Rumaihi (1976), p. 194.

population. The Al-Khalifa rulers hoped the oil industry would provide an alternative source of employment and so insisted on including a particular chapter in the concession agreement with SOCAL, stipulating that Bahrainis should be prioritized for employment in BAPCO.[64] The problem was that although they formally engaged to hire Bahrainis as far as practicable, the oil company managers were first and foremost looking for competent workers, something the tiny Bahraini islands, whose population had no previous experience of industrial employment, could not supply. In the first instance, the company mainly relied on Iranian manpower for a set of practical reasons. Iranians in search of job opportunities on the Arabian coast were residing in Bahrain on a permanent or seasonal basis. As some of them had already worked in the oil industry in their country, where oil had been discovered twenty years before (1911), they needed little professional education. Another non-negligible incentive for hiring them was that they had less salary expectations than Bahrainis.[65]

The dependence of the nascent Bahraini oil industry upon Iranian manpower was far from satisfactory for both the Bahraini rulers and their British protectors, who feared that an enhanced Iranian presence in the country would sustain the Shah's claim over Bahrain. This is why they pressured BAPCO to get rid of its Iranian workers. As most Bahrainis were still unable to fill the requirements of a good employee, the company decided to import Indian labourers to staff the intermediate semi-skilled and skilled positions. The logical result was that in the early oil industry, Bahrainis were a minority among BAPCO employees. Some sources even estimate that a significant part of those officially registered as Bahrainis were actually Iranian migrants or were born from Iranian parents.[66] While the proportion of Bahrainis constantly increased due to the pressure from the rulers as well as BAPCO's investment in vocational training, in the 1950s they were still in a minority and, moreover, at the bottom of the employment scale. Labour inside the company was segmented and stratified along strict ethno-national lines: "Westerners in management positions, Indians and Pakistanis in intermediate positions and Bahrainis at the bottom in lower clerical and labour jobs".[67] Most of the Bahrainis were employed on a daily non-contract basis which rendered their situation precarious.

---

64   Ian J. Seccombe and Richard I. Lawless, "Foreign Worker Dependence in the Gulf, and the International Oil Companies: 1910-50", *International Migration Review*, vol. 20, n° 3, autumn 1986, p. 551.

65   *Ibid.*, p. 559-60.

66   *Ibid.*, p. 559.

67   Willard A. Beling, "Recent Developments in Labor Relations in Bahrayn", *The*

This situation logically fuelled discontent among BAPCO Bahraini employees who felt they were being deprived of the benefits of their country's natural resources. This was an important source for the development of what remains a feature of Bahraini social fabric: the relative lack of social integration between the Baharna and the 'Ajam, the Arab Shias and the Iranian Shias, manifested not only by the scarcity of intermarriages but also by palpable tension. While the 'Ajam do not display particular animosity towards their Arab co-religionists, bitterness towards them is widespread among the Baharna. There are two main sources of grievances. First, the 'Ajam are accused of supporting the regime. It is hence commonplace to hear that, contrary to the Baharna, the 'Ajam felt little empathy with the Islamic revolution that put an end to the Shah's rule in 1979 and sparked enthusiasm among the Shias of the Gulf. The 'Ajam generally strongly deny this and it is difficult to assert the accuracy of the Baharna's language in this respect. What is sure is that the perception that the 'Ajam chose the Al-Khalifa against Ruhollah Khomeini does not reflect the fact that several 'Ajam supported the exportation of the revolution to Bahrain (cf. chapters 4 and 5). It is probably grounded in the memory of the good relations built between the rulers and the Iranian merchant class in the nineteenth century and on the fact that the Iranian notability of Bahrain has long remained politically silent. Another element likely to explain Bahrani resentment is the pattern of recruitment in the early oil industry. It is indeed commonplace to hear from Baharna that the 'Ajam monopolize management positions in the oil company as well as in all the big state-owned companies. As the sources show, this is an old claim since it was at the heart of the first Bahraini labour movement in the late 1930s. Angry at the preferential treatment of Iranian workers in BAPCO, the Bahraini workers set up quasi trade unions and organized strikes to demand the overall improvement of working conditions and wages, as well as better representation of Bahrainis in the company's staff. This embryonic labour movement, which became the most powerful of the Arabian emirates, began to crystallize in 1938 following a tense regional political context that witnessed the establishment of the Legislative Council by the Kuwaiti merchant oligarchy, followed by a similar move in Dubai. In Bahrain, Sunni and Bahrani urban merchants then launched an initiative to demand further reforms, including the improvement of the judiciary system, a better representation of Bahrainis in the municipal administration and the preference for Bahraini workers in employment at BAPCO.[68] The petition was supported by a strike by Bah-

---

Middle East Journal, vol. 13, n° 2, 1959, p. 159.

68   Rumaihi (1976), pp. 198-201.

raini BAPCO employees, who were mainly driven by the hope of improving their working conditions. Finally, a committee – the Society of Free Youth – was created to articulate a set of demands of which the main point was the formation of a council of six representatives – three Baharna and three Sunnis – to advise the ruler.[69]

While the 1938 initiative came from the ranks of both the Sunni and Arab Shia notability, the available literature does not provide details on the sectarian affiliation of the Bahrainis employed in BAPCO, who constituted a core element of the mobilization. As the pearl industry was mainly handled by the Sunni tribes and employed many Sunnis of modest background, one can surmise that the latter turned to the oil industry when the pearl trade collapsed. Shias were also present in BAPCO's rank; the Bahraini staff was therefore probably religiously mixed. Anyhow, one should note that a singular feature of this early period of politicization as compared with the situation of the 1920s was that it transcended sectarian cleavages on all rungs of the social scale. Several reasons can be advanced to explain it. First, the traditional elite probably realized that in order to exercise more leverage on the government, they had to take into consideration the particular grievances of the Baharna, in particular of BAPCO workers. Second, the embryonic bureaucracy fostered the emergence of a new kind of social actor both among the Sunnis and the Baharna. While they often came from the urban merchant notability, they also came from families with no particular social weight and were generally driven by an ethos of efficiency. Third, they were influenced by the political atmosphere of the time, which was characterized by the diffusion of Arabism and its message centred on the unity of the Arab nation beyond religious differences. Fourth, the fact that BAPCO's internal organization was marked by a clear hierarchy of status and wages between Bahrainis and foreigners fostered a sense of common interests and belonging among Bahrainis. They were discriminated against as Bahrainis, not as Shias or Sunnis, and had therefore to fight together. Fifth, the administrative reforms launched by the British led to an endeavour to categorize the residents of the islands according to their nationality, this in order to determine on which judiciary system they depended, the ruler's or the British's. Therefore, the period also corresponded to the creation of the very category "Bahraini" which, although it never succeeded in overwhelming totally the old ethno-religious categories, also contributed to the emergence of a sense of a shared identity.

---

69   *Ibid.*, pp. 196-208.

The 1938 initiative finally reached an impasse as most of the demands were dismissed but it opened the way to increasing organization of civil society in both the Sunni and Shia sectors of the population. In particular, Bahrain witnessed the creation of the first clubs and societies, which acted as substitutes for the officially banned political parties and trade unions. While some of them were clearly established on an ethno-religious basis, like the Firdawsi[70] club, which was established in 1946 by rich Shia Iranian merchants and had no clear political stance, others were more politicized in that their members, without directly opposing the regime, embraced the tenets of Arab nationalism. This was the case of the most famous of them, the 'Uruba club (the club of the "Arabness"), created in 1939 by a handful of Bahrani wealthy traders together with Bahrani high civil employees in order to "fight religious sectarianism accordingly with the principles of Arab nationalism".[71] It was still in existence at the time of writing, when its premises regularly hosted important political meetings.

In the 1950s, the pattern of political mobilization remained almost unchanged, revolving around a religiously mixed coalition of Bahraini BAPCO employees, the new intelligentsia and mostly urban notables. The Baharna as a group did not constitute a consistent political actor and mobilized along with their Sunni fellow citizens. However, mobilization gained in intensity, leading to an event which has since become a central reference point in Bahraini collective memory: the *intifada* (uprising) of 1956. Everything began with a series of sectarian clashes between Sunnis and Shias following an initial incident during the 1953 'Ashura procession. The sources are too scarce to permit a fully accurate evaluation of the event. However, the fact that it occurred in the above-mentioned context of increasing trans-sectarian political mobilization against the rulers and the British renders convincing the hypothesis of a deliberate attempt by the latter to put an end to the phenomenon. This is all the more likely since the initial clash broke out after a member of the Al-Khalifa family insulted the 'Ashura procession in Manama, sparking anger among the penitents and leading to the attack on one Bahrani village by a Sunni crowd. Other clashes took place up to 1954, including between BAPCO workers. A Sunni was killed. A trial followed and, as the Baharna felt they were unfairly considered responsible for the incidents, they decided to organize a demonstration of protest which was brutally quelled by the police, leading to the death of four Bahrani demonstrators. Understanding that the clashes were a threat to their political ambitions,

---

70   Abu al-Qasem Firdawsi is a famous Iranian poet of the tenth century.

71   Khuri (1980), p. 175.

Sunni and Bahrani leading members of the Arab nationalist clubs decided to organize to bring them to an end and formed a secret network of activists and notables. This finally led to the creation of the High Executive Committee (November 1954), which comprised 120 members and the leadership of which was composed of four Sunnis and four Baharna. The Committee's main objective was to pressure the government to enact new reforms, mainly the establishment of an elected legislative council, the draft of a fair criminal and civil law, the authorization to set up trade unions and the creation of an appeal court.[72] Then began a difficult process of negotiation between the Committee and the rulers, whose aim was to buy time. As for the opposition, it was far from being united and the Committee was subject to contradictory demands from part of its popular base. In particular, while the leadership of eight proved ready to compromise with the rulers and were reluctant to organize strikes or any kind of mass demonstrations, more radical elements in the population hoped to take over power. Therefore, the negotiations between the Committee and the rulers were punctuated with clashes when the radicals tried to make their views prevail by force and intimidation. Eventually, the Committee came to posit itself as an alternative to the rulers, practising conflict resolution within the population and even constituting an embryonic militia with arms smuggled from Iran. Things ended following the October 1956 war when, after the Egyptian president Nasser decided to nationalize the Suez Canal, British and French armies aided by the Israeli troops attacked Egypt. A mass rally was organized by the Higher Executive Committee in Manama which degenerated into riots and violence against British interests. This was the pretext for the rulers and their British allies to quell the opposition, whose main leaders were sentenced to prison and deported, once and for all. However, they were quickly pardoned and allowed to come back to Bahrain.[73] While some chose to establish themselves in Egypt or Iraq, others returned home and continued to play an important political role throughout the 1960s and the 1970s. Among the 120 members of the High Executive Committee, many were co-opted by the government, which offered them positions in the high administration.[74]

---

72   Rumaihi (1976), p. 214.

73   Details on the 1953-56 events are mainly to be found in Rumaihi (1976), pp. 209-345 and Khuri (1980), pp. 194-217.

74   Khuri (1980), p. 224.

The Role of the Oil Industry in Saudi Arabia

Compared to Bahrain where, as folk wisdom reckons, "there is a demonstration every week and a popular uprising every ten years", Saudi political life appears rather quiet. Despite the numerous discriminations they were faced with, the Shias did not rise against the regime after the failed and limited attempt by Sh. Mohammed al-Nimr in the late 1920s. As in Bahrain, many Shias had chosen to flee the country rather than rising against the unjust rulers and those who remained, aware of their minority status, had confined to a wait-and-see attitude. Their resentment had failed to be articulated by any kind of organized political action.

Like in Bahrain again, when trends of politicization re-surfaced in the Shia population, it had little to do with a religiously oriented revolt against the Saudi regime as such and was mainly driven by the new socio-economic conditions that radically transformed the landscape of the Shia areas. Driven by their success in Bahrain, the American oil companies began to prospect Saudi soil in 1933 and discovered hydrocarbons in commercial quantities in 1938. Commercialization began after the Second World War in 1946. The wells happened to lie in the heart of the Shia land around the oases of Qatif and Hasa. Like BAPCO in Bahrain, ARAMCO, the Arabian American Oil Company, to which the Al-Saʻud had given the concessions, recruited many foreign workers to fill its manpower needs. Westerners of course came to occupy the administrative and the technical positions. Probably because of the unfriendly religious atmosphere, no Iranians came to work in the Saudi oil industry, but many Arabs came from countries such as Palestine, Egypt, Lebanon or Yemen. Skilled workers even came from nearby Bahrain as ARAMCO's salaries were known to be higher than BAPCO ones.[75]

Unlike BAPCO however, ARAMCO was successful in quickly integrating nationals into its ranks so that in the early 1950s, around 65 per cent of its employees were Saudis.[76] Many of these came from the lower ranked Sunni tribes and originated from almost all the regions of the kingdom. However, as the oil fields were located in the Eastern Province, the bulk of ARAMCO Saudi employees were poor Shias who barely succeeded in earn-

---

[75] Khuri (1980), p. 135; Ian Seccombe and Richard Lawless, *Work Camps and Company Towns: Settlement Patterns and the Gulf Oil Industry*, Durham, University of Durham, 1987, pp. 37-9.

[76] 10,400 of the 13,400 Aramco employees, according to Antony Cave Brown, *Oil, God and Gold. The Story of Aramco and the Saudi Kings*, Houghton Mifflin, Boston, 1999, p. 140.

ing their lives as peasants or craftsmen.[77] Like their Sunni fellow employees, they considered wage work a way to secure a regular though modest income. ARAMCO administration, however, considered the Shias as harder working than Bedouins who tended to despise manual work and were reputed more efficient as guards or drivers.[78] While Saudi workers began to work in poor conditions in non-skilled employment, a lot of them were able to access to vocational training organised by ARAMCO and to climb the rungs of the ladder. One of ARAMCO's aims indeed was to secure a stable and loyal workforce rather than relying on the fluctuating expatriate workforce, whose turnover was very high. The most promising Saudi employees were sent to Egypt and subsequently more and more to the United States, becoming not only fluent in English but also able to occupy higher paid skilled positions in the company. Therefore, while initial working conditions were harsh for the Saudi employees, their situation never ceased to improve throughout the years. By the end of the 1950s, two-thirds of them were skilled or semi-skilled workers and 3,000 had reached managerial positions.[79] Their wages followed suit, rising from 3,800 ryals in 1953 to 17,800 on average in 1971.[80] Moreover, in the absence of a developed state apparatus, ARAMCO quickly turned into a kind of quasi-welfare state for its employees and their families, providing them with education, healthcare and even housing loans. In the little towns surrounding the oil fields, one finds to this day what Saudis call "ARAMCO quarters". These are ARAMCO lands which the company gave to its employees with a loan to build a house. Virtually all the inhabitants are the company's cadres and, generally speaking, the quarters count among the best-off areas.

In the first instance, the Shias' enrolment into the harsh industrial employment despised by other Saudis reflected their lower status within society. As in Bahrain, the Shias and the Saudis overall were at the bottom of the wage ladder within the oil company during the early stages.[81] However, as ARAMCO Saudi employees progressively developed into a privileged

---

77   Georges Arthur Lipsky (ed.), *Saudi Arabia. Its People, its Society, its Culture*, HRAF Press, New Haven, 1959, p. 90. See also Madawi al-Rasheed, *A History of Saudi Arabia*, Cambridge, Cambridge University Press, 2002, pp. 97-8.

78   Vassiliev (2000), p. 424.

79   William Rugh, "Emergence of a New Middle Class in Saudi Arabia", *Middle East Journal*, vol. 27, n° 1, 1973, p. 16.

80   *Ibid.*, p. 16.

81   On ethnic relations within ARAMCO, see Robert Vitalis, *America's Kingdom. Mythmaking on the Saudi Oil Frontier*, Stanford: Stanford University Press, 2007, pp. 88-120.

class among Saudi wage workers, employment in the oil industry quickly became an opportunity to circumvent discrimination for the Shias. While few of them reached the top administrative positions of the company monopolized by Westerners and later on by Sunni Saudis whom the rulers judged more loyal, over the years Shias nonetheless succeeded in securing a strong position within ARAMCO, which they were able to retain up to the 1980s. To this day, Shias who have been or are ARAMCO employees form an elite in the Shia population, and have been a key element of the various political movements which have developed since the 1950s. As clearly underlined by Madawi al-Rasheed, "ARAMCO not only facilitated the emergence of the first wave of Saudi administrators, technocrats, civil servants and oil millionaires, but also the first political prisoners, dissidents, exiles and opposition literary figures".[82] It was among ARAMCO employees that new ideologies began to circulate in Saudi Arabia, and new modes of political mobilization to emerge. Strikes in ARAMCO became a regular matter of concern for the company's managers as early as 1945. They were mainly driven by the foreign Arab workforce who demanded better working conditions and wages, and denounced the preferential treatment reserved for Westerners in the company.[83] This early stage of mobilization only marginally concerned the Saudi workers. Not accustomed to labour mobilization like their foreign colleagues who had previously been politically socialized in their home countries, Saudis preferred to maintain a low profile and to avoid conflict with the ARAMCO hierarchy.

A few years later however, some of the Saudis who had returned from vocational training abroad participated in an attempt to set up a trade union together with their foreign colleagues. They demanded official recognition from the administration board and articulated a set of claims pertaining to work conditions and wage increases. As their demands were dismissed and a dozen of their leaders arrested, they organized the first large scale strike in 1953, with 20,000 workers involved from a total of nearly 30,000.[84] The trial of strength lasted two weeks, with martial law declared at the oil fields and the army deployed to contain the strikers. Work resumed after the administration finally agreed to grant the trade unionists most of what they claimed except the right actually to exist as an official trade union. But mobilization did not end and soon began to articulate political slogans under the impact of regional events and the spread of "anti-imperialist"

---

82   Al-Rasheed (2002), p. 100.

83   Vitalis (2007), p. 93.

84   Vassiliev (2000), p. 336.

trends throughout the Middle East which had followed events like the na-tionalization of the Anglo-Persian Oil Company by Mossadegh in Iran in 1951 and the coup by Nasser in Egypt in 1952. In short, the movement departed from strictly labour-oriented demands to espouse a global revolu-tionary rhetoric echoing worrying events for the Saudi monarchy which, at this time, happened itself to be subjected to internal strife.

In 1953 indeed, King 'Abd al-'Aziz, who had unified the kingdom died and his sons started a battle for a share of power and wealth. Sa'ud, the new king, soon revealed himself incompetent and let the kingdom fall into a deep financial crisis. Among the population, he had the reputation of be-ing only preoccupied with building luxurious palaces. He had to meet the opposition of his brother and Crown Prince, Faysal, who claimed a bigger share of power and had different views on how to administer the kingdom's wealth.[85] This overall context explains why King Sa'ud was welcomed by a mass demonstration of protestors upon his arrival in the oil city of Dhah-ran in July 1956. Besides the traditional labour demands for increasing wages and equality between local and American employees of the company fully articulated in a petition presented to the King, the demonstrators carried anti-imperialist slogans.[86] One should add that the events probably seemed particularly threatening for the Saudi rulers since similar events were also taking place in Bahrain at the same time, and on an even larger scale as this ended in a true uprising. Saudi informants who were working in ARAMCO at that time attested that the Saudi strikers tried to somehow coordinate with the Bahraini ones.[87] This information seems all the more accurate since many Bahraini and Saudi Shias were tied by family links and, as mentioned above, many Bahrainis had been incorporated into the ARAMCO workforce.

This overall context explains why King Sa'ud decided to turn a deaf ear to ARAMCO workers' demands. He ordered the banning of strikes and demonstrations as well as the arrest and beating of the movement's leaders. This led to another strike where, this time, the demonstrators made precise political claims such as the establishment of a constitution and the right to form political parties and trade unions. As underlined by historians, the workers' movements of the 1950s, although unprecedented and denoting the working of new socio-political trends among the Saudi population, were far from manifesting the existence of a real popular movement among

---

85   Al-Rasheed (2002) pp. 106-110.

86   Vassiliev (2000), p. 337.

87   Personal interviews, Saudi Arabia, 2004.

the Saudi population overall, and more particularly among the Shias of the Eastern Province.[88] That's why they finally ended in a political impasse. However, they left a legacy of leftist political activism among the Shia population. Although its leader was not a Shia but a Sunni from Najd – Nasir Sa'id – the Shias were well represented among the members and sympathizers of the National Reform Front which came out of the strike of 1953. Following the dominant political ideology of the time, it was pan-Arab in inspiration and displayed socialist-like leanings. In the 1960s, it associated with dissident members from the Al-Sa'ud family clustered around Prince Talal bin 'Abd al-'Aziz and backed by Nasser's Egypt. Their programme for Saudi Arabia was to organize a popular referendum asking the Saudis to choose between a constitutional monarchy and a republic. They also of course wanted to renegotiate the concession agreements with ARAMCO.[89] The National Reform Front was rather short lived and, once the support of the rebel princes was lost in the mid-1960s, it quickly vanished. In 1975, the Communist current within the Front decided to create the Communist Party of Saudi Arabia, the founding congress of which was held in Beirut. Like the National Reform Front, it demanded a constitution, a parliament, political pluralism and the nationalization of the oil resources, but it was unambiguously aligned with the USSR.[90] The Communist Party had an even more Shia outlook than the National Reform Front, although it had always represented a marginal trend among the Shias. Some of its cadres even issued from prominent families of science, like Najib al-Khunaizi, whose close relatives have monopolized the position of *qadhi* of Qatif since King Abd al-Aziz.[91] Others were sons of members of the trade union set up during the strike of 1953. Many were educated in the USSR or other countries of the Communist bloc.

---

88   Vassiliev (2000), p. 339; Al-Rasheed (2002), p. 110.

89   Ghassane Salameh, "Political Power and the Saudi State", *Merip Report*, n° 91, October 1980, p. 20.

90   *Ibid.*, p. 21.

91   They lost this position in 2006 when the overall system of Shia religious courts was reformed following events which will be described in chapter 7. Najib al-Khunaizi was among the thirteen people arrested in September 2003 for demanding the establishment of a constitutional monarchy.

2

THE SHIAS IN THE AMBIT OF THE STATE

"We are Kuwaitis, yes we are. In my view, the Shias even constitute the foundations of the Kuwaiti state. However, according to the constitution, power falls within the hands of the Al-Sabah family. Mohammed Rafi' [Husein al-Ma'rafi] was richer than the Al-Sabah. So was Marrad Bahbahani… Today, Marrad Bahbahani is not officially an adviser to the Emir but he enters the Emir's house when he wants. This comes from the time of the foundation of the Kuwaiti state, from the time of the wars. The Kuwaitis were besieged in the Red Castle in Jahra. He who rescued them was Mohammed Rafi', from the sea. When the Al-Sabah came back to Kuwait city, the Ma'rafi welcomed them. They told them: 'you the Al-Sabah, you have the power to rule but in exchange we want freedom of trade'. From then onward, it became a duty for the Emir to visit Mohammed Rafi' for each national commemoration. It's part of his obligation. The Shias in Kuwait have their place. But we are working in silence, because the state is Sunni and because we don't like problems. I want to do business: the government doesn't bother me, I don't bother it."[1]

As this excerpt of an interview with a Kuwaiti Shia shows, Kuwaiti Shias consider themselves as being a structural element of the state. With around 25 per cent of its national population professing the Shia creed and a rather active presence of Shia Islamic groups usually labelled "radicals", it is one of the Gulf monarchies where Shiism is an important and often deemed potentially destabilizing socio-political and geopolitical factor. Aside from the pessimistic estimates however, the situation of the Shias in Kuwait has been rightfully described by observers as a "success story".[2] The Shias themselves are the first to say it: Shias have found their place in Kuwait; they enjoy a good relationship with the rulers, have a fair share of the national wealth and benefit from ample religious freedom. How do we explain that?

---

1   Personal interview, Kuwait, June 2003.

2   Graham Fuller and Rend Rahim Francke, *The Arab Shi'a. The Forgotten Muslims*, New York: Palgrave, 2001, p. 155.

THE SHIAS IN THE FORMATION OF THE KUWAITI STATE

By contrast with their Bahraini and Saudi co-religionists, Kuwaiti Shias have been fully-fledged actors in the process of state formation. This is in great part due to the nature of the Shia social fabric in Kuwait, as well as the particular modality of the state formation process.

A Mix of Diasporas

Here is how another Kuwaiti Shia puts the history of his family in the context of the history of Kuwait itself:

"Kuwait was created by a group of tribes and families. They came from outside and settled in Kuwait. Some came from Saudi Arabia, Iraq and Iran. Of course, most of the Kuwaiti Shia families came from Iran. Some families came from outside one hundred, one hundred and fifty, or even two hundred years ago. It depends. Our family is one of those who came around one hundred years ago from Iran and established themselves in Kuwait. They had good revenues at the time, doing commerce. They owned boats. They came to Kuwait where they played a positive role."[3]

This way of presenting the Shias' position within Kuwaiti society is very representative of the dominant Shia discourse in Kuwait. Rather than the language of the age old character of Ancient Bahrain, Kuwaiti Shias tend to accentuate the fact that Kuwait is a relatively young state as compared with its neighbours. Kuwait, they say, was born out of the gathering of tribes and families of various geographic origins. Some of them were Shia, others were Sunni. What matters is that they all arrived from "outside" from the eighteenth century onward and that they all contributed to the development and prosperity of the country. While the stories of Bahraini and Saudi Shias revolve around the theme of the rights attached to the status of native, the stories told by of their Kuwaiti co-religionists are about movements, journeys and forced exodus. Kuwait is described as a haven where merchants could trade in peace and where persecuted people could begin a new life.

This way of experiencing things is grounded in basic data of Shia settlement in Kuwait. Contrary to Baharna and Saudi Shias who developed a group identity based on a claim to prior settlement, Kuwaiti Shias share many patterns typical of diasporic populations. While often displaying overt Kuwaiti patriotism to the point of presenting themselves as the guardians of Kuwaiti territorial integrity and independence, they simul-

---

3   Personal interview, Kuwait, June 2003.

taneously keep their place of origin as a central referent of their collective identity. Hence, although political mobilization cuts across ethno-regional divisions, ordinary social life, and in some cases religious life, is organized according to membership of three main categories: 'Ajam (sing. 'Ijmi, from Iran), Hasawiyyin (sing. Hasawi, from Hasa) and Baharna (sing. Bahrani, from Bahrain).

The diasporic pattern is reflected in the strong family ties Kuwaiti Shias have kept with relatives settled in the regions their forefathers left, even when relocation dates back more than one hundred and fifty years. For example, it is not uncommon for 'Ajam to marry women they select in Iran from among remote relatives. In summer time when the heat is difficult to bear, many choose to cross the sea to a summer house in Iran, to relatively fresher air. By the same token, at times of hardship, be it economic difficulties, political instability or family conflict, 'Ajam can also find it convenient to settle in Iran for a while. Finally, while many 'Ajam have arabized their names and speak standard Gulf Arabic fluently, they nevertheless often speak Persian in their family circle.

Intense cross-border family networks are not only the privilege of 'Ajam, and Hasawiyyin and Baharna also often keep close contacts with their relatives in Hasa and Bahrain. Moreover, as with Hasawiyyin and Baharna settled in other parts of the Gulf, they keep ties with other Hasawi and Bahrani communities in Oman, Qatar, the United Arab Emirates, Iran and south Iraq (the region of Basra). Although not systematic, these family cross-border networks can play a political role. For example I was told that during the Saudi municipal elections of 2005 for which the Shias had particularly mobilized, a wealthy Kuwaiti Hasawi financed the campaign of one of his relatives who was a candidate for a seat in the council of Hufuf-Mubarraz.

Shias of Iranian descent form the most important group demographically speaking. The first of them came around the second half of the eighteenth century,[4] shortly after the Bani 'Utub's settlement. Most of them were maritime traders from the coastal areas of Iran and were first and foremost motivated by developing their economic activities. Such was the case, for example, of the al-Ma'rafi family, to date one of the wealthiest Shia families of Kuwait and the owner of the oldest *huseiniyya*, built in 1905. Among these old Shia families one also counts the al-Mazidi, who gave Kuwait several high level *'ulama* as well as politicians, including 'Isa al-

---

4   Sami Naser al-Khaldi, *The Islamic Parties in Kuwait. The Shias, the Muslim Brotherhood, the Salafis* (in Arabic), Kuwait, Dar al-Naba' lil Nashra wal-Tawzi', 1999, p. 91.

Mazidi, who was regularly appointed as minister between 1981 and 1992 (Transport, Oil).

The flow of Iranians to Kuwait continued throughout the following centuries. It was influenced by internal Iranian developments as well as by the growing prosperity of the Arabian emirates as compared with the southern coastal regions of Iran. First, these regions witnessed regular harsh climatic conditions by the end of the nineteenth century, with a drought hitting the region of Bushehr which forced hundreds of families to the Arabian shore.[5] Second, many Iranian merchants took up residence in Kuwait as well as in the other Arabian emirates to escape the new fiscal measures of the Iranian government. Faced with a severe financial crisis, the Qajar regime endeavoured to enforce its effective control over the remote provinces which had become *de facto* autonomous areas, including the southern areas bordering the Gulf. In 1902 it decided to impose high customs dues for goods imported and exported through the Gulf's ports like Bushehr, Bandar 'Abbas or Bandar Linga. This directly threatened the commercial activities of the merchant class, eventually pushing many traders to leave for the Arabian ports, which consequently became the main ports of call for Indian goods.[6] With the accession to power of the Pahlavi dynasty in 1926, poor Iranians from rural backgrounds were severely hit by new reforms[7] like mandatory military service, land reform and the forced abandonment of traditional clothes, including the veil for women. This pushed many in the southern regions to cross the sea to Arabia.[8]

Furthermore, one should bear in mind that just as the Arab tribes used to cross to the Iranian side of the Gulf, Iranians used to go to the Arabian shore in search of better life conditions or economic opportunities. Thus the Iranian presence in Eastern Arabia was part of a classical pattern of border migration.[9] With the exponential expansion of the pearling industry from the nineteenth century onward and the subsequent development of the oil industry from the 1930s, the Arabian side became even more attrac-

5 Fuccaro (2005), p. 45.

6 Frauke Heard-Bey, *From Trucial States to United Arab Emirates*, Dubai: Motivate Publishing, 2004, pp. 244-5.

7 M. Reza Ghods, "Government and Society in Iran, 1926-34", *Middle Eastern Studies*, vol. 27, n° 2, April 1992, pp. 223-6.

8 Shahnaz R. Nadjmabadi, "Travellers between 'The World' and 'The Desert': Labour Migration from Iran to the Arab Countries of the Persian Gulf", unpublished paper presented at the Bellagio Conference on Transnational Migration in the Gulf, June 2005, p. 3.

9 *Ibid.*, p. 1.

tive for Iranians. They provided significant contingents of workers in the early oil industry, in Kuwait as well as in the other Gulf emirates. Many had had previous working experience in the oil industry of their own country and were therefore valuable manpower compared to the locals. For the Iranians, working on the Arabian side was motivating because the oil companies there offered higher wages than in Iran. Besides industrial working, Iranians also engaged in all possible kinds of professional occupations from civil servants to construction workers, from bread makers to taxi-drivers.

Many Hasawiyyin and Baharna also settled in Kuwait in the second half of the eighteenth century, either for commercial reasons or to escape persecution and/or political instability. Shias of course fled Hasa following the various episodes of the Saudi conquest of Eastern Arabia, taking up residence in Kuwait and other Gulf emirates, but also in southern Iran, southern Iraq, India and present-day Pakistan.[10] Hasawi families are numerous in Kuwait. Among them one can mention the al-Wazzan, that gave Kuwait politicians like 'Abd al-Wahhab al-Wazzan who, in the late 1990s, reached the office of minister of Commerce and Social Affairs, and of Commerce and Industry. The al-Qattan family is very active in running Hasawi community institutions. The al-Baghli family has been active in the secular political movements, with 'Ali al-Baghli being appointed Minister of Oil in the 1990s. Hasawiyyin in Kuwait have traditionally displayed a particularly well developed group identity since their common geographical origin is coupled with belonging to a particular current of Twelver Shiism: Sheikhism, that follows the teachings of Ahmed al-Ahsa'i (*cf.* chapter 1). In the Shia world, Kuwait actually counts amongst the important Sheikhi centres, not the least because Kuwaiti Shias overall, and Hasawiyyin in particular, are affluent. A line of Sheikhi *marja'*, the al-Ihqaqi family originating from the city of Usko in Iranian Azerbaijan, also took up residence in the emirate in the 1950s to lead the community's religious affairs. Mirza 'Ali al-Ihqaqi, the first Sheikhi *marja'* who became established in Kuwait, had lived among the Sheikhi community of Hasa but had been compelled to leave following a rift with local Shia *'ulama* who, like many Shia scholars, considered the ideas of Ahmed al-Ahsa'i to deviate from Islamic doctrine.[11] His descendants have since continued to live in Kuwait where they progressively constituted themselves into an important financial force with numerous religious and charity activities. The religious institutions in many

---

10   Sa'ada (1997), p. 72; al-Hasan (1993), pp. 78-81.

11   Personal interview with 'Ali al-Mahdi, a Kuwaiti Hasawi historian and journalist, Kuwait, May 2006. One should note that while the Sheikhi consider themselves as *usuli*, they are often denied this status by non Sheikhi scholars.

respects serve as community institutions. Hence, the heart of the Sheikhi community is the al-Sadiq mosque, a complex which, besides the prayer hall, comprises a *huseiniyya*, a library and a *diwaniyya*: that is, a traditional Kuwaiti and Gulf in general semi-private place of meeting.[12]

As for the Baharna, some left Bahrain before the Al-Khalifa conquest in the mid-seventeenth century when, following the decline of the Safavid state, the islands were subjected to regular raids from coastal tribes and Omani rulers. A second wave left immediately after the Al-Khalifa arrival. The flow never really ceased afterwards, as the country was regularly submitted to harsh political conditions. The archipelago suffered a brief occupation by Saudi warriors in 1811 following which the country was placed under the Saudi sphere of influence, which entailed the implementation of discriminatory regulations against the Shias.[13] Later on in 1843, a factional strife between two contenders for rulership inside the Al-Khalifa family bled Bahrain dry and was a major cause for the exodus of Shia families.[14] While their role has not been as central as that of Iranian and Hasawi families in the religious and political life of Kuwaiti Shias, Baharna nonetheless count among them influential families in Kuwait, be it in the economic field, like the wealthy businessman 'Ali al-Matruk, or in the politico-religious field, like S. Husein al-Qallaf, a religious scholar who was the first Shia cleric ever elected to Parliament in 1996, 1999 and 2003.

As a conclusion on the absence of an integrated Shia community in Kuwait, one should note that the boundaries of each of the Shia groups identified above are often fluctuating. They are the product of a social construction rather than the automatic expression of a geographic origin. At the individual level indeed, it is not uncommon to find people whose parents are from two different groups and whose position in the "social organization of culture difference"[15] is the result of the particular history of their parents – the preferred social network they were inserted in – as well as their own personal religious, political and professional choices. Moreover, fami-

---

12 Called "*majlis*" in other Gulf countries, the *diwaniyya* is either a particular room in a private house or a small independent house generally located close to the house of the owner. The *diwaniyya* plays a central role in the political life of Kuwait, being a place of free debate and gathering. *Cf.* Fatiha Dazi-Héni "Hospitalité et politique. La *diwaniyya* au Koweït", *Maghreb-Machrek*, vol. 142, n° 1, 1994.

13 Al-Hasan Vol. I (1993), p. 173.

14 Fuccaro (2005), p. 43.

15 By reference to Fredrik Barth's concept outlined in "Introduction" in Fredrik Barth (ed.), *Ethnic Groups and Boundaries. The Social Organization of Culture Difference*, Boston: Little, Brown and Company, 1969.

lies who have circulated from one place to another and consequently have networks of connections in virtually all the countries of the Gulf shores are not uncommon. The al-Muhri families are typical in case. The al-Muhri are two different families of science from which two of the most influential religious scholars of Kuwait were born: S. 'Abbas al-Muhri (d. 1988) who enjoyed close relations with Ruhollah Khomeini whose main representative in Kuwait in the 1970s and 1980s he was, and S. Mohammed Baqer al-Muhri, the president of the Shia '*Ulama*'s Assembly (*Tajammu' al-'Ulama al-Shi'a*) created in 2001 with the ambition to become the representative body of the Shia clerics in Kuwait. The two al-Muhri families originate from the village of Twaithir in Hasa but migrated to south Iran somewhere during the nineteenth century to escape the Wahhabi exactions. They settled in empty territory around Shiraz where they founded a village which they named Muhr following a misunderstanding with the local governor. The latter had told them that he would give them a "*muhr*", a stamp in Persian, which would ascertain of their right to settle on this piece of land. Having little understanding of Persian, they understood that "*muhr*" was the name of the land. After installation in Muhr, the two families took the name of Muhri following the traditional Iranian usage according to which family names indicate the locality from which those persons originate. In the early twentieth century, two religious men from the family went to study and live in Najaf, and from there came to Kuwait, residing between the two countries. At the independence of Kuwait, they were granted Kuwaiti citizenship although continuing to reside in between Kuwait, Iraq and Iran. In such cases, membership of one particular community is difficult to asses other than with empirical data on the actual situation of this or that person. 'Abbas al-Muhri, who arrived in Kuwait in the 1940s from Najaf, was for example considered as the religious leader of the 'Ajam community. Although enjoying continuous networks of family relations with Twaithir in Hasa, he had little relations with the Hasawi community in Kuwait, mainly because he abhorred Sheikhism. Within the family circle, he used to speak Persian. The same can be said today of Mohammed Baqer al-Muhri who, although he refuses to identify himself as a member of this or that particular group, is identified by most of the Shias as an " 'Ijmi".

A Vested Interest in Co-operation

While fully accountable historical sources are lacking on the real circumstances of the Bani 'Utub settlement in Kuwait, most historians date their arrival back to somewhere in the first half of the eighteenth century.[16] It is not exactly known who then inhabited the area. In any case, the population was scarce as the Kuwaiti harbour was hardly more than a fishing port under the formal rule of the Bani Khaled, the then dominant tribal power of Eastern Arabia. The latter however only maintained a small fortress with provision of foodstuff and arms and they had no problem with letting the Bani 'Utub establish themselves there. They perhaps even entrusted them with the administration of the area. Be that as it may, the Bani 'Utub did not have to subdue a native population by the sword. On the contrary, their presence appears to have been a major incentive for others to come: tribes from the Arabian Peninsula and Iraq but also the above mentioned Shias from Iran, Hasa and Bahrain.

In brief, Kuwait gradually developed into a thriving port engaged in pearling, caravan trade and long distance commerce to India and Eastern Africa following the progressive clustering of tribes and traders from diverse horizons who, for the sake of commerce and prosperity, had a vested interest in cooperating peacefully together. This is how Kuwait progressively developed as a city state whose residents shared a deep feeling of community which needed to be protected at any cost. The Shias, for their part, were no more than one of many segments of this nascent society.

Following the decline of Bani Khaled rule in Eastern Arabia, the little blooming port found itself without any effective military power to protect it from Bedouin raids or from the lust of emerging regional powers. Around the mid-eighteenth century the elders of the main families came together to designate a ruler able to provide military protection but also to arbitrate wisely in conflicts of interests. Sabah, one the Bani 'Utub leaders, was chosen.[17] The reasons for the choice are the object of various tales by Kuwaitis. A common version among the members of the merchant oligarchy, who formed the core element of the opposition to the ruling family, is that Sabah issued from a minor clan of the Bani 'Utub and accepted the job because the others had more interesting things to do, i.e. get richer.[18] The historian Jacqueline Ismael gives a more interesting account than this common Kuwaiti wisdom by stressing the fact that, unlike other clans from the Bani 'Utub, the Al-Sabah were not engaged in maritime trade and "remained oriented towards the desert".[19] Involved in caravan trade, they had

16   Abu Hakima (1983), pp. 3-4.

17   *Ibid.*, pp. 5-6.

18   Mary Ann Tétreault, *Stories of Democracy. Politics and Society in Contemporary Kuwait*, New York: University of Columbia Press, 2000, pp. 33-4.

19   Ismael (1982), p. 27.

kept relations with the nomadic tribes with whom they intermarried and maybe received a tribute as recognition of their superior status. In brief, they could command the allegiance of the tribes and therefore protect the city against Bedouin razzias. Because of their ties to the desert also, and contrary to the sea traders who had to travel extensively, they remained in Kuwait on a permanent basis. What is important to bear in mind here is that the different economic interests and occupations of the various Bani 'Utub clans led to the emergence of a "functional division of power"[20] between the Al-Sabah and the class of maritime traders.

The Shias in the Kuwaiti Founding Myth

Another important element to explain the Shias' situation in Kuwait is the fact that, unlike Bahrain, the country never felt threatened by Iranian irredentism and even enjoyed good relations with its neighbour for most of its history.[21] With the notable exception of the 1980s at the peak of Iranian revolutionary activism, threats always came West, from Saudi Arabia and North, from Iraq.

Like the other Arabian emirs, Kuwaiti rulers resorted to British protection to guarantee Kuwait's territorial integrity. However, this did not totally deter the neighbouring states from irredentist claims over the emirate. Kuwait was subjected to Saudi attacks early after the formation of the first Saudi state in the eighteenth century. Around 1760-70, Kuwaitis undertook to build a wall around their city in order to better rebuff assaults from the Wahhabi Ikhwan. Showing magnanimity as well as probably hoping to reduce the al-Sa'ud ambitions to conquer Kuwait, the Al-Sabah offered them asylum after the fall of the second Saudi state in 1865, helping them to regain strength sheltered from their enemies. This was a miscalculation however, as the alliance proved anything but reliable. As soon as they recovered and began the military campaign to rebuild their state, the Al-Sa'ud strove to bring Kuwait under their domination and launched the Ikhwan against their ex-protectors. The latter massacred a detachment of Bedouin soldiers from the private guard of Emir Salim in April 1920.

What followed became not only the most important event of Kuwait history; it was magnified to constitute a founding myth with deep implications not only for the structuring of Kuwaiti citizens' collective memory but for the formal organization of citizenship. The attack by the Ikhwan

---

20   Ibid., p. 28.

21   Amir Sajedi, "Iran's Relations with Kuwait", Strategic Analysis, 1993, vol. 16, n° 7.

pushed the Emir to imagine an overall plan to defend Kuwaiti territory and first and foremost the city of Kuwait. He decided to consolidate and extend the city's wall, initially built of mud, in order to make it a fully-fledged fortification. According to the tradition, in an exemplary sign of cohesiveness and what is now termed "national" solidarity, Kuwaiti men and women joined forces to build a new wall. Working tirelessly day and night, they succeeded in erecting the fortification in only two months.[22] In October 1920, Kuwaitis aided by British gunboats and planes defeated the Ikhwan in Jahra, a little oasis 40 kilometres West of Kuwait city. This marked the end of Saudi irredentism over Kuwait.

The role of the Shias in the battle of Jahra remains a subject of controversy in Kuwait. Indeed, leading members of the merchant oligarchy have accused them of having refused to fight the Ikhwan militarily. Saif al-Shamlan, a Kuwaiti historian who wrote in 1959 one of the most commonly studied histories of Kuwait in Kuwaiti classrooms, makes no mention of the Shias' role during the battle. He only mentions incidentally that at the end of the battle, when the inhabitants of Kuwait city thought their army had been defeated and that the Ikhwan were marching in to the city, the 'Ajam went to demand protection from the British representative, arguing that "they were not Arabs but Iranians".[23] This version is contested by the Shias, who refer to another history of Kuwait published afterwards in 1965 by Husein Khalaf al-Sheikh Khaz'al. The latter wrote a detailed history of Kuwait in five volumes. Contrary to al-Shamlan who is part of a well-known family of the Sunni merchant oligarchy, the latter is a Shia descending from Sheikh Khaza'l, the ruler of Muhammara, today Khoramshahr in the Iranian province of Khuzistan which hosts an important Arabic speaking population. Sheikh Khaz'al was deposed by the Shah in 1925. He enjoyed a close relationship with the successive Kuwaiti rulers, who helped him several times. Molla Salih, the personal secretary of Mubarak the Great, the most famous of the Kuwaiti emirs (d. 1915) for the role he played in the consolidation of the dynastic principle of succession, had been provided to Mubarak by Sheikh Khaza'l. He played a leading role in the subsequent life of the city, and in particular in mobilizing the Shias at times of political crisis. In the fourth volume of his history dealing with the reign of Salim Mubarak Al-Sabah, Husein Khalaf al-Sheikh Khaza'l writes two pages devoted to the role of the Shias during the battle of Jahra which are widely referred to by Kuwaiti Shias as being the proper

---

22   Abu Hakima (1983), p.133.

23   Saif Marzuq al-Shamlan, *About the History of Kuwait* (in Arabic), Cairo: Matba' Nahdat Misr, 1959, p. 192.

account of what happened. According to him, the Shias in fact did not fight militarily but this was the result of a concerted decision with the rulers of Kuwait. When the Shias, led by their then main religious leader, S. Mahdi al-Qazwini (1865-1940), went to see the rulers to ask them for a provision of arms in order to join the army, the latter responded that it was not a good idea for the Shias to be physically on the battlefield. The rulers were afraid that if they knew that there were Shias among the Kuwaiti warriors, the Ikhwan would take it as a religious duty to defeat them, and their military fierceness would be reinforced. They therefore asked the Shias to stay inside the wall to defend Kuwait city in case of siege. While this is not exactly documented by al-Sheikh Khaza'l, the Shias say that their ancestors contributed to the rescue of the Kuwaiti fighters when they were besieged in the fort of Jahra, the Red Castle, threatened with starvation. Kuwaitis who had remained in the city sent them boats to resupply them with water, foodstuff and arms.[24]

The memory that Sunnis and Shias have kept of the battle of Jahra is a telling example of the competing historical narratives that one finds about the Shias' role in Kuwaiti nation building. Further evidence will help to understand better why some Sunnis adhering to Arab nationalist ideals have attempted to deny the Shias their place. At this stage of the analysis, what is important to bear in mind is that Kuwaiti Shias are eager to insist on their full participation in the building and defence of the state. Contrary to their Bahraini and Saudi co-religionists, their narrative is about inclusion and not about exclusion.

The Shias in Kuwaiti Social Stratification

Another factor explaining the Shias' good integration to Kuwaiti society is their position in Kuwaiti social stratification. The sectarian division between Sunnis and Shias is no doubt an important structuring element of Kuwaiti society but it is transcended by at least two other important and interrelated divides opposing original and naturalized Kuwaitis on the one hand, *hadhar* and *bedu* Kuwaitis on the other hand.

The split between original (*asli*, pl. *asliyyin*) and naturalized (*mutajannis*, pl. *mutajannisin*) Kuwaitis has several dimensions. First, it opposes those who fought against the Ikhwan at the battle of Jahra in 1920 and therefore proved their commitment to the project of an independent and sovereign

---

24   This is mentioned by 'Abd al-Muhsin Yusuf Jamal, *A Survey of the History of Shias in Kuwait from the Birth of Kuwait to the Independence* (in Arabic), Kuwait: Dar al-Naba lil-Nashr wa al-Tawzi', 2006, p. 53.

Kuwait, to those who, literally, came after the battle to merely enjoy the benefits of a dearly won peace. In the words of Mary Ann Tétreault, the battle of Jahra operated in Kuwaiti collective representations as a "citizenship myth" which "solidified perceptions by Kuwait's urban residents of their engagement in a common political enterprise but also initiated a system of differential status and rights".[25] The distinction between original and naturalized Kuwaitis has been institutionalized by the 1959 nationality law which defines the original Kuwaitis as those who were residing in Kuwait before 1920 and who therefore supposedly fought at the battle of Jahra. Naturalized Kuwaitis are those who became established in Kuwait afterwards. In a country like Kuwait which has a pluralistic political life with elected assemblies since 1921, the distinction between original and naturalized Kuwaitis has had direct implications in terms of political rights as the naturalized Kuwaitis did not have the right to vote before 1966, when an amendment to the nationality law granted them voting right after a thirty-year period from the date of the law's promulgation.

As shown by Anh Nga Longva, the divide between original and naturalized Kuwaitis partly overlaps with the traditional *hadhar/badu* split. Unlike in Bahrain and Saudi Arabia, it does not refer to a religious or regional identity since *hadhar* include both Sunnis and Shias from different regions. Neither does it refer to a practical difference between settled and nomadic people as Kuwaiti citizens, like the vast majority of the Gulf population, are all sedentary. In the Kuwaiti context, being *hadhar* or *badu* refers to the modality and chronology of the establishment in Kuwait: the *hadhar* are those who came to Kuwait before the oil era and, although sometimes initially Bedouin like the Al-Sabah family itself and most of the merchant oligarchy, settled upon their arrival and worked as traders, sailors, fishermen and pearl divers. The *badu* on the other hand, left Saudi Arabia and settled in Kuwait in the 1950s and the 1960s.[26] The *hadhar*, who see themselves as the true Kuwaitis, tend to consider the *badu* as alien elements who did not contribute to the construction of the Kuwaiti nation and whose establishment in the city is only motivated by capturing the allowances of the welfare state. They are said to be of dubious loyalty to Kuwait, a country they left en masse just after the invasion by Iraqi troops in 1990 while the *hadhar* were, allegedly, the only ones to organize resistance. The disdain and suspicion *hadhar* feel towards the *badu* is manifested in a geo-

---

25   Tétreault (2000), p. 43.

26   Anh Nga Longva, "Nationalism in Pre-Modern Guise: The Discourse on *Hadhar* and *Badu* in Kuwait", *International Journal of Middle East Studies*, n° 38, 2006, p. 172.

graphic divide. Initially, the *hadhar* used to live in the centre of Kuwait city, inside the area circumscribed by the wall of 1920. This is because, they said, they participated in its erection. When the wall was destroyed in the 1950s, and housing patterns changed following population growth as well as official housing policy, the *hadhar* population moved outside of the wall area but rarely went beyond a zone delimitated by the sixth ring road. Beyond lie the peripheral areas of Kuwait city, in majority inhabited by the *badu,* and which are commonly referred to as the "outlying areas" (*manatiq kharijiyya*).[27]

Although not located at the top of the social hierarchy dominated, in Kuwait like elsewhere in the Gulf, by the Sunni families from the central regions of the Arabian Peninsula, the Shias count nonetheless among the socially valued segments of the population as a great part of them rank among the original Kuwaitis and all of them cannot but define themselves as *hadhar*. Shias are even particularly inclined to castigate the *badu* crude manners and opportunism which, beyond their adhesion to the overall *hadhar* narrative, can also be explained by the *badu*'s leaning toward the Sunni Islamic movements' since the 1980s,[28] which often leads them to display overt hostility towards Shia beliefs and practices. Contrary to their co-religionists in Bahrain and Saudi Arabia therefore, Kuwaiti Shias have been able to espouse Kuwaiti founding myths and to integrate in the official representation of collective self promoted by the rulers and the socially valued segments of Kuwaiti society.

MODES OF POLITICIZATION

Mirroring their overall position in Kuwaiti society, the politicization process of Kuwaiti Shias stands in sharp contrast to the Bahraini and Saudi examples. It was not influenced by the establishment of the oil industry and, above all, it did not take the form of an opposition movement to the rulers.

The Kuwaiti Rulers and the Merchant Oligarchy

A distinctive feature of Kuwait as compared to its neighbours is the existence of an old mechanism of power sharing between the ruling family and the merchant class. Designated by the merchants, the formal political leader was meant to continue ruling in coalition with them and important

---

27   Longva (2006), p. 175.

28   Shafeeq N. Ghabra, "Balancing State and Society: The Islamic Movement in Kuwait", *Middle East Policy*, vol. 5, n° 2, May 1997, p. 61.

decisions were to be taken after consultation.[29] This arrangement was materialized by a pattern of intermarriage between the rulers and the main trading families. In terms of social prestige, the ruler was not above the main merchants, especially since most of them were actually better off than he was. As the state formation process deepened, the merchants became chief contributors to the rulers' treasury through loans and taxes on imported goods. Power was diffuse rather than hierarchic and decision making consensual rather than authoritarian. At the elite level, ruling therefore implied a form of consociational arrangement: it was a pact between the representatives of various tribal, ethnic and sectarian groups for the sake of a common enterprise.[30] However, the nucleus of the merchant class who kept the Al-Sabah rulers in check were from one of the Bani 'Utub clans and therefore did not count any Shia figures among them. Overall, and while the Shias included very affluent merchants like the above mentioned Mohammed Rafi' Husein al-Ma'rafi, the latter were never at the level of the Najdi Sunni tradesmen.[31] And in fact, the rich Shia merchants never intermarried with the rulers. This was of course because they were not part of the oligarchy but also most probably because of the difference of religious belonging.

The consultative mode of ruling was affected negatively after the accession to power of Mubarak the Great (1896) who, breaking the principle of consultation with the city's merchant notables in the matter of succession, imposed himself by eliminating physically his two rival brothers and by allying with the British who agreed to protect him against his rivals in exchange for the signing of an Exclusive Agreement (1899) which placed Kuwait under their protectorate. A turning point in Kuwaiti history, the event marked the switch to a more and more dynastic mode of ruling. But while the rulers grew stronger in face of the merchants, they never succeeded in totally subjugating them and, until the oil era in the mid-1940s, the merchant oligarchy was able to retain a strong bargaining power in front of the Al-Sabah.[32] If discontented with the rulers, the merchants would resort to the "migration weapon", so to speak, and leave Kuwait for another Ara-

---

29   Jill Crystal, *Oil and Politics in the Gulf: Rulers and Merchants in Kuwait and Qatar*, Cambridge: Cambridge University Press, 1990; Ghanem al-Najjar speaks about a "shared power" (*hukm mushtarak*) between the emir and the society: *Introduction to the Political Development of Kuwait* (in Arabic), Kuwait: Qurtas, 2000 (first edition in 1985), p. 8.

30   The presence of consociational forms of ruling in the Gulf monarchies has been well underlined by Nazih N. Ayubi, *Over-Stating the Arab State. Politics and Society in the Middle East*, London: I. B. Tauris, 1995, p. 245.

31   Jamal (2006), pp. 68-9.

32   Crystal (1990).

bian port. This is what several big pearl traders did in 1909 after Mubarak the Great tried to establish tighter control over their activities. As pearling was a chief source of capital for the city, their departure harmed the entire economy and, consequently, the ruler's own interest. He had to make the merchants many concessions to bring them back to Kuwait.[33]

Following the reinforcement of the dynastic nature of power, the merchant class felt that the principle of power sharing had been destroyed. In 1921, following the death of Emir Salim, the heads of the most influential merchant families thought they had a unique opportunity to regain their lost leverage and sought to institutionalize power sharing.[34] By taking sides in the internal rivalries that tore the Al-Sabah family apart, they could pressure for a reversion the initial principle of consultation in succession matters. They assembled in what they named the Consultative Council (*al-Majlis al-Istishari*) composed of twelve members all chosen among the affluent Sunni merchants. Beyond the role they hoped to play in case of internal disputes between the Al-Sabah contenders for rulership, their ultimate objective was to build a strong position for themselves in the decision-making process. As the succession finally occurred peacefully, the council did not play a role this time and although recognized by the new Emir, quickly dissolved after two months of existence because of factional quarrels between its members.

An expression of the Sunni merchant oligarchy's common interests, the council did not include Shia representatives. However, this was probably not the result of a deliberate policy. On the one hand indeed, because the Shias were not part of the merchant oligarchy who claimed power sharing with the rulers, they did not feel concerned by their battle.[35] On the other hand, before its dissolution the council had time to write down statutes stipulating that it should include two Kuwaitis of Iranian descent to be elected by their fellow-ethnics.[36] It is interesting to note that, at that time, the main social split in the eyes of the trading class divided Arabs from Iranians and not Sunnis from Shias. The two cleavages did not totally overlap indeed, as there were many Iranians professing the Sunni creed in Kuwait. There are only scarce sources on the 1921 council and the way the Shias overall took part or not in the project. The most commonly held view among Kuwaiti Shias is that having a say in the dynastic succession was not

---

33 Ismael (1982), p. 58.

34 Al-Najjar (2000), p. 23.

35 Jamal, (2006), p. 69.

36 Falah 'Abdallah al-Mdayris, *The Shia Movement in Kuwait* (in Arabic), Kuwait, Qurtas, 1999, pp. 10-11.

among their priorities because they felt their interests were perfectly well defended by the system as it was.[37]

The real turning point in both the political history of Kuwait and the Shias' involvement in it occurred later with the episode of the 1938 Assembly, commonly referred to as "The Assembly Movement" (*Harakat al-Majlis*). The event originated in a difficult context at the diplomatic, political and economic levels.[38] On the international level, the events in Palestine (the so-called 1936 "Arab revolt") fostered new political awareness among the educated Kuwaitis, who mobilized to send arms to the Palestinian fighters. As most of the educated Kuwaitis had studied in Iraq, political activism was also very much influenced by the Iraqi political developments. Arab nationalism became the dominant oppositionist ideology in Kuwait, leading to the formation of a group of young activists named the National Bloc (*al-Kutla al-Wataniyya*) which was the direct emanation of an Arab nationalist youth movement in Iraq.[39] Several members of this movement overtly militated in favour of the incorporation of Kuwait into Iraq and therefore espoused the Iraqi point of view that, as a previous part of the Ottoman province of Basra, Kuwait was an integral component of Iraq. On the internal political level, dissatisfaction with the Emir was growing among Kuwaitis as the latter did little spending for public services and tended to keep the whole state budget, which was actually not distinguished from his own, for his personal use. On the economic level, the merchant class had difficulties recovering from the collapse of the local pearl trade and many Kuwaitis faced tough life conditions.

Supported by the British who came to the conclusion that the only way to guarantee the city's stability and counter Iraqi irredentism was to find a way to accommodate the Kuwaitis' grievances,[40] the merchants assembled once again to pressure the ruler to agree to the creation of an assembly of fourteen members to be elected by the heads of the leading 150 families of Kuwait. The assembly was to have legislative powers and, among other things, total control of the state's budget.[41] While having no other choice than to acquiesce to the merchants and the British, the Emir simultaneously strove to undermine its legitimacy. He tried to buy the loyalty of some of its

37   Jamal (2006), p. 72.

38   Al-Najjar (2000), pp. 24-32.

39   Kamal Osman Salih, "The 1938 Kuwait Legislative Council", *Middle Eastern Studies*, vol. 28, n° 1, January 1992, p. 70.

40   Simon C. Smith, *Kuwait, 1950-1965. Britain, the al-Sabah, and Oil*, Oxford: The British Academy/Oxford University Press, 1999, pp. 8-9.

41   Osman Salih (1992), p. 77.

members and, after he failed, he dissolved the assembly authoritatively after only six months of existence. Refusing the decision, the council's members took refuge in a fortified citadel, which the ruler besieged with the support of Bedouin warriors, forcing his opponents to surrender. Several of them were arrested in the following months, while others fled to Iraq. In order to calm down the tensions, the ruler however agreed to proceed to the election of another council with a wider electorate than the previous one, which turned out to be an advisory body more than a legislative one and, in the context of growing Iraqi irredentism, was also quickly dissolved.[42]

Broadly speaking, the failure of the Assembly Movement was symptomatic of the new autonomy the Kuwaiti rulers had gained over their society following the signing of the concession agreement with the Anglo-American oil companies in 1934, and the discovery of the first oil well in 1938. As the emir had direct control of the oil revenues that were transferred directly to him by the oil companies, he did not depend anymore on the financial strength of the merchant class: "since he no longer needed the merchants' taxes, he no longer needed to listen to their ideas on policy".[43] The failure was also due to the mishandling of the situation by the oppositionist merchants. According to Jill Crystal, two elements precipitated the breakdown of the council: the fact that the merchants appeared to many as instruments of Iraqi irredentism and their inability to widen their social base and, in particular, to include the Shia residents.[44]

The Shias in Kuwaiti Coalition Politics

During the 1938 events, the Shias allied to the ruler against the Sunni merchants and played a key role in the collapse of the assembly. There were a number of reasons for this. The more frequent explanation is that the Shias did not feel represented by the assembly which, in fact, had no Shia member.[45] At first glance, as in 1921, the reasons for the absence of Shia representatives in the 1938 assembly lay in the socio-political reality of the Shia population in Kuwait, who included few wealthy merchants. Moreover, Shias felt they had a direct access to the ruler through the Emir's chief secretary, Molla Salih, "who had for some forty years been in effect

---

42   Osman Salih (1992), pp. 92-3.

43   Jill Crystal, *Kuwait. The Transformation of an Oil State*, Boulder: Oxford University Press, 1992, p. 20.

44   *Ibid.*

45   *Ibid.*, pp. 20-1; al-Mdayris (1999), p. 12; al-Khaldi (1999), pp. 93-2.

the Government of Kuwait".[46] As mentioned previously, the latter was an Iranian professing the Sunni creed who had been asked by Sheikh Khaz'al to assist the Kuwaiti emirs. He was abhorred by the merchant class because of his role in the breaking down of the principle of consultation during the reign of Mubarak the Great, but he was much appreciated by Iranian Shias. Upon the formation of the assembly, Molla Salih endeavoured to turn the Shia Iranian population into a pro-Emir constituency. This in turn brought the assembly's members to demand his dismissal, which naturally aroused the anger of the Shias who felt they were going the lose a master card in the representation of their interests.[47] Molla Salih was effectively dismissed by the Emir, but immediately replaced by his son 'Abdallah. This however did not calm the Shias who mobilized under the leadership of the leading religious authority of the time, Mahdi al-Qazwini, aided by his brother S. Jawad al-Qazwini and his nephew S. Mohammed al-Qazwini. Mahdi al-Qazwini sent a letter of protest to the council in which he articulated a set of demands: a fair Shia representation in the council, the opening of a special school for the Shias, the creation of a Shia religious court, the presence of Shia representatives in the municipal council of Kuwait city and, finally, fair recruitment in the nascent public administration.[48] As the council refused to accept the demands, some 4,500 Shias went to the British representative to ask for the British citizenship, expressing their feeling of exclusion from the nascent Kuwaiti nation.[49] In retaliation, the council issued a law stipulating that any Kuwaiti applying for a foreign citizenship would be expelled from the country. Faced with such an affront, Mahdi al-Qazwini incited the Shias to take to the streets to call for the disbanding of the assembly, which led to the first political demonstration of Kuwait's history. Jawad al-Qazwini would even have brought armed men to participate in the final siege of the assembly's members.[50]

In a book published in Kuwait in 2006, *A Survey of the History of Shias in Kuwait from the Birth of Kuwait to the Independence*, 'Abd al-Muhsin Jamal endeavoured to shed a new light on what he considers to be the conventional wisdom on the Shias' role in the Assembly Movement. A doctor of political science and also a leading member of the main Shia Islamic movement of Kuwait, the Islamic National Alliance, which he represented in the

---

46   Osman Salih (1992), p. 83.

47   *Ibid.*, pp. 85-86; Crystal (1990), p. 54.

48   Al-Mdayris (1999), p. 12.

49   Osman Salih (1992), p. 86; Crystal (1990), p. 54.

50   Personal interview with S. 'Ala al-Qazwini, a grand son of Mahdi al-Qazwini who keeps the family's archives, Kuwait, December 2006.

Kuwaiti parliament between 1981 and 2003, Jamal challenges the idea that the Shias did not participate in the movement. In line with his own political stance which always tried to overcome sectarian divides in political matters in order to favour the unification of an opposition to the government based on pure political considerations, he acknowledges that the aim of his book is "to avoid depicting the facts in sectarian terms".[51] According to his own sources, some Shias did actually participate in the National Bloc and were not, as such, barred from standing in the elections.[52] As he explains indeed, the whole election process was not as formal as it is today and there was no list of candidates. First, the 150 families whose members voted and ran for elections were not designated following an institutionalized procedure. The chosen people were rather self-designated by a process of self-mobilization and imposed themselves on the rulers by mobilizing their social networks. Second, as there was no list of candidates, the voters simply wrote the name of a person on a white paper and put it in the ballot box which was placed in the *diwaniyya* of 'Abdallah Saqr, a renowned merchant who was himself among the elected persons. Therefore, nobody as such was prevented from being candidate and, although the bulk of the voters were Sunni, "many Sunni families did not participate while many Shia families did participate".[53] By the same token, the assembly's opponents were to be found both among the Sunnis and the Shias. Jamal's explanation stops here and he does not say a word about the role of Molla Salih, and he does not even mention the Shia demonstration against the assembly.

Jamal's explanation tends to suggest that the reason why no Shia was elected to the 1938 assembly lies in a mere social fact: the Shias were not part of the merchant oligarchy of which the 1938 council was an expression. However, he tends to elude an important ideological factor which concurred to the Shias' exclusion. As mentioned above, many of those who launched the movement of the assembly were deeply influenced by Arab nationalist ideas and, more precisely, by Arabism the Iraqi way. Due to the particular context of Iraqi state formation – frontier tensions with Iran and the special political role played by the Shia *'ulama* of Iranian descent – a distinctive feature of Iraqi Arabism was its obsession with Iranian expansionism and plot to weaken the Arab nation. While, in the name of Arab solidarity, Syrian and Yemeni Arabs had no problems in obtaining an unconditional Iraqi citizenship and in working their way to

---

51   Jamal (2006), p. 84.

52   *Ibid.*, pp. 81-2.

53   *Ibid.*, p. 82.

important political positions,[54] long-time Iranian residents were granted a special identity card mentioning their Iranian nationality (*taba'iyya*), as a way to single them out as potential Iranian fifth columnists. This proved to be a precious instrument when the Ba'th government undertook to massively deport them in the 1970s and 1980s. Kuwaiti Arab nationalists borrowed this anti-Iranian prejudice from their Iraqi friends and, together with their claim for power sharing, also expressed refusal of further Iranian migration to Kuwait.[55] The strong anti-Iranian position of Kuwaiti Arab nationalists persisted long after the Assembly Movement and even aggravated in the 1970s when Iran became the regional power in the Gulf and was systematically accused of using its diaspora to advance its interests in the Arab states of the Gulf.[56]

This anti-Iranian stance naturally added to the Iranian Shias' defiance towards the 1938 council and, interestingly, they succeeded in winning over to their cause the Bahrani and Hasawi Shias. On the one hand, one can surmise that it was due to the pre-eminence of the Iranian notability both economically and religiously among the Shias overall, which allowed it to mobilize the different segments of the population. On the other hand, as the transformation of Shiism into the religion of the Iranian state in the sixteenth century prompted the Sunnis to regard any Shia either as an ethnic Iranian or at least as an agent of the Iranian state, one cannot rule out that by referring to "the Iranians", the nationalist merchants meant the Shias all together. This in turn could have led the Shias to coalesce behind the Iranian notability and to function as a single political actor.

From the 1938 events stemmed a particular pattern of relationship between the Shias and the ruling dynasty that lasted up to the 1980s. As the Kuwaiti political scene was dominated by the heirs of the Assembly Movement, the Shias and the Al-Sabah remained objective allies. Shias were regularly elected to the Parliament established in 1962 but most of them were so-called pro-government deputies. It is only with the Arab nationalist current's loss of influence in the late 1970s, the emergence of Shia Islamic movements and the concomitant advent of the Islamic revolution in Iran, that this pattern of silent Shiism shifted to a much more confrontational

---

54   The main example being that of Sati' al-Husri, the father of Iraqi Arab nationalism, who was actually born in Aleppo and exerted great influence on the Iraqi education system. See William L. Cleveland, *The Making of an Arab Nationalist: Ottomanism and Arabism in the Life and Thought of Sati' al-Husri*, Princeton, New Jersey: Princeton University Press, 1971.

55   Al-Mdayris (1999), pp. 13-14.

56   *Ibid.*, p. 20.

one reminiscent, although only superficially as we shall see, of the ones in Bahrain and Saudi Arabia.

PART II

CENTRE AND PERIPHERY

In the course of the 1970s, Shia modes of politicization in the Gulf monarchies witnessed a dramatic shift. Like in the other regions of the Middle East, the humiliating defeat of the Arab nationalist regimes by Israel in June 1967 wore down the legitimacy of the Arab nationalist ideology that dominated the political scene. Both among the Sunnis and the Shias, the Islamic movements took the opportunity to reassert their solution for the predicament of the Arab world. They stressed that, in order to fight Western imperialism and defeat Israel, Muslims should overcome what they considered first and foremost to be a moral crisis. This should be done by returning to a strict practice of Islam.

Sunni Islamic movements had been created as early as 1928 with the foundation of the Society of the Muslim Brotherhood in Egypt by Hasan al-Banna. From Egypt, the Society spread to other countries and in particular Iraq, where the movement took root in the 1940s.[1] The Shias, however, had failed to articulate their own Islamic political ideology and to translate it into fully-fledged political organizations. It is in Iraq, at the heart of the Shia learning community based in the shrine cities, that the first Shia Islamic movements appeared in the late 1950s and 1960s. Al-Da'wa and the Shiraziyyin, the two leading groups of the time, soon extended to the neighbouring Arab countries, including Lebanon but – more significantly – in the Gulf monarchies and in particular Kuwait, Bahrain and Saudi Arabia. From this time on, political developments affecting the Shia population in these countries were intimately tied to the events in Iraq. Furthermore, the diffusion of the Iraqi Shia movements to the Gulf countries was part of a much broader process of establishment of a centre-

---

1   Abdul-Halim al-Ruhaimi, "The Da'wa Islamic Party: Origins, Actors and Ideology", in Faleh Abdul-Jabar (ed.), *Ayatollahs, Sufis and Ideologues. State, Religion and Social Movements in Iraq*, London: Saqi Books, 2002, p. 149.

periphery pattern between the clerical class of the Iraqi shrine cities and their counterparts in the Gulf.

3

MEANWHILE IN IRAQ

Understanding the process by which the Iraqi Shia movements extended to the Gulf monarchies necessitates adopting a long term perspective by bringing to light the method of the lengthy centralization process of religious authority in the shrine city of Najaf in present-day southern Iraq. This was the result of a series of historical circumstances and doctrinal developments that, in the nineteenth century, led to the constitution of broad patronage networks of Shia religious professionals spread out across the Shia world. This provided the twentieth century Islamic activists with a ready-made infrastructure of circulation through which to spread across the borders.

THE FORMATION OF A CENTRAL RELIGIOUS AUTHORITY

Before the Occultation in the ninth century, the Imams had trained agents whose task was to intermediate between them and the ordinary believers.[1] In the vacuum of religious guidance left by the Occultation, these agents logically gained in strength and importance and progressively constituted into a fully-fledged corps of religious professionals. They played a central role in helping the Shias to survive the predicament of Occultation by exercising a legal-traditional leadership that substituted for the Imam's charismatic direction.[2]

---

1   Liyakat N. Takim, *The Heirs of the Prophet. Charisma and Religious Authority in Shi'ite Islam*, New York: State University of New York Press, 2006.

2   Wilfred Madelung, "Authority in Twelver Shi'ism in the Absence of the Imam", in George Makdisi (ed.), *La notion d'autorité au Moyen-Age: Islam, Byzance, Occident*, Paris: Colloques Internationaux de La Napoule, 1982, p. 166.

The Formation of the Shia Clerical Class

Since its inception, two schools of thought on the role of the *'ulama* have been opposed. The Akhbari current considered that the disappearance of the Imams was of little consequence since the latter had provided the believers with many statements that would help them to elaborate Islamic law during the Occultation. According to them, *ijtihad*, the inferring of religious norms, should therefore be exercised on the basis of two sources: the Quran on the one hand and, on the other, the statements by the Prophet and the Imams (*akhbar*). In opposition to the Akhbari school, the Usuli current considered that these two sources were insufficient to elaborate Islamic law and that the scholars, thanks to their great knowledge, could legitimately practice *ijtihad* by using two other sources: speculative reasoning (*'aql*) and consensus between the scholars (*ijma'*). While they did not claim infallibility like the Imams, Usuli *'ulama* insisted that they could act as the Hidden Imam's legitimate representatives (*na'ib*, pl. *nuwwab*) during the Occultation and formulated the doctrine of "general deputyship" (*niyaba 'amma*).[3]

According to historical circumstances, Shia scholars tended to gather in territories under benevolent powers, like the Mesopotamian shrine cities under the rule of the Shia Buyyid dynasty (945-1055) or, from the thirteenth century onward, the region of Jabal 'Amil (present-day southern Lebanon), which hosted an important Shia population that managed to stay out of the grip of Sunni powers at various moments in time.[4] With the establishment of the Safavid dynasty (1501-1722) in Iran and the subsequent transformation of Shiism into the Iranian state religion, Iran became the main centre of Shia learning, attracting many of the most qualified scholars of the Shia world. The latter were assigned the task of providing the new regime with its religious legitimacy as well as actively implementing the Shiaization of this then predominantly Sunni country. An essential component of state power, the religious professionals grew in number and reached for the first time the status of a fully-fledged hierocracy, an institution with unprecedented coercive means to enforce its grip on lay society.[5]

---

3   Ahmad Kazemi Moussavi, "The Establishment of the Position of Marja'iyyat-i Taqlid in the Twelver-Shi'i Community", *Iranian Studies*, vol. 18, n° 1, winter 1985, pp. 35-8; Heinz Halm, *The Shiites. A Short History*, Princeton, New Jersey: Markus Wiener Publishers, 2007, pp. 95-102.

4   Moojan Momen, *An Introduction to Shi'i Islam. The History and Doctrines of Twelver Shi'ism*, New Haven, Connecticut: Yale University Press, 1985, pp. 75-104.

5   Arjomand (1984), pp. 122-59.

Under the leadership of 'Ali al-Karaki (d. 1534), a leading scholar from Jabal 'Amil whom the Safavid invited to their court, the scholars, most of them affiliated to the Usuli school of thought, developed the concept of general deputyship to its ultimate logic. They obtained from the second Safavid sovereign an official proclamation of 'Ali al-Karaki as the Imam's representative.

In the course of the eighteenth century, a series of historical events in Iran led to the relocation of hundreds of religious scholars from Iran to the Mesopotamian shrine cities. The most decisive one was the fall of the Safavid dynasty in 1722 following the invasion of Iran by Sunni Afghan tribes who proved particularly hostile to the Shia religious professionals. The dynasty that succeeded the Safavid, the Afsharid (1736-1750), opted for a different approach to state-religion relations. Threatened by Sunni powers, it endeavoured to put an end to Iranian religious particularism by declaring that Shiism was no more than the fifth school of religious law of Sunni Islam (*madhhab*), with the same status as the other four.[6] This meant, among other things, that Shia religious law had no particular divine authority compared to Sunni law. Consequently, the Afsharid put an end to the various privileges of the Shia scholars, therefore putting an end to the symbiosis between the Iranian state and the clerical class. Deprived of the governmental endowments that constituted a major source of power for them, many *'ulama* left Iran, mainly for India and Mesopotamia. This is how the centre of Shia scholarship shifted from Iran to the Mesopotamian shrine cities, mainly Karbala and later on Najaf.[7]

At that time under a largely nominal Ottoman rule, south Mesopotamia formed the Marches of the Ottoman Empire. It was a frontier zone constituting the main front line of the rivalry between the Ottoman and the Iranian empires, a region of regular military confrontation of which a main object was the control of the shrine cities hosting the tombs of the Imams.[8] The special location of the Mesopotamian shrine cities, more particularly Najaf and Karbala, made them ideal places to establish a kind of *de facto* extra-territorial clerical power independent both from the Ottoman and the Iranian states. Independence from the state was an advantage in terms

---

6   Sunnism is divided into four schools of Islamic law (*madhhab*, pl. *madhahib*) deriving from the thought of four Islamic jurists (*faqih*, pl. *fuqaha*): Shafeism, Malekism, Hanbalism and Hanafism. On the Afsharid period, see Ernest S. Tucker, *Nadir Shah's Quest for Legitimacy in Post-Safavid Iran*, Gainesville: University of Florida Press, 2006.

7   Momen (1985), pp. 127-8.

8   Nakash (1994), p. 14.

of freedom of thought and deeds, but it also posited very concrete problems of financing. Deprived of state support, the clerics had to find other sources of funding. This meant relying on the voluntary contributions of the lay population and, therefore, launching an active campaign of conversion of the Mesopotamian tribes to Shiism. As shown by Yitzhak Nakash, the vital necessity to increase the number of Shias in order to assure the religious professionals' material survival explains the relatively late shiaization of the Mesopotamian populations, that was only achieved in the course of the nineteenth century.[9] The expansion of Shiism throughout Mesopotamia provided the clerics with a population to whom they could provide religious services of various sorts in exchange for payment. However, the main feature of the clerical class based in the Mesopotamian shrine cities was that their economy was largely extrovert. Money came from abroad, mainly Iran but also India. The financial dependence upon Iranian sources of funding can be explained by the fact that the bulk of the clerics, and in particular the higher ranking scholars, were of Iranian descent and had therefore kept close contacts with Iran.[10] By the end of the nineteenth century, the 'ulama of Mesopotamia benefited from the conflict between the wealthy Iranian merchant class and the Qajar regime (1781-1925). Looking for a way to solve its fiscal crisis, the Iranian government opted for a deliberate policy of favouring foreign trading firms over the local merchants who had heretofore been major contributors to its budget. This deeply harmed the interest of the bazaari, the Iranian urban merchants, who turned to the scholars of Mesopotamia whose support they gained in their struggle against their government's policy. A strong alliance was forged after the tobacco episode (see below) of 1891, where the scholars of Mesopotamia succeeded in forcing the Shah to cancel the monopoly over tobacco exploitation it had granted to a British firm. In exchange for extensive funding, the 'ulama provided the bazaari with political support when needed. By the same token, the scholars of Mesopotamia gained religious pre-eminence over their colleagues based in Iran, whose credibility had been undermined by their subservience to the regime.[11]

But funding was not the only problem of the Shia scholars of Mesopotamia. They had also to guarantee the stability of their environment by making sure that the shrine cities would be safe from outside attacks, be it tribal razzias, attacks by the Wahhabi Ikhwan or attempts by the Otto-

---

9   *Ibid.*, pp. 25-48.

10   *Ibid.*, pp. 184-201.

11   *Ibid.*, p. 210.

man central state to impose a tighter control. In the absence of a strong central power able to monopolize violence, Najaf and Karbala were under the thumb of gangs who extorted money from the inhabitants but also provided them with armed protection at times of need and were the defenders of the cities' independence. This was very much to the convenience of the 'ulama. In Karbala, for example, local gangs ensured that the Ottoman Sultan's name was not pronounced in Friday sermons as should have been the case in a city under formal Ottoman rule.[12] In Najaf, the Zuqurt and Shumurt gangs shared control of the city's four quarters from the time when, in the early nineteenth century, a prominent Arab scholar had undertaken to recruit warriors from among the locals to protect Najaf from Wahhabi attacks.[13]

The Centralization of Religious Authority in Najaf

Under the Qajar dynasty, the link between the Iranian state and the Shia clerical class was progressively re-established but Iran nonetheless remained a secondary centre of learning as compared with the Mesopotamian shrine cities. In Iran, because of their privileged relation with the state, the clerics were integrated within a formal hierarchy based on institutional positions granted by the Shah. In Mesopotamia, by contrast, in the absence of effective state control the society of the scholars was essentially a loose self-regulated milieu revolving around individual scholars who all behaved as free electrons competing for financial resources, religious influence and, sometimes, also political power.

This society has been described in detail by Meir Litvak for the nineteenth century period. He showed that beyond the absence of formalized forms of organization, the clerical class had developed regular patterns of behaviour that resulted in the formation of a fully-fledged institution, which the Shias came to refer to as the "*hawza 'ilmiyya*".[14] Literally meaning "the territory of learning", this Arabic expression defines the scholars as a body of religious professionals whose main task is to teach and learn. A generic term collectively designating the teachers and the students, the word *hawza* also refers to the community of learning in one particular place. One will for example speak of the *hawza* of Najaf or the *hawza* of

---

12   On the gangs of Karbala, see Cole, (2002), chapter 6, "Mafia, Mob and Shi'ism in Iraq" (with Moojen Momen), pp. 99-122.

13   Meir Litvak, *Shi'i Scholars of Nineteenth-Century Iraq. The 'Ulama' of Najaf and Karbala'*, Cambridge: Cambridge University Press, 1998, pp. 123-6.

14   Litvak (1998), p. 22.

Qom. In the contemporary period that witnessed the diffusion of more formalized modes of learning, the word *hawza* also came to refer to a particular religious school and is hence synonymous with the word "*madrasa*", that is, "school" in Arabic. The higher ranks of the *hawza* were constituted by the *mujtahid*, the scholars who had reached the level of *ijtihad*, that is obtained a sufficiently wide knowledge to formulate independent interpretations of the religious law. The *mujtahid* gave classes at the mosque, in the shrine courtyards or even at their private homes. They were tied to their students and to the lower ranking *'ulama* by patronage bonds. Due to the absence of a central administration as well as to the scarcity of religious endowments (*waqf*, pl. *awqaf*) providing financial support to the students, the latter were indeed dependent upon their teachers for their very material survival. This was all the more so since most of the students were actually *immigrés*, often teenagers, who had no other means of living than the stipends granted by their teachers. The teacher-student relationship, however, was essentially interdependent as the students had significant leverage on the teachers. In this highly competitive system indeed, they could shift freely from one *mujtahid* to another, a more learned or, more basically, one providing higher stipends. Moreover, the teachers' reputations among their peers depended on the number and quality of their students. The latter would spread their ideas by writing down their lessons and compiling their legal rulings (*fatwa*). When needed, they could also transform into vigilantes intimidating their teacher's rivals when, as sometimes happened, a dispute between *mujtahid* was resolved by force.[15] Often, the circle of students of one *mujtahid* developed a group identity based on the pride of being the disciples of a particular scholar as well as on antagonism with a rival network of students.[16]

While the Usuli doctrine tended to consider that the general deputyship of the Imam during the Occultation was the collective responsibility of the *mujtahid*, a practical and doctrinal consensus progressively crystallized on the idea that the *hawza* should have one single *mujtahid* as its head. In theory, his leadership position would be based on the pre-eminence of his religious knowledge, that is on his status as the most learned of the *mujtahid*.[17] Before the second half of the nineteenth century however, supreme religious authority was only a local reality. A religious leader was recognized as such only at the level of a city. Hence, when two leaders competed for

---

15   *Ibid.*, p. 27.

16   *Ibid.*, p. 29.

17   *Ibid.*, p. 55.

supremacy, the loser of the contest often left for another town where he would try to establish himself, knowing that his rival's authority would be contained within the borders of Najaf, Karbala or any other shrine city.[18] The landscape of the community of learning was therefore geographically polycentric, structured around multiple centres that, although connected to each other, constituted autonomous entities as far as the practical exercise of religious leadership was concerned. This pattern began to shift towards an increasingly centralized model of religious authority when, in the mid-nineteenth century, the city of Najaf emerged as the main geographical centre of religious learning among the many competing centres. This was achieved thanks to the skilfulness of S. Mohammed Hasan Najafi (d.1850), who became the religious leader of the Najafi *hawza* in 1846 and subsequently succeeded for the first time in establishing himself as the premier *mujtahid* beyond the borders of Najaf, in the Mesopotamian cities but also in Iran.[19] Mohammed Hasan Najafi benefited from a historic leadership vacuum both in Iran and Iraq. In Iran, the scholars had lost religious prestige by getting too involved in the state apparatus and the concomitant administration of justice and religious endowments. The population accused them of corruption and, more and more, Iranians turned to the *mujtahid* of Mesopotamia for religious guidance. The leadership vacuum was also true in Mesopotamia where several leading *mujtahid* died without successors.[20]

In a society based on networks of interpersonal relations, Mohammed Hasan Najafi achieved his position of pre-eminence thanks to his ability to build patronage networks within Najaf but also beyond the city. In order to cut across the local boundaries that had heretofore constrained religious authority, he introduced a new form of interpersonal relations that provided the model on which subsequent transnational networks were built. He dispatched his disciples, mainly to Iran but also to other Mesopotamian shrine cities and India, with a mandate to judge as well as to collect religious alms on his behalf. He hence built a whole network of representatives (*wakil*, pl. *wukala*) that acted as his delegates in the main centres of religious learning.[21] This pattern of delegation of authority had an obvious practical advantage as it gave him the ability to be everywhere at once. He

---

18   *Ibid.*

19   Ahmad Kazemi Moussavi, "The Institutionalization of the Marja'-i Taqlid in the Nineteenth Century Shi'ite Community", *The Muslim World*, vol. 83, n° 3-4, July-October 1994, p. 280.

20   Litvak (1998), p. 65.

21   *Ibid.*, p. 67.

did not have to travel physically to Iran to raise funds, as the *mujtahid* used to do before him, and he actually set up the basis of a centralized management of the religious authority that has been emulated by his successors up to the present day.

A practical reality under Mohammed Hasan Najafi, the idea of leadership by a single scholar was systematized conceptually in the middle of the nineteenth century by his successor, Murtadha Ansari (d. 1864). The accession of the latter to supreme religious leadership in Najaf and beyond resulted from a totally new procedure. Contrary to the traditional habit according to which a *mujtahid* rises to leadership thanks to his knowledge and social capital, he was indeed formally designated as his successor by Mohammed Hasan Najafi on his deathbed, in front of an assembly composed of the leading *mujtahid* of the time.[22] The fact that he thenceforth effectively imposed himself as the senior scholar even beyond the level of his predecessor indicates the scope of the effective power gained by the latter. Indeed, although an eminent scholar, Murtadha Ansari was not recognized as a possible contender for supreme religious leadership by his peers upon the death of Mohammed Hasan Najafi. Nonetheless, his designation was unchallenged by his potential rivals. In order to consolidate his position, he distinguished himself not only by his virtuosity in *ijtihad* but also by his exemplary ascetic style of living that contrasted with that of his predecessor. He also undertook to lay down the doctrinal bases of supreme religious leadership, which shifted to the status of an undisputed doctrine that has become a central pillar of the Shia religious institution to this day.

Murtadha Ansari actually systematized the idea, found in many treaties by *mujtahid* for several decades previously, that the *hawza* should be headed by a senior scholar who would be the most learned of the *mujtahid*. He formulated the doctrine known as the *marja'iyya al-taqlid* (the source of emulation) by stipulating that, during the period of Occultation, ordinary believers as well as clerics who have not reached the level of *ijtihad* must follow the opinions of a senior living *mujtahid* on a wide range of issues falling within the realm of religious law, going from purely ritualistic issues, to men and women's physiology[23] and political matters. Practically, the *mujtahid* recognized as the supreme leader would also be the only one entitled to collect religious taxes and spend them for the maintenance of the *hawza*, the spreading of Islam and assistance to the needy. Actually, Murtadha Ansari set out the basis of a hierarchy of *'ulama*, as attested by

---

22   *Ibid.*, p. 70.

23   That is, issues pertaining to the functioning of the body as far as it has implications for the performance of religious ritual or for the ethic of sexuality.

the progressive introduction of honorific titles joined to the clerics' name in theory according to their degree of religious knowledge: grand *ayatollah* (the sign of God) for the most learned, *ayatollah, hujjat al-Islam* (the proof of Islam), sheikh.[24] The *mujtahid* would be called *marja'* (pl. *maraji'*) *al-taqlid*. Since its inception, the weakness of the *marja'iyya* doctrine resided in the method of choosing the *marja'*. Indeed, the doctrine of the *marja'iyya*, while introducing a measure of centralization in the amorphous institution of the *hawza*, did not solve the problem of the absence of formal procedures for the designation of the *mujtahid*. Since deciding who is the most learned is a highly subjective matter, the absence of formal procedure helped reproduce the highly competitive and factionalized character of the society of *'ulama*. According to the doctrine articulated by Murtadha Ansari, the choice is indeed incumbent on the followers themselves who, after a close examination made in all conscience, must decide who they will emulate. Practically, this means that, while the emulation of a single *marja'* by the entire community of believers has remained an ideal horizon, there has almost always been several *marja'* at the same time. This explains the appearance of the title of "supreme *marja'*" (*marja' 'a'la*) to distinguish senior *marja'* from less popular and supposedly less knowledgeable ones. But again, there are often several *mujtahid* who claim the status of supreme *marja'*. As we shall see, their relations can oscillate between mutual respect and overt hostility.

How does one become a *marja'*, today, when the institution of the *marja'iyya* is a well anchored reality? With no procedure of appointment, and no election by peers, a *marja'* is said to "emerge" (*baraz*) following a lengthy process of mobilization of the clerical milieus, the wealthy laity and the ordinary believers.[25] This means that while being a *marja'* is ideally a status based on pre-eminence in religious knowledge, it is actually founded on "practicalities of leadership".[26] The candidate must first of all establish his reputation within the *hawza*. To assert himself in this milieu, the applicant must be recognized as a senior *mujtahid* by his peers. His teachers must give him certificates attesting to his ability to practice *ijtihad*.

---

24   Moussavi (1994), pp. 295-9.

25   Sabrina Mervin, "Les autorités religieuses dans le chiisme duodécimain contemporain", *Archives des sciences sociales des religions*, n° 125, January-March 2004, p. 67.

26   Abbas Amanat, "In Between the Madrasa and the Marketplace: The Designation of Clerical Leadership in Modern Shi'ism", in Said A. Arjomand, *Authority and Political Culture in Shi'ism*, Albany: State University of New York Press, 1988, p. 101.

To further substantiate his claim, the candidate should also have lots of students attending his classes, as well as writing down and publishing his lectures. Another criterion is the style of living of the candidate: he must be particularly pious and upright. But as *marja'iyya* is as much a matter of social weight as of religious knowledge, influence in the religious arena is not enough and any candidate must also have economically potent supporters among lay society. Historically, *marja'* have been tightly linked to the merchant and landowner notability who have greatly contributed to the funding of their religious and charitable activities. Up to today, a chief source of funding has been the collection of religious taxes like the *zakat*, which is common to Sunnis and Shias, and the *khums*, the specific Shia Islamic tax consisting in one fifth of the yearly surplus income of a family. The fact that people chose to give these religious incomes to a particular *mujtahid* is a sign that he is recognized as a *de facto marja'*, even though he may not have announced it publicly. Some also receive state financial support as governments often mix in *marja'iyya* affairs in order to support a candidate considered more prone to serve their interests. These various sources of financial support permit the *mujtahid* to sustain their students but also to penetrate the poorer segments of society by providing a wide range of social services. Once his position is sufficiently assured, the candidate can prepare to "announce his *marja'iyya*" (*ya'lan marja'iyyatuhu*), as the expression goes. But this should not be done without following a set of tacit rules. He should first of all wait until he reaches a venerable age. This rule is not mandatory in principle but it is a well established tacit imperative risky for any candidate to circumvent. Second, he has to publish a treaty of religious behaviour (*risala 'amaliyya*) in which he sets out his views on a wide range of legal matters. The treaty is seldom innovative and often consists of mere footnotes on the manual of a previous *marja'*.[27] As a last step, most of the candidates wait for the death of a senior *marja'* before declaring themselves publicly. Indeed, as the Usuli doctrine forbids emulation of a dead *marja'*, an applicant can hope to capture the following of one of his predecessors. Often but not always, a living *marja'* promotes one of his former students to be his successor after his death so that the network of institutions and followers can pass from one *marja'* to another. In the contemporary period,

---

27   Chibli Mallat, *The Renewal of Islamic Law. Muhammed Baqir as-Sadr, Najaf and the Shi'i International*, Cambridge: Cambridge University Press, 1993, p. 48; Linda S. Walbridge, "The Counterreformation. Becoming a *Marja'* in the Modern World", in Linda S. Walbridge (ed.), *The Most Learned of the Shi'a. The Institution of the Marja' al-Taqlid*, Oxford: Oxford University Press, 2001, p. 231.

this is what happened between S. Abu al-Qasem al-Khu'i (1899-1992) and S. 'Ali al-Sistani (b. 1930).

Religious Authority and Politics

The long-distance networks that were progressively built within the framework of the centralization of the *marja'iyya* in Najaf from the mid-nineteenth century on had no political dimension as such. Not the support of a particular political project, they were merely the means through which the clerical class of the Mesopotamian shrine cities asserted its position in the face of its peers from other areas of the Shia world. However at certain moments in time, these networks happened to play a key role in major political issues, and in particular in the opposition to the established worldly powers. During the Safavid period in Iran, the Shia clerics had largely served to legitimize the regime to the point that their religious authority was largely derived from the state/clergy symbiosis. The rise of Najaf as an extra-territorial pole of Shia religious authority entailed a totally different type of state/clergy relation characterized by confrontation.[28] Sheltered in the shrine cities, the *mujtahid* of Mesopotamia, the majority of whom were Iranian *immigrés* or were born from families of Iranian migrants, developed into a contest for power with the Qajar sovereigns. In 1890, in order to find new state budget sources to face a deep financial crisis, the Qajar sovereign decided to grant a British company a fifty-year monopoly on the cultivation and commercial exploitation of Iranian tobacco. The decision prompted protests all over the country, in particular among the merchant class whose interests the decision directly hurt. They urged the *'ulama* of Iran to petition the Shah, but the latter stayed inflexible, showing that the opinion of the local clerical class was of little weight. In the meantime in Mesopotamia, S. Mirza Hasan Shirazi had established himself as the uncontested successor of Murtadha Ansari as the *marja'* of the era. Contrary to his predecessor who had benefited from the financial and political support of the Iranian rulers, Mirza Hasan Shirazi had from the start refused to compromise with the Qajar. This was mainly due to the close ties he maintained with the merchant class of south Iran and particularly Shiraz, the town where he was himself born.[29] These ties had proved decisive in the consolidation of his position as the leading *marja'* in the course of the con-

---

28   Faleh Abdul-Jabar, "The Genesis and Development of *Marja'ism* versus the State", in Faleh Abdul-Jabar (ed.), *Ayatollahs, Sufis and Ideologues. State, Religion and Social Movements in Iraq*, London: Saqi Books, 2002, pp. 61-89; Arjomand (1984), pp. 238-57.

29   Amanat (1988), p. 116.

test that followed the death of Murtadha Ansari. Therefore, Mirza Hasan Shirazi could not ignore the call by these merchants when they asked him to support the rulings of local *'ulama* who wished to forbid the use of tobacco to any Muslim as long as the British would hold the concession. The legend tells how all Iranians suddenly stopped smoking, including the wives of the Shah himself who removed all the water-pipes from his palace so he was himself unable to smoke. Faced with this large boycott, the Shah finally had no choice but to put an end to the agreement with the British company.[30]

Another famous event shows the scope of the influence of the shrine cities' scholars on Iranian political affairs. Between 1905 and 1911, Iran witnessed a revolution that saw the population mobilize to demand the transformation of the authoritarian Qajar state into a constitutional monarchy with an elected parliament. From Najaf, three Iranian *mujtahid* played a leading role in mobilizing the *hawza* in favour of constitutional ideas and in imposing the scholars as chief political actors: Mirza Husein Tihrani, Mohammed Kazem Khorassani and Abdallah Mazanderani.[31] The latter were approached directly by their colleagues in Tehran who asked them to send letters and telegrams to the Shah asking for the creation of a parliament. As during the tobacco episode, the scholars based in Iran had reached the conclusion that the influence of their colleagues based in Mesopotamia far outstripped their own. In 1909, as the struggle between pro- and anti-constitutionalists intensified in Iran, it is in Najaf that Mohammed Na'ini wrote one of the most important books of Shia political philosophy, *The Awakening of the Islamic Community and the Purification of the Nation*. Written to support the constitutional movement, the book was in many respects revolutionary as it articulated the link between Islamic concepts of government and the Western concepts of constitution and rule by the people.

Principally involved in Iranian political affairs up to the First World War, the *'ulama* of the Mesopotamian cities also participated actively in the various episodes in the formation of the modern Iraqi state. While they had always been anxious to keep the Ottoman state at distance, the clerics chose to side with it following the penetration of British troops into Mesopota-

---

30   On the details of the tobacco affair, see Ann K. S. Lambton, "The Tobacco Regie: Prelude to Revolution I", *Studia Islamica*, n° 22, 1965 and "The Tobacco Regie: Prelude to Revolution II", *Studia Islamica* n° 23, 1965.

31   Abdul-Hadi Hairi, *Shi'ism and Constitutionalism in Iran. A Study of the Role Played by the Persian Residents of Iraq in Iranian Politics*, Leiden: Brill, 1977, pp. 98-100.

mia in 1914, preferring coexistence with a Sunni state rather than the prospect of occupation by a foreign and un-Islamic power. They enacted *fatwa* urging the population to join the Ottoman army and themselves led tribal militias that caused heavy losses to the British troops although they were not able to defeat them.[32] After the final fall of the Ottoman Empire (1918) and the installation of the British in the three ex-Ottoman provinces that were to constitute Iraq, the *'ulama* petitioned the Society of Nations to demand the creation of an independent Iraqi state governed according to Islamic law and the rulings of the *mujtahid*.[33] When the British occupation was legitimized by an official mandate from the international community in 1920, the Shia clerics launched a revolt which has since stayed in the collective memory of Iraqis as one of the most important episodes of their history. The "Revolution of 1920" was led by a prominent Iranian *mujtahid*, Mohammed Taqi Shirazi, based in Karbala. Composed of tribal leaders as well as of young clerics and sons of clerics, his army succeeded in ousting the British from the south in only a few days, which enabled the scholars to form an independent government in Karbala.[34] The experience was short-lived as the British finally defeated the insurgents and imposed the formation of an Iraqi state under protectorate over which the Shia scholars had little if any influence. Several of them were exiled or chose voluntarily to leave the country to establish themselves in Iran, where they were unable to influence the events in Iraq. The ones who finally decided to return to Iraq were marginalized, signalling the beginning of a period of decline of the *hawza* in what was now Iraq.

A direct consequence of the weakening of the *hawza* was the rebirth of the Iranian centres of learning and, in particular, the progressive emergence of the city of Qom. Hosting the grave of Fatima, the sister of the eighth Imam 'Ali al-Redha, Qom was then a shrine city where several Safavid and Qajar sovereigns had been buried over the centuries. It had also hosted a vital community of learning that had however collapsed in the early nineteenth century after the death of the last renowned teacher.[35] In 1920 after the rout of the Shia *mujtahid* in Iraq, dozens of teachers and students left the Iraqi shrine cities for Iran. The growing flow of refugees necessitated the

---

32   Pierre-Jean Luizard, *La formation de l'Irak contemporain. Le rôle politique des ulémas chiites à la fin de la domination ottomane et au moment de la création de l'Etat irakien*, Paris: CNRS, 1991, pp. 319-35.

33   *Ibid.,* p. 370.

34   *Ibid.*, pp. 403-13.

35   Michael M. J. Fisher, *Iran. From Religious Dispute to Revolution*, Madison, Wisconsin: The University of Wisconsin Press, 1980, pp. 107-8.

restoration of the local infrastructures of learning and it was in this context that the *hawza* of Qom was rehabilitated. Qom emerged as a major centre of learning after 'Abd al-Karim Ha'iri-Yazdi, an eminent *mujtahid* repatriated from Najaf, decided to establish himself there.[36] In order to strengthen his leadership, the latter avoided supporting his colleagues who, in contrast to him, had actively engaged in the opposition to the British and envisaged their stay in Iran as temporary, a way to regain force in order to return to Iraq in a position of strength. He rather endeavoured to establish Qom as a new major centre of Shia learning[37] Meanwhile in Iraq, the Arab *mujtahid* took the opportunity to challenge the position of the Iranians with the backing of the Iraqi government staffed by Arab nationalists eager to put an end to the pre-eminence of the Iranian scholars.[38] Under the influence of nationalist ideologies on both sides of the frontier, a pattern of relative nationalization of the Shia clergy then emerged both in Iraq and Iran. In other words, the frontier that had been highly volatile in the previous period was rigidified. Iranian *'ulama* were denounced by the Iraqi government as agents of Iranian irredentism and the Arab Shia population of Iraq, the bulk of whom supported the project of the Iraqi state and disregarded the position of the Iranian *mujtahid*, either distanced themselves from the religious institution, or turned to Arab clerics deemed better qualified to understand the needs of the Arabs.[39] In Iraq, the Arab *'ulama* again reached high positions within the clerical hierarchy, in contradistinction with the Ottoman period. In Iran, the clerics progressively gained in strength under successive regimes and became a potent opposition force that was able to challenge the Shah successfully in 1979. At this date, the advent of the Islamic Republic of Iran further enhanced the status of Qom as a major centre of Shia learning across the entire Shia world, establishing a durable pattern of bipolarization of the Shia learning community between Najaf on the one hand, and Qom on the other.

THE *HAWZA* IN IRAQI POLITICS

It is in this context of overall decline of the Shia religious institutions that the first Shia Islamic political movements emerged in Iraq. Contrary to their Sunni counterparts that were founded by devoted but nonetheless lay personalities who regarded the religious establishment with contempt,

36   *Ibid.*, p. 109.
37   Nakash (1994), p. 83.
38   *Ibid.*, p. 85.
39   *Ibid.*, p. 86.

the Shia movements were created in intimate connections with the clerical hierarchy. Indeed, while displaying a reformist stance towards some aspects of the religious institution's functioning which they sometimes harshly criticized, they simultaneously claimed to speak in the name of the supreme religious authority, whose support they were eager to garner. This explains why the Shia Islamic movements were deeply marked by the clerical institution's traditional conceptions of religious and political authority.

Al-Da'wa, the Political Expression of the Hawza

The creation of Hezb al-Da'wa al-Islamiyya (the Party of the Islamic Call) in 1958 was the direct result of the awareness by the clerical class of Iraq that the *hawza*, as an institution, was in real jeopardy in the face of the rise of secular ideologies. In particular, the growing audience for the Communist party among the poorer and newly urbanized segments of the Shia population was a major source of concern. Sons of *mujtahid* were said to leave the turban to embrace the tenets of social revolution. For the religious establishment, the period was all the more critical since a military junta backed by the Communists had overthrown the monarchy in 1958 and established a republic. The progress of secular ideologies did not only represent a moral defeat for the Shia clerics. It had also far reaching economic implications. Indeed, since the endowment of their institutions was chiefly based on the voluntary contributions of dedicated believers, the shrinking of their audience translated into a sharp diminishing of their resources for material survival. Moreover, the government of 'Abd al-Karim Qasem set up after the 1958 coup promulgated several laws which the Shia clerics considered alien to Islamic principles. This was so, in particular, of the family law which deprived them of a major domain of activity as judges. They were also concerned with the agrarian reform which abolished the system of big land tenures by tribal leaders and therefore eliminated a class of traditionally major contributors to their institutions.[40] The merchants of the shrine cities, whose revenues were tied to the continuous flow of pilgrims and who were also chief sources of funding for the *hawza*, were also severely hit by secularization and eager to take action to halt the process. Together with the tribal leaders, they were the allies of the clerics.

The 1958 regime change was decisive in prompting the clerics to react and reassert their prerogatives. A handful of laymen and junior clerics from

---

40   Faleh Abdul-Jabar, *The Shi'ite Movement in Iraq*, London: Saqi Books, 2003, p. 76; Joyce N. Wiley, *The Islamic Movement of Iraqi Shi'as*, Boulder, Colorado: Lynne Rienner Publishers, 1992, p. 33.

Najaf leaded by S. Mohammed Baqer al-Sadr (1931-1980) reached the conclusion that creating a fully-fledged political party was the most efficient tool to fight secularization. Mohammed Baqer al-Sadr was in many respects a pure product of the *hawza*, born into an old prestigious family of clerics descending from Prophet Mohammed and possessing branches in Iran and Lebanon. At the time of the founding of al-Da'wa, he was still a junior yet very promising cleric, one of the most brilliant students of S. Muhsin al-Hakim (d. 1970), the then leading *marja'* and head of the *hawza* in Najaf. Besides writing the statutes of the al-Da'wa and defining its overall programme of action and concrete organization, Mohammed Baqer al-Sadr distinguished himself as the author of seminal contributions to Islamic contemporary thought, in particular *Our Philosophy* (1959), in which he deconstructed Marxist theory, and *Our Economics* (1961), in which he exposed the outline of an entire Islamic theory of political economy. Often considered as a forerunner of Ruhollah Khomeini's conceptions, his work has inspired some basic tenets of the Islamic Republic of Iran.[41]

In accordance with the cautious attitude they had adopted after the 1920 Revolution, the higher ranking *mujtahid* did not directly enlist in al-Da'wa. Neither did they publicly express support for it. However, Muhsin al-Hakim is usually considered as having tacitly backed al-Da'wa, whose goals – the spread of Islam through the revivification of the religious institution and the fight against secular political ideologies – he shared. Some sources reckon that the founding meeting of the party was actually held in his house in Najaf.[42] What is sure is that one of his sons, S. Mahdi al-Hakim (d.1988), was among the chief founders of al-Da'wa and, according to some, involved in the project even before Mohammed Baqer al-Sadr.[43] One should also mention that the senior *mujtahid* organized in 1960 into a body named the Society of Scholars (*Jama'at al-'Ulama'*) which had no organizational links to al-Da'wa but in which some key positions were held by leading figures of the party: Mohammed Baqer al-Sadr who was the editor of the Society of Scholars' publication, *The Islamic Lights* (*al-Adhwa al-Islamiyya*); Mahdi al-Hakim, and the two Lebanese, S. Mohammed Husein Fadlallah (b. 1935) and Mohammed Mahdi Shams al-Din (1936-2001).[44]

---

41   Mallat (1993), pp. 59-78.

42   Al-Ruhaimi (2002), p. 151.

43   T. M. Aziz, "The Role of Muhammed Baqir al-Sadr in Shi'i Political Activism in Iraq from 1958 to 1980", *International Journal of Middle East Studies*, vol. 25, n° 2, May 1993, p. 209.

44   For the membership of the Society of Scholars, see Abdul-Jabar (2003), pp. 111-12.

Like al-Da'wa, the Society aimed at reviving religion and did that through the extensive publication of books and booklets explaining Islam's point of view on chief issues of the time such as the rights of workers or the redistribution of wealth, as well as by setting up a wide network of religious schools and charitable associations throughout Iraq.

Far from being a mere reassertion of the clerical establishment's prerogatives, the birth of al-Da'wa also expressed the rise of new ideas and patterns of action among the scholars. The statutes of the party written by Mohammed Baqer al-Sadr contained sometimes audacious innovations which many among the more conservative circles of the *hawza* considered as deviating from Islamic doctrine. A main source of contention was the dual principle of authority: the activists were to obey the formal party leadership on the one hand but, on the other, vow allegiance to the *marja'iyya*. As noted by Faleh Abdul-Jabar, "the notion of party obedience involves an irresolvable contradiction with Shia theology" as it *de facto* nullifies the very principle of *marja'iyya*.[45] The two principles could have been reconciled were Mohammed Baqer al-Sadr be the formal head of the party as well as a recognized *marja'*. While being among the contenders for Muhsin al-Hakim's succession, he reached the status of *marja'* only at the end of his life. After al-Hakim's death in 1970, his successor at the head of the *hawza* was another student of his, namely S. Abu al-Qasem al-Khu'i who did not support al-Da'wa the way his predecessor did.

Another sign of al-Da'wa's modernity was the links it established with Sunni Islamic organizations settled in Iraq, most notably the Muslim Brotherhood and the Hezb al-Tahrir (Liberation Party). The two were explicitly mentioned by Mohammed Baqer al-Sadr in al-Da'wa's statutes as models both to emulate and to surpass. The works of their spiritual mentors like Hasan al-Banna or Sayyid Qutb were part of the indoctrination programme in which the activists were educated. Mohammed Baqer al-Sadr borrowed from them the idea of the organization of political action into several stages, adding one fourth stage to the three step programme of the Muslim Brotherhood: the propaganda step, the political step of forming an organization and training activists, the revolutionary step of seizing power, and the final step of establishing the Islamic polity.[46] As in the Sunni Islamic movements' doctrine, the Islamic state as envisioned by Mohammed Baqer al-Sadr would encompass the entire territory of the *umma*, the community of Muslims, as well as the as yet non-Islamized parts of the world over which it would claim authority by virtue of the universal character of

45   Abdul-Jabar (2003), p. 80.
46   *Ibid.*, p. 81; al-Ruhaimi (2002), p. 153.

Islam. Contrary to his Sunni counterparts however, Mohammed Baqer al-Sadr added that the Islamic polity would be placed under the guidance of the *marja'iyya*. While the executive and legislative powers would be elected by the people, they would also be placed under the final supervision of a body comprising senior *mujtahid*. Its role would be to ascertain that the laws voted into existence matched Islamic principles. In the case of conflict, the scholars would have the final say over the elected bodies.[47]

While al-Da'wa enjoyed the tacit backing of Muhsin al-Hakim, Mo-hammed Baqer al-Sadr's views were far from achieving consensus within the *hawza*. This explains why, during the 1960s, the clerics retreated from their direct involvement in the party, feeling that this could endanger their position by alienating them from powerful segments of the *hawza*. Probably following advice from Muhsin al-Hakim himself, Mohammed Baqer al-Sadr chose to leave his functions in the party to dedicate him-self to his religious career. He was followed by Muhsin al-Hakim's son, Mahdi. Therefore, and although it continued to claim a link to the *hawza*, al-Da'wa became more and more a party whose hardcore activists issued from the young lay educated classes. This shift in the type of recruitment was fostered by the advent of a new regime in 1963, which undertook the brutal suppression of the two secular parties in which the Shias had massively engaged: the Communist party, which had backed the Qasem regime, and the Ba'th, which advocated Arab nationalism and briefly seized power in 1963 before being expelled by a junta of Sunni militaries.[48] Under the leadership of 'Abd al-Salam 'Arif and then his brother 'Abd al-Rahman in 1966, the new regime quickly took on a narrow sectarian and localist basis. It relied both on the army, which was by tradition staffed by Sunnis, and on the familial solidarity of a handful of clans mainly issuing from the Sunni village of Tikrit, north of Baghdad. This trend of excluding Shias from chief positions in the state apparatus was to be pursued following the Ba'thist coup of 1968 which brought Saddam Husein to power. The circumstances were ripe for al-Da'wa, which more and more appeared to the Shias as the only political body capable of defending their interests by opposing successive Iraqi regimes.

The Conflict with the Iraqi Regime

The logical outcome of this process was open confrontation between al-Da'wa and the Iraqi regime, which finally saw the re-engagement of the

---

47   Wiley (1992), pp. 125-8.
48   Abdul-Jabar (2003), p. 131.

'ulama in political matters. The first clash arose in 1969 when matters of foreign policy added further to internal tensions. Since the creation of the modern Iraqi state, the relation between Iraq and Iran had always been characterized by mistrust and suspicion. Because Iran tended to consider the Iraqi shrine cities as its natural constituency, the Iraqi rulers suspected the Shias, and in particular the clerical establishment, of being a fifth column of Iranian irredentism. This suspicion had been materialized in the 1924 law establishing Iraqi citizenship, which had created the special category of "Iraqis of Iranian nationality *(taba'iyya iraniyya)*".[49] These were the residents of the three ex-Ottoman provinces which became Iraq who had previously held Iranian citizenship. Their Iranian nationality was displayed on their identity cards so that they would quickly and easily be identifiable. Border disputes between Iraq and Iran were common matters, in particular in the south area of Shatt al-'Arab which constituted the only access Iraq had to Gulf waters. Following the umpteenth episode of tension in this zone, and the refusal by Muhsin al-Hakim to condemn the Iranian government, the Ba'th regime decided to expel some 20,000 so-called "Iranians", i.e. Iraqi citizens of Iranian descent or long-time Iranian residents of the shrine cities who had never relinquished their Iranian citizenship. Many among them were seminarians of the *hawza*. As the dispute escalated, Mahdi al-Hakim was arrested and tortured for being a Zionist spy. A few months later, in 1970, an alleged Iranian coup to overthrow the Iraqi regime was the pretext to denounce the Shia religious hierarchy as agents of the Shah. Many chose to leave the country to stay alive. The massive expulsion of Shias continued with the deportation of some 40, 000 Shias Kurds (Faylis) and 60,000 "Iranians" in 1971 after Iran occupied the three Emirati islands of Abu Musa and Great and Little Tunb in the Gulf.[50]

The 1970s were a period of escalating suppression of the *hawza*, whose ranks were systematically decimated. While visas for foreigners wishing to study in the religious seminars of Najaf were curtailed, hundreds of Iraqi clerics were imprisoned, tortured, murdered and executed. Dozens of others were exiled to the neighbouring countries: Lebanon, Syria, Iran and the Gulf monarchies, Kuwait and the United Arab Emirates in particular. The advent of the Islamic revolution in Iran and the starting of the Iran-Iraq war (1980-1988) marked the peak of the confrontation with the arrest and execution of Mohammed Baqer al-Sadr and his sister Bint al-Huda

---

49 Samir Khalil, *Republic of Fear*, Berkeley: University of California Press, 1989, p. 136.

50 Wiley (1992), pp. 48-9.

(April 1980). The al-Hakim family was also severely hit, with dozens of its members arrested and assassinated. The repression dealt a severe blow to the *marja'iyya* which, under the leadership of the quietist Abu al-Qasem al-Khu'i, not only retreated from politics but also saw its sources of funding curtailed.

THE SHIRAZIYYIN: RELIGIOUS
FACTIONALISM AND POLITICAL ACTIVISM

The *marja'iyya* is an institution that reproduces itself through the sometimes harsh factional struggles regularly opposing contenders for religious authority. Indeed, while the pattern of centralization has been constantly reinforced over the years, the fact that the successive *marja'* never succeeded in establishing undisputed patterns of designation created a quasi-permanent situation where the one who controls the *marja'iyya* is contested by challengers resorting to various means to weaken his legitimacy. As the aim of these struggles is to conquer the centre, they help consolidate it by favouring its identification as the centre and helping anchor the idea that there should be a centre. At the same time however, they can result in the development, although at an embryonic stage, of alternative centres of religious authority. At the beginning of the 1960s, it was such a commonplace quarrel over religious authority that led to the birth of another Shia Islamic movement that has succeeded in gaining a wide audience in the Gulf to this day.

The Birth of a Clerical Dispute

From a long term perspective, the clerical dispute originated in an old rivalry between Najaf and Karbala. Located some fifty miles north of Najaf, the city of Karbala hosts the mausoleum of Imam Husein, the third Imam, who chose to rise up against the caliph and was massacred with the bulk of his family in 680. Facing the shrine of Husein lies the tomb of 'Abbas, Husein's half-brother who was also killed during the battle of Karbala. Like Najaf which hosts the tomb of Imam 'Ali, Karbala was a pilgrimage town and its economy revolved around the flow of pilgrims, mainly coming from Iran. During the Safavid period, Karbala like Najaf had been endowed with plentiful gifts by the Iranian rulers, which allowed the development of magnificent shrine complexes. Following the fall of the Safavid dynasty in 1722 and the Shia clerics' exodus to Mesopotamia, Karbala became the alternative centre of learning to Isfahan in Iran, which heretofore had hosted the most dynamic clerical community. The choice of Karbala was motivated by the fact that the city had a good water supply system and a flourishing economy thanks to the development of the road from Baghdad that facilitated the travel of pilgrims from the north.[51] With the weakening of Ottoman central power during the second decade of the nineteenth century, local gangs expelled the Sunni governors of the city and established their dominion in alliance with the Shia clerics, so that Karbala became a virtually independent city-state.[52] In 1843 however, in the framework of a vast centralization endeavour through which they aimed to reassert their control, the Ottomans launched a military campaign against Karbala.[53] After a siege and a fierce battle with local gangs in which fifteen per cent of the city's population was killed, the Ottomans occupied Karbala and decided to put a complete end to its autonomy. They appointed a Sunni governor, a Sunni prayer leader and a Sunni judge entitled to arbitrate conflicts even between Shia parties.[54] This prompted thousands of citydwellers to leave for more auspicious lands, including many religious scholars who relocated to Najaf.

After the campaign against Karbala, the Ottomans intended to impose their effective rule on Najaf but the city's notables decided to surrender peacefully. Najaf was therefore preserved from Karbala's tragic fate and became the most suitable place for learning activities.[55] Karbala progressively recovered but experienced a process of Iranization of its population. With the defeat of the gangs, who recruited members from the tribal Arab population of the city, the Iranian merchants and religious notables indeed gained a *de facto* position of strength. While the Iranization process also affected Najaf, the city by contrast retained a "strong Arab character" due to its position alongside the desert.[56] Despite its recovery, Karbala was never able to regain its status of main centre of learning in the face of the ascent of Najaf. When Mohammed Hasan Najafi undertook to expand his authority beyond Najaf, the *mujtahid* of Karbala, and primarily Ibrahim Qazwini, experienced it as an unacceptable encroachment on their authority. This was all the more so since Mohammed Hasan Najafi devoted himself to staining the reputation of his rivals and, for example, refused to recognize

---

51   Nakash (1994), p. 22.

52   Cole and Momen (2002), pp. 104-6.

53   Litvak (1998), pp. 135-44.

54   Cole and Momen (2002), p. 118.

55   Nakash (1994), p. 22.

56   *Ibid.*, pp. 20-1.

the validity of Ibrahim Qazwini's rulings as well as the *ijtihad* certificates of his students.[57]

The birth of the group that quickly came to be known as the "Shirazi-yyin" is in many respects the product of the marginalization of Karbala as a learning centre and the subsequent rivalry that developed between its *mujtahid* and their Najafi counterparts. The group was named the Shirazi-yyin (i.e. the partisans of the al-Shirazi) because it was closely associated with the al-Shirazi family of Karbala, and more particularly the charismatic figures of S. Mohammed al-Shirazi (1926-2001) and his younger brother S. Hasan al-Shirazi (1934-1980).[58] Mohammed and Hasan al-Shirazi were born into a prestigious clerical family claiming descent from the Prophet. They came to Iraq from Shiraz in south Iran in the course of the nineteenth century.[59] The first to leave Shiraz for the shrine cities of Mesopotamia was Mirza Hasan Shirazi in 1838, the successor of Murtadha Ansari at the head of the *hawza* and the enactor of the famous tobacco *fatwa* in 1891. One of his brothers, S. Mirza Agha Bazraq Shirazi, settled in Karbala around the same period with his sons, among whom S. Mirza Habib Allah Shirazi. The latter married a sister of Mohammed Taqi al-Shirazi, the *mujtahid* who led the 1920 Revolution against the British. Of this marriage was born S. Mirza Mahdi al-Shirazi, the father of the two protagonists in question, Mohammed and Hasan al-Shirazi. To sum up, Mirza Hasan Shirazi was their great-paternal uncle and Mohammed Taqi al-Shirazi was their great-maternal uncle.[60]

The father of Mohammed and Hasan al-Shirazi, Mirza Mahdi al-Shirazi (1884-1960), was born in Karbala and completed his religious education in Najaf. He returned to Karbala in the 1930s where he established himself as the leading *mujtahid*. He founded a religious school which he ran until

---

57   Litvak (1998), p. 67.

58   I shift here to an Arabized version of the Persian names, with the definite article "al" preceding them since from the time of Mohammed and Hasan al-Shirazi, the members of the family based in Iraq underwent a marked process of Arabization like most of the Iranian residents who chose to remain in Iraq after the creation of the state. Moreover, since they are mainly known among the Arabic speaking Shia populations, their names are generally known in their Arabized form.

59   Michael M. J. Fisher has drawn a partial genealogical tree of the Shirazi family. See Fischer (1980), p. 90.

60   To our knowledge, the most complete account of the Shirazi family's genealogy is to be found in an article by 'Abd al-Husein al-Salihi Al-Shahid al-Thalith, "The al-Shirazi and the History of the Great *Marja'iyya*" (in Arabic), *Al-Naba'*, n° 69, ninth year, Dhu al-Qa'da 1423/January 2003, pp. 9-20.

his death. In the 1950s, he distinguished himself by enacting several *fatwa* condemning adherence to the Communist Party, going as far as stating that a true Muslim could not buy meat from a communist butcher. All of his four sons were educated in his *hawza* under his direction and became *mujtahid*: Mohammed, Hasan, Sadiq and Mujtaba. According to his hagiographers, Mohammed the elder attained the level of *ijtihad* at the early age of twenty. After the death of his father, he succeeded him at the head of the *hawza* and quickly announced his *marja'iyya*. He was then thirty-three years old.

What followed is rather unclear, and the true history has yet to be investigated in detail. What is important to keep in mind is that Mohammed al-Shirazi's claim to the *marja'iyya* was dismissed or at least not recognized by the *mujtahid* of Najaf. In fact, he had circumvented several of the tacit rules of the *marja'iyya*. First, he had kept aloof from the Najafi seminars as most of his teachers resided in Karbala. Second, he was much too young. According to the *marja'iyya*'s gerontocratic standards indeed, he should at least have waited forty more years before declaring himself. The announcement of his *marja'iyya* was taken as an open challenge to the religious institution. While Muhsin al-Hakim seems to have merely ignored the pretension of Mohammed al-Shirazi, his successor, Abu al-Qasem al-Khu'i, took the matter personally. In 1970 at the death of Muhsin al-Hakim, Mohammed al-Shirazi reasserted his claim to the *marja'iyya*, which amounted to an open challenge to the *marja'iyya* of Abu al-Qasem al-Khu'i who had quickly established himself as the legitimate successor of Muhsin al-Hakim. The latter felt offended enough to become one of the fiercest enemies of Mohammed al-Shirazi and his followers to the point of enacting several rulings dismissing Mohammed al-Shirazi's scholarly credentials.

The conflict between Mohammed al-Shirazi and the *marja'iyya* assumed the aspect of a traditional dispute for religious leadership. It notably included the mobilization of the strong localist feelings of Karbala's population, which were chiefly expressed in the form of resentment against the domination of Najaf. While his religious authority was not recognized in Najaf, Mohammed al-Shirazi rapidly succeeded in establishing himself as the leader of Karbala. He continued the pattern of forging strong alliances with the most potent families of the city, both within the clerical class and the merchant notability, both among the Iranians and the Arabs. The al-Shirazi were for example related to the al-Qazwini Iranian clerical family, the descendants of Ibrahim Qazwini who had unsuccessfully opposed the leadership of Mohammed Hasan Najafi during the nineteenth century. They were also related to the al-Ma'ash, a potent Arab merchant family

with a tribal background. Not only did Mohammed al-Shirazi use his social capital within Karbala as a tool to assert his religious leadership, but he
also made his local roots an ideology. Among the Shiraziyyin indeed, it is
commonplace to hear that Karbala, as the place of Husein's martyrdom,
hosts a peculiar spirit which the Shiraziyyin have been able to catch better
than anybody else: the spirit of revolution, and – following Husein's own
example – of sacrifice in the path of God.[61] The bond linking the Shiraziyyin to Karbala is so obvious that the Shiraziyyin are frequently designated
by outsiders as the "Karbala group" (*jama'at Karbala*).

Another aspect that gives the dispute a very traditional flavour is that
it has extensively mobilized family capital. On the one hand, Mohammed
al-Shirazi used the symbolic capital which his prestigious ancestry granted him in order to substantiate his claim to supreme religious authority.
This is a sensitive point in the society of Shia scholars. While the resort
to a prestigious ancestor to support the quest for religious leadership has
been common throughout the learning community's history, it has always
been considered as a deviation from the *'ulama*'s code of ethics, of which
a central pillar is the idea that religious authority should only be the result of knowledge and not of descent.[62] By the same token, while the idea
that religious leadership could be transmitted from father to sons has been
strongly fought, it nevertheless remains true that the society of Shia religious scholars is by and large structured around dynasties of clerics, often
descending from the Prophet and generally referred to as the "families of
science" (*al-'usra al-'ilmiyya*). While the *marja'* do not always issue from
such families, these dynasties have generally sought to sustain an eminent
position within the religious landscape so that a member of such a family
struggling for leadership not only fought for his own personal prestige but
for the honour of the entire family. Therefore, and while he never pretended to have inherited religious eminence of his forefathers, Mohammed al-
Shirazi and his followers have always sought to emphasize their prestigious
lineage in their quest for religious authority. In the eighties, they published
a book of almost 480 pages giving the details of the family's genealogy and
of its members' personal achievements, named *The Good Tree* (*Al-Shajara
al-Tayba*).[63]

---

61   See the interview given by S. Mohammed Taqi al-Mudarrisi, Mohammed al-
      Shirazi's nephew, to 'Adel Ra'uf, *Islamic Action in Iraq. Between Marja'iyya and
      Parties. A Review over Half a Century (1950-2000)* (in Arabic), Damascus: Iraqi
      Centre for Information and Research, 2000, p. 235.

62   Litvak (1998), p. 104.

63   Anonymous, *The Good Tree. The al-Shirazi Family: Its History, its Thought and its*

The other facet of the family dimension of the Shiraziyyin phenomenon is that it is based on the alliance between a handful of Iranian clerical families claiming descent from the Prophet who gathered in Karbala in the course of the nineteenth century. At the centre of the alliance lies the al-Shirazi family, led by Mohammed and his brother Hasan. The latter outlined some essential threads of the political theory that supported the Shiraziyyin's claim to religious seniority (*cf.* below). He was killed by Iraqi agents in Beirut in 1980, leaving Mohammed, who had anyway a higher religious standard, as the undisputed leader of the family. Other members of the al-Shirazi family played a leading role in the subsequent years. Sadiq al-Shirazi succeeded Mohammed as a *marja'* after his death in 2001. Mujtaba al-Shirazi took care of the group's interests in London. At the time of writing, the sons of Mohammed (six) and Sadiq (four), all of them turbaned and the bulk of them already *mujtahid*, were taking a more and more important role in the perpetuation of the group. S. Mohammed Redha al-Shirazi, the eldest son of Mohammed, in his forties at the time of writing, will probably be the next *marja'* of the family after his uncle's death. Additionally, the sons play a central role in sustaining the vast transnational network of the group.

After the members of the al-Shirazi family proper, one finds another family of foremost importance: the al-Mudarrisi. The al-Mudarrisi are a clerical family who came from Mashhad in north Iran to Karbala. There, they intermarried with the al-Shirazi so that a sister of Mohammed al-Shirazi espoused a cleric from the al-Mudarrisi family. They gave birth to four boys, all of them embracing the clerical career: Mohammed Taqi, Hadi, 'Abbas and Mohammed Baqer. The first two, S. Mohammed Taqi al-Mudarrisi (b. 1945) and S. Hadi al-Mudarrisi (b. 1946), who also claimed to have attained *ijtihad* in their twenties, were key in the political organization of the Shiraziyyin in Iraq and the Gulf monarchies. Another important family related to the al-Shirazi are the al-Qazwini. They are a clerical family who came from Qazvin to Karbala before the al-Shirazi and are related to them by marriage. They are one of the oldest clerical families of Karbala.

Beyond this very traditional dimension of a clerical dispute with familial resonance however, the Shiraziyyin as a social phenomenon also demonstrated the encroachment of reformist ideas among the clerical class. The central theme of their discourse was the need to reform the *hawza* which risked becoming an ossified institution headed by a handful of gerontocrats remote from public affairs and the concerns of the laity. In their view, the *hawza* needed to be taken on by younger *'ulama* who, because better in

---

Fight, (in Arabic) Beirut: Dar al-'Ulum, no date.

touch with modern society, would better be able to regain the favours of the masses attracted by secular ideologies. While striving to consolidate the *hawza* in Karbala, Mohammed al-Shirazi opened professional schools and charitable institutions. Like the founders of al-Da'wa, he thought that the *marja'iyya* should not be afraid to tackle the debates of the age by addressing political and economic problems rather than confining itself to debating scholarly matters. Moreover, he thought that the scholars, while continuing to concentrate on high level religious matters, should also write booklets aimed at the masses and that therefore should be written in simple language. Mohammed al-Shirazi himself, who has the reputation of having written 1,200 books, published many little fascicules destined to simplify arduous religious debates for the average Muslim. This is a source of criticism for his detractors, who often say that he might indeed have written 1,200 books but none of them is worth reading by qualified scholars.

Contrary to many other reformist scholars however, Mohammed al-Shirazi did not strive to fight popular rituals, and in particular the bloody practice of *tatbir*. Also called "*haidar*", the *tatbir* is mainly performed during 'Ashura, the tenth day of the month of Muharram, as a means of lamenting Husein's martyrdom. After arraying themselves in white clothes, the penitents make incisions on their foreheads that they hit with a sword to make the blood flow. Reformist scholars, whose aim was to purify Islam from the scoria of non-Islamic conceptions and for whom rational knowledge was considered as the only legitimate means to accede to the truth of the Quranic message, usually considered *tatbir* as leading to misconceptions and un-Islamic behaviour.[64] The *tatbir* quickly became one of the Shiraziyyin's privileged modes of mass mobilization, in a situation where many cadres of al-Da'wa condemned it as backward and insane practice.[65] For them, the Shiraziyyin's insistence on *tatbir* was further proof of their weak standard in terms of religious knowledge. The Shiraziyyin replied that, on the contrary, the *tatbir* was an essential ritual through which the Shias showed their attachment to Imam Husein. They liked to explain that al-Da'wa's reluctance to endorse this practice reflected the elitist spirit of this party, which concentrated its recruitment on the more educated seg-

---

64   For the scholars' attitudes on this matter, see Werner Ende, "The Flagellations of Muharram and the Shi'ite 'Ulama", *Der Islam*, vol. 55, n° 1, 1978; Sabrina Mervin, *Un réformisme chiite. Ulémas et lettrés du Gabal 'Amil (actuel Liban-Sud) de la fin de l'Empire ottoman à l'indépendance du Liban*, Paris: Karthala, 2000, p. 257.

65   Abdul-Jabar (2003), p. 220.

ments of society while neglecting the people.[66] Furthermore, al-Da'wa's disapproval of *tatbir* was seen as a proof of its lack of engagement in Husein's path, a path stressing the value of popular enthusiasm as a mean to achieve revolution.

Finally, while the *marja'iyya* in Najaf embodied a form of "charisma of office",[67] Mohammed al-Shirazi possessed an undeniable personal charisma which he played perfectly. In other words, while the charisma of the official *marja'* resided in their institutional status, that of Mohammed al-Shirazi was a matter of personal virtuosity. This helps explain why, contrary to many *marja'* who generally avoided too much interaction with the common herd and preserved their authority by keeping their distance from society, Mohammed al-Shirazi relied very much on personal interactions with the common people. His house was open so that everybody could have the opportunity to meet him personally. Accounts by those who met him are often full of dithyrambic details on the scope of his modesty and asceticism, on his ability to convince the people of his ideas and to push them to act in order to spread Islam. Almost everyone has a history to recall about someone of known to them who came out of a meeting with Mohammed al-Shirazi totally transfigured. Overall, Mohammed al-Shirazi's followers tend to speak about him as an unknown genius who was attacked by his contemporaries because he revolutionized Shia thought. The mention of his 1,200 books is quasi-systematic, with people often reckoning that he wrote so much that his right-hand fingers were distorted. This authentic personality cult is well served by another talent of the Shiraziyyin that appeared during the 1990s and from then on continued to develop: their ability to self-promote through the most modern communication means, especially web sites where emphatic portraits of Mohammed al-Shirazi are drawn ad nauseam. After his death in December 2001, it is essentially through the web that the idea that Mohammed al-Shirazi was the "*mujaddid*" of the fifteenth Hegirian century has been introduced. Literally meaning the "the one who renewed", the word "*mujaddid*" refers to a belief shared by Sunnis and Shias that every Hegirian century witnesses the coming of a man who renews the Islamic doctrine and hence guides the believers on the right path. Needless to say, all these assertions are dismissed by those who emulate other, more established, *marja'*. While, as we shall see, these critics have pushed some to distance themselves from the Shiraziyyin,

---

66   Ra'uf (2000), p. 236.

67   For the notion of "charisma of office", see Max Weber, *Economy and Society. An Outline of Interpretative Sociology*, edited by Guenther Roth and Claus Wittich, New York: Bedminster Press, 1968, pp. 1140-1.

the fervour of Mohammed al-Shirazi's emulators has also been reinforced by these critics who have strengthened their feeling of belonging to the privileged ones who fully understand the scope of Mohammed al-Shirazi's genius. This is in line with a strong leaning of Shia religious identity overall, which tends to represent the Shias as a minority who, because they hold the truth, are persecuted by a sightless majority. This no doubt helps to further explain the remarkable permanence of the Shiraziyyin phenomenon in a rather hostile environment.

The Passage to Politics

Initially confined to the religious arena, the conflict between the Shiraziyyin and the Najafi *marja'iyya* soon assumed a political aspect when al-Da'wa tried to expand its networks to Karbala. Its leaders apparently contacted Hasan al-Shirazi to convince him to be part of the preliminary discussions on the formation of the party. The al-Shirazi agreed to the proposal but, probably realizing that they would only be able to play a secondary role in the project, quickly decided to retreat to pursue their own agenda.[68] The rivalry between al-Da'wa and the Shiraziyyin then regularly took a violent turn, especially after al-Da'wa succeeded in taking control of the Islamic Charity Association's board which Mohammed al-Shirazi had created in Karbala in 1962. Taking advantage of the mass effect created by the 'Ashura procession, the al-Shirazi's partisans sacked the office of the association and succeeded in ousting al-Da'wa from Karbala.[69]

The Shiraziyyin diverged with al-Da'wa on the very notions of religious and political authority. Indeed, they considered the concept of a political party as alien to Islam because it entailed the negation of the *marja'iyya*'s supreme authority. In this, the Shiraziyyin were actually in line with the conception of the most conservative ranks of Najafi establishment. However, unlike the quietist scholars who abhorred any idea of political action and distinguished between religious and political authority, the al-Shirazi thought it was part of the clerics' duty to engage in politics. Like Mohammed Baqer al-Sadr and al-Da'wa's activist clerics, they were deeply convinced that, in the face of the rise of secular ideologies, the time was ripe for taking direct political action to make Islam prevail. In their view however, to be in full accordance with Islam, any political action should be placed under the supervision of the *marja'iyya*. In their eyes therefore, the dual source of authority endorsed by the statutes of al-Da'wa was unaccept-

---

68   Abdul-Jabar (2003), p. 104.

69   *Ibid.*, pp. 220-1.

able. Actually, the Shiraziyyin's argument was very similar to the doctrine of the *wilayat al-faqih* theory formulated by Ruhollah Khomeini in 1970 and which entrusted the *marja'* with supreme political authority, that is government of the state in the absence of the Imam. According to Ahmed al-Katib, who was a follower of Mohammed al-Shirazi from his Karbala days and wrote a critical biography of him, Mohammed al-Shirazi actually formulated a doctrine which he named "the government of the jurisprudents" (*hukumat al-fuqaha*), which was articulated by his younger brother Hasan in a book published in 1963 entitled *The Word of Islam* (*Kalimat al-Islam*).[70] This doctrine was reformulated after the Islamic revolution as "the council of the jurisprudents" (*shurat al-fuqaha*). Like Ruhollah Khomeini, it affirmed that in the absence of the Imam, the *marja'* were invested with his political temporal power. The similarity of political conceptions helps to explain why Mohammed al-Shirazi developed a close relationship with Ruhollah Khomeini. He was the only *mujtahid* to organize a formal ceremony of welcome upon Ruhollah Khomeini's arrival in Iraq in 1965, after he was exiled by the Shah. Mohammed al-Shirazi had previously organized demonstrations to protest against Ruhollah Khomeini's harassment by the Iranian regime and the two men held each other in mutual respect. When Ruhollah Khomeini arrived in Iraq, he paid Mohammed al-Shirazi a personal visit in Karbala, which amounted to a profound mark of respect since Mohammed al-Shirazi was younger than him.[71] Mohammed Taqi al-Mudarrisi, the nephew of Mohammed al-Shirazi, explained that his aim was actually "to draw the outline of the theory of *wilayat al-faqih* which was later on embodied by the Imam Khomeini".[72] In brief, the Shiraziyyin were ardent advocates of the political engagement of the *'ulama* but, as Falah Jabar insightfully noticed, their reluctance on the concept of political parties "reflected the stance of a group of *'ulama* who, on the one hand, realized the need for militant activism but, on the other, abhorred the prospect of losing command and control to a new form of militancy (a political party) they were asked to legitimize".[73]

The rift between the Shiraziyyin and the Najafis finally led to the creation of a second Shia Islamic movement in the second half of the 1960s. The move occurred thanks to the organizational skilfulness and pragmatism of Mohammed Taqi al-Mudarrisi. The latter was in his early twenties in the

---

70   Personal interview, London, July 2007.

71   Abul-Jabar (2003), p. 219.

72   An interview he gave to 'Adel Ra'uf (2000), p. 235.

73   Abdul-Jabar (2003), p. 218.

mid-1960s and, according to his hagiography, had already reached the level of *ijtihad*.[74] Realizing the need for a more formal organization than the loose group that had clustered around his two uncles, he undertook to transform it into a fully-fledged movement. The exact date of creation is unknown. Like al-Da'wa, it probably crystallized gradually during several years from an informal network of individuals and institutions into a coherent body. Mohammed Taqi al-Mudarrisi himself claimed that the organization was founded following the Arab-Israeli war of June 1967 as part of the "Islamic alternative" that emerged stronger from the rout of the nationalist Arab regimes. Observers of the Iraqi scene have raised doubts about the veracity of this account and think the organization was actually created after the Islamic revolution in Iran.[75] In fact, the movement only took its definitive name after 1979: the Islamic Action Organization (*Munazzamat al-'Amal al-Islami*), which it has retained to this day. Before, it was known under several names: the Movement of the Messengers' Vanguard (*Harakat al-Tala'i' al-Risaliyyin*), the *Marja'iyya* Movement (*Harakat al-Marja'iyya*), the Message Movement (*al-Harakat al-Risaliyya*).[76]

In line with his uncles' conceptions and to distinguish clearly from al-Da'wa, Mohammed Taqi al-Mudarrisi consciously avoided using the term "party" (*hezb*) to name his organization. In reality however, al-Da'wa and the Islamic Action Organization shared lots of features. First, they endeavoured to create a pyramidal structure of command and both advanced the idea that loyalty to the leader was central to the efficiency of political action. In principle, the two only diverged on the nature of command: while al-Da'wa, as an assumed political party, considered this should lie *in fine* within the formal leadership of the party, the Islamic Action Organization claimed the ultimate decision should fall in the hands of the *marja'*– namely Mohammed al-Shirazi. In practical terms however, and this is a second point of resemblance, the two movements were linked to the *marja'iyya* but operated largely as autonomous bodies. Indeed, most of the Shiraziyyin's outsiders and insiders agree that while he gave it his support, Mohammed al-Shirazi never agreed to become formally the leader of the Islamic Action Organization and was not part of its command structure. The real leader has always been Mohammed Taqi al-Mudarrisi who was indeed a *mujtahid* but announced his *marja'iyya* only in the late 1990s. A third point of resemblance between the two rival movements was their elitist character.

---

74   www.almodarresi.com/biography.htm
75   Ra'uf (2000), pp. 238-41.
76   *Ibid.*, p. 236.

Indeed, while the Shiraziyyin greatly relied on popular religion to establish their position, the Islamic Action Organization itself was not conceived as a mass movement but rather as a secret revolutionary avant-garde. Like al-Da'wa, the Organization recruited chiefly in the clerical and lay educated sectors. It thought it was better to rely on the quality of the leadership rather than on the quantity of members. A fourth common feature was that both al-Da'wa and the Islamic Action Organization swiftly engaged in violent action against the Iraqi regime.

Like al-Da'wa the Shiraziyyin suffered harsh repression from the authorities. While their political activism was a major reason for their persecution, their status as Iraqis of Iranian nationality exposed them to particular suspicion from the regime. Hasan al-Shirazi was the first to be arrested in 1969. After months of harsh torture, he fled Iraq to Lebanon and Syria. In the months following his departure, the members of the whole al-Shirazi and al-Mudarrisi families also took the road of exile and finally relocated in Kuwait and, from there, dispersed to several Gulf monarchies.

FROM PRE-NATIONALISM TO TRANS-NATIONALISM

Both al-Da'wa and the Shiraziyyin emerged from the need of the Shia clerical class to deal with the particular socio-political context of Iraq and, as such, their political agendas were dictated by Iraqi issues and events. Since their inception however, they also conceived themselves as universal missionary movements with a much wider goal than the mere overthrowing of the Iraqi secular regimes. The missionary vocation was intimately linked to the dominance of the clerical element within the two groups. Indeed, more than the lay cadres, for whom the spreading of Islam may have been an aim as such but was also very much an efficient political ideology to achieve temporal political objectives, the clerics' main goal remained what it had always been: the worldwide diffusion of the Islamic message and the empowerment of the religious institution. As shown by the clerics' temporary retreat from al-Da'wa in the 1960s, this goal superseded the political one if the fight against the unjust rulers put in jeopardy the religious institution and its Islamization activities.

Beside the missionary ethos, another important feature of the society of the clerics led them to consider a much wider field of action than did the lay activists: the Shia clerics were typical of what I would call a pre-national religious corporation. Born long before the formation of nation-states in the Middle East, in a time of porous political borders and indefinite ethno-national boundaries, they established themselves as an extra-territorial power on disputed territory on the Marches of two rival empires where cultural mixture was an everyday social experience. Therefore, the clerics felt part of a much larger world than Iraq. As the focal point of a bundle of long-distance networks, the shrine cities were cosmopolitan places hosting students and teachers from all corners of the Shia world. Each came with his own language and with his own folk customs, but also with his own way to practice the various Shia rituals. While rivalries between different ethnic groups were a structuring element of the shrine cities' daily social life,[77] attesting that common religious belonging never succeeded in transcending ethnic differences and in pacifying social relations, interactions across the ethnic boundaries also led to syncretic cultural and religious forms. Self-mortification rituals for examples, which were practised in northern Iran from the seventeenth century, were only introduced in the Mesopotamian shrine cities in the course of the nineteenth century through Iranians who had themselves borrowed those practices from Central Asian Shias.[78]

Beside the fact that cosmopolitanism was a daily way of life and a socio-cultural condition for the clerics of the Iraqi shrine cities, it was also invested with a philosophical and even ideological dimension.[79] Following the formation of the Iraqi state, many Shia *'ulama* probably accepted the nation-state as a unavoidable "fact of life"[80] they needed to deal with, but many also continued to stick to the traditional Islamic worldview stipulating that the only legitimate division of the social body is that opposing Muslims to non-Muslims and that a Muslim is always at home within the territory of Islam (*dar al-Islam*), that is, where Muslims rule.[81] This posture of principle led them to refuse the concepts of nation and nation-state, which they considered as a blameful innovation introducing irrelevant distinctions between the Muslims and preventing them from travelling freely within the geographic realm of Islam. While the idea of the essential illegitimacy of the very concept of nation-state was also to be found in Mohammed Baqer al-Sadr's work, Mohammed al-Shirazi appeared particularly

---

77   Litvak (1998), pp. 30-5.

78   Nakash (1994), pp. 142-54.

79   I draw here on the analysis by Steven Vertovec when he describes the various ways one can be cosmopolitan, "Fostering Cosmopolitanism: A Conceptual Survey and a Media Experiment in Berlin", Oxford: Economic and Social Research Council, Transnational Communities Programme, Working Paper WPTC-2K-06 (www.transcomm.ox.ac.uk).

80   James P. Piscatori, *Islam in a World of Nation-States*, Cambridge: Cambridge University Press, 1986, pp. 82-3.

81   On this matter, see Franz Rosenthal, "The Stranger in Medieval Islam", in *Arabica*, vol. 44, n° 1, 1997.

resentful towards the idea of a world of nation-states. A central theme of his thought was the denouncement of what he castigated as "the blameful innovation (*bid'a*) and the laws the West exported to the Islamic countries and implemented by its agents".[82] He considered himself a victim of "the game of nationality and identity cards, the game of residence permit and passport, [...] the imposture of false geographic frontiers inside the united Islamic homeland (*watan*)".[83]

The reason for the particular anger Mohammed al-Shirazi felt towards nations and nation-states had probably something to do with his personal history. Unlike the al-Sadr or the al-Hakim families who had deep roots in Iraq and, although they had family ties to Iran, could claim an Arab descent matching the Arab nationalist ideology articulated by the Iraqi state, the al-Shirazi had a much more recent past in the country. The same could be said of several of Karbala's other clerical families allied with the al-Shirazi, who were all of rather "fresh" Iranian descent. Mohammed al-Shirazi himself spoke Persian within his family circle. He did not even carry Iraqi citizen-ship and, as he himself explained, this was a deliberate choice: "because I was opposed to this religiously illicit innovation [nationality], I did not ask for identity papers nor passports and I did not want to possess a national-ity or a residence permit."[84] According to his son S. Mahdi al-Shirazi, his father actually carried Iranian citizenship.[85] Not that he was particularly attached to this country but, as he had decided to ignore the national ad-ministrative categorizations, he never bothered to engage in a procedure to change his initial citizenship. Actually, the only relevant regional identity Mohammed al-Shirazi seemed to have been ready to assume was Karbala's. The members of the al-Shirazi family, most of whom had relocated to Iran at the time of writing, continued to call Karbala their homeland (*watan*). Here, they referred not so much to a physical locus than to a religious to-pography. Local identification is allowed insofar as the locus is inhabited by the spirit of Imam Husein and the memory of his martyrdom.

In brief, as in other contexts of radical nationalism where cosmopolitans, because they do not belong to the single cultural identity the state claims to embody and defend, are seen as disloyal, the Shia clerics were considered as a threat by the state elites. This largely explains why the clerics' ideological

---

82   Great *ayatollah* Imam S. Mohammed al-Huseini al-Shirazi, *How and Why Was I Expelled from Iraq?* (in Arabic), Beirut: Mu'assasat al-Mujtaba lil-Tahqiq wa al-Nashr, 2002/1422, pp. 12-13.

83   *Ibid.*

84   *Ibid*, p. 13.

85   Personal interview, Iran, July 2005.

commitment to cosmopolitism found expression in a cosmopolitan politi-cal project of building Islamic institutions circumventing the authority of the existing nation-states and linking together the different geographical poles of the Shia world. Far from being unique, this project was typical of Islamic reformists of the nineteenth and twentieth century, who in-tended to oppose a concept of an Islamic state to the Western notion of nation-state.[86] However, with its long-distance networks and its ability to project religious authority beyond national frontiers, the institution of the *marja'iyya* offered the ideal infrastructure through which the project could actually be implemented. The creation of the Shia Islamic movements at the heart of the religious institution constituted the specifically political instrument to carry out the project since they enacted the transformation of the pre-national ethos of the clerical class into a trans-national one. They articulated the passage from a mere ethos born out of a social experience to a conscious ideology.

---

86   This was in particular the essence of the political vision of S. Jamal al-Din al-Afghani. See Nikki Keddie, *An Islamic Response to Imperialism: Political and Religious Writings of Sayyid Jamal al-Din al-Afghani*, Berkeley: University of California Press, 1968.

4

FROM IRAQ TO THE GULF

Sociologists of diffusion have long shown that the best way to transmit an item is direct face-to-face ties.[1] Drawing on this basic idea, scholars interested in the transnational diffusion of political ideas and forms of action reached the conclusion that, even in an era of mass-media, what they call "relational diffusion" remains the most effective vehicle for the spreading of ideas across national borders.[2] Organized around transnational interpersonal bonds of patronage between higher and lower-ranking scholars, the Shia religious institution therefore provided the ideal framework through which to diffuse political ideologies. This is in fact what happened in the Gulf monarchies where, in the course of the 1970s, al-Da'wa and Shiraziyyin established what local actors call "branches" (fara', pl. furu'). At a time when mass media was still underdeveloped and when, above all, the political activities of the two groups were clandestine, the interpersonal transnational networks were central to the diffusion process. This means that the transnational ties linking activists in Iraq and the Gulf did not develop *ex nihilo* through the action of voluntarist brokers[3] but rather followed "previously established lines of interaction".

---

1   Elihu Katz, "Theorizing Diffusion: Tarde and Sorokin Revisited", *Annals of the American Academy of Political and Social Sciences*, vol. 566, November 1999, p. 151.

2   Doug McAdam and Dieter Rucht, "The Cross-National Diffusion of Movement Ideas", *Annals of the American Academy of Political and Social Sciences*, vol. 528, July 1993; Sidney Tarrow and Doug McAdam, "Scale Shift in Transnational Contention", in Donatella della Porta and Sidney Tarrow (eds), *Transnational Protest and Global Activism*, Lanham: Rowman & Littlefield Publishers, 2005, p. 127.

3   What Tarrow and McAdam (2005) have called "brokerage".

ACTING THROUGH THE INSTITUTION: AL-DAʿWA

As shown previously, Bahrain and Saudi Arabia have an old and vivid tradition of Shia learning. However, the conquest by the Najdi Sunni tribes in the course of the eighteenth century, and the subsequent establishment of modern states in which they were marginalized and even openly persecuted, logically led to the progressive decline of the local learning tradition. The centralization process of supreme religious authority in Najaf further contributed to weakening local learning centres, which were integrated in the centre-periphery pattern linking Najaf to the other corners of the Shia world. This means that the religious legitimacy of Bahraini and Saudi clerics in face of their local flock became a factor of their proximity with the centre. Only the clerics trained in Najaf's seminaries could hope to climb up to the higher rungs of the religious hierarchy and gain wide social recognition.

Najaf, the Common Matrix

At the time al-Daʿwa began to exercise a growing influence among the Najafi *hawza*, Bahraini and Saudi students were among the many foreign apprentice scholars following the teachings of Mohammed Baqer al-Sadr and others. While no Saudi student appears to have been attracted into the ranks of al-Daʿwa, several Bahrainis, on the other hand, enrolled in the party or were politically socialized by associating with its activists and sympathizers. They transported al-Daʿwa to Bahrain by giving a precise ideological framework to a group of some twenty young religious activists in their twenties. Most of these men originated from Diraz, a village with an old tradition of religious learning, known more particularly for hosting the al-ʿAsfur family of science, the descendants of the aforementioned Yusuf al-Bahrani who promoted the revival of Akhbari thought in the eighteenth century. It is in this village that, at the initiative of Jaʿfar al-Shihabi (b. 1945), an informal religious society began to crystallize in 1968. With a modest social background – his father was tailor – Jaʿfar al-Shihabi had become a petroleum engineer after unversity studies in London with, as often happened, a scholarship from BAPCO. His aim was to enhance religious awareness in Bahrain in the framework of an association that, after five years of unofficial existence, was finally recognized by the government in 1972 under the name of the Islamic Enlightenment Society (*Jamaʿiyyat al-Tawuʿiyya al-Islamiyya*).[4] It is under the influence of the clerics returned

---

4   These details were provided by Saʿid al-Shihabi, the brother of Jaʿfar al-Shihabi and a leading figure of the Islamic Enlightenment Society. Personal interview, London, July 2007.

from Najaf that the group, that had no clear political identity, embraced the ideology of al-Da'wa and that the Islamic Enlightenment Society became the front of al-Da'wa in Bahrain.

There is a dispute about who first created al-Da'wa in Bahrain as an organized political movement. The polemic was made public following the release of a series of articles published in a Bahraini daily, in 2005 and 2006. Entitled "The Story of Political Islam in Bahrain" (*Qissat al-Islam al-Haraki fi al-Bahrain*), it consisted mainly of interviews conducted by the journalist Wissam al-Saba' with leading Shia and Sunni activists. In this context, 'Isa al-Sharqi (b. 1953), a member of al-Da'wa from the beginning, affirmed that the late Sh. Suleiman al-Madani (1939-2003) was the prime founder of al-Da'wa.[5] This was by the way an idea commonly held among Shia Islamic activists in Bahrain. Suleiman al-Madani had settled in Najaf in the early 1960s to undertake religious training and was politically socialized with the clerical cadres of al-Da'wa in Iraq. He disseminated their ideas in Bahrain during his regular visits home. Born in the village of Jidd Hafs, he preached mainly in the countryside and, in 1968, upon his definitive return to Bahrain, he created the party. Wisam al-Saba', the journalist who interviewed 'Isa al-Sharqi, afterwards published an interview he had done with Suleiman al-Madani in 2002, a few months before his death.[6] Al-Madani did not speak about his personal role in al-Da'wa but rather elaborated on his younger brother, 'Abdallah al-Madani (1939-1976), whom he confirmed played a central part in the foundation of al-Da'wa. He gave precious details, in particular on the circumstances of his brother's assassination by leftist militants in 1976.

'Abdallah al-Madani was born like his brother in 1939, probably from a different mother than Suleiman's. He began his political career as an Arab nationalist activist while he was working as an employee of the Health Ministry. He was active in various cultural and sport clubs, which at the time served as the main channels for political activities. In 1961-62, he visited his brother Suleiman in Najaf, where he met with activists of al-Da'wa who offered him a totally different avenue for activism than the one he had previously embraced. Already feeling uncomfortable with the socialist outlook of the Arab nationalists, he definitively shifted away from his previous political engagement and enrolled in al-Da'wa in Iraq. A few years later, he decided to undertake religious studies in Najaf. When he came back

---

5   *The Story of Political Islam in Bahrain* n° 1 and n° 2, *al-Watan* (Bahrain), 13 December and 14 December 2005.

6   *The Story of Political Islam in Bahrain* n° 7, *Al-Watan* (Bahrain), 24 December 2005.

to Bahrain in the early 1970s, he founded a journal named *Al-Mawaqif* (the Stances) the aim of which was to fight the secular political currents then dominating the Bahraini scene. He and his brother also distributed the books of Mohammed Baqer al-Sadr in Bahrain specifically aimed at refuting Marxist theories, in particular *Our Philosophy* and *Our Economy*. According to 'Isa al-Sharqi, the principal objective of the al-Madani brothers was rather to fight the influence of the secular political movements than to fight the Bahraini regime, with which they were perfectly well accommodated and tended to ignore. What they borrowed from al-Da'wa in Iraq therefore, was not the radical project of establishing an Islamic state after the revolutionary overthrowing of the impious regime, but the idea that the religious institution, in order to fight secular political parties efficiently, should create fully-fledged Islamic political parties. The al-Madani brothers' focus on the fight against the secular organizations explains the fact that once the audience of the latter actually went into decline, maybe not so much thanks to al-Da'wa's efforts proper than because of repression by the authorities, the al-Madani brothers tended to retreat from political action. This was so in particular of Suleiman, who quit al-Da'wa in the mid-1970s after he estimated his work was done, but also after the party began to enter into tense relations with the regime which threatened to undermine his own good relations with several leading members of the royal family. Not an oppositionist but a traditionalist concerned with the revival of Shia Islamic ethic, Suleiman al-Madani subsequently pursued the career of religious official at the Ja'fari court. Until his death in 2003, he was well known in Bahrain to be a "man of the government", which owned him to be appointed president of the Ja'fari court of appeal in 1997. This no doubt explains why he did not speak about his own role in the foundation of al-Da'wa during his interview and why 'Isa al-Sharqi's interview aroused the anger of his entourage. They sent a right of reply to the newspaper, the main idea of which was that Sh. al-Madani had never been a activist of al-Da'wa or any other party, be it in Bahrain or in Iraq.[7] In support of this, they quoted Sh. 'Ali al-Kurani, one of the leading cadres of al-Da'wa in Iraq up to the 1980s, who confirmed that Suleiman al-Madani had never looked for anything but religious knowledge during his time in Najaf, and did not join the ranks of al-Da'wa there.

According to 'Isa al-Sharqi, it is only at a later period that Sh. 'Isa Qasem (b. 1943) appeared on the stage. Sa'id al-Shihabi (b. 1954), also a figure

---

7   *The Story of Political Islam in Bahrain* n° 8, *Al-Watan* (Bahrain), 28 December 2005.

of al-Da'wa, agreed that he rose to prominence rather belatedly.[8] At the time of writing, he was politically the most influential Shia cleric of Bahrain thanks to his unofficial status of *eminence grise* of al-Wifaq (the Concord), the main Shia Islamic party since 2001. Like Suleiman al-Madani, 'Isa Qasem undertook religious studies in Najaf in the mid-1960s. He was born into a modest family – his father was a fisherman – in Diraz. In his in-depth and to date unequalled anthropological study of Bahrain, Fuad Khuri gave particularly useful details on the circumstances in which 'Isa Qasem returned to Bahrain in 1972.[9] Following the withdrawal of the British from all their Arabian military bases in 1971,[10] Bahrain, Qatar, the United Arab Emirates and Oman became formally independent. In Bahrain, the rulers decided to surrender to popular pressure and agreed to organize elections. A two-step process, the ballot was meant to establish a Constituent Assembly by the end of 1972, composed of forty-two members of whom twenty-two would be elected by Bahraini male citizens. Once the constitution was voted on by the Assembly, new elections would be held during the year 1973 in order to elect the first Parliament. 'Abdallah al-Madani immediately enrolled as the official registration of candidates began. He was elected to the two assemblies. As for 'Isa Qasem, he was then still in Najaf with his wife and children and apparently felt little concerned with Bahraini political affairs. In his native village of Diraz however, people were organizing for the electoral competition. The political arena was progressively becoming polarized between the various leftist and Arab nationalist currents, who would describe themselves as the "progressives" (*taqaddumiyyin*), and those who wished to maintain an amount of religiously oriented moral order, who would call themselves the "religious" (*mutadayyinin*).

Faced with the impressive academic credentials of many progressive candidates, who held university degrees and had socially valued professional occupations like lawyer or doctor, the religious felt they needed candidates equally endowed with symbolic capital to match their adversaries. Being endowed with the authority of the *marja'iyya*, the students of the Iraqi religious seminaries appeared to them as being perfect. In Diraz, after a

---

8   Personal interview, London, July 2007.

9   Khuri (1980), pp. 226-9. Khuri chose to describe 'Isa Qasem's career using the fictitious name of 'Ali Qasim. It is however an open secret in Bahrain that 'Ali Qasim is actually 'Isa Qasem.

10   The British decision to withdraw from its military bases in the Arabian Peninsula reflected purely domestic British concerns, when the Labour Party undertook drastically to reduce Britain's military expenditures which it considered weighed too heavily on the public purse.

consultation with the notables of the village, the board of the Islamic Enlightenment Society decided to call upon 'Isa Qasem to represent their
constituency in the elections. As the latter did not answer favourably in the
first instance, his brother undertook the trip to Najaf to convince him, and
in the end succeeded in bringing him back for good to Diraz. A rather similar process occurred with one of 'Isa Qasem's colleagues in Najaf who also
happened to be his childhood friend, Sh. 'Abbas al-Rayyas. They both won
a seat in the Constituent Assembly in 1972 and in Parliament in 1973,
with 'Isa Qasem achieving the most impressive score: for the Constituent
Assembly, he won 984 of the 1260 valid votes in his constituency.[11]

The elections greatly contributed to the institutionalization of al-Da'wa.
Indeed, while Bahraini rulers refused to allow the participation of formal
political parties in the ballot, they did not oppose the creation of associations with cultural, social or religious calling and, moreover, greatly liberal-
ized the conditions by which they could be granted formal authorization.
Bahrain therefore witnessed the blossoming of associations, some of which
were actually no more than a fig leaf for political parties. This was particularly so of the Islamic Enlightenment Society, which acted as the legal front
of al-Da'wa.

It is also in the context of the parliamentary elections that Sh. 'Abd al-
Amir al-Jamri (1937-2006) began his political career, following a very similar path to 'Isa Qasem's. Like his companions in al-Da'wa, he was trained
in Najaf where he stayed between 1962 and 1973. In 1973, he was brought
back from Najaf by his fellow villagers of Bani Jamra to be their candidate,
and he succeeded in gaining a seat in Parliament. In the meantime, he had
been appointed the deputy-general secretary of the Islamic Enlightenment
Society. 'Abd al-Amir al-Jamri became the most popular of the Shia religious scholars in Bahrain in the 1990s thanks to his role during the uprising of 1994-98 which earned him the nickname "*al-Sheikh al-Mujahid*",
i.e. the "combatant Sheikh". At that time, 'Isa Qasem was in Iran to round
off his religious education and was not among the protagonists of these
events. When 'Isa Qasem came back to Bahrain in 2001, 'Abd al-Amir
al-Jamri was already seriously ill and had retreated from political affairs. It
was a sign of his wide popularity that when he died in December 2006 his
funeral aroused one of the biggest popular rallies ever held in Bahrain.

The last important name to bear in mind is that of S. 'Abdallah al-
Ghurayfi (b. 1944). He is a member of an old clerical family claiming descent from the Prophet, which produced dozens of *'ulama*, some of whom
relocated to Iran and Iraq in the course of the eighteenth century. Unlike

---

11   Nakhleh (1976), p. 158.

the vast majority of the Bahrani clerics, many al-Ghurayfi scholars shifted to Usulism probably in the early twentieth century. 'Abdallah al-Ghurayfi's uncle, S. 'Allawi al-Ghurayfi, converted thousands of Baharna to Usulism in the 1960s. For a long time he ran one of the most prestigious *hawza* of Bahrain, located in the village of Na'im in the outskirts of Manama. The al-Ghurayfi are also present in Iraq to this day. A close aid to 'Ali al-Sistani, S. Mohammed Redha al-Ghurayfi was a member of the committee that drafted the Iraqi constitution after the fall of Saddam Husein in April 2003 and has been the prayer leader of the mosque of the Imam Ali shrine in Najaf since 2004. As for 'Abdallah al-Ghurayfi himself, he was trained like the others in Najaf and is said to have been particularly close to Mohammed Baqer al-Sadr, with whom he enjoyed a close personal relationship. He came back to Bahrain at the time of the 1973 elections, in which he ran unsuccessfully against a Ba'thist candidate. In the 1980s, 'Abdallah al-Ghurayfi spent sometime in Dubai where he took the direction of the *ja'fari waqf* administration. He then moved to Syria to Sayyida Zaynab, where he officiated as the director of the *hawza* created by Mohammed Husein Fadlallah. The Lebanese *mujtahid*, who announced his *marja'iyya* in 1995, was born in Najaf and, if not strictly speaking a member of al-Da'wa, was at least a close associate of its leaders (*cf.* chapter 3). 'Abdallah al-Ghurayfi's ties with Mohammed Husein Fadlallah were probably forged from this time the two men spent in Najaf, and continued to be reinforced over the years. At the time of writing, 'Abdallah al-Ghurayfi was the main representative of Mohammed Husein Fadlallah in Bahrain and a major broker of the influence of this particular *marja'* in the Gulf, who has continued to gain ground over the years. It is a commonly held opinion in Bahrain that 'Abdallah al-Ghurayfi could be the successor of Mohammed Husein Fadlallah as a *marja'*. According to Wissam al-Saba' who is a connoisseur of Shia Islamic movements in Bahrain, 'Abdallah al-Ghurayfi did not play a central role in setting up al-Da'wa's organizational structure in Bahrain and was always more dedicated to religious learning than to political activity as such.[12] He is by all standards one of the most learned of the Bahraini *'ulama* but also enjoys the respect of the Islamic activists. He is said to be the other spiritual leader of al-Wifaq with 'Isa Qasem, with whom he is friends. Many say, including people from his family entourage, that 'Abdallah al-Ghurayfi is in regular and close contact with the Iraqi leadership of al-Da'wa. He would "advise" (sic) the two successive Iraqi prime ministers of Iraq post-Saddam Husein: Ibrahim al-Ja'fari and Nuri

---

12   E-mail exchange with Wissam al-Saba', February 2007.

al-Maliki, both lay cadres of al-Da'wa who spent many years in Syria at the time he himself resided there.

As the case of Kuwait will illustrate by contrast, the way the Iraqi Shia movements spread to Bahrain was shaped by the structure of the local clerical class. Indeed, the fact that the Bahrani 'ulama had long been connected to the big centres of Shia learning in Iraq and Iran did not prevent them from being pretty parochial. Residing quasi-exclusively in rural communities, far away from the cosmopolitan life of Manama whose moral deliquescence they abhorred, they tended to view non-locals as intruders. This probably explains why I have been unable to find significant information indicating that, as is the case in many other Shia regions, the Bahrani clerical class was nourished by a constant supply of foreign scholars. Bahrain of course hosted many peripatetic *mulla* and preachers coming regularly to emcee religious ceremonies but few strangers established themselves in Bahrain and integrated into the local religious establishment. In other words, although Bahrain exported many scholars throughout its history, it did not import many. The case of Sh. 'Abd al-Husein al-Hilli (1883-1955), an Iraqi native who set up the Bahraini *Ja'fari* court system in 1935, was an exception in that respect. As a matter of fact, he lived in Manama and not in the rural areas, a sign that he might not have been welcomed by the Bahrani clerical class and came to Bahrain because he was asked by the rulers to create an administration meant to curb the autonomy of the local clerics in the management of Shia personal status law.

The resilience of the Akhbari school of thought can be interpreted as another manifestation of the parochialism of the Bahrani clerical class. In the context of foreign encroachment of all sorts, it was a defensive doctrine that protected the local clerics from outside interference. It helped maintain the clerical class's cohesion, its sense of belonging to a besieged elite. Furthermore, one should note that al-Da'wa in Bahrain was born out of the Akhbari milieu, although the political thought it carried was typically Usuli, with its insistence on the role of the scholars as vice-regents of the Imam. 'Isa al-Sharqi made clear that, in the 1970s, many members of al-Da'wa were emulators of Yusuf al-Bahrani (known as Yusuf al-'Asfur in Bahrain), the famous eighteenth century Akhbari scholar. In his eyes, this should not be taken as a contradiction because, like most of the lay cadres of al-Da'wa be it in Bahrain or Iraq, he considered that al-Da'wa's doctrine was against the idea of any kind of fusion between the *marja'iyya* and the party.[13] This idea was of course not shared by the clerical cadres, who represented the

---

13   *The Story of Political Islam in Bahrain* n° 2, *al-Watan* (Bahrain), 14 December 2005.

wing of the movement attached to the idea of the pre-eminence of religious authority. The latter could not ignore the contradiction between adhering to al-Da'wa's ideas and continuing to be Akhbari. Nevertheless, the "founding patriarchs" of al-Da'wa in Bahrain were still reluctant to drop their Akhbari outlook at the time of writing. It is hence commonly held in Bahrain that 'Isa Qasem is still Akhbari, despite the fact that, as we shall see later, he is said to promote the *marja'iyya* of S. Ali Khamene'i, the successor of Ruhollah Khomeini at the head of the Islamic Republic of Iran. 'Abd al-Amir al-Jamri also remained Akhbari.

This poses questions less about the religious coherence of the politicized Bahrani clerics than about the transformation of Akhbari thought following the growing encroachment of Usulism. The matter is out of the scope of this book and would need the collection of further empirical evidence and a deeper examination by experts, but the idea that Akhbarism in Bahrain is little by little being emptied of its doctrinal specificity seems a plausible hypothesis. This suggestion was at least the outcome of a conversation I had with a Bahrani scholar of a famous Akhbari family of science, the al-Sittri. At the time I met him, he had left his profession of businessman to undertake religious training in Sayyida Zaynab in Syria. The last of the scholars of his family had died and he was expressly asked to continue the family tradition of religious learning. He was also willing to preserve the Akhbari tradition but tended all the way through to minimize the doctrinal differences between Akhbarism and Usulism. According to his view, Akhbarism's only characteristic was that it recognized only two sources for the elaboration of *fiqh*: the Quran and the Imam's reports. For the rest, it admitted the idea of emulation of a *marja'*, with the difference from Usulism being that Akhbarism allows the emulation of a dead *marja'*. As for political quietism, he also denied that Akhbarism was in itself politically silent. He gave as a proof precisely the fact that 'Isa Qasem was an Akhbari...[14] It may well be that one day Akhbarism in Bahrain will be reduced to a mere diacritical mark sustaining the sense of a Bahrani specificity.

Dual Positioning

Because the structure of the local clerical class was totally different from that in Bahrain, the pattern of transnationalization of al-Da'wa was totally different in Kuwait and, incidentally, in the United Arab Emirates. There, al-Da'wa penetrated through the physical presence of some of its chief cadres. A typical case study was that of Sh. 'Ali al-Kurani (b. 1944). Upon his

---

14   Personal interview, Syria, February 2005.

arrival in Kuwait in 1968, he was a young Lebanese cleric in his twenties trained in Najaf. Like many young scholars, he had been enthusiastic about the ideas of Mohammed Baqer al-Sadr and was among the first recruits of al-Da'wa, of which he soon became one of the most prominent leaders. In the meantime in Kuwait, the al-Naqi family had completed the building of a new mosque in the Shia quarter of Dasma and had contacted the office of the *marja'* Muhsin al-Hakim in Najaf to ask him to provide them with a competent cleric to officiate as the prayer leader at the new mosque. Muhsin al-Hakim dispatched 'Ali al-Kurani, who would also act as his official representative in Kuwait.

Far from being unusual, this kind of occurrence was characteristic of the way the Kuwaiti clerical class formed itself so that, here again, we are faced with a process of diffusion drawing on previously established patterns of interaction. There were indeed hardly any clerics among the Shia who came to settle in Kuwait, and there was therefore no tradition of high level Shia scholarship in the emirate. The mosques and the *huseiniyya* were generally built at the initiative of merchant families, of which they bore the names. The upper merchant class was the main broker of relations with the *marja'iyya* in Najaf. Merchants would contact the *marja'iyya* to ask for a prayer leader for the mosque they were patronizing, as much for the religious edification of the Shia as for their own personal social prestige. Having a scholar from Najaf officiating at one's mosque was definitely more rewarding than the usual local self-taught "*hajj*".[15] This was, for example, the way Mahdi al-Qazwini, who played such a critical role in rallying the Shia to the Al-Sabah in 1938 (*cf.* chapter 2), arrived in Kuwait in 1908. One of the main Shia mosques, the al-Mazidi mosque, then lacked a prayer leader. The owners of the mosque turned to the *marja'* Mohammed Taqi Shirazi, then residing in Najaf and who would hereafter lead the 1920 Revolution in Iraq, to send a scholar to replace the prayer leader who had just died.[16] The *marja'* chose Mahdi al-Qazwini. The latter stayed only seventeen years in Kuwait but, as previously mentioned, left a deep imprint on the community where he contributed to forging the relationship with the rulers by acting as its *de facto* political leader. He then returned to Iraq, where he officiated in Basra until his death in 1940, but had in the meantime asked his brother, S. Jawad al-Qazwini, to replace him in Kuwait. After the death of the latter in 1950, one of the al-Mazidi mosque's flock undertook the

---

15   I.e. someone who had made the pilgrimage to Mecca. The title "*hajji*" or "*hajj*" is often conferred on old men who not only made the pilgrimage but are also known for their particular religious devotion.

16   Personal interview with S. 'Ala al-Qazwini, December 2006.

trip to Basra to bring one of Mahdi al-Qazwini's sons, S. Amir Moham-med al-Qazwini, who settled in the emirate.[17] His sons, all clerics, were still living and officiating in Kuwait at the time of writing. This is how a fully-fledged family of science were established in Kuwait, with the status of first category Kuwaiti citizens.

The arrival of 'Ali al-Kurani in Kuwait was thus part of an old pattern. The question remains as to whether Muhsin al-Hakim sent a representa-tive who was also a political activist on purpose. Kuwaiti informants who frequented 'Ali al-Kurani during his stay generally think that the choice of the *marja°* was made on the criteria of efficiency. 'Ali al-Kurani was indeed an incisive preacher. He himself denied his appointment was politi-cally motivated and insisted he set up in Kuwait in order to represent the *marja'iyya* and not to create secret cells of al-Da'wa.[18] This of course has to do with the fact that, like many clerical leaders of al-Da'wa who thereafter left the party to pursue a religious career and did so most often following harsh internal quarrels, 'Ali al-Kurani is reluctant to speak about his past political engagement. A reminder of the tricky political manoeuvres with which he has been associated could indeed harm his current religious ca-reer. As he stressed, his experience in al-Da'wa led him to the conclusion that political engagement contradicts probity and is therefore detrimental to the religious scholars' moral requirements.

But the insistence on the idea that his stay in Kuwait was part of the *marja'iyya*'s framework also reveals that his success as a political ideologue stemmed from his dual positioning as an activist and an envoy of the cen-tral religious authority. In the words of a Kuwaiti informant, 'Ali al-Kurani was a "*haraki hawzawi*", that is a member of a political movement (*haraka*) and of the *hawza*. Being a delegate of the *marja'iyya* allowed him to stay in good terms with the Kuwaiti authorities for whom he was no more than a religious scholar doing his job in a population known for its loyalty to the ruling family. In actual fact, 'Ali al-Kurani officiated among a population for whom politics essentially meant preserving the *status quo* of good rela-tions with the ruling dynasty, and which was therefore little interested in embracing anything that could appear as a potentially oppositionist politi-cal ideology. On the other hand however, as we shall see, the novelty of his religious discourse and of his political positioning seduced the younger Shia generation wanting to break with past practices. The strategic value

---

17   On the life of Mahdi al-Qazwini, see Mansur Hajji Isma'il Khaldi, "Moham-med Mahdi al-Qazwini. A Forgotten Figure of Kuwaiti History" (in Arabic), *al-Qabas* (Kuwait), 7 December 2006.

18   Personal interview with 'Ali al-Kurani, Iran, July 2005.

of 'Ali al-Kurani's dual positioning was well illustrated by his high degree of religious opportunism. Upon the death of Muhsin al-Hakim in 1970, 'Ali al-Kurani in fact became the official representative of Abu al-Qasem al-Khu'i in Kuwait. In many respects the paragon of the quietist *marja'*, the latter is generally considered by the Shia Islamic activists as the one who operated the *marja'iyya*'s withdrawal from the political arena to the point of compromising with the Ba'thist regime. 'Ali al-Kurani's shift to Abu al-Qasem al-Khu'i shows that while militating inside al-Da'wa, he was always keen to preserve his connection to the most powerful figures of the religious institution even when this contradicted his ideological commitment.

'Ali al-Kurani left Kuwait after seven years to return to Lebanon. His departure may have been precipitated by the tensions his presence raised among the Shia population. Indeed, even those who appreciated him often consider that his "aggressive" (*haddi*) style of speech generated regrettable conflicts within a community who had been used to a much softer way. He then played a rather obscure role in the foundation of the Lebanese Hezbollah. When asked directly, he denies having played a part in Hezbollah's foundation.[19] Yet, he is often described as having played at least an ideological role in the process.[20] Be that as it may, 'Ali al-Kurani subsequently ceased any formal political activity to dedicate himself to preaching and writing. At the time of writing, he was still residing in Qom where, among other things, he has pursued a successful career as a TV preacher in Iranian Arabic-language broadcasting.[21] As an individual, he is still in touch with his acquaintances in Kuwait and the Gulf monarchies overall. He is one of the regular foreign preachers invited on the occasion of various religious ceremonies, where his eloquence ensures him a full house.

Transnationalization and Domestic Political Weakness

Internal political developments in Iraq and, to a lesser extent, in Iran, were another key factor in the transnationalization process of al-Da'wa, which was also the unintended consequence of the party's failure to implement its project of overthrowing the Ba'thist regime and the subsequent closure of the domestic political arena. By setting themselves up in Kuwait, the

19   Personal interview, Iran, July 2005.

20   Magnus Ranstorp, *Hizb'allah in Lebanon. The Politics of the Western Hostage Crisis*, London: Macmillan, 1997, p. 37; Ra'uf (2000), p. 225. 'Ali al-Kurani is the author of a book on the Lebanese Hezbollah: *Hezbollah's Approach to Islamic Action* (in Arabic), Beirut: Al-Dar al-Islamiyya, 1406 A.H. (1985).

21   See 'Ali al-Kurani's web site where, among other things, there are photographs of his stay in Kuwait: www.alameli.net.

main aim of the Iraqi activists was not to lay the foundations of a transnational political movement but, more prosaically, to guarantee their physical integrity. Transnationalization was a stopgap solution for activists chased out of their country by repression and transformed into exiles reduced to conducting politics from abroad. But here again, one finds out that it is the exiles' ability to wear two hats that has facilitated their relocation to Kuwait. They were not mere refugees looking for a haven but were also seen as delegates of the *marja'iyya*. Typical of this is the case of Sh. Mohammed Mahdi al-Asefi, a companion of 'Ali al-Kurani in al-Da'wa to whom 'Ali al-Kurani offered his office as prayer leader of the al-Naqi mosque upon his departure in 1974. At that time, he was in search of an asylum to escape the persecution of both the Iraqi and the Iranian governments. An Iraqi of Iranian descent, he had been expelled to Iran with thousands of other ethnic Iranians at the beginning of the 1970s. Although he apparently enjoyed good connections with some pro-Shah clerics,[22] he underwent pressure from the Iranian government following a brief period of rapprochement between Iran and Iraq in 1975, after the signature of the Algiers Agreement which ended – temporarily – the border dispute between the two countries. According to all accounts, Mohammed Mahdi al-Asefi had a much smoother personality than his predecessor and, Kuwaitis deem, much better adapted to the Kuwaiti context. This allowed him to somehow ease the tension 'Ali al-Kurani had created with the old-fashioned sectors of the Shia population, who feared his presence might have endangered the Shias' relationship with the rulers. Mohammed Mahdi al-Asefi stayed five years in Kuwait, leaving for Iran soon after the beginning of the Iran-Iraq war in 1980. He gained further in prominence at the beginning of the 1980s when he became the official spokesman of al-Da'wa.

The arrival of Mohammed Mahdi al-Asefi in Kuwait marked the opening of a new period in the relationship between Kuwait and the Iraqi shrine cities: that of the arrival of political exiles following growing repression by the Ba'th regime. Several other cadres of al-Da'wa followed Mohammed Mahdi al-Asefi, among whom were again prominent figures of the party. S. Mohammed Bahr al-'Ulum for example, who was among the founders of al-Da'wa but quickly quit in early 1960,[23] also established himself for a short period in Kuwait before reaching London. He did not stay long in Kuwait and none of my informants mentioned him as having left any political heritage in the emirate. Such was not the case with 'Azz al-Din Salim (Abu Yasin) (d. 2004) whose real name was 'Abd al-Zahra 'Othman

---

22   Ra'uf (2003), p. 73.

23   Abdul-Jabar (2003), p. 256.

Mohammed. The latter was not a cleric but a so-called "*effendi*", i.e. a lay cadre of al-Da'wa. A teacher by education, he had been responsible for the library created by Muhsin al-Hakim in the city of Qarna in the vicinity of Basra in southern Iraq. Wanted in Iraq, he arrived in Kuwait in 1977 where he became a teacher of history and geography at the National *Ja'fariyya* School (*al-Madrasa al-Wataniyya al-Ja'fariyya*). The school had been created in 1939 shortly after the crisis of the Assembly Movement by a group of Shia notables supported by the Emir. The establishment was the first and to date only school specifically aimed at Shia pupils. In the 1970s, it employed several teachers from among the Iraqi activists of al-Da'wa. This institutional framework provided them with a unique tool to spread their ideology among the Shia youth. 'Azz al-Din Salim also participated in the creation of a cultural association, Dar al-Tawhid (the House of the Unity), the aim of which was the publication of religious books. He also animated circles of reflection in several Shia mosques.[24] 'Azz al-Din Salim played a leading role in al-Da'wa, mainly in a splinter group that was closely associated with Iran after the Islamic revolution (*cf.* chapter 5). After the fall of Saddam Husein's regime in April 2003, he was elected president of the Transitory Council of Government, which led to him being assassinated in May 2004 in a suicide attack.

The career of Mohammed Mahdi al-Asefi and 'Azz al-Din Salim in Kuwait are a further example of the benefit entailed by dual positioning. In fact, as a state, Kuwait did not have a policy of granting refuge to political opponents. It was typical of those states to agree to host political opponents while being careful to avoid possible reprisals.[25] As mentioned previously, Kuwait always had a tense relationship with Iraq. This explains why the authorities welcomed those combating the Iraqi regime, considered as would-be rulers with whom it would be possible to have better relations. But because Kuwait was a militarily weak state, it could also have suffered from direct retaliation by Iraq, which might have considered Kuwait's asylum policy as a *casus belli*. This is why Kuwaiti rulers did not authorize al-Da'wa exiles to undertake political action against the Iraqi regime from their territory and only tolerated religious activities. In this context, the fact

---

24   Hamed al-'Abdallah, "'Azz al-Din Salim. The Assassination of a Thinker" (in Arabic), *al-'Asr*, n° 35, August 2004, p. 27. *Al-'Asr* is a cultural monthly published in Kuwait by people who are intellectually and politically the heirs of al-Da'wa current in Kuwait. Hamed al-'Abdallah is himself professor in political sciences at the University of Kuwait and one of the young men who assiduously attended the lectures of 'Azz al-Din Salim in the 1970s.

25   Yossi Schain, *The Frontier of Loyalty. Political Exiles in the Age of the Nation-State*, Ann Arbor: The University of Michigan Press, 2005, p. 121.

that the Iraqi exiles continued to use the framework of the *marja'iyya* to legitimate their presence proved again a decisive resource as it contributed to allaying the stigma attached to the status of political exile. As a matter of fact, al-Da'wa teachers at the National *Ja'fariyya* School did provide their students with an introduction to Shia Islamic jurisprudence (*fiqh*) but this was through the *fatwa* of Abu al-Qasem al-Khu'i and not the thought of Mohammed Baqer al-Sadr. By the same token, in the mid-1970s, they opened a small *hawza* under the patronage of the same Abu al-Qasem al-Khu'i. It no longer existed at the time of writing, having been replaced by a well known centre of Islamic teaching and publication named Dar al-Zahra (the House of Zahra)[26] which was considered the meeting place of al-Da'wa activists at the time of writing. As for Mohammed Mahdi al-Asefi, although he settled in Kuwait because he was looking for shelter, he was like his predecessor 'Ali al-Kurani a delegate of Abu al-Qasem al-Khu'i. He was perceived as such by many. "He did not behave like a political activist but as a religious scholar", reckoned a Kuwaiti who used to frequent his circle of students at the al-Naqi mosque. Like 'Ali al-Kurani, he was also unwilling to speak about his political past when I interviewed him, and the status of delegate of the *marja'iyya* is the only one he agreed to assume.[27] As a matter of fact, Mohammed Mahdi al-Asefi was rather close to Abu al-Qasem al-Khu'i whom he apparently preferred to emulate rather than Mohammed Baqer al-Sadr.[28] This choice could of course have been based on the intimate conviction that Abu al-Qasem al-Khu'i was the most learned of the *mujtahid*. But it also most probably reflected the fact that, springing out of the *marja'iyya*, al-Da'wa could not allow itself to cut ties with it and, even more, was highly dependent on it. The *marja'iyya* provided al-Da'wa cadres not only with a religious legitimacy but also with an infrastructure within which to circulate as well as means to sustain oneself outside of Iraq. The transnational networks of al-Da'wa and the *marja'iyya* were so tightly intermingled that it was often impossible to separate the religious and the political rationales accounting for the physical mobility of al-Da'wa members.

It is significant that this pattern was also the case for al-Da'wa lay cadres and not only for the clerical leaders. The former were indeed closer to the

---

26   Zahra is one of the names of Fatima, the daughter of the Prophet Mohammed and wife of Imam 'Ali.

27   Personal interview, Kuwait, May 2006.

28   'Adel Ra'uf, *Iraq without Leadership. Lecture of the Crisis of the Shia Religious Leadership in Iraq* (in Arabic), Damascus: Al-Markaz al-'Iraqi lil-I'lam wal-Dirasat, 2003, p. 66.

status of pure political exiles than the latter, as their installation in Kuwait could not be justified by their professional status. However, their stay in Kuwait was also facilitated by their inclusion in the realm of the central religious institution. For example, the fact that 'Azz al-Din Salim had worked as director of an Islamic library created and funded by Muhsin al-Hakim allowed him to boost his credentials to the *Ja'fariyya* school's board. In Kuwait, his inclusion in the inner circles of Mohammed Mahdi al-Asefi also further reinforced his legitimacy. In brief, the Kuwaiti Shia notability did not receive him as an exiled political activist but as an associate of the *marja'iyya*.

Al-Da'wa in the United Arab Emirates

The way al-Da'wa spread to the United Arab Emirates is a further argument militating in favour of the idea that the mode of transnationalization is partly modelled by the initial structure of the local clerical class. Like in Kuwait, and for the very same reasons, there was no real Shia local clerical class in the UAE. The merchants were the main actors of the religious life, that was centred on ritual practices rather than on scholarship and learning. The merchants built the mosques and the *huseiniyya*. All the Shia religious endowments (*waqf*) were owned mainly by Bahrani and 'Ijmi families who, as in Kuwait and for the same reasons, had migrated from Bahrain and Iran mostly in the course of the nineteenth century. The link with the central religious institution was more tenuous than in Kuwait, with no established pattern of resident *'ulama* representing the *marja'iyya* and acting as the spiritual leaders of the community. There was therefore no Shia family of science.

In this context, the implantation of al-Da'wa could only occur as a direct result of the forced exile of al-Da'wa cadres, with the arrival in 1971 of Mahdi al-Hakim in the emirate of Dubai. As mentioned previously (*cf.* chapter 3), he was the son of Muhsin al-Hakim, a close aid to Mohammed Baqer al-Sadr and among the nucleus of those who founded al-Da'wa. In 1969, he was arrested and tortured on suspicion of having participated in a plot to unseat the Ba'th.[29] After his release, he fled to Pakistan among relatives from a branch of the al-Hakim family based there.[30] A few months later, he took a plane to Dubai where he was received by the Bahrani merchants, who welcomed him as the official representative of the *marja'iyya*. His establishment in Dubai did not entail far reaching political implica-

---

29   Abdul-Jabar (2003), p. 204.

30   Wiley (1992), p. 77.

tions but led to a complete reorganization of the local religious institution. Mahdi al-Hakim indeed pushed the merchant families of Dubai and Sharjah to abandon their prerogatives over the religious endowments and to hand them over to an administrative board that would manage it in the best interests of the Shias. According to Emirati informants, the reason why the merchants accepted handing over the *waqf* was because they had many endowments and had themselves realized that they could not manage them the proper way without a centralized body. This was in contrast to the merchants of Abu Dhabi, who had fewer *waqf* which they wanted to keep under their control.

Dubai and Sharjah merchants therefore agreed to ask the Emir of Dubai to release an official decree instituting the *Ja'fari Waqf* Administration. While the decree appointed a representative of the powerful al-Fardan Bahrani family as the official director of the body, Emirati informants deem that Mahdi al-Hakim was the real executive manager. This was an effect of his exteriority to local conflicts between the merchants. He was perceived as a neutral arbiter able to stand above the factions. Only such a man, Shia Emiratis reckon, would have been able to unite the excessively factionalized Shia merchant notability. Mahdi al-Hakim stayed nine years in Dubai. He left in 1980 after the beginning of the Iran-Iraq war because his life was no longer safe. He left for London where he established a charitable association – Ahl al-Bayt (the Family of the Prophet) – and was subsequently assassinated by Iraqi agents during a trip in Sudan in 1988.[31] Before his departure, Mahdi al-Hakim handed over his function as the unofficial supervisor of the *ja'fari* endowments to 'Abdallah al-Ghurayfi, whom he had met in Najaf and who was one of those who had contributed to spreading al-Da'wa ideas in Bahrain (*cf.* infra). 'Abdallah al-Ghurayfi also stayed roughly nine years in the UAE where he completed the institutional work of his predecessor. He more particularly built a strong personal network of relationships in Abu Dhabi where the bulk of the Shias are Bahrani. In the mid-1990s, the latter have become the nucleus from where the *marja'iyya* of Mohammed Husein Fadlallah spread in the UAE. On the other hand, the stay of 'Abdallah al-Ghurayfi did not go without creating numerous tensions inside the local Shia population. According to Emirati informants, he had a tougher personality than Mahdi al-Hakim, being in particular less tolerant towards certain ritual practices he deemed backward and deviating from true religion. Furthermore, because he thought that the administration of religious life should fall within the hands of the clerics – that is, himself – he encroached upon the big merchants' prerogatives, making

31   *Ibid.*

several of them angry. This apparently was the reason why he was asked to leave the UAE in 1989 and took a plane to Syria where he became the director of Fadlallah's *hawza*. The merchants had deliberately tarnished his reputation by suggesting to the Emirati authorities that he was a pro-Iranian agent wishing to export the revolution.

CIRCUMVENTING THE INSTITUTION: THE SHIRAZIYYIN

The case of Mohammed al-Shirazi and his followers also follows the pattern of the political exiles described above. There was however a sharp and decisive difference with al-Da'wa exiles: because they were in conflict with the *marja'iyya*, their sojourn was unmediated by its networks. This contributed to reinforcing their profile as religious and social innovators.

Mohammed al-Shirazi as a "Freelance Preacher"[32]

Uprooted from Karbala, the al-Shirazi and al-Mudarrisi families, soon followed by several members of the al-Qazwini, sought refuge first in Lebanon and Syria. Hasan al-Shirazi established good contacts with the Syrian regime which authorized him to create the first Shia learning institution in Sayyida Zaynab in 1975. Mohammed al-Shirazi joined his brother in Lebanon and Syria in 1970. A few months later in 1971, he had the opportunity of settling in Kuwait with most of his family: his wife and children, his two younger brothers Sadiq and Mujtaba, as well as his nephews Mohammed Taqi and Hadi al-Mudarrisi.

The installation of Mohammed al-Shirazi in Kuwait was rendered possible by connections with Kuwaiti merchants he had made during the Karbala days. The locus of Imam Husein's martyrdom, Karbala was a place of pilgrimage which people from all the corners of the Shia world used to visit regularly. This was particularly the case for Kuwaitis, for whom Karbala was not such a remote place. Therefore, the name of Mohammed al-Shirazi was not totally unknown to some Kuwaitis. A handful of them had met him on the occasion of regular pilgrimages to the holy city and contributed to financing his activities. While not among the best off of the merchant class, they had social weight among the Shia population of Kuwait and were able to arrange his stay in the emirate. Moreover, all Kuwaiti informants agree that, in the early 1970s, the quarrel with the Najafi establishment had not crossed the frontiers of Iraq so that many ignored it or at least did not attach importance to it. As underlined by Saleh 'Ashur, a leading political fig-

---

32 To borrow from Michael Walzer, *The Revolution of the Saints. A Study in the Origins of Radical Politics*, London: Weidenfield and Nicolson, 1965, p. 14.

ure of the Shiraziyyin in Kuwait and a member of Parliament since 1999, "we thought it was a matter of personal rivalry. We were not aware that it was also a matter of divergence between two political organizations"[33]. This also explains why Mohammed al-Shirazi had the support of important Kuwaiti Shia scholars, most notably S. 'Ali Shubbar (d. 1973), who was the main representative of the Najafi *marja'iyya* among the Hasawi and Bahrani populations, and S. 'Abbas al-Muhri (1912-1988), who acted as the religious leader of the 'Ajam. While they might have doubted the legitimacy of Mohammed al-Shirazi's *marja'iyya*, they supported him out of a reflex of corporate solidarity: he was a religious scholar who needed help, and was moreover the descendant of a prestigious family of science. At the time one of the most powerful Shia religious men in Kuwait, 'Abbas al-Muhri used his influence to provide Mohammed al-Shirazi with a visa and personally asked a local merchant, Haji Barun, to lend him a house he owned in the old Shia quarter of Bneid al-Gar, where Mohammed al-Shirazi and his followers established their quarters.

Far from being content to just sit and wait for more favourable days to go back to Karbala, Mohammed al-Shirazi proved particularly active during the nine years he stayed in Kuwait. In many ways, he revolutionized the landscape of organized religion in a country in which religiosity was mainly expressed in prayer at the mosque and participation in religious rituals. Thanks to the support of key figures of the merchant class, including wealthy and politically influential ones like Mohammed Qabazard, he built quickly a whole set of religious and charitable institutions, which survived his departure to Iran in 1979. Of course, he created a mosque, a *huseiniyya*, a library and a *diwaniyya*. He also founded a charitable institution, the Association *Ahl al-Bayt*, which is today run by Saleh 'Ashur and is one of the most important Shia associations in Kuwait, financing numerous religious and charitable projects mainly in Iran and Iraq, but also in Pakistan and Azerbaijan: restoration, refurbishing and building of mosques and *huseiniyya*, help to indebted clerics, medical treatments for poor people, etc. The novelty, and probably Mohammed al-Shirazi's main institutional legacy in Kuwait, was the creation of the first *hawza* of the country, the *Hawza* of the Supreme Prophet (*Hawzat al-Rasul al-A'dham*).[34] The aim of Mohammed al-Shirazi was therefore to contribute to the formation of a local clerical class. This in his view necessitated the presence of a religious learning institution in Kuwait itself, as the political circumstances had made the

---

33   Personal interview, Kuwait, December 2006.

34   Another one was founded in 1999 by the proponents of the so-called Hezbollah current, which is in many respects the heir of al-Da'wa in Kuwait (*cf.* chapter 6).

hawza of Iraq and Iran very difficult to access for foreign students. Having a religious school close by would attract more Kuwaiti young people to the profession of cleric.

Besides contributing to the diffusion of religious learning among Kuwaiti Shias, Mohammed al-Shirazi continued using one of his favourite means of mobilization: religious rituals. As one of the regulars of 'Ali al-Kurani reckoned with a disdainful pout: "he was distributing candies during the feasts.[35] That's how he hoped to gain the hearts of the masses ". This was all the easier for him since he had gained the support of figures of the merchant notability, who played a central part in popular religion. For the merchants, financing popular rituals was a way to reinforce their economic and social standard by a moral one. Following a rationale reminiscent of ancient Rome's evergetism, they responded to a tacit social norm demanding that the rich contribute to public good.[36]

The question remains of how Mohammed al-Shirazi managed to be so successful considering his marginal position towards the *marja'iyya*. In many respects, aside from his personal charisma, the key to his success was precisely linked to his status as a stranger both in relation to Kuwaiti society and the Najafi religious establishment. Georg Simmel has emphasized the fact that newcomers in a society enjoy a freedom unknown of the locals, who are much more bound to established patterns of behaviour from which it would be socially dangerous for them to deviate.[37] In this sense, strangers are often social innovators who, more than others, have the ability to break important social taboos. The estrangement of Mohammed al-Shirazi from the central religious authority forced him further to resort to innovation to legitimate his marginal status. Significantly, this pattern of behaviour has also been underlined by Michael Walzer in his description of the sixteenth century puritan clerics. He described them as "freelance preachers" whose original style and tactics of penetrating foreign milieus were framed by their estrangement from the legitimate religious authority and their experience of exile. In rupture with the corporate church, they were compelled to run away from their homeland to escape persecution

---

35   The distribution of candies is a tradition during the celebration of the birth of the twelve Imams, but more particularly for what the Shias call "*nusf Sha'ban*" the mid-Sha'ban month when they celebrate the birth of the Hidden Imam.

36   For the notion of evergetism, see Paul Veyne, *Bread and Circuses. Historical Sociology and Political Pluralism*, Penguin Books, 1990 (translation from *Le pain et le cirque*, Paris: Seuil, 1976).

37   Georg Simmel, *The Sociology of Georg Simmel*, translated, edited and with an introduction by Kurt H. Wolff, Glencoe, Illinois: The Free Press, 1950, pp. 404-5.

but were able to transform this apparently initial weakness into strength: "their exile had taught them the style of free men; its first manifestation was the evasion of traditional authority".[38] In other words, their estrangement from the traditional chains of authority and power pushed them to radicalize their already non-conformist profile, and to break further conventional rules in their speech, and style of preaching.

It was by following this very same logic that Mohammed al-Shirazi, stigmatized by the central religious institution and therefore no longer feeling compelled to follow all of its rules, acted as a social innovator and a religious reformer. First, he did not behave socially as *marja'* usually do. Until today, the preferred way for *marja'* to affirm their status is to put distance between them and society. They relate to it through intermediaries, often their sons or close relatives. They intervene directly only on important occasions and in a highly ritualistic manner. All the accounts of those who met Mohammed al-Shirazi tally in saying that his personal behaviour was contrary to this old *habitus*. He was not afraid of losing his religious prestige by relating directly to people. In his *diwaniyya*, he received anybody wishing to talk to him. Moreover, he did not wait for people to come to him and himself went to visit the house of this or that person. If one of the young men he had gathered around him missed the prayer at the mosque or did not appear at the *diwaniyya*, he would give him a phone call or even knock at his door. His voluntarism did not stop here, as he asked, and obtained, a meeting with the Emir and other political personalities. By doing this, he broke another taboo, that of the independence of the *marja'* towards the temporal political power, which for many should be demonstrated by the absence of direct intercourse.

On another level, Mohammed al-Shirazi proved innovative in his strategy to attract people into religion, especially the younger generation whom he thought should be addressed in their own language rather than with the dryness of the traditional scholarly language. For example, in a country where leisure activities were rather restricted at the time – "going to the beach or doing sport" said one informant – Mohammed al-Shirazi played documentary films in his library. Saleh 'Ashur, who was then responsible for the project, was touring the foreign embassies to pick up various documentaries on the life of Martin Luther King, the Mahatma Gandhi or any other subjects likely to contribute to enhancing the awareness of believers about the great issues of the time. While many disapproved of the project and accused Mohammed al-Shirazi of having opened a cinema, something by then considered highly reprehensible, it also attracted many among the

---

38   Walzer (1965), p. 121.

younger generation. Young people were encouraged not just to be the recipients of religious preaching but also to be active participants in the religious revival. Mohammed al-Shirazi pushed them to write booklets of their own so that young people could be addressed in their own words. Keen to reach all segments of society, Mohammed al-Shirazi also encouraged women to go to the mosque and participate in religious life in general. For that purpose, he built a prayer hall for women in his mosque and encouraged the other mosques to do the same.

Although it is not the country where the Shiraziyyin have the greatest political weight, as we shall see, Kuwait has remained to this day their main base. In the 1970s, the *Hawza* of the Supreme Prophet in Bneid al-Gar became a centre of political training in both ideological and practical terms. The majority of the students were Saudis, Bahrainis and Iraqis. For those who would not engage in studying the whole year, the *hawza* organized summer training courses. As those who went through the *hawza* often recount, while the rooms of the first floor hosted traditional religious lectures, the second floor was reserved for political education. This was dispensed by Mohammed Taqi al-Mudarrisi, the leader of the Message Movement (later on the Islamic Action Organization) and the mastermind behind the whole political strategy of the Shiraziyyin. Beyond the books of theology, Mohammed Taqi al-Mudarrisi initiated his students into reading of the main ideologues of the Islamic revival as a whole. Far from being sectarian, he thought that authors like Hasan al-Banna, Sayyid Qutb or Abul 'Ala Mawdudi, all Sunnis whose works are among the "classics" of the Sunni Islamic movements, were as essential to know as Ali Shariati, the main Shia religious intellectual whose approach to religion inspired generations of Shia Islamic activists. Mohammed Taqi al-Mudarrisi, who was convinced that the success of secular political ideologies among the Shias was largely due to the incapacity of the *hawza* to integrate modern scientific knowledge, was also a fervent adept of neuro-linguistic programming, which was an integral part of the activists' training. Conceived in the United States in the 1960s, this school of psychology aimed at developing individual potential through the study of successful personalities and the building of formal models of successful behaviour.[39]

---

39   Recently, Mohammed Taqi al-Mudarrisi's brother, Hadi al-Mudarrisi, has specialized in writing small books inspired by neuro-linguistic programming, published by the Arab Scientific Publishers and the Arab Cultural Centre (Lebanon) in 2002: *The Keys of Success, The Factors of Success, The Styles of Success, The Art of Success, The Faces of Failure, You Also Can Have Success, How to Overcome Failure* (in Arabic).

Besides ideological education, the activists were also learned in clandestine political action and, upon their regular returns home, the students were given propaganda materials to distribute to those around them. The *hawza* also served as a regular meeting place of the Gulf and Iraq activists with well-known Iranian opponents to the Shah like Sh. Mohammed Montazeri (d. 1981) and S. Mehdi Hashemi (d. 1987). After the Islamic revolution in Iran, the latter supervised the transnational networks of Iranian sponsored "liberation movements", that is Shia Islamic movements aiming at exporting the revolution worldwide (*cf.* chapter 6).

Concerning the strictly political aspect of the activities of the Shiraziyyin in Kuwait, one should note that they were essentially "externalized", so to speak, in the sense that they did not target the Kuwaiti regime but the neighbouring countries. An important aim was of course to continue to work against the Ba'thist regime in Iraq but this was not done openly because, as already mentioned, the Kuwaiti government did not authorize such activities. Therefore, while some Kuwaiti, Bahraini and Saudi activists were used to forward propaganda material to Iraq because they could easily travel there without arousing the suspicion of the authorities, the publishing of propaganda material denouncing the Iraqi regime was coordinated from Beirut by Hasan al-Shirazi. Military training in order to educate activists in arms drill and other things useful for people hoping to overthrow a government, was also done in Lebanon. The cadres of the Message Movement were indeed trained by various groups of the Palestinian Liberation Organization (PLO) established in the refugee camps there. It is there that they forged strong relations with Mohammed Montazeri and other figures of the Islamic opposition to the Shah, who also frequented the PLO camps. Incidentally, the military education was undertaken together with al-Da'wa activists. This was possible because the Shiraziyyin avoided mentioning their affiliation and even passed themselves off as members of al-Da'wa when necessary.

More than Iraq, the activities of Mohammed Taqi al-Mudarrisi in Kuwait therefore targeted the Gulf countries where the relation between the Shias and their governments was conflictual, namely Bahrain and Saudi Arabia where segments of the Shias had witnessed a previous process of politicization in opposition movements. In fact, there were few full time Kuwaiti students in the *Hawza* of the Supreme Prophet, the most notable exception being the director of the *hawza* from 2002, Sh. Rajab 'Ali Rajab. Saleh 'Ashur and 'Abd al-Husein al-Sultan, the two leading political figures of the Shiraziyyin in Kuwait, only occasionally frequented the *hawza*. Therefore, while an entire generation of Saudi activists who hoped to bring

125

about a revolution in their country – and duly organized to do so – were educated in the *Hawza* of the Supreme Prophet, no Kuwaiti revolutionary organization went out from the *hawza*. With a strong presence of wealthy notables well connected to state elites, the social basis of the Shiraziyyin in Kuwait was not propitious to the kind of radical ethos that, as we shall see, prevailed among many of the Bahraini and Saudi activists. In this context, Kuwait was always more a base than a field for political action. It was a hub for the co-ordination of activities targeting other countries rather than a target in itself. When politicians from the Shiraziyyin rose to prominence in the end of the 1990s they quickly acquired the reputation of being "yes men" owing their success to the support of the government. This on the whole explains why, unlike in Bahrain and Saudi Arabia where they quickly assumed the reputation of a radical Shia current with revolutionary undertone, the Shiraziyyin in Kuwait were always perceived as a "traditional" trend not confronting the established political power.[40]

Hadi al-Mudarrisi in Bahrain

The career of Hadi al-Mudarrisi in Bahrain will help to further document the peculiar features of the penetration strategy of the Shiraziyyin in the Gulf countries. It will also further illustrate how the initial social fabric of one society influenced this strategy, in this case the parochial character of the local clerical class.

While his brother Mohammed Taqi stayed in Kuwait, Hadi al-Mudarrisi went to check out the other Gulf monarchies. He settled for a while in Sharjah with another of his brothers, S. 'Abbas al-Mudarrisi. The latter was never mentioned by our informants as having played a decisive part in the diffusion of the Shiraziyyin's network in the Gulf countries, and was probably among the many go-betweens who relayed the activities of his relatives worldwide. Be that as it may, the two brothers took over a disused *huseiniyya* among the Lawati[41] community, which they made the locus of their activities. Local informants had only a vague memory of the al-Mudarrisi brothers' rather short stay in the emirate. One can surmise that their attempts at establishing themselves as religious scholars was impeded by the well anchored networks of the Najafi *marja'iyya* and al-Da'wa. Hadi and 'Abbas al-Mudarrisi nonetheless succeeded in building good connec-

---

40   Al-Khaldi (1999), p. 110; Fuller and Francke (2001), p. 160.

41   The Lawati (sing. Luti) are Shias from Sind in Pakistan who came to settle mostly in the UAE (Dubai and Sharja) and Oman between the eighteenth century and the first half of the twentieth century. For further details, see further in this chapter.

tions twith the Al-Qasimi ruling family who granted them Emirati citizenship at the time of the federation's creation and independence from British rule in 1971. This was despite the fact that the then ruler, Sheikh Khaled bin Mohammed Al-Qasimi, adhered to Arab nationalist tenets. According to Hadi al-Mudarrisi, his naturalization was part of the Sheikh's general policy of attracting Arab elites of all persuasions to his country[42]. The fact that the al-Mudarrisis were actually 'Ajam and had been expelled from Iraq precisely because of their Iranian descent did not bother him or, because he was probably ignorant of the subtleties of the Iraqi social fabric beyond the Arabist ideology deployed by the state, remained unnoticed by him.

It was only later that Hadi al-Mudarrisi decided to establish permanently in Bahrain, a country he had only visited from time to time since his departure from Iraq. Here again, his arrival did not occur in a vacuum and, like his uncle in Kuwait, he benefited from personal relations previously established at the time he was in Karbala. While Mohammed al-Shirazi only had contacts among some middle range merchants upon his arrival in Kuwait, Hadi al-Mudarrisi could benefit from the mediation of members of an important Shia merchant family of the country, the al-'Alawi family. As their name indicates, the al-'Alawi descend from the Prophet through Imam 'Ali. While not all such families hold a socio-economic status congruent with their noble lineage, the al-'Alawi family comprised prominent figures of the Bahraini political and economical scenes. An indicator of its social status was the fact that it was a *tawwash* family. The *tawwash* (pl. *tawawish*) are the pearl merchants possessing their own fleet of boats. After the conquest by the Al-Khalifa, only a few Shia *tawwash* families were able to continue engaging in pearling, an activity that had come to be monopolized by the Sunni tribes. After the collapse of the pearling industry at the end of the 1920s, the al-'Alawi had shifted to various activities like real estate and import-export of goods and manufactured products. They were urban notables based in Manama where, to this day, they own many lands, including one where they built a *ma'tam* at the beginning of the twentieth century, the *Ma'tam* al-Qassab (*ma'tam* is a synonym of *huseiniyya*, a word more in use in Bahrain).

Like all the *tawwash* Shia families who had often been able to keep pearling thanks to their loyalty to the rulers, the al-'Alawi were close to the Al-Khalifa. S. Mahmud al-'Alawi, the president of the *Ma'tam* al-Qassab board of trustees in the 1960s, was for a long time the Minister of Finance and National Economy. This earned him the status of *ex officio* member of the 1972 and 1973 National Assemblies. In 1970, he personally paid

---

42   Personal interview, Iran, July 2005.

for the entire renovation of the *ma'tam* and had the great privilege to have the then Emir of Bahrain, Sheikh 'Isa bin Salman Al-Khalifa, attend the inauguration. At the time Hadi al-Mudarrisi arrived in Bahrain in the early 1970s, Mahmud al-'Alawi's son, S. Kadhem al-'Alawi, had succeeded his father as the administrator of the *ma'tam*. He was a personal adviser of the Emir and also one of the heads of the General Council for the *Huseini* Processions (*al-Hay'a al-'Amma lil-Mawakib al-Huseiniyya*) which was officially charged with organizing the 'Ashura processions in the capital. He had been among the Shia notables involved in the 1956 *intifada* as a full member of the Supreme Executive Committee, some meetings of which were held in his house. The profile of Kadhem al-'Alawi indicates that while having more than excellent relations with the rulers, the al-'Alawi were intermediaries with the State, strictly speaking, and not agents of it. They fitted the classical model of notable drawn by Albert Hourani quite well as they had "a social power of their own"[43] stemming from their wealth and role in the organization of popular religion. Therefore, they acted as intermediaries with the rulers because they had the ability to represent civil society, and it is as such that they had been partly co-opted in the higher administration. But they could also use their social power to pressure the rulers and did not hesitate to do so.

By the end of the 1960s, a young and up to then rather obscure member of the al-'Alawi family, S. Mohammed al-'Alawi, went on a pilgrimage to Karbala with a group of friends. Until then, he had never heard about Mohammed al-Shirazi and his followers, but was struck upon his arrival in the holy city to see portraits of al-Shirazi covering the walls and hanging in the main streets. Curious to know more about the man, he went to his *majlis* hoping to meet with him. There, he met Hadi al-Mudarrisi with whom he talked while waiting for Mohammed al-Shirazi who was giving a lecture a few blocks away. Mohammed al-'Alawi was deeply impressed by this young scholar of roughly the same age as himself, with whom he spoke about the corruption of society under growing foreign encroachment. Hadi al-Mudarrisi expressed his intention to visit Bahrain in the coming months, and the two men agreed that Mohammed al-'Alawi would arrange his stay. The conversation went on with the arrival of Mohammed al-Shirazi, who warmly welcomed his visitor. Mohammed al-'Alawi was particularly impressed by the fact that Mohammed al-Shirazi had precise information on

---

43   Albert Hourani, "Ottoman Reform and the Politics of Notables" in William Polk and Richard L. Chambers (eds), *Beginnings of Modernization in the Middle East. The Nineteenth Century*, Chicago: The University of Chicago Press, 1968, p. 46.

Bahrain, knowing for example the number of cinemas opened in the country. Mohammed al-Shirazi enjoined his visitor to act in order to put an end to Bahrain's growing moral corruption. The two men agreed that upon his return to Bahrain, Mohammed al-'Alawi would set up a religious association placed under Mohammed al-Shirazi's religious authority, aiming at reviving Islamic values. This is how the first institution of the Shiraziyyin was set up in Bahrain, under the name of the Association of the Islamic Guidance (*Jama'iyyat al-Irshad al-Islami*) which, according to Mohammed al-'Alawi, counted around two hundred members.[44]

While Mohammed al-'Alawi was the first member of the al-'Alawi family to meet with the Shiraziyyin, others soon followed. Kadhem al-'Alawi who ran the *Ma'tam* al-Qassab and the General Council for the *Huseini* Processions went to Karbala soon afterwards with two of his sons, in particular the youngest one, S. Ja'far al-'Alawi. Then aged ten, he was to become a leading figure of the Shiraziyyin in Bahrain a few years later. In Karbala, the family met with Mohammed al-Shirazi through the mediation of one of his students, Sh. 'Abd al-Hamid al-Muhajir, whom they had met in Bahrain during a stay he had made to the emirate in 1970.[45] According to Sa'id al-Shihabi, he had been invited by his brother Ja'far and his group, who formed the nucleus of the Islamic Enlightenment Society, to lead the religious ceremonies and give lectures in the main *ma'tam* of Diraz during the month of Ramadan.[46] Those who thereafter identified as activists of al-Da'wa, but whose political identity had not yet crystallized, had met him during previous trips to Karbala. They had books of Mohammed al-Shirazi in their library, which were sent them free of charge from Beirut. This shows that, before the arrival of Hadi al-Mudarrisi in Bahrain, Mohammed al-Shirazi had already begun a propaganda campaign, so to speak, targeting Bahrain and probably the other Gulf monarchies too.

THE REPRODUCTION OF *MARJA'IYYA* FACTIONALISM

Be it in Kuwait, Saudi Arabia or Bahrain, many informants stressed that the quarrel between the Shiraziyyin and the Najafi establishment developed on an unprecedented scale during the period when some of its main protagonists stayed in the Gulf countries. In other words, the Shia activist transnational networks did not only carry political ideas and a general

---

44   Personal interview, Bahrain, December 2006.

45   Ja'far al-'Alawi, *The Story of Political Islam in Bahrain* (in Arabic) n° 23, *al-Watan* (Bahrain), 2 June 2006.

46   Personal interview, London, July 2007.

worldview but also brought with them this founding quarrel between the Najafi and the Karbala'i trends, between the dominant actors of the religious institution and their challengers. One would have thought that this rather parochial dispute, in which localist and familialist *habitus* played a leading role, would have had little resonance in Gulf societies but, on the contrary, a striking feature of this dispute was its ability not only to travel but to perpetuate itself by following the outlines of domestic conflicts.

A Travelling Quarrel

The first step of the transposition of the dispute between al-Da'wa and the Shiraziyyin occurred in Kuwait. Many reasons can be given for that. First, Kuwait was the main place of refuge for the activists of the Iraqi Shia movements so that, literally, the actors of the quarrel were transplanted from one country to another. Gathered in a tiny city state, it was logical that al-Da'wa and the Shiraziyyin would resume with their dispute. Second, Kuwait was, as many Shia Islamic activists put it, the "milk cow" of Shia religious activities of all sorts. The country was among the wealthiest of the Gulf emirates so that while only a minuscule population by contrast with the millions of Shias living in Iraq, Kuwaiti Shias were more financially powerful. The average Kuwaiti Shia was by far better off than the average Iraqi Shia. As for the higher strata, even if no Shia merchant ever matched the fortune of the Sunni oligarchs, their wealth far outstripped that of their Iraqi counterparts. Here one should remember that a main feature of the Shia religious institution in Mesopotamia and then Iraq has always been its relative inability to attract funds from its local constituencies and its heavy reliance on external, mainly Iranian and Indian, sources of revenue.[47] This pattern was reinforced after the establishment of the Iraqi state, the strain in Iran-Iraq relations, the accelerated secularization of Iraqi society and, finally, the suppression of the clerical class. More than ever in this context, the Najafi *mujtahid* had to look for outside sources of funding, in the Gulf, Pakistan, India or East Africa. The petrodollars of Gulf citizens, therefore, constituted a manna that greatly contributed to the worsening of the dispute between the Najafi *marja'iyya* and the Shiraziyyin. Abu al-Qasem al-Khu'i has the reputation of having understood before the others the financial importance of the Gulf countries, where he has been a particularly skilful fundraiser.[48]

---

47   Nakash (1994), p. 205.

48   Walbridge (2001), p. 239.

It is against this background that one must set the stark reactions of al-Da'wa representatives to the arrival of Mohammed al-Shirazi and his followers in Kuwait in 1971. Then established for three years in the emirate, 'Ali al-Kurani quickly understood that Mohammed al-Shirazi would be a hard competitor in the battle for resources. Besides, Mohammed al-Shirazi began to raise a sensitive issue among local Shias. One of his favourite credos was that while Kuwaitis were great contributors to the financing of the *marja'iyya*, they had received little in return. Kuwaiti money was flowing to Najaf and did not serve to further the religious edification of Kuwaiti Shias. The Najafi *marja'iyya* had never spent money on building a *hawza* in Kuwait and therefore had not contributed to the formation of a class of local clerics. In his view, this was a lack and should be corrected. In other words, he told Kuwaitis that he would not take their money to spend it in Iraq but would use it to improve their own situation at home. Because all his assets in Iraq had been confiscated by the regime, he had anyway no other place to spend the money endowed to him.

On the other hand, Mohammed al-Shirazi invented new and more efficient methods of fundraising. He created a system of moneyboxes to be put in every Shia house, in which the family would put a few coins every day and give it to the office of Mohammed al-Shirazi once full. Moreover, he was skilful in seeking the financial help of big Kuwaiti merchants. He would never solicit them to pay religious alms *per se* but would always present them with a concrete project – building this or that religious institution, organizing this or that activity – which their money would permit him to achieve. The contributors would then see the concrete result of their contribution and, as all the projects concerned Kuwait, saw furthermore an occasion to enhance their local social prestige.

In order to weaken his rival, 'Ali al-Kurani resorted to the direct help of the Najafi *marja'iyya*. As the official representative of Abu al-Qasem al-Khu'i, he forwarded to Kuwait several inflammatory communiqués in which the *marja'* was denouncing the illegitimacy of Mohammed al-Shirazi's *marja'iyya*. 'Ali al-Kurani went so far in denouncing his rival that he almost succeeded in having Mohammed al-Shirazi expelled from Kuwait. Indeed, in 1972, a tract, attributed to those frequenting the al-Naqi mosque, circulated accusing Mohammed al-Shirazi of having come to Kuwait in order to create a political party. It was only thanks to the intervention of Mohammed Qabazard, an influential Shia trader who had direct access to the Emir, that the threat was overcome. Therefore, while Mohammed al-Shirazi had initially been supported by leading figures of the religious class, his presence soon became the source of a major split among the Shia population. As a Kuwaiti partisan of the Shiraziyyin put it: "In our books, we are told that the basis of the divide between Sunnis and Shias is the second Caliph. From my point of view, I think that the divergence between the Shias in Kuwait and their division in two groups originated in the al-Naqi mosque and 'Ali al-Kurani".[49]

I found various accounts of the way the quarrel diffused to Bahrain. According to one testimony coming from the direct entourage of 'Abdallah al-Ghurayfi, some figures of the local clerical establishment had heard about the conflict and built a negative opinion of Mohammed al-Shirazi and his followers well before Hadi al-Mudarrisi established himself in the country. Here is how the story was recounted to me. After the decease of Muhsin al-Hakim in 1970, Mohammed al-Shirazi judged the moment was ripe to assert his claim to the *marja'iyya* more strongly. He sent a delegation to Bahrain to the only Usuli *hawza* of the country then, headed by 'Allawi al-Ghurayfi (*cf.* supra). 'Allawi al-Ghurayfi had been the chief representative of Muhsin al-Hakim in Bahrain and, like the other agents of the deceased, was waiting to see who would emerge as the next *marja'*. It was in this context that Mohammed al-Shirazi's messengers presented themselves at 'Allawi al-Ghurayfi's place carrying a document showing a verse of the Quran framed by the photographs of Mohammed al-Shirazi and Muhsin al-Hakim facing each other, which the delegation presented as an official statement by Muhsin al-Hakim that Mohammed al-Shirazi was legitimate to exercise the *marja'iyya*. Presenting such a document implicitly amounted to a demand that 'Allawi al-Ghurayfi himself announced that he recognized Mohammed al-Shirazi as the heir of Muhsin al-Hakim. The attempt ended in complete failure as 'Allawi al-Ghurayfi considered the paper as a mere statement of *wikala* and not an *ijaza*: it was a document authorizing Mohammed al-Shirazi to act as Muhsin al-Hakim's agent and not an official recognition of Mohammed al-Shirazi's entitlement to the *marja'iyya*. Like most scholars of the Arabian countries, 'Allawi al-Ghurayfi recognized Abu al-Qasem al-Khu'i as the most learned and became his representative. According to the informant, the episode cast a shadow on the reputation of Mohammed al-Shirazi, who appeared as someone of dubious religious credentials using circuitous routes to impose himself.

Bahraini Shiraziyyin strongly denied this episode ever happened, basing this on the fact that, until late 1974, major figures of al-Da'wa like 'Isa Qasem and 'Abdallah al-Ghurayfi gladly agreed to undertake joint projects with Hadi al-Mudarrisi. They held conferences and religious ceremonies together. This was confirmed by activists of al-Da'wa. According

---

49   Personal interview, Kuwait, June 2003.

to Sa'id al-Shihabi who was among the first recruits of al-Da'wa, the respective political identities did not crystallize until the mid-1970s.[50] Before that, activists of al-Da'wa and the Bahraini followers of Hadi al-Mudarrisi were unaware of the conflict opposing Mohammed al-Shirazi to the Najafi establishment. They were mixing and cooperating for the sake of the propagation of Islam. In particular, they worked together in the framework of the Islamic Library (*al-Maktaba al-Islamiyya*), an institution aiming at spreading Islamic culture created a few years before by a local pious notable from the al-'Asfur family and whose premises were based in Manama, in the vicinity of the *Ma'tam* al-Qassab administered by the al-'Alawi family. The Shiraziyyin were part of the library's board under the name of an independent association, the *Huseini* Social Fund (*al-Sunduq al-Huseini al-Ijtima'i*).[51] But details on the conflict between Mohammed al-Shirazi and the Najafi *marja'iyya* finally spread among the Bahraini religious activists so that relations between al-Da'wa and the Shiraziyyin progressively deteriorated. The Shiraziyyin began to feel a growing irritation on the part of the cadres of al-Da'wa around 1974. The latter distanced themselves from Hadi al-Mudarrisi and his followers. According to Mohammed al-'Alawi, this was due to the fact that al-Mudarrisi was gaining influence and began to be perceived more and more as a serious competitor.[52] This was probably a direct result of the naturalization of Hadi al-Mudarrisi, who was granted Bahraini citizenship precisely in 1974. This made local clerics realize that he was not actually another of these travelling preachers coming and going but was here to stay. The analysis made by al-Da'wa is clear in that respect: "S. Hadi al-Mudarrisi became a fully-fledged actor of the Islamic social action in Bahrain in 1974. He obtained Bahraini citizenship this year".[53] From then on, tension continued to grow, reaching a peak in 1976 when the members of the *Husein* Social Fund decided to quit the Islamic Library, a privileged arena of joint activities with al-Da'wa. According to al-Da'wa,

---

50   Personal interview, London, July 2007.

51   According to an anonymous article written in 1999 by the Islamic Bahrain Freedom Movement (IBFM, an offshoot of Bahraini al-Da'wa created in London in 1982, *cf.* chapter 6) entitled "An Overview of the Bahraini Islamic Movement" (in Arabic), the *Huseini* Social Fund was denied official recognition from the Ministry of Labour and Social Affairs. This is why it tried to get control of the Islamic Library. The article is available on the IBFM's web site: www.vob.org. According to Mohammed al-'Alawi however, it was the first association of the Shiraziyyin, the Association of the Islamic Guidance created in 1969, and not the *Huseini* Social Fund, that was not granted official recognition.

52   Personal interview, Bahrain, December 2006.

53   Islamic Bahrain Freedom Movement (1999).

the motive of the conflict was the fact that "the *Huseini* Fund tried to present Hadi al-Mudarrisi as the only religious scholar able to solve the intellectual and moral problems of the youth".[54] The conflict was so intense that the Shiraziyyin and al-Da'wa were often fighting mosque by mosque and *ma'tam* by *ma'tam*. In the village of Bani Jamra, the stronghold of 'Abd al-Amir al-Jamri, where the Shiraziyyin succeeded in gaining recruits, including Sh. Mohammed 'Ali al-Mahfuz, the future leader of the Islamic Front for the Liberation of Bahrain, Hadi al-Mudarrisi and 'Isa Qasem were regularly announced as speaking at the same mosque or *ma'tam* the same evening.

Although some individuals espoused the ideas of al-Da'wa, the movement did not succeed in establishing cells in Saudi Arabia as it did in Kuwait and Bahrain. This explains why the quarrel between the Shiraziyyin and the Najafi trend was not politicized and remained at the level of the traditional competition for religious authority. In the words of Fouad Ibrahim, himself a leading lay cadre of the Shiraziyyin in Saudi Arabia, it opposed the so-called "traditional" (*taqlidi*) and "conservative" trend that shifted to Abu al-Qasem al-Khu'i after the death of Muhsin al-Hakim to a "progressive and revolutionary trend" linked to Mohammed al-Shirazi and his nephews.[55]

Notables and Young Men in Kuwait

The resilience and further development of the quarrel was also due to its capacity to follow the outlines of previously existing lines of conflicts in Gulf societies. This was particularly so in Kuwait and Bahrain.

At the beginning of the 1970s, when the Iraqi exiles established themselves in Kuwait, the Shia society was still dominated by a notability of traders who were among the most reliable allies of the Al-Sabah. The Iranian notability tended to dominate the Shia political representation in the Parliament.[56] As during the episode of the Assembly Movement in 1938, the Shia notables and the rulers were united against the remnants of the Sunni merchant oligarchy as well as the proponents of Arab nationalism who monopolized the political opposition to the regime. The latter had even radicalized their stance against the Shias, demanding that Iranian mi-

---

54   In the words of an anonymous member of the library's board quoted in The Islamic Bahrain Freedom Movement (1999), p. 3.

55   Fouad Ibrahim, *The Shi'is of Saudi Arabia*, London: Saqi Books, 2006, p. 107.

56   For an overview of the political representation of the Shias since 1962, see Michael Herb's Kuwait Politics Data Base on the web site of Georgia State University: www2.gsu.edu/~polmfh/database/database.htm

gration to Kuwait be stopped and that Kuwaiti nationality be given to Arabs only. The idea of a plot by the Shah to subvert the Arab identity of Kuwait through the sending of a mass of the poorest and most backward of his subjects was publicly articulated.[57] Paranoia naturally increased when Iran became the *de facto* dominant regional power after the British troops left the Gulf in 1971. The radicalization of the Arab nationalists' positions had led the few Shias who had joined their ranks to separate and create their own movement, which they named the Young Men's National and Constitutional Assembly (*Tajammu' al-Shabab al-Watani al-Dusturi*).[58]

In 1963, in the context of the political liberalization that followed Kuwait's formal independence from British rule in 1961, the emirate witnessed a blossoming of societies of various callings, some of which actually acted as legal fronts for political currents, most notably the Arab nationalists.[59] The Shia notables took the opportunity to create the Social Society for Culture (*Jama'iyyat al-Thaqafa al-Ijtima'iyya*). Partly funded by the Ministry of Labour and Social Affairs, it was deemed to provide the Shias with a kind of unified institutional framework to promote what its members called the "Shia culture" (*thaqafat al-Shia*). However, instead of organizing rituals and conferences aimed at increasing the population's religious awareness, the Society's aim was the release of publications on various subjects written by Shias. The concept of "Shia culture" therefore amounted to works by people socially identified as "Shias", the Shia category here referring to an inherited social status and not to a particular degree of piety and religious practice. This conception was perfectly in line with the ethos of the notability that promoted the project. They considered the Shias as a natural constituency on which to exercise their influence, as well as a captive electorate. The Social Society for Culture was meant to operate as a kind of rallying point for the whole Shia community.

The way the notability was managing the affairs of the Shia community was however far from satisfying everybody among the Shia population. This was true in particular of the way they exercised political representation at the parliamentary level. Some people were surprised for example that despite their unfailing loyalty to the rulers, the notables had never been able to obtain a minister portfolio. In the beginning of the 1970s, a group of younger Shia men emerged who aspired to organize Shia political activity better in order for them to get a greater and more effective representation

---

57   Al-Mdayris (1999), pp. 20-1.

58   Al-Khaldi (1999), p. 108.

59   Shafeeq Ghabra, "Voluntary Associations in Kuwait: The Foundation of a New System?", *The Middle East Journal*, vol. 45, n° 2, Spring 1991, p. 202.

in the National Assembly. Their platform of expression was a "*diwaniyya*" named the *Diwaniyya* of the Young Men.[60] Designating themselves as "the young men" (*shabab*) the group was very heterogeneous in its social setting and not always clearly distinguishable from the notables other than, precisely, their young age and their determination to "change things". As often in the Arab world, the generational dichotomy served as an idiom for expressing the rupture with past political and religious practices.

Some of the "young men" belonged to the dominant families, as did Musa al-Ma'rafi for example, and were present on the board of the Social Society for Culture. Others were of more middle class background, with a significant number frequenting the al-Naqi mosque, the stronghold of al-Da'wa under the leadership of its prayer leader 'Ali al-Kurani. All claimed to be better educated and better informed on the management of political affairs than their elders, with some having completed higher studies abroad. This was the case for S. 'Adnan 'Abd al-Samad, who subsequently had the longest and most successful political career of all the Shia political activists. At the time of writing, he was still a member of Parliament. Born in 1950, 'Adnan 'Abd al-Samad had obtained a BA in political science and economy from the University of Cairo where he had spent four years. Upon his definitive return to Kuwait in 1970, he was recruited to the Ministry of Finance, the position he held when he emerged as one of the main leaders of the "young men". Although related to the prestigious clerical family of the al-Mazidi, he was from a minor branch of the family. His legitimacy stemmed mainly from his technical abilities in politics, duly certified by his diploma, as well as from his commitment to the defence of the interests of the "*madhhab*" (the sect) and "*Ahl al-Bayt*" (the family of the Prophet). He was indeed a regular at the al-Naqi mosque and had been deeply convinced of the necessity for the Shias to change their conception of the link between religion and politics. He also thought that the Shias should adopt a more rewarding political strategy[61].

In 1972, at the occasion of the elections for the renewal of the board of the Social Society for Culture, the "young men" took control of the society. From a gathering of notables, the Social Society for Culture therefore became the legal front for al-Da'wa in Kuwait, and the "young men" became progressively designated as the "line (*khatt*) of the Society for Culture". Their views were made known through periodical publications which, although consisting of no more than a handful of sheets, were nonetheless a useful instrument of social visibility.

---

60   Al-Khaldi (1999), p. 104.

61   Personal interview with 'Adnan 'Abd al-Samad, Kuwait, May 2006.

The second step of the "young men's" strategy was participation in the Parliamentary elections of 1975. As 'Adnan 'Abd al-Samad himself explained, their objective in that respect was first and foremost to increase Shia representation in Parliament: "we must act in order to increase as much as possible the number of members of the sect (*ta'ifa*), even if they are sheep".[62] The best way to achieve this aim was to unite the ranks of the Shias and to diversify the profiles of the parliamentarians. In his opinion, and despite the fact that he had a completely different worldview than the notables, this implied supporting candidates from the notability whose social weight, he thought, could not yet be matched by candidates from the middle class, even if they were more ideologically aware and more politically competent.[63] One must add that the period was very propitious for such a project as the electoral law had just been changed so that it was henceforth possible for candidates from different constituencies to exchange votes.[64] For the "young men", this was an opportunity to forge a broad Shia alliance at the level of the whole country. For the first time, the political stakes would be negotiated not only inside the constituencies but inside the Shia population itself, therefore constituting it as a political actor as such. The calculus proved to be accurate as, at the 1975 elections during which the law was first implemented, the Shias won ten representatives out of forty in Parliament, an unprecedented score. This allowed them to negotiate the appointment of the first Shia minister, namely 'Abd al-Mutallib al-Kadhimi who took the Ministry of Oil, a portfolio which from then on has regularly been held by a Shia. A close associate of 'Abd al-Mutallib al-Kadhimi, 'Adnan 'Abd al-Samad was appointed his principal private secretary.

The dissolution of Parliament in 1976 put a brutal end to the collaboration between the "young men" and the notables. In the aftermath of the dissolution, the ten Shia deputies joined forces with other members of Parliament to organize the signing of a petition condemning the ruler's decision and demanding the return to normal parliamentary life. Pressured by the government, nine of the ten Shia deputies subsequently removed their names from the petition. The only one to stand firm on his position was Khaled Khalaf, the representative of the Young Men's National and Constitutional Assembly[65] and therefore the only one who had competed on the basis of an articulated ideological agenda. The others were notables

---

62   Quoted by al-Khaldi (1999), p. 104.

63   Personal interview with 'Adnan 'Abd al-Samad, Kuwait, May 2006.

64   Al-Najjar (2000), p. 97.

65   Al-Khaldi (1999), p. 105.

for whom personal ambitions and the preoccupation of maintaining a good relationship with the rulers had finally prevailed. The defection of the nine disclosed the extent of the social and political gap between the notables and the young men, which had been only temporary concealed by an artificially created communal consensus. For the "young men" indeed, the decision of the government was unacceptable and should be fought whatever the price. Those who accepted the suspension of parliamentary life were not worthy to represent the community. This conception was explicitly articulated in a petition they circulated among the Shia population: it denied the nine deputies any right to claim to represent the Shia community.[66]

The event marked a major shift in the political history of the Shias in Kuwait. In terms of their relation to the rulers, it was the first time that a significant segment of the Shia population had publicly opposed a government decision. Far from being an occasional episode, this was only the beginning of a new stage in the Shias' relation to state power. The "young men" came to dominate the political representation of the Shias. They won a resounding victory in the 1981 elections, with 'Adnan 'Abd al-Samad, 'Abd al-Muhsin Jamal (b. 1950) and Naser Sarkhu (b. 1947), the historic leaders of the "young men" and to date the "heavyweights" of Shia politics in Kuwait, winning their first electoral mandate. In terms of the Shia internal balance, 1976 marked the definitive retreat of the notables and the accession to power of a new generation of political men. These were not only younger. They carried new ideological conceptions but also new ways of conceiving Shia identity. Henceforth, being a true Shia equated with displaying a certain degree of religiosity. This meant not only the practice of the traditional rituals, which had always operated as a strong identity marker for the Shias, but also a certain amount of familiarity with the practice of legal reasoning through reading the works of the *'ulama*, attending religious conferences and lectures and, of course, a belief in the indissoluble link between religion and politics. Being a Shia was no longer a matter of heritage. It meant being "aware" (*wa'i*) of one's identity by understanding the reasons why the Shia way of conceiving Islam was the right one and should be defended *per se*.

Another consequence of the rupture between the notables and the "young men" was the reinforcement of the relationship between Mohammed al-Shirazi and the notables. The subversion of the socio-political make-up of the Social Society for Culture had naturally raised tensions inside the association, as many of its "old" figures had not well accepted being deprived of their prerogatives by the young generation. The cohabitation

66   *Ibid.*

went well as far as the two groups pursued common political objectives at the parliamentary level, but the conflict that arose following the disbanding of Parliament led logically to a split inside the Society when many of the notables merely slammed the door. Several others got nearer to Mohammed al-Shirazi. The latter's reputation as a peaceful religious scholar only preoccupied with the spreading of religious education in front of the "revolutionary" partisans of al-Da'wa was henceforth further established.

This was all the more so since the Shiraziyyin had not striven to participate in the Parliamentary elections as an independent faction, leaving the stage to the notables whom they had no interest in antagonizing. The political battle with al-Da'wa rather occurred at the university where a handful of Shiraziyyin created a student list to compete in the yearly elections to the National Union of Kuwaiti Students (al-Ittihad al-Watani li-Talabat al-Kuwait), the representative organ of the students of Kuwait University. The list, which had ceased to exist at the time of writing, was named the Free List (al-Qa'ima al-Hurra) and competed with the Islamic List (al-Qa'ima al-Islamiyya) set up by the "young men" of the Social Society for Culture. While none of the list ever succeeded in gaining a single seat in the Union because they were never able to gain votes outside of their Shia constituency, it was, up to the late 1990s, the only real occurrence of an organized political competition between the Shiraziyyin and al-Da'wa in Kuwait.

Rural and Urban in Bahrain

The Bahraini context offered another aspect of the combination of *marja'iyya* factionalism with local divides as the Shiraziyyin and al-Da'wa started their recruitment in fairly different social milieus.

Al-Da'wa in Bahrain began in the countryside, in a handful of villages long known for hosting *hawza* and circles of religious learning: Diraz, Bani Jamra, Jidd Hafs and Sittra to mention only the most noteworthy. The clerical leaders of al-Da'wa were born in those villages, but so were the lay cadres like Sa'id al-Shihabi, who was from Diraz as was 'Isa Qasem, and 'Isa Sharqi, who was born in Jidd Hafs as were the al-Madani brothers. Because it accounted for the greatest number of cadres as well as the most prominent among them, Diraz was the main stronghold of al-Da'wa. It was there that the office of the Islamic Enlightenment Society was opened in 1972. The fact that al-Da'wa began in Diraz is significant. Along with Bani Jamra – 'Abd al-Amir al-Jamri's village – Diraz was always one of the places most resistant to Al-Khalifa rule. Fuad Khuri recounts that the two villages were particularly heavily taxed because they produced little agricultural surplus and that their leading families did not render services to the ruling dynasty, therefore being considered of dubious loyalty.[67] In villages such as these, he reports, those inhabitants who acted as tax leviers and representatives of the Al-Khalifa had to leave to Manama to escape reprisal after the reform of the 1920s that entailed the progressive abolition of the feudal estate system. As opposed to the leftist and nationalist political movements whose base was essentially urban, al-Da'wa in Bahrain therefore began as a rural phenomenon and it was only at a later stage that it spread to the cities. This move was greatly favoured by the 1972 and 1973 elections, which offered al-Da'wa's cadres the occasion to articulate their ideas at a national level.

While al-Da'wa spread from the villages to the cities, the Shiraziyyin spread from the cities to the villages. At that time, there were two places worth calling cities in Bahrain: Manama, the capital, and Muharraq. Muharraq was initially the Al-Khalifa's place of residence upon their arrival in Bahrain. It was a small island separated by a few oarstrokes from the main island of the archipelago, to which it was linked up by a bridge in the 1940s. Like Manama, Muharraq was religiously mixed and generally cosmopolitan. It was more particularly host to a dynamic community of Iranian merchants. Because the urban environment was the most propitious for their commercial activities and also the most open to the settlement of strangers, Iranian merchants used to settle either in Manama or Muharraq upon their arrival in the country.

Because of his privileged links to the al-'Alawi family, Hadi al-Mudarrisi settled in the old *suq* of Manama close to the *Ma'tam* al-Qassab, in a house the al-'Alawi arranged for him. His first recruits were naturally made in the direct environment of the family and one finds a clear pattern of family linkage between many of the Shirazi cadres in Bahrain, in particular among those who henceforth formed the nucleus of the Islamic Front for the Liberation of Bahrain (*al-Jabha al-Islamiyya li Tahrir al-Bahrain*) founded by Hadi al-Mudarrisi after the Islamic revolution (*cf.* infra): brothers and cousins, families linked by old marriage or patronage bonds, childhood friends. While they did not all come from wealthy merchant families like the al-'Alawi, the vast majority of al-Mudarrisi's followers were sons of traders of both Iranian and Bahrani descent, many of whom had long been involved in the organization and financing of popular rituals.

Murtadha Badr, who was later elected mayor of Manama (2002-2006), is typical of the Shirazi Iranian recruits. Born in 1955 in Manama, his ancestors were involved in pearl trade on both the Iranian and the Ara-

---

67   Khuri (1980), p. 48.

bian shores of the Gulf and came to settle in Bahrain during the second half of the nineteenth century. After the collapse of the pearl industry in the 1930s, his grandfather and his father engaged successfully in transit trade and contributed to the financing of the Shia religious institutions in the capital. The family kept an eye on the political developments in Iran much more closely than on what happened in Bahrain, a rather common behaviour among the Iranian diaspora. The family and its entourage were fervent supporters of Mohammed Mosaddegh and therefore opponents to the Shah, whom they considered as a traitorous agent of America. Murtadha Badr recalls that his first participation in a political demonstration occurred when he accompanied his father to a cortège in support of Mosaddegh after he was deposed by a CIA coup in 1956.[68] Later on in the 1970s, Murtadha Badr, who became a university student of science in Kuwait and then Bahrain, took a particular interest in Ali Shariati's texts, which were distributed to Bahrain and translated into Arabic by members of the 'Ijmi community. As he himself reckons, he became a regular of Hadi al-Mudarrisi's teaching circles simply because he was a guy from the same old Makharqa district where the latter was living and preaching. Because all Manama's mosques had their prayer leaders, Hadi al-Mudarrisi had appointed himself as the prayer leader of a disused little mosque of the district's cemetery, where he gathered his followers for daily prayers. Because he was himself an 'Ijmi and spoke both Persian and Arabic fluently, he preached regularly in both the Bahrani and the 'Ijmi mosques. He was not only a regular of the *Ma'tam* al-Qassab but a customary lecturer at the *Ma'tam* al-'Ajam al-Kabir (literally the "Grand *Ma'tam* of the 'Ajam"). Built by the leading Iranian merchants of Bahrain, it was one of the main religious convening centres of the 'Ijmi community and was located only a few meters from the *Ma'tam* al-Gassab.[69]

One should add that, for obvious structural reasons pertaining to the fact that 'Ajam did not live in the villages, al-Da'wa did not recruit among the 'Ijmi population as did the Shiraziyyin and remained a typically Bahrani phenomenon. There was therefore a difference in ethnic background between the two movements. However, one should not exaggerate this empirical fact to the point of saying that the activists of al-Da'wa were Baharna while the Shiraziyyin were 'Ajam.[70] What is

---

68   Interview in *Story of Political Islam in Bahrain* n° 17, *al-Watan* (Bahrain), 26 February 2006.

69   On the history of the *Ma'tam* al-'Ajam al-Kabir, see Fuccaro (2005), pp. 48-9.

70   As did Falah al-Mdayris, *The Political Movements and Groups in Bahrain*

sure on the other hand is that the difference in ethnic background was used by al-Da'wa as an argument to further dismiss the legitimacy of the Shiraziyyin, who were denounced as an alien political current imported by an "Iranian born in Karbala",[71] implanted among the Iranian community and with only marginal roots among the original inhabitants of Bahrain. The rural/urban cleavage therefore added fuel to the previously existing Baharna/'Ajam antagonism. Some cadres of al-Da'wa like Sa'id al-Shihabi even talked about the necessity to "Bahranize" (*bahrana*) the Shia Islamic movement in Bahrain. It is hard to say what such an ambiguous statement might mean. Sa'id al-Shihabi himself claimed it meant to define an endogenous politics in which outsiders would not interfere.[72] This is in line with the subsequent evolution of al-Da'wa (*cf.* chapter 6). In the context of the 1970s however, "Bahranize" was interpreted by the Shiraziyyin as a denunciation of their supposed exclusively Iranian ethnic social base.

The urban background of Hadi al-Mudarrisi's first followers ensued from his strong ties with the al-'Alawi family. It also stemmed from the fact that the city constituted a more favourable environment structurally for strangers than the villages. But one can construct a more strategic reading of this fact. Indeed, being close to the urban notability offered several advantages Hadi al-Mudarrisi could not ignore. First, it was of course a good way to ensure access to sources of funding. Second, the merchant notability provided Hadi al-Mudarrisi with access to the ruling circles, to whom the Shia urban merchants were the main intermediaries with the Shia society. Indeed, like his uncle did in Kuwait, one of Hadi al-Mudarrisi's way to overcome his marginal status as both a challenger of the Najafi *marja'iyya* and a stranger to the rather parochial Bahrani clerical class was to gain the support of the state elite. One has often the *a priori* idea that Shia activist networks spread in a clandestine and secret way, using back doors in order not to attract the attention of the authorities. But the Shiraziyyin extended to the Gulf monarchies in exactly the opposite way, through a process in which the state was present at all levels. While they sometimes established their quarters in disused mosques and *huseiniyya* as Hadi al-Mudarrisi did in Sharjah and Bahrain, this was not because they wanted to remain in the shadow but because they had to occupy premises not already under the physical

---

1938-2002 (in Arabic), Beirut: Dar al-Kanuz al-Adabiyya, 2004, p. 100.

71   IFBM (1999).

72   Personal interview, London, July 2007.

control of the local clerical class. Otherwise, they strove successfully to gain the support of the rulers because it was, after all, the best way to get some means to reach to the masses. It is of public notoriety that Hadi al-Mudarrisi met with the Emir Sheikh 'Isa bin Salman Al-Khalifa several times and developed a relationship of trust with his son and heir apparent, Sheikh Hamad bin 'Isa Al-Khalifa, then the Chief of the Armed Forces (and King of Bahrain since 1999). This was emphasized by Hadi al-Mudarrisi himself during the interview we had, where he spontaneously elaborated on his contacts at the highest level of the Bahraini state. This is how he obtained regular access to the local media. This is how he was granted Bahraini citizenship in 1974, through the intercession of another member of the al-'Alawi family, S. Musa al-'Alawi, who was then working at the Emir's cabinet (*diwan*).[73]

A third reason for Hadi al-Mudarrisi's endeavour to target the mercantile community was its central role in performing popular rituals. In Bahrain, the 'Ajam claim to have been the first to organize 'Ashura processions outside the *ma'tam* in the surrounding streets, according to a practice they imported from Iran. In fact, up to the 1970s, the *Ma'tam* al-'Ajam al-Kabir was the only one to organize public processions along with the *Ma'tam* Bin Rajab administered by the Bin Rajab family, another of the few Shia *tawwash* families well-known for being very "loyal" to the rulers. At this time, the processions were only performed in Manama and the cortèges were small, including only a few hundred penitents. Before the 1980s, no procession had ever been organized in the villages where people used to celebrate the martyrdom of Imam Husein inside the mosques or the *huseiniyya*. In the course of the 1970s, the *Ma'tam* al-Qassab of the al-'Alawi family began organizing its own 'Ashura cortège as a direct result of Hadi al-Mudarrisi's encouragement.

THE CASE OF SAUDI ARABIA

The case of Saudi Arabia needs to be addressed separately as it offers a mixed picture that does not fit either of the two models of penetration detailed above completely. This is due to the particular situation of the Shias in this country where, because of the state sponsored ideology, Shia religious activities were perceived as a form of deviance and even protest. In these circumstances, maintaining a vivid religious life was much more

---

73 *The Story of Political Islam in Bahrain*, n° 23, *Al-Watan* (Bahrain), 2 June 2006.

difficult for the Shias of Saudi Arabia than for their Bahraini and Kuwaiti co-religionists. This was all the more so since, as mentioned previously, the younger Shia generation had yielded to secular ideologies and did not envisage the Shia doctrine as providing an efficient way to resist the Saudi regime. In this context, the numbers motivated towards a religious career were, logically, in decline.

Keeping the Tie to the Marja'iyya

In this rather inhospitable environment however, ties with the big religious centres of the Shia world had not been totally cut off. Some families had kept in touch with the *marja'iyya* in Najaf and, in the 1970s, there were even a handful of students in the Iraqi religious seminaries. Many however, chose to stay there to make a life rather than to return to Saudi Arabia, where the possibility of making a living from the profession of religious scholar was rather limited. A good example in that respect is that of the al-Khunaizi family. An old clerical family of Qatif, they held the position of religious judge (*qadhi*) in the last years of Ottoman rule. In the conquest by the Al-Sa'ud in 1913, the *qadhi* Sh. 'Ali Abu 'Abd al-Karim al-Khunaizi led the group of notables who negotiated the peaceful surrender of the city.[74] This led them to be granted a virtual monopoly over the position of *qadhi* of Qatif, which passed from father to son and from brother to brother during the whole twentieth century. Only in 2006 was the last al-Khunaizi *qadhi*, Sh. 'Abdallah al-Khunaizi, replaced by an outsider. Yet even the members of this renowned family who largely leaned on the support of the Saudi regime to perpetuate their religious position, had difficulty sustaining themselves as religious professionals in the 1970s. This is illustrated by the case of 'Abdallah al-Khunaizi, who had studied in Najaf with Abu al-Qasem al-Khu'i in the 1970s, making an important investment by settling with his wife and children in the city. Upon his return to Qatif however, he could not find a way to live from his status as a scholar and had to work in customs administration.

On the other hand, many Saudi informants recounted that Iraqi and Iranian preachers regularly managed to make their way to the Eastern Province, often on the occasion of the pilgrimage to Mecca, when they would take advantage of their presence in the country to drive up to Qatif and Hasa. To my knowledge however, no Iraqi or Iranian Shia religious professional made long stays in this country inhospitable to the Shias. In Saudi Arabia therefore, the initial pattern found in Bahrain of an extrovert

---

74   Al-Hasan (1993), p. 14; Steinberg (2001), p. 244.

clerical class circulating widely throughout the Shia world but being only marginally penetrated by foreign elements was reinforced by the particular religious context. The Shia Islamic ideology was not brought to the country through agents of the *marja'iyya* and exiles. Nor was it brought by Saudi students coming back home after a stay in the Najafi seminars. But the general pattern found in Kuwait and Bahrain remains nonetheless valid for Saudi Arabia, of political ideas diffusing through previously established lines of interactions. Indeed, the nucleus of the Shia Islamic activist class was constituted by people who, mostly by family tradition, had managed to keep in touch with the *marja'iyya*.

This is clearly the case of the most well-known Shirazi figure and, in many respects, the mastermind behind the past and current political evolutions of Saudi Shias: Sh. Hasan al-Saffar. The latter was born in 1958 in Qatif to a family with several turbaned forebears. While not himself a religious professional but a merchant, his father was particularly devoted and used to bring his son with him to the mosques and *huseiniyya*. He also encouraged him to read and study the Quran under the supervision of the few local *'ulama* among whom, as a child, he gained many acquaintances. Hasan al-Saffar's father also used to travel regularly to the Iraqi shrine cities, where he liked to pay regular visits to the scholars. Brought up in this environment, Hasan al-Saffar acquired the reputation of a rather eloquent preacher early in childhood, while he was around twelve years old. People even used to refer to him as "*Molla* Hasan". The Persian word "*molla*" commonly designates a preacher, that is a religious man who does not deal with the legal aspects of religious life but is involved in the recounting of the life of the Imams and leads religious ceremonies. Informants who spent time with Hasan al-Saffar at this period also recall that he was nicknamed "little Shami" (*al-Shami al-saghir*) by reference to S. Husein al-Shami –"Big Shami" – an Iraqi preacher popular in Qatif where he used to lecture regularly, and whose style Hasan al-Saffar apparently emulated.

Hasan al-Saffar read books by Mohammed al-Shirazi for the first time in his father's library in the late 1960s. A while later in 1970, he accompanied his father on a trip to Iraq where, among others, he met with Mohammed al-Shirazi. Although not decisive in this respect, the encounter further fortified his will to engage in a religious career and, a few months later in 1971, when he was thirteen, he decided to take the plunge: he moved to Najaf to begin his religious education. In the meantime, Mohammed al-Shirazi and his family had left for Kuwait, so the two men did not have the opportunity to develop their relationship in that period. Hasan al-Saffar enrolled in the *hawza* of Abu al-Qasem al-Khu'i, a natural choice as it was the school with the best reputation. Neither was the stay in Najaf the occasion for him to spend time with al-Da'wa's activists. As he explained himself, the context of the early 1970s was too tense for him to venture outside the realm of strict religious education.[75] Foreign students of the *hawza* in particular were tightly monitored by the security apparatus. After two years, following an umpteenth wave of arrests of foreign students, he chose to leave Iraq. Rather than joining Mohammed al-Shirazi in Kuwait however, he chose to go to Qom in Iran, where many foreign students of the Iraqi seminaries had already resettled to pursue their education. As Hasan al-Saffar explained, Mohammed al-Shirazi had not yet opened his *hawza* at that time, so Kuwait did not appear a good option. One can surmise that, aged fifteen, his personal ideological setting had not yet clarified and that he was still mainly motivated by a rather traditional religious career. What mattered for him was to live in the most suitable environment to pursue his education and this is what Qom offered. There, he naturally enrolled in one of the most prestigious *hawza*, that of Sh. Mohammed Kazem Shariat-Madari (1904-1985), then the leading *marja'* of Iran who thereafter became involved in the Islamic Revolution.

It was only in 1974 that Hasan al-Saffar joined Mohammed al-Shirazi in Kuwait and his religious orientation shifted to become much more political, in particular through regular association with Mohammed Taqi al-Mudarrisi, with whom he came to collaborate. Not only a mere religious student at the *Hawza* of the Supreme Prophet, he then became closer to being a peripatetic preacher travelling extensively in the Gulf. Upon his regular visits back to Saudi Arabia, his main activity was to recruit students willing to undergo religious education at the Kuwaiti *hawza*, either full time or for short training courses during the summer period. This is how a whole generation of religious scholars was formed, as virtually all the Shirazi clerical leadership in Saudi Arabia passed through the *Hawza* of the Supreme Prophet: Hasan al-Saffar, his closest associate Sh. Tawfiq al-Seif; his two brothers Sh. Fawzi al-Seif and Sh. Mahmud al-Seif; Sh. Yusuf al-Mahdi, and Sh. Hasan al-Khuweildi to mention only the most noteworthy.

Hasan al-Saffar in Oman

Another field of action for Hasan al-Saffar was Oman, where he spent close to five years between 1974 and 1979. He established himself in Muscat among the small Bahrani community, whose leaders facilitated his stay in

---

75   Personal interview, Saudi Arabia, September 2004. Most of the biographical details given here were collected during this interview.

the country.[76] His stay there followed the pattern described in the case of 'Ali al-Kurani in Kuwait. In Oman, where there was no indigenous clerical class in the sense of a long-established community of scholars with regular patterns of recruitment, Shia notables used to contact the *marja'iyya* in Iraq or Iran to ask for a prayer leader. It is in this context that a merchant of the Bahrani community contacted Mohammed al-Shirazi in Kuwait. The choice to send Hasan al-Saffar was his. Hasan al-Saffar undertook to create several religious institutions in Oman, in particular three libraries of which one was still open at the time of writing, the Library of the Supreme Prophet (*Maktabat al-Rasul al-A'dham*) in the mosque run by the Lawati in Mutrah.

The most numerous and socially visible Shia group in Oman, the Lawati (sing. Luti) came from the city of Hyderabad in present day Pakistan in between the mid-eighteenth century and the end of the nineteenth.[77] They initially spoke a vernacular language called Khodjki close to the Sindi and Gujarati dialects. This led Western orientalists and experts to consider them as Hindus who converted to Ismaeli Shiism in the fifteenth century.[78] They would then have shifted to Twelver Shiism in the nineteenth century following a dispute over the succession of the Aga Khan, the leader of the Ismaeli Indians. One must note however that this version of the Lawati's history is contested by Lawati themselves who are eager to stress their Arab descent. A myth of origin circulates in the community, stressing that the Lawati actually descend from an old Arab tribe (whose eponymous ancestor would be al-Hakam bin 'Awanat al-Lat) from the Hijaz who left the Arabian Peninsula to participate in the Muslim conquest of India. They stress that this tribe embraced the cause of 'Ali from the beginning. This, they reckon, is proven by the name Hyderabad which comes from the association of two Arabic words: "Haidar", one of 'Ali's nicknames meaning "the Lion" and "*badiyya*" meaning the Bedouins.[79]

While he was called upon by the Baharna, Hasan al-Saffar essentially attracted young Luti men. He encouraged them to be more involved in religious practices and, for example, convinced them to perform the

---

76   Marc Valéri, *Les chiites d'Oman entre visibilité socioéconomique et quête de reconnaissance*, unpublished research paper, 2006, p. 15.

77   J. E. Peterson, "Oman's Diverse Society: Northern Oman", *The Middle East Journal*, vol. 58, n° 1, winter 2004, p. 41.

78   Calvin H. Allen Jr., "The Indian Merchant Community of Masqat", *Bulletin of the School of Oriental and African Studies*, vol. 44, n° 1, 1981, p. 49; Peterson, (2004), p.41.

79   I was told this story by a Luti of Sharjah in November 2005.

'Ashura procession in the streets rather than in the *huseiniyya* as was then the habit. He also briefly published a periodical – *Al-Wa'i* (the Awareness) – aimed at spreading religious culture in a community that had then apparently rather limited leanings to religiosity. Like his fellow-activists in Kuwait and Bahrain however, Hasan al-Saffar was caught in the middle of local rivalries that mixed with *marja'iyya* factionalism. Therefore, while his style and message appealed to many young Shias, his open criticism of "the traditional way to see religion" – as the expression goes – equally irritated many notables who were not ready to see their way of life criticized by a young outsider.[80] It is apparently in this context that, as with Mohammed al-Shirazi in Kuwait, a communiqué by Abu al-Qasem al-Khu'i arrived in Oman, through which the *marja'* intended to make publicly known that he considered Hasan al-Saffar as a dubious individual working for someone – Mohammed al-Shirazi – of no less dubious credentials.

As in Kuwait, one can surmise that the issue was also financial. Omani Shias are indeed a particularly wealthy community. The Lawati in particular are economically powerful. At the zenith of the Omani maritime empire during the first half of the nineteenth century, together with Hindu merchants, they dominated the financial sector of the country as well as the triangular trade between Muscat, Zanzibar and Bombay.[81] They had a virtual monopoly on the importation of foodstuffs unavailable in the Omani hinterland. At the time of writing, the al-Baqer family still played a central role in the importation of Indian tea and rice into the country.[82] The Lawati's strong economic position was further consolidated in the twentieth century, which moreover saw their investment in higher education in prestigious universities of the Arab world at a time when the Omani population was still largely illiterate and lacked modern skills. Their economic strength has naturally led them to occupy important political positions. The most well known and significant example is that of the al-Sultan family, which heads a leading holding company (W. J. Towell and Co) and whose members have also occupied political posts: 'Ali bin Sultan (d. 1999) was the president of the first consultative institution established in 1979 to advise the Sultan on economic matters (the Council on Agriculture, Fisheries and Industry), he was then vice-president of the State Consultative Council between 1981 and 1983 and presided over the Chamber of Commerce

---

80   Valéri (2006), p. 15.
81   *Ibid.*, p. 6.
82   *Ibid.*, p. 9.

and Industry for almost twenty-five years.[83] At the time of writing, his son Maqbul bin 'Ali Sultan had been the minister of Commerce and Industry since 1993.

83   *Ibid.*, p. 8.

PART III

IN BETWEEN THE TRANSNATIONAL AND THE INTERNATIONAL

The advent of the Islamic Republic of Iran in 1979 impacted on the centre-periphery pattern within the Shia world in at least two respects. On the one hand, the centre moved geographically since, following the suppression of the religious seminaries in the Iraqi shrine cities, Qom further gained in prominence as a centre of learning. Because it continued to host the most widely emulated *marja'* worldwide, namely Abu al-Qasem al-Khu'i and his successor 'Ali al-Sistani, Najaf remained a foremost locus of religious authority. However, because the opportunities to study there were very restricted for foreigners and even for Iraqis, the city lost its pre-eminence as a place of study. From 1979 on, the vast majority of those wishing to undertake religious education went to seminaries in Qom. The city provided a secure environment as well as adequate infrastructure for learning. Leading *mujtahid* also established their premises in Qom, including a handful who had been compelled to leave Iraq. While many might have been less knowledgeable than Abu al-Qasem al-Khu'i and 'Ali al-Sistani, they played a more important role in terms of religious education. In other words, there was a disjunction between the centre of religious authority and the centre of study.

On the other hand, by elaborating the doctrine of *wilayat al-faqih* (government by doctor in religious law), Ruhollah Khomeini extended the area of application of the traditional norm of religious authority to include the government of the state.[1] The traditional understanding of the notion of deputyship of the Imam limited the authority of religious scholars to the religious and legal sphere. During the Occultation, they could interpret

---

1   Said Amir Arjomand, *The Turban for the Crown. The Islamic Revolution in Iran*, Oxford: Oxford University Press, 1988, p. 180.

religious law following certain well codified rules and levy religious alms but there was a general consensus that they were not entitled to exercise the political powers of the Imam. This was the opinion of Murtadha Ansari himself, who formulated the doctrine of the *marja'iyya* and who considered that it would be "absurd to reason that because the Imams should be obeyed in all temporal and spiritual matters, the *faqih* are also entitled to such obedience".[2] This had led to a general tendency of the Shia *'ulama* to accommodate *de facto* temporal powers, based on the principle that since religious law could not be fully implemented during the Occultation, one could accommodate with virtually all established regimes, be they Shia or Sunni.[3] Ruhollah Khomeini's interpretation of religious authority represented a rupture with this traditional conception as it considered that religious scholars could legitimately appropriate even the temporal powers of the Imam and rule the state. Moreover, Ruhollah Khomeini went against the traditional idea that the general deputyship of the Imam was the collective charge of the *mujtahid* by claiming that the government of the Islamic state should be assumed by one single *marja'*.[4] The justification for such an interpretation was purely practical, based on the idea that government by one person was better for the stability of the state. Furthermore, the ruling *marja'* was not necessarily the most learned of the *mujtahid* but should be obeyed by the others because of his personal political achievements: if a *marja'* succeeded in forming an Islamic government, then he should be followed by the others.[5] It was a matter of practice and not of doctrine.

Such a revolutionary understanding of the notion of religious authority had implications far beyond the borders of Iran. Indeed, while recognizing the legal validity of the Iranian nation-state, the 1979 Constitution stipulated that Ruhollah Khomeini was the Supreme Guide of the Iranians but also of all Muslims. He therefore remained faithful to the traditional worldview of the Shia clerical class in regarding religious authority as something not confined to the frontiers of a particular national territory. Consequently, in his speeches, he regularly denied that the revolution in Iran was an Iranian revolution. It was an Islamic revolution in the sense that it was the first step of a process concerning the entire *dar al-Islam*, the territories

---

2   *Ibid.*, p. 178.

3   Norman Calder, "Accommodation and Revolution in Imami Shi'i Jurisprudence: Khumayni and the Classical Tradition", *Middle Eastern Studies*, vol. 8, n° 1, January 1982, p. 4.

4   Calder (1982), p. 16; Arjomand (1988), p. 179.

5   *Ibid.*

inhabited by the Muslims.[6] In this respect, the Islamic Republic of Iran should be considered as the prefiguration of a future broad Islamic state encompassing the entire *umma*. This vision underlay the so-called policy of "exportation of the revolution" that characterized the foreign policy of Iran after 1979. With Lebanon and Afghanistan, the Gulf monarchies were the main theatre where Iran endeavoured to export its model. As we shall see, this had far reaching implications on the strategies for the Shia movements and on their relations with the regimes they opposed.

---

6   Farhang Rajaee, *Islamic Values and Worldview. Khomeini on Man, the State and International Politics*, Lanham: University Press of America, 1983.

5

SOCIETIES FACE THE ISLAMIC REVOLUTION

Most of our interviewees described the advent of the Islamic revolution as a psychological shock that entailed a genuine change of conscience in them. But the political impact of this event did not consist of simply an emulation process. It is true that, contrary to the clandestine activities of the Iraqi Shia movement, the Islamic revolution received broad international media coverage. Moreover, one of the first moves of the new Islamic regime was to create an efficient broadcasting apparatus diffusing information and propaganda in several languages, and more particularly in Arabic. While important however, the media apparatus played a back-up rather than a primary role in the diffusion of revolutionary fervour. The media completed the work done via the very same transnational interpersonal networks that had developed previously from Iraq, whose political conceptions and overall worldview were similar in content to those promoted by the leaders of the Islamic Republic. Therefore, the impact of the Islamic revolution on the Gulf monarchies varied according to the type of position these networks had established in the domestic political spaces. This means at least two things. First, that the the Islamic revolution's modes of diffusion, at least in the early years, did not depart from the pattern heretofore described of a networking endeavour by religious professionals trained in the Iraqi shrine cities. Second, it means that the domestic political structures were more important than Iranian efforts in shaping the various modalities of the Islamic revolution's impact.[1] Here, one finds again the great dichotomy drawn out initially between Bahrain and Saudi Arabia on the one hand, and Kuwait on the other hand. Indeed, in all three countries, a direct outcome of the Islamic revolution was the passage to political violence by Shia

---

1   As noted by Gregory Gause III, "Revolutionary Fevers and Regional Contagion: Domestic Structures and the 'Export' of Revolution in the Middle East", *Journal of South Asian and Middle Eastern Studies*, vol. 14, n° 3, 1991.

Islamic activists. But beyond the apparent similarity of the situations, this violence had different meanings and was perpetrated to achieve different aims.

INSURRECTIONARY POLITICS IN
BAHRAIN AND SAUDI ARABIA

In Bahrain and Saudi Arabia, where the domestic contexts were character-ized by historically tense relations between the ruling dynasties and the Shia communities, the Islamic revolution was seen as a unique opportunity for radical change. Consequently, it aroused a series of civil disturbances mainly orchestrated by the Shiraziyyin.

The Shiraziyyin's Radical Shift in Bahrain

In Bahrain, the Islamic revolution occurred in a rather fraught political con-text where the relationship between the Shia Islamic movements and the rulers had deteriorated significantly, mainly because of the political choices made by the so-called "Religious Bloc" (*al-Kutla al-Diniyya*). The Religious Bloc was a parliamentary group mainly constituted by the deputies of al-Da'wa elected in the 1973 elections. Unsurprisingly, it distinguished itself by advocating the establishment of a more strict religious public ethic, op-posing, for example, the mixing of men and women in public spaces and the free selling of alcohol. It also wanted to make blasphemy a civil crime. This contradicted the choices made by the rulers, who wanted on the whole to maintain their country's "liberal" reputation, maybe because of their own personal worldview but, more significantly, because they knew that Bahrain had only limited oil and gas resources that would soon be depleted and had therefore to develop other economic activities. Tourism was one sector they had bet on and this entailed a not too heavy application of religious ethic. The pressure to impose more religion in the public sphere was not in itself a motive for serious conflict between the government and the Shia religious faction. The clash occurred when, contrary to the expectations of the rulers who had hoped to use the Religious Bloc against the progressives whom they considered as the main threat, the deputies of the Religious Bloc trans-formed into an opposition movement that grew more and more powerful.

In December 1974, the government, which was appointed by the ruler without consultation or approval from the elected representatives, decided unilaterally to enact a security law granting the ruler the right to arrest and imprison for three years without trial any person deemed to pose a security threat. The progressives and the religious faction put aside their ideological differences and joined forces to demand that the law be submitted to the Parliament's approval before implementation. A trial of strength followed between the Parliament and the government, with the government trying to convince the Religious Bloc that the law was not targeting them, but rather the progressives, and the Religious Bloc would be allowed to go on freely with their activities. The government also tried to negotiate the breaking of the alliance by promising the Religious Bloc the enactment of laws forbidding the selling of alcohol and enforcing the closure of brothels. The bargaining almost succeeded but in the end failed once the government decided that such measures would too severely endanger the economic viability of the country. It decided that an authoritarian disbanding of Parliament was the best solution to its predicament. This eventually occurred in August 1975, with the reinstatement of the Assembly becoming the rallying cry of all the segments of the opposition, be they of secular or religious calling.[2]

The Shiraziyyin were largely absent from this political trial of force. They had not presented candidates to the Parliament and had adopted a low profile during the whole campaign. As in Kuwait, they lacked the kind of social base necessary for institutional political action. They preferred to exercise discrete influence at the elite level rather than entering into open political competition. But the enactment of the state security law and the subsequent dissolution of Parliament made the Shirazi local activists pass a psychological threshold. In the words on one of them: "people began to say to themselves that the government was bad and that one needed to do something. We began to tell ourselves that we were actually doing politics and not only spreading Islamic culture".[3] A decisive step in the Shiraziyyin's passage to politics occurred in 1976 with the writing and printing in Lebanon of an anonymous book entitled *The Struggle of the Bahraini People* (*Kifah Sha'b al-Bahrain*), which was distributed clandestinely in Bahrain. The book gave a historical overview of the history of Bahrain, particularly insisting on the discrimination suffered by the Shias under the rule of the Al-Khalifa. In contrast to al-Da'wa, which remained committed to the doctrine of progressive action through legal channels and did not envisage any kind of "military escalation"[4] with the regime, the Shiraziyyin

---

2   For details of the crisis which led to the disbanding of Parliament, see Khuri (1980), pp. 231-3; Nakhleh (1976), p. 169.

3   Personal interview, Bahrain, December 2006.

4   According to 'Isa al-Sharqi, *Story of Political Islam in Bahrain* n° 2, *al-Watan* (Bahrain), 13 December 2005.

began seriously to consider the option of armed opposition to the Bahraini regime. This is attested by the fact that several of the main cadres of the organization undertook military training in the Palestinian refugee camps in Lebanon, under the supervision of the PLO. This was made possible through the contacts Hadi al-Mudarrisi had built with Ruhollah Khomeini and his followers during their stay in Najaf in the second half of the 1960s (*cf.* chapter 4). Because Iran was then a key ally of Israel in the region, the opponents of the Shah had naturally allied with the PLO, who provided them with military training in Lebanon. The Iranians arranged for Iraqis and Bahrainis to benefit from the PLO's military expertise despite the fact that the Palestinians had clearly made it known that they refused to train any opponents to Arab regimes supporting its struggle against the "Zionist entity". This was more particularly true of the Gulf regimes, which hosted an important diaspora of Palestinian refugees who greatly contributed to financing the PLO. Their situation could have been jeopardized had the PLO supported the Gulf regimes' opponents. This is why, with Iranian complicity, Bahrainis passed themselves off as Arab citizens of Iran from the region of Khuzistan, a region of dense Arab settlement bordering Iraq.

While al-Da'wa was determined to continue opposing the Bahraini regime through political means, the Shirazyyin were therefore prepared to confront it more brutally several years before the Islamic revolution. The fall of the Shah served only as a release mechanism. It was interpreted as the founding event of a new phase of political action: that of mass mobilization. Shortly after the revolution, Hadi al-Mudarrisi announced he was the official representative of Ruhollah Khomeini in Bahrain and, building on this legitimacy, he initiated a series of demonstrations during the year 1979 with various aims: expressing support for the Islamic Republic, celebrating "Jerusalem Day", which Ruhollah Khomeini had encouraged the Muslims to celebrate on the last Friday of Ramadan. While some members of al-Da'wa participated in these demonstrations, the leadership of the movement did not endorse them and was largely absent from the scene at this early stage. Actually, the Islamic revolution contributed directly to the reversal of the initial balance of power between al-Da'wa and the Shiraziyyin. Indeed, Al-Da'wa was caught on the hop by the speed of the events in Iran. The revolution showed them another way, that seemed more efficient than their strategy of non-escalation and negotiation with the Bahraini regime. Compared to the Shiraziyyin who had long opted for the revolutionary strategy, they lacked responsiveness. This occured to the extent that some cadres began to envisage the disbanding of the party, considered as no longer a useful political tool.

While the Shiraziyyin's demonstrations were tolerated by the authorities, the latter did not totally feel comfortable, especially after public declarations by a certain S. Sadiq Rohani. In June 1979, Sadiq Rohani had denounced the agreements in which the Shah had renounced any territorial claim on Bahrain. In Sadiq Rohani's view, Bahrain was actually the fourteenth province of Iran and should be reintegrated into the motherland unless it adopted a regime complying with Islamic tenets.[5] It is difficult to ascertain the scope of Sadiq Rohani's connection to the Iranian government but most experts tend to think that he was only speaking for himself and was not mandated by either of the factions participating in Iranian decision making.[6] Bahraini informants assessed the facts the same way. Moreover, contrary to what was written, no Bahraini source ever confirmed the presence of Sadiq Rohani on Bahraini soil as mentioned by some.[7] Overall, Sadiq Rohani seems to have had little if no personal connection to Bahrain and certainly never played a role in mobilizing Bahraini Shia for the Islamic revolution.

Still, for the Bahraini rulers, Sadiq Rohani's public declarations rendered suspect any manifestation by Ruhollah Khomeini's supporters. In August 1979, they arrested Sh. Mohammed al-'Akri, a Shia scholar politically active although not enrolled in any organization. The latter had just returned from Tehran where he was suspected of having met with Sadiq Rohani. Hadi al-Mudarrisi immediately organized a demonstration to demand his release. Although it was modest in proportion, gathering no more than one thousand people,[8] the demonstration was quelled by the security forces, who arrested a handful of demonstrators. The situation deteriorated and regional tensions rose, resulting in the deportation of Hadi al-Mudarrisi who was by the same token stripped of his Bahraini citizenship. He reached the United Arab Emirates where he was still a citizen and, after a few months, went to Tehran where he publicly announced the creation of the Islamic Front for the Liberation of Bahrain.

The deportation of Hadi al-Mudarrisi hampered the activities of his supporters but did not stop them. The *Huseini* Social Fund was officially

---

5   Christin Marschall, *Iran's Persian Gulf Policy. From Khomeini to Khatami*, London: Routledge Curzon, 2003, p. 27.

6   *Ibid.*

7   Joseph Kostiner, "Shi'i Unrest in the Gulf", in Martin Kramer (ed.), *Shi'ism, Resistance and Revolution*, Boulder, Colorado: Westview Press, 1987, p. 176; Fuller and Francke (2001), p. 126.

8   According to Fred H. Lawson, *Bahrain. The Modernization of Autocracy*, Boulder, Colorado: Westview Press, 1989, p. 86. Kostiner (1987) p. 176 mentions five hundreds demonstrators.

closed by the authorities but the Iranian revolution had helped to further clarify the political identity as well as the objectives of its members. As Mohammed al-'Alawi put it: "before the revolution the leadership of the Front was already formalized but we were not aware of constituting a po-litical organization strictly speaking and our objective was not clear."[9] In December 1981, the Bahraini government announced it had thwarted a coup by the IFLB. Three hundred persons were arrested and seventy-three were tried. The majority of them (sixty) were Bahraini but there were also a significant number of Saudis (eleven), as well as one Kuwaiti and one Omani.[10] This confirms the interconnection of the various Shirazi cells in Iraq and the Gulf monarchies. The IFLB activists who had escaped the first wave of arrests either fled the country for Iran or were imprisoned. Mohammed al-'Alawi had left for Iran before the coup, and was suspected of having participated in its organization. His cousin Ja'far al-'Alawi, who had remained in Bahrain, was arrested and only left jail eighteen years af-terwards, in 1999. His father, who had always been a trusted interlocutor of the regime but in whose garden his son had apparently hidden weapons, lost the trust of the ruler and consequently his status as the organizer of the 'Ashura processions.

The biggest popular demonstration in the aftermath of the revolution was the one organized in April 1980. The Shiraziyyin claim they organized it but many al-Da'wa activists and sympathizers also participated. Indeed, they could not but join the march, which was organized to protest the ex-ecution of Mohammed Baqer al-Sadr by the Iraqi regime. Although not di-rectly linked to the revolution, the demonstration clearly signalled a shift in popular mobilization. Until then, it had been rather limited in scope, prob-ably reflecting the Shiraziyyin's estrangement from the clerical mainstream, as well as al-Da'wa's reluctance to participate in anything organized by Hadi al-Mudarrisi and its overall cautiousness not to spark further repres-sion from the government. Although not specifically directed against the Bahraini regime, the demonstration was quelled violently. One of the dem-onstrators, Jamil al-'Ali, died under torture, sparking rage and anger among the Shia youth. Jamil al-'Ali was a regular at the *Huseini* Council (*al-Hay'a al-Huseiniyya*), a *ma'tam* frequented by many young people sympathizing with either the Shiraziyyin or al-Da'wa. Many were not even aware of the factional rift between the two currents and recognized themselves in the

9   Personal interview, Bahrain, December 2006.

10   Kostiner (1987), p.180; R. K. Ramazani, "Shi'ism in the Persian Gulf", in Juan R. I. Cole and Nikki Keddie (eds), *Shiism and Social Protest*, New Haven: Yale University Press, 1986, p. 49.

message of the Islamic revolution. In memory of the first "martyr" of the Islamic cause in Bahrain, they renamed the *Huseini* Council the "*Ma'tam* of the Martyr" (*Ma'tam al-Shahid*), which soon became the rallying point for young activists of Shia political Islam. Although it was not officially authorized to organize an 'Ashura procession by the General Council for the *Huseini* Processions dominated by the Shia notability, the *ma'tam* held one on its own. According to Bahraini informants who participated in it, it attracted around three thousands penitents from Manama and the Shia villages. In contrast, the other *cortège* did not exceed the usual number of a few hundred. This marked the beginning of the use of the 'Ashura *cortège* as a political display of strength for the Shia Islamic activists, both al-Da'wa and the Shiraziyyin who marched together in the procession of the *Ma'tam* of the Martyr. This lasted during almost one decade up to 1989 when the *ma'tam*, under pressure from the authorities who arrested several of its regulars, ceased its procession but was soon succeeded by other funeral houses.

The Intifada of Muharram 1400 in Saudi Arabia

It is noteworthy that the scope of popular demonstrations fostered by the advent of the Islamic revolution was much greater in Saudi Arabia than in Bahrain. In a country that, unlike Bahrain, lacked a culture of popular demonstrations to articulate political demands, the events signalled a departure from the well-established quietist pattern of behaviour adopted by the majority of the Shias after the definitive conquest of the Eastern province by the Al-Sa'ud in 1913. Known as the "*Intifada* of Muharram 1400", that is the uprising of the month of Muharram of the year 1400 of the Hegirian calendar, the events constituted a watershed in the political mobilization of Saudi Shias. Most of the activists interviewed mentioned it as a turning point in their personal story. This was particularly so since, at the time of the *intifada*, the bulk of the Shirazi current was constituted by teenagers and young men for whom the uprising was experienced as a baptism of fire amounting to a rite of passage to adulthood and political awareness. An activist from Qatif who was fifteen at the time, said: "before the *intifada* and the advent of the Islamic revolution, we were children. We were attending religious debates and discussions but we were not aware of political matters."[11] The *intifada* marked the passage from a general religious revival orchestrated by the activists of the Shirazi current to clear political slogans calling for revolution.

---

11   Personal interview, Syria, February 2005.

The riots were concentrated in the region of Qatif and spared the region of Hasa. The *intifada* was hence another example of the different political cultures of the two Shia zones of the Eastern Province. Because the Hasawi population is equally divided between Sunnis and Shias, the latter tended to remain discreet, favouring escapism over protest. Drawing on hitherto unpublished material as well as interviews with eye witnesses, Toby Craig Jones has recently well documented the process that led to the uprising.[12] The events themselves display the classical pattern of a string of demonstrations and repressions. As in the demonstrations of April 1980 in Bahrain, the falling of the first "martyr", Husein al-Qallaf, a young student from the ARAMCO education centre, exacerbated the anger of the crowd. The funerals of the deceased signalled the escalation of a bloody confrontation with the security forces. The violence of the reaction of the authorities, who fired live ammunitions at the demonstrators and killed several of them,[13] can be explained by the particular timing of the uprising. Indeed, it followed by only a few days the seizure of the Grand Mosque of Mecca by a group of Sunni orthodox rebels led by Juhaiman al-'Utaibi. The occupation lasted three weeks and was only brought to an end with the help of the French Special Forces. While the events were unrelated and obeyed two different socio-political logics,[14] the sequential correspondence between the two events was enough to worry the Saudi regime about the consequences of an all-out Islamic revival cutting across sectarian boundaries. For the rulers, the 'Ashura processions were no less than the opening of a second front of a single contestation in the heart of the petroleum rich region.

Toby Craig Jones also documented the political networks that framed the demonstration. He pointed to the presence of communist activists among the demonstrators, showing that the uprising was the occasion of the activation of all the partisan networks present among the Shia population. This was confirmed by my own findings. Even if they were aware that religious empathy with Iran was a major driver of the events, the leftist activists participated in the uprising because they also wanted to see in it a salutary manifestation of civil society's vitality. Many, especially the

---

12   Toby Craig Jones, "Rebellion on the Saudi Periphery: Modernity, Marginalization, and the Shi'a Uprising of 1979", *International Journal of Middle East Studies*, n° 38, May 2006, p. 215.

13   Jacob Goldberg writes that there were seventeen dead, but there remains doubt to this day as to how many people were killed: "The Shi'i Minority in Saudi Arabia", in Cole and Keddie (1986), p. 240.

14   Thomas Hegghammer and Stéphane Lacroix, "Rejectionist Islamism in Saudi Arabia: The Story of Juhayman al-'Utaybi Revisited", *International Journal of Middle Eastern Studies*, vol. 39, n° 1, 2007, p. 112.

younger ones, were also driven to demonstrate purely out of feelings of communal solidarity as well as desire for expressing their revolt. They reported that the events far transcended the boundaries of political affiliations and that once the bloody circle of demonstration and repression was engaged, all segments of Shia society, even the less politicized, felt empathy for the demonstrators, helping them to hide from the police and providing assistance to the injured ones.

However, it remains that while leftist activists and sympathizers participated in the uprising, they were not the initiators of it but rather followed something that was initiated by the Shia Islamic activists from the Shirazi current. As shown by Toby Craig Jones, three months before the uprising, the Shiraziyyin had announced their intention to celebrate 'Ashura by organizing public processions.[15] Besides the fact that any kind of public march was at odds with Saudi political culture, this constituted a clear breaking off of the initial agreement between the Al-Sa'ud and the Shia leaders that the performance of the Shia rituals would remain confined inside the walls of the mosques and the *husseiniyya*. Moreover, what was meant to be a religious cortège turned quickly into a political demonstration when the penitents flourished portraits of Ruhollah Khomeini, now no longer a mere religious authority but the head of a foreign state whose diplomacy was becoming increasingly hostile to the Saudi monarchy. Moreover, they chanted slogans hostile to the Al-Sa'ud, like "Oh King Khalid release your hands from power, the people do not want you".[16] The planned character of the events is confirmed by the fact that a few days before the first demonstration, the Shiraziyyin sent threatening letters to the Western residents of the Eastern province and more particularly the American employees of ARAMCO, warning them of forthcoming retaliation for the harmful role they were playing in Saudi Arabia by exploiting the natural resources and taking an hostile position towards the Islamic Republic of Iran.[17]

Facts tend therefore to show that the uprising was the result of planned action by the Shiraziyyin, who had reached the conclusion that, due to the changing regional context, the time was ripe for an intensification of pressure on the regime, including by violent means. This is not to say that the details were premeditated and that the exact objectives were clear. Actually, participants today acknowledge that they proved particularly unprepared and naïve. Lacking a sustained strategy of mobilization beyond religious

---

15   *Ibid.*, p. 222.

16   *Ibid.*, p. 223, n. 49.

17   *Ibid.*, p. 225.

awareness-raising and enthusiasm, they were not clearer about their exact aims beyond their willingness to express their anger. That said however, the question remains of the role of the existing linkage between the Saudi Islamic activists and the Shirazi Iraqi leaders, all based in Iran at the time. In his account of the events, Toby Craig Jones tended to favour internal over external factors and relativized the importance of the transnational dimension of the Saudi events: "members of the OIR [the Organization for the Islamic Revolution in the Arabian Peninsula, created by the Shiraziyyin in the aftermath of the uprising] certainly took inspiration from revolutionaries in Iran, even appropriating their symbols. However, it seems likely that relations did not surpass the level of the symbolic".[18] To substantiate his argument, he points to the fact that Mohammed al-Shirazi, the religious authority who inspired the Saudi activists around Hasan al-Saffar, was not a supporter of Ruhollah Khomeini's ideas to the point that the two men had tense relations. He is right in stressing that the Shirazi network that framed Shia political mobilization was initially autonomous from the Iranian networks but it is an anachronism to say that Mohammed al-Shirazi and Ruhollah Khomeini disagreed and were even in conflict. As we shall see in detail in the following chapter, there was indeed a bitter conflict between the two men but it arose well after the Saudi uprising, in 1982 and more so in 1986 when the Iranian pragmatists eliminated the faction that supported the Shiraziyyin's activities. In 1979, relations between the Shiraziyyin and the leaders of the Islamic Republic of Iran were at their zenith. While it is true that, before the Islamic revolution, Mohammed al-Shirazi had formulated a doctrine of Islamic government that differed slightly from that of Ruhollah Khomeini (for more details, *cf.* chapter 6), his nephews Mohammed Taqi and Hadi al-Mudarrisi, who were the political executives, had unrestrainedly embraced the doctrine of *wilayat al-faqih* and acted rather autonomously from Mohammed al-Shirazi. Moreover, the brothers became the main brokers of the exportation of the Islamic revolution to the Gulf monarchies. This explains why in Bahrain, Hadi al-Mudarrisi acted both as Mohammed al-Shirazi's and Ruhollah Khomeini's representative and was behind the failed coup in 1981. Besides, for many activists in Saudi Arabia and the Gulf, the two *marja'* were not really distinguishable because they enjoyed a particularly good relationship. Many explained that, at this time, they emulated them both.

What follows is that while domestic factors, and in particular the blatant discriminatory policies of the Saudi regime towards the Shias, were certainly central in explaining why the Saudi Shias responded so enthusiastically

---

18   *Ibid.*, p. 215.

to the Iranian impulse, the external factor of the Islamic revolution did not operate merely at a symbolic level on the domestic situation. The ideology of the revolution, as well as what was perceived as its concrete *modus operandi* – mass demonstrations led by enthusiastic people – was conveyed through interpersonal networks of activists. The question remains as to the level of coordination of events. Was the uprising the result of a pure domestic initiative or of a project formulated in Iran by the Iraqi Shirazi leaders and their Iranian supporters? It is probably impossible to give a definitive answer to this question, which remains a highly sensitive one. At the time of writing, in a context where the Shiraziyyin were striving, and succeeding, to constitute themselves into a legitimate political actor in the eyes of the Saudi regime, they were tending to systematically downplay the scope of their relationship to Iran in the past. They want to promote the idea that, ultimately, the Saudi activists were always autonomous from their transnational religious and political authorities and that the decision-making process was essentially domestic. However, considering the Iraqi Shiraziyyin's project to create a wide transnational network of Shia revolutionaries emulating the Iranian model, it is doubtful that the events of November 1979 in Saudi Arabia were the result of a purely domestic initiative. The details of the action were probably planned by the local activists but it is at least not unlikely that the initial impulse was given from Iran by the Iraqi agents of the network and their Iranian mentors. Besides, accounts by participants in the uprising show that, during the events, communication with the Iraqi leaders was unbroken. Indeed, several informants recounted the presence of Murtadha al-Qazwini at the time of the events. The latter had been a companion of Mohammed al-Shirazi in Karbala. The al-Qazwini and the al-Shirazi were old families of science related by marriage (*cf.* chapter 3). Murtadha al-Qazwini had followed Mohammed al-Shirazi to Kuwait in the early seventies, where he became one of his right-hand men. He was one of the most active teachers at the *Hawza* of the Supreme Prophet there. This is how he got close to the Saudi activists, who succeeded in getting him come to Saudi Arabia to lead religious ceremonies and give speeches during Muharram. None of my informants said that Murtadha al-Qazwini came to Saudi Arabia on purpose to coordinate events or assume some kind of leadership position over the Saudi activists. What is sure however, is that he made inflammatory sermons from a *huseiniyya* in Qatif that was a rallying point for many demonstrators.

The events of Muharram constituted the peak of the uprising and were followed by other sporadic little demonstrations and skirmishes in the following months, with at least one serious episode in February 1980 on the occasion of the first anniversary of Ruhollah Khomeini's accession to power.[19] Violence quickly calmed down however. It was probably thanks to a significant shift in Saudi public policy towards the Eastern region. Realizing that violence was as much the result of obvious neglect of the Shia population from the part of the central state as of Shia Islamic activism, the Saudi authorities made an effort to fill the gap. New infrastructures were built so that old grievances were at least partially addressed. On the eve of 'Ashura in 1980, the government announced a new development plan and released several prisoners arrested during the *intifada*. This explains why 'Ashura went off without incident that year and in the following years. According to many informants, during the 1980s, while systematically suppressing the Shia Islamic activists, the authorities also showed more tolerance towards the public display of Shia religiosity, even letting the muezzins call to prayer according to the ritual Shia formula "Mohammed is the prophet of God and 'Ali is the entrustee of God" (*Mohammed rasul Allah wa 'Ali wali Allah*). Overall, despite its religious commitment to Sunni ultra-orthodoxy, the Saudi regime displayed much more flexibility and skillfulness than the Bahraini one in handling the Shia problem. This is probably due to the fact that the Shias, as a weak minority, always represented a less dangerous threat to the Al-Sa'ud than to the Al-Khalifa, who had to confront a deeply politicized and revanchist Shia majority.

A landmark in the collective memory, the *intifada* of Muharram 1400 marked a turning point for the nature of the Shia Islamic movements' activities. First, as in Bahrain, the Shiraziyyin officially announced the creation of the Organization for Islamic Revolution in the Arabian Peninsula (*Munazzamat al-Thawra al-Islamiyya fi al-Jazira al-'Arabiyya*) with Hassan al-Saffar as its head. As its names indicates, the organization was clearly revolutionary and aimed at no less than overthrowing the Saudi regime with the help of Iran. As recalled by an informant who was among the exiles at the time: "we were really persuaded that we would bring down the Saudi regime within ten years, twenty years maximum".[20] For this purpose, the movement started to publish a monthly review the title of which was also unambiguous: *The Islamic Revolution* (*al-Thawra al-Islamiyya*). The tone and the content of the articles were uncompromising as Hassan al-Saffar's position was that no negotiation was possible with the impious Saudi regime.[21]

---

19   Ramazani (1986), p. 46; Goldberg (1986), p. 240.

20   Personal interview, Saudi Arabia, September 2004.

21   Mamoun Fandy, *Saudi Arabia and the Politics of Dissent*, London: Macmillan, 1999, p. 198.

A second consequence of the *intifada* was that, in a way even more pronounced than in Bahrain, the entire Shirazi leadership was de-territorial-
ized. Most of the leaders relocated to Iran, while some of the lay cadres
established themselves in Western Europe and North America. In Iran,
most of the activists established themselves in Tehran where the Saudis
constituted the bulk of the students at the *Hawza* of the Imam of the
Age (*Hawzat al-Qa'im*). The school had been established by Mohammed
Taqi al-Mudarrisi on the model of the *Hawza* of the Supreme Prophet in
Kuwait: more than just a religious school, it served as an education centre
for the Shirazi activists mainly from the Gulf and Iraq. Only one cleric,
Sh. Yusuf al-Mahdi from Safwa, stayed uninterruptedly in Saudi Arabia
during the 1980s. He was among Mohammed al-Shirazi's students in Kuwait and after the closure of the *Hawza* of the Supreme Prophet in 1980,
he decided not to pursue religious studies in Qom or Tehran like most of
his counterparts. Despite the fact that he was arrested and imprisoned several times, he thought his moral and religious duty was to stay among his
flock so as not to leave the ground to hostile forces. For this reason, Shias
pay him particular respect to this day and he is one of the most popular
preachers in Saudi Arabia.

KUWAIT: THE BIRTH OF A SHIA OPPOSITION

As in Bahrain and Saudi Arabia, the Islamic revolution has had a great
impact on the various actors of the Islamic *renaissance* in the Kuwaiti Shia
population. Political violence was also a major feature of the revolution's
aftermath but it never took the form of civil unrest. Revolutionary enthusiasm was rather reinvested within the modes of action proper to the old
pluralistic Kuwaiti political culture.

A Failed Social Movement

While both al-Da'wa and the Shiraziyyin displayed overt support for the
Islamic revolution, it was a figure who had previously remained discreet in
the political arena who emerged as the main broker of revolutionary zeal in
Kuwait: S. 'Abbas al-Muhri. Much false information has circulated about
him, in particular that he was the brother-in-law of Ruhollah Khomeini.[22]
In reality, he had no family tie with the leader of the Islamic revolution
but was related by marriage to S. Mahmud Shahrudi (d. 1974), an Iranian

22   Kostiner (1987), p. 177; Crystal (1990), p. 101; Marschall (2003), p. 31.

born cleric who was counted among the grand *mujtahid* of Najaf.[23] 'Abbas al-Muhri himself was from a clerical family from Hasa who had fled to southern Iran in the eighteenth century.[24] In the 1930s, he went to Najaf to complete his religious education. Some years later in the early 1940s, following the pattern described previously, a group of Kuwaiti tradesmen from the region of Tarakma in southern Iran contacted Mahmud Shahrudi to ask him to look for a cleric ready to come to Kuwait and act as the religious leader of the 'Ijmi community which then lacked, at least according to the merchants, any scholar of great stature to contribute to its religious edification. Mahmud Shahrudi transmitted the invitation to 'Abbas al-Muhri, but the latter was unwilling to bury himself in what he considered a small backward country. He was ultimately convinced when the merchants proposed to build a mosque especially for him, which was eventually erected and named the Sha'ban mosque. 'Abbas al-Muhri quickly became a socially influential cleric. In the late 1950s, he threatened to organize a boycott of the great Shia businessman Marrad Bahbahani's numerous companies if he did not fire the handful of Bahais he employed. The latter had no choice but to comply. 'Abbas al-Muhri began to take interest in Ruhollah Khomeini's activity after the latter began his public diatribes against the Shah's regime in the early 1960s, which one of his sons translated into Arabic and distributed in Kuwait. He even visited him once in Qom and attended one of his lectures. The man made a deep impression on him so that when he was arrested and imprisoned in 1963, 'Abbas al-Muhri issued a communiqué asking for his immediate release. When Ruhollah Khomeini went in exile to Najaf in 1965, 'Abbas al-Muhri immediately undertook the trip to the holy city accompanied by several of his sons, particularly Ahmed and Murtadha. The latter decided to remain in Najaf to begin his religious studies with Ruhollah Khomeini. In Kuwait, 'Abbas al-Muhri's other sons had regular contact with activists of the Iranian opposition from the entourage of Ruhollah Khomeini, particularly the famous Mohammed Montazeri who became the spearhead of the exportation of the Islamic revolution after the fall of the Shah (*cf.* chapter 6). When Ruhollah Khomeini was expelled from Najaf in 1978 and needed asylum, Ahmed al-Muhri drove him by car to the Kuwaiti frontier hoping that his father would be able to arrange his stay in Kuwait. His efforts were aided by Mohammed al-Shirazi, who also though Kuwait would be a good sanctuary for Ruhollah

---

23   Personal interview with S. Mohammed Redha al-Muhri and S. Mohammed Jawad al-Muhri, the sons of 'Abbas al-Muhri, Kuwait, December 2006.

24   In the village of Muhr, *cf.* chapter 2.

Khomeini. The attempt failed and Ruhollah Khomeini finally took a plane for France before coming back triumphantly to Iran in February 1979.

When the revolutionaries seized power in Iran, 'Abbas al-Muhri was Ruhollah Khomeini's official representative in Kuwait for many years. While he confined himself to a religious role, his sons, and more particularly Ahmed, undertook to mobilize Kuwaiti Shias on a political platform. In February 1979, only a few days after Ruhollah Khomeini had returned to Iran, they organized a march from their father's house to the Iranian embassy in order to support the new regime in Tehran. The demonstrators apparently succeeded in substituting the former regime's flag with one mentioning "God is the greatest" (*Allahu al-akbar*).[25] Another aim of the demonstrators was to take the embassy's archives, but this was not achieved.[26] More importantly, in August 1979, Ahmed al-Muhri decided to organize a series of weekly conferences entitled "Revising the concept of equality in Kuwaiti society" (*Tashih Mafhum al-Musawa fil-Mujtama' al-Kuwaiti*). They were held in the Sha'ban mosque of which his father was prayer leader. Contrary to previous forms of Shia political mobilization in Kuwait, the conferences were not focused on Shia community demands but addressed issues of general concern for all residents of Kuwait. Ahmed al-Muhri criticized the existence of various unequal categories of Kuwaiti citizenship. He particularly focused on the problem of the so-called "*bidun*", the stateless residents who, although long residents of Kuwait and not bearing the citizenship of any other state, were unable to become officially Kuwaiti citizens. He also denounced the disbanding of the Parliament in 1976 and the consequent suspension of the democratic life. He also launched scathing attacks against the corruption of the administration. His weekly sermons attracted a wide audience. Because they had not previously been involved in Shia factional politics, the al-Muhri were able to transcend the dispute between al-Da'wa and the Shiraziyyin, who both came to listen to Ahmed al-Muhri's speeches. Many Sunnis were also to be found among the listeners. Even more significant and threatening for the regime, Ahmed al-Muhri succeeded in attracting the sympathy of the Arab nationalists, who had proved so hostile to the Shias in the past. At that period, the latter were under the growing influence of Marxist ideas so that they had shifted to a more open approach to the concept of Arab identity.[27] Moreover, in the context of the shrinking of public freedoms, of which the

---

25   Al-Mdayris (1999), p. 24.

26   Personal interviews with Mohammed Redha and Mohammed Jawad al-Muhri, Kuwait, December 2006.

27   Al-Mdayris (1999), p. 25.

disbanding of Parliament was only one among many manifestations, they felt the need for a greater collaboration of all the opposition movements.

The diversity of the audience, as well as the themes that were broached, gave Ahmed al-Muhri's conferences the potential to transform into a social movement. In fact, people *a posteriori* referred to the conferences as the "Movement of Sha'ban". Although Kuwaiti political life had traditionally enjoyed a good deal of freedom, especially by Arab standards, politics had rarely taken the form of mass gatherings and rallies like the one at the Sha'ban mosque. The Shia demonstration of 1938 which, as mentioned previously, was organized in order to support the ruling family against its opposition (*cf.* chapter 2), was an exception in that respect. So was the march of February 1979 to the Iranian embassy. In a country where politics had always been done in the semi-private space of the *diwaniyya* and was more a matter of bargaining between various centres of power revolving around individuals than of popular mobilization, an event like the weekly gathering at the Sha'ban mosque was seen as somehow worrying by the regime. It first tried to use its customary allies to counter the movement. Shia notables met with Ahmed al-Muhri to propose to him a joint action in order to improve the lot of the Shia population. They proposed to pressure the rulers to authorize the construction of more Shia mosques and *huseiniyya*. In other words, they suggested a return to the traditional modes of Shia mobilizing focused on pure sectorial demands rather than on general political reform.[28] After Ahmed al-Muhri refused to alter his movement, the government took a radical step. Referring to a law promulgated after the disbanding of the Parliament which forbade the gathering of more than twenty persons, it banned the conferences and arrested Ahmed al-Muhri in the aftermath of his fourth conference. It eventually deported the entire al-Muhri family to Iran, striping all its members of their Kuwaiti citizenship.

In Iran, 'Abbas al-Muhri remained closed to Ruhollah Khomeini and continued to engage in religious activities. He died there in 1988. His son Ahmed emerged as an important figure of Ruhollah Khomeini's entourage, to the point that the rumour spread that he was related by marriage to the latter's family. Between 1980 and 1982, he played a central role in the administration of the Foundation of the Deprived (*Bonyan i-Mostazafin*). This foremost institution, which soon became a huge financial power in Iran, had been created in the aftermath of the revolution in order to administer the goods expropriated from figures of the former regime: lands, buildings but also companies. The aim was to redistribute the profits to the needy. Ruhollah Khomeini had appointed a committee of six persons,

---

28   Al-Mdayris (1999), p. 27.

all of them clerics, to run the Foundation but was wary of their actual administrative competence. The first director of the Foundation had been accused of corruption and dismissed. The second director was Ali-Akbar Mohtashami, who subsequently became minister of Interior and played a key role in spreading Iranian influence in Lebanon when he was ambassador in Syria in the mid-1980s. Ahmed Khomeini, the son of Ruhollah Khomeini, feared he would be unable to properly administer the Foundation and asked Ahmed al-Muhri to assist him in his task. During two years, Ali-Akbar Mohtashami was the official director but Ahmed al-Muhri was the real manager, totally autonomous thanks to his close relationship with the Supreme Guide. He then quit to return to his personal buisiness.[29]

After the Gulf War, which closed the tense interlude of the 1980s with the end of the systematic suspicion towards the Shias (*cf.* chapter 7), all the sons of 'Abbas al-Muhri, with the notable exception of Ahmed, were authorized to come back to Kuwait and regain their citizenship. As for Ahmed, he never went back to Kuwait and decided to establish himself in London in the aftermath of the Gulf War. His choice was motivated by his refusal to undertake the official procedures necessary to get back his Kuwaiti citizenship. In his view, the governement should have given it back to him spontaneously, as a way to admit that it had been wrong in the beginning in targeting him. He did not stay in Iran either since his relations with the new rulers, after the death of Ruhollah Khomeini in 1989, were marked by reciprocal suspicion. Afraid of being caught in Iranian factional disputes, he preferred to leave Iran. At the time of writing, he was running a religious web site in Arabic from London.[30]

Significantly, the deportation of 'Abbas al-Muhri and his sons marked the end of the dynamic of the social movement they had initiated. Although his sons had somehow tried to organize into a political party at some stage, as underlined by a Kuwaiti informant from al-Da'wa, 'Abbas al-Muhri was a "*hawzawi* one hundred percent". For the same reasons as he had helped Mohammed al-Shirazi to become established in Kuwait, he supported Ruhollah Khomeini out of corporate solidarity with a religious scholar and a *marja'*. What was at stake for him was the preservation of the religious institution in the face of the impious regime of the Shah and subsequently the defence of a state run by the clerics. Beyond that, he had himself no clear political project and, furthermore, he was deeply hostile to the very idea of a political party. For this reason he had bitter relations with

---

29   These details were provided by Ahmed al-Muhri, personal interview, London, July 2007.

30   www.ahmadmohri.org.uk

the activists of al-Da'wa and had not participated in their effort to enhance the representation of the Shias in Parliament. While his son Ahmed obviously had a political project for Kuwait, he was never able to transform his audience into an organized political movement and did not leave a legacy after his departure. This explains why, after the short period of mobilization at the Sha'ban mosque, the "young men" of al-Da'wa took back the lead by transforming the dynamic created by the al-Muhri into concrete political gains at the parliamentary level.

The 1981 elections, which marked the return of democratic life after the disbanding of the National Assembly in 1976, were decisive in that respect. They were in many respects a turning point in the political history of the Shias in Kuwait. A new electoral law promulgated in 1980 brought substantial changes that deeply affected the scope of the Shia parliamentary representation. The number of constituencies was increased from ten to twenty-five. The two old Shia constituencies, the first and the seventh, were left untouched but saw their number of representatives drop from five to two each.[31] Besides, contrary to the previous elections where voters could vote in any constituency, they had henceforth to vote in the constituency where they resided. This was done in the context of a massive population move to new quarters outside the traditional perimeter of the city. The Shias tended to become diluted in new quarters where they did not systematically constitute a demographic majority. The new electoral law certainly did not occur aimlessly, especially considering the worsening of the geopolitical context. After the open manifestations of support for the Islamic revolution, the Iran-Iraq war had further increased fears that the Shias would act as an Iranian fifth column. Between two evils – Iraqi irredentism or Iranian exportation of the revolution – the Kuwaiti rulers chose what they thought the lesser: they sided unambiguously with Iraq. The results of the elections confirmed the rulers' impression that their Shia citizens had shifted their political orientation. While, as a result of the new electoral law, the Shia parliamentary representation dropped from ten to four deputies, the latter were all members of the Social Society for Culture, that is of al-Da'wa.

Terrorist Violence

As in Bahrain and Saudi Arabia, a consequence of the Islamic revolution in Kuwait was the passage to violence by the Shia Islamic activists. Unlike

---

31   Kamal Osman Salih, "Kuwait's Parliamentary Elections: 1963-1985: An Appraisal", *Journal of South Asian and Middle Eastern Studies*, vol. 16, n° 2, winter 1992, p. 20.

in Bahrain and Saudi Arabia however, the pattern of political violence in Kuwait strictly speaking fits the definition of terrorism. Indeed, it was not the climactic expression of the process of formation of a social movement contesting the established order but rather the result of the failure of the embryonic social movement initiated by the al-Muhri.[32] Although details about the real relationship between those who perpetrated the violence and the semi-official Shia Islamic movements are still difficult to ascertain, it is most probable that violence was not orchestrated by the mainstream of the Shia movements and did not enjoy the support of a significant part of the Shia population. This is clearly manifested in the fact that, contrary to their Bahraini and Saudi counterparts, the Kuwaiti cadres of the Shia Islamic movements denied any responsibility for the violence of the 1980s when interviewed. Indeed, Bahrainis and Saudis have no problems in acknowledging that, in the aftermath of the Islamic revolution, they contemplated violence as the most efficient way to achieve their goals but have since reconsidered their position. Kuwaitis stick to the idea that violence was undertaken by marginal elements while the mainstream never departed from a strictly political strategy. Their objective was not to export the Islamic revolution to Kuwait but to gain more political weight in the framework of the pluralist political institutions, in order to pressure the rulers to restore the Parliament disbanded in 1976 and grant it more powers, but also to enhance the political and social relevance of the Shias overall.

The terrorist rationale behind Shia political violence in Kuwait explains why violence did not occur in the framework of popular demonstrations degenerating into unrest galvanized by anti-regime slogans. It took the form of attacks targeting Kuwaiti as well as foreign institutions based in Kuwait. The first attacks occurred in December 1983 when a series of explosions hit the American and French embassies, an American compound, the control tower of the airport, the ministry of electricity and water and a big industrial zone named Shu'aiba.[33] Among the twenty-five persons arrested for having participated in the attacks, only three were Kuwaiti nationals and two were stateless residents in Kuwait. Three were Lebanese but the bulk – seventeen – were Iraqi activists of al-Da'wa.[34] It appears that the attack was perpetrated by a splinter group of mainstream al-Da'wa,

---

32   This following the analysis by Michel Wieviorka, *The Making of Terrorism* (translated by David Gordon White), Chicago: The University of Chicago Press, 1988, pp. 3-24.

33   Kostiner (1987), p. 180.

34   *Ibid.*

named al-Da'wa al-Islamiyya.[35] It was led by activists who had been in exile in Kuwait, and had therefore built networks there. These were, among others, 'Ali al-Kurani and 'Azz al-Din Salim. According to 'Adel Ra'uf – himself an activist of al-Da'wa with keen knowledge of the party – the split originated in the first place in a personal dispute between 'Ali al-Kurani and Mohammed Baqer al-Sadr himself, after the latter had decided to quit the party without previously informing the former.[36] One can also surmise that, because he was living far away from Iraq and was moreover not an Iraqi, 'Ali al-Kurani was progressively marginalized within the party apparatus. This hypothesis is corroborated by the fact that he eventually joined forces with other dissatisfied members of the party from Basra led by 'Azz al-Din Salim, who deemed they were not given satisfactory representation in a party dominated by the Najafis. Be that as it may, 'Adel Ra'uf reckoned that 'Ali al-Kurani and his allies failed to gain the support of the majority of the general assembly which gathered in 1982, and that this was the decisive path in the creation of al-Da'wa al-Islamiyya, which became known in the activists' circles as al-Da'wa al-Islamiyya – Basra faction (*khatt Basra*).[37] For his part, Faleh Abdul-Jabar emphasized that 'Ali al-Kurani and the Basra group splintered because they rejected the introduction of elections to designate the party's governing body, arguing that the leadership should be appointed according to the activists' individual achievements.[38] Considering the numerical dominance of the Najafiyyin, it is very possible that they refused the elections not because they were against them in principle but because the system of one man one vote would prevent them from reaching a higher position inside the party apparatus. Be that as it may, the alliance between 'Ali al-Kurani and the Basra activists was short-lived and the two separated shortly afterwards. Formally headed by 'Azz al-Din Salim, the Basra group integrated into the Supreme Assembly for the Islamic Revolution in Iraq (SAIRI), created under Iranian auspices in 1982 in order to unite and better control the Iraqi opposition exiled on its soil. It stayed in SAIRI even after al-Da'wa mainstream quit in 1986 and SAIRI transformed from an umbrella organization to a party in its own right, closely tied to Iran. Another feature of the group responsible for the terrorist attacks in Kuwait was therefore that it was a proxy of Iran. This was confirmed recently in February 2007 when CNN revealed that one of the

---

35   Ranstorp, (1997), p. 91.

36   Ra'uf (2000), p. 224.

37   *Ibid.*

38   Abdul-Jabar (2003), pp. 257-8.

Iraqis convicted for the attacks and sentenced to death *in absentia*, Jamal Ja'far Mohammed, had been sitting in the Iraqi parliament since December 2005 and had served as an adviser to Iraqi Prime Minister Ibrahim al-Ja'fari.[39] A member of al-Da'wa in the 1970s, Jamal Ja'far Mohammed became a member of al-Da'wa al-Islamiyya and then a cadre of SAIRI.

The implication of al-Da'wa al-Islamiyya and the small proportion of Kuwaitis involved in the attacks confirm that the terrorist acts in Kuwait are to be analysed more as the playing out of external conflicts on the Kuwaiti scene than as the expression of an internal state-society conflict. The first wave of attacks was conceived as a way to support the strategic interests of Iran in its war against Iraq. The aim was to bring Kuwait round to dropping its huge contribution to the Iraqi war effort against Iran.[40] Furthermore, the attacks were part of Iranian pressure on the United States and France, two countries that supported Iraq and constituted serious obstacles to Iranian objectives in Lebanon. The attacks in Kuwait appear to have been part of a broader sequence of strikes against countries supporting the Iraqi war effort. They took place a few weeks after similar attacks against American and French interests in Lebanon by a Hezbollah front organization: the Islamic Jihad. The attacks in Kuwait were a joint operation by Lebanese Hezbollah activists and Iraqi al-Da'wa al-Islamiyya.[41] More particularly, the Lebanese were activists of the Lebanese chapter of al-Da'wa, created in the 1970s under the religious guidance of Mohammed Husein Fadlallah and several Lebanese students coming back from the Najaf seminaries.[42] The party was dissolved in 1980 after the execution of Mohammed Baqer al-Sadr, with many of its members integrating into the Amal party, created by Musa al-Sadr in 1974 initially under the name of the Movement of the Deprived. In 1982, a splinter group of Amal named Amal Islamiyya, which included many former al-Da'wa activists, integrated into a new Shia Islamic organization created at the initiative of Iran named Hezbollah. The links between Kuwaiti, Iraqi and Lebanese activists of al-Da'wa help explain the implication of the Lebanese in the attacks perpetrated on Kuwaiti soil. 'Imad Mughniyya, a leading member of Hezbollah, specializing in armed operations and previously an activist of Lebanese al-Da'wa, was suspected of having planned the attacks together with his brother in

---

39   James Glanz and Marc Santora, "Kuwait Court Convicts Iraqi Lawmaker in 1983 Bombings that Killed Five Americans", *The New York Times*, 7 February 2007.

40   Kostiner (1987), p. 181.

41   Ranstorp (1997), p. 91.

42   *Ibid.*, pp. 25-30.

law, Mustafa Badr al-Din.[43] The latter was arrested and sentenced to death in Kuwait with several of his companions. The subsequent attacks in Kuwait were most probably organized by the same 'Imad Mughniyya with the narrow objective of setting free his companions sentenced in Kuwait.[44] In 1984, he hijacked a Kuwaiti airplane to Mashhad in northern Iran hoping to bargain for their release. As the Kuwaitis refused to give up, he organized an attempt on the life of the Kuwaiti Emir in 1985, by a suicide bomber. The ruler was only slightly hurt but the event marked the intensification of suspicion against the Shias, and the launching of a wave of deportations to Iran as well as the purging of sensitive sectors of the administration.

---

43   Carlyle Murphy, "Bombs, Hostages: A Family Link", *The Washington Post*, 24 July 1990.

44   Ranstorp (1987), pp. 91-100; Kostiner (1987), p. 181.

6

EXPORTING THE REVOLUTION

Because they had different conceptions of political action as well as different domestic resources, al-Da'wa and the Shiraziyyin related differently to the Islamic Republic. The Shiraziyyin were tightrope walkers who chose to associate intimately with the apparatus of exportation of the revolution while at the same time struggling to retain their independence. Thanks to its bigger domestic social base in Iraq and in the Gulf, al-Da'wa benefited from more room for manoeuvre towards the Islamic republic. Hence, while it resorted to Iranian support, it cautiously avoided appearing as the Trojan horse of Iranian foreign policy. In the long run however, it was the final winner of the battle it had engaged in with the Shiraziyyin to appropriate the legitimacy of the Islamic revolution and use it domestically.

THE PREDICAMENT OF EXILE POLITICS

A distinctive feature of the Shiraziyyin as compared with al-Da'wa was that the major part of its Iraqi and Gulf leaders relocated to Iran in the aftermath of the revolution. There, they became closely associated with the apparatus of safeguarding and exporting the revolution in various respects. While this gave them unprecedented tools to consolidate their position within the Shia world, this also rendered them highly dependent on the good will of their hosts.

Associating with the State Apparatus

In line with Ruhollah Khomeini's own conceptions, the Shiraziyyin did not see the revolution as an Iranian event but as the first step on the path of a world revolution in which they intended to be a fully-fledged actor. Drawing on this, they considered it was fully legitimate for them to meddle in the affairs of the revolution in Iran itself. Hence, they did not behave like political exiles usually do, avoiding getting too involved with the host society beyond what is strictly necessary for the needs of their domestic political struggle.[1] For the Shiraziyyin, Iran was not only a back base for political activities targeting their respective home countries, it was a country where they had the unique opportunity to put in practice their conception of the ideal Islamic society. The new Iranian leaders shared this point of view and solicited their help. For example, many were employed as vigilantes in the Arab-speaking regions of Khuzistan. In this restive province where autonomist claims re-emerged in the direct aftermath of the revolution, their task was to spread the ideology of the revolution in the vernacular language.[2] Both Iraqis and Gulf activists spent some time in Khuzistan. This was the case for Hasan al-Saffar, for example. Overall, the use of foreign Arab revolutionaries of all persuasions in Khuzistan has been a constant feature of the Islamic republic of Iran to this day.

The Shiraziyyin's high degree of connection with the new Iranian ruling elite was the direct result of the interpersonal links they had established, before the fall of the Shah, with people who became key figures of the Islamic Republic. Furthermore, the trust they enjoyed from some Iranian leaders was a result of, and a reward for the help they had provided in times of hardship. This consisted not only in moral but operational support, in which the Bahraini activists of the IFLB played a role of their own. This was underlined by Murtadha Badr in an interview he gave in March 2006 to a Bahraini daily: "The late Imam al-Shirazi and his followers in the Gulf put all their weight and means at the service of the Islamic revolution. They gave to some of the revolution's leaders money, false passports and plane tickets to leave Iran and meet Imam Khomeini in France. And this is not to mention all the propaganda work we did in the media. The Front [IFLB] sent some of its representatives to Neauphle-le-Château where Imam Khomeini was living and where his communiqués were translated into Arabic and disseminated in the region [Middle East] through the Message Movement in the Gulf. Years before the advent of the revolution, Sh. Hashemi Rafsandjani arrived in Syria with the intention of meeting Imam Khomeini in Iraq. The Message Movement provided him with false documents and drove him to Iraq".[3]

---

1   Stéphane Dufoix, *Politiques d'exil*, Paris: PUF, 2002, pp. 241-3.

2   For more details, see the interview of Ja'far al-'Alawi, *al-Watan* (Bahrain), *The Story of Political Islam in Bahrain*, n° 24.

3   *The Story of Political Islam in Bahrain*, n° 18, *Al-Watan* (Bahrain), 4 March 2006.

More specifically, the Shiraziyyin enjoyed strong ties with figures of the Guardians of the Revolution, better known under their Persian name as the "Pasdaran". This body was created soon after the revolution by the institutionalization of the revolutionary committees that had mobilized the population against the Shah. Independent from the command of the Iranian army, it was a tool in the hands of the religious radicals clustered around Ruhollah Khomeini, who wished to have an armed force of their own they could use against the rival factions contending for power, most notably the leftist movements.[4] Many of those who formulated the Pasdaran project had been trained in the PLO camps in the 1970s together with Iraqi exiles of both al-Da'wa and the Shiraziyyin. This was particularly so of Mohammed Montazeri (d. 1981) and Mehdi Hashemi (d. 1987). The former was the son of Ay. Husein Ali Montazeri (b. 1922), Ruhollah Khomeini's heir apparent until 1989, whose role in the policy of armed exportation of the revolution was a particularly active one. Accounts by Bahraini Shiraziyyin confirm that he was actually the most important interlocutor of the so-called "liberation movements" that established their headquarters in Tehran after the revolution.[5] Mehdi Hashemi was also related to Husein Ali Montazeri by family ties, being the brother of Montazeri's son-in-law. After the revolution he rose as the head of a radical pressure group through which he attempted to circumvent the central government.[6] Several witnesses on visits to Kuwait and Bahrain saw both Mohammed Montazeri and Mehdi Hashemi regularly, where they spent time particularly with the Shiraziyyin as well as frequenting the *diwaniyya* of 'Abbas al-Muhri.

A kind of a Praetorian Guard for the Islamic regime protecting the Islamic Republic from its enemies from within, the Pasdaran quickly became a critical instrument of Iran's foreign policy.[7] This role was formalized in 1981 with the creation of the Office of the Liberation Movements, headed first by Mohammed Montazeri and then by Mehdi Hashemi, after the former died in the bombing of the headquarters of the Islamic Republic Party in Tehran. Its task was to co-ordinate and handle the armed op-

---

4   Shaul Bakhash, *The Reign of the Ayatollahs. Iran and the Islamic Revolution*, London: I. B. Tauris, 1985, p. 63.

5   *The Story of Political Islam in Bahrain* n° 6, *Al-Watan* (Bahrain), 22 December 2005 (interview of 'Abd al-'Adhim al-Muhtadi) and n°s 17 and 18, 26 February and 4 March 2006 (interview with Murtadha Badr).

6   Michael Rubin, *Into the Shadows. Radical Vigilantes in Khatami's Iran*, The Washington Institute for Near East Policy, 2001, pp. 31-4.

7   Kenneth Katzman, *The Warriors of Islam. Iran's Revolutionary Guard*, Boulder, Colorado: Westview Press, 1993, pp. 95-107.

erations of the liberation movements against the "oppressive rulers" of the neighbouring countries.[8] The main targets were Iraq, Bahrain, Saudi Arabia, Lebanon and Afghanistan whose Shia movements were given material support as well as wide coverage in the media. The Pasdaran's most famous success in this respect remains the creation of Hezbollah in Lebanon in 1982.

There has been much speculation about the role of Mohammed Taqi al-Mudarrisi in the Office of the Liberation Movements. Several Western sources mentioned him as having been the head of a body dedicated to the exportation of the revolution that would have been tied to the Office, or even as the head of the office.[9] Mohammed Taqi al-Mudarrisi himself denied any such role when I asked him the question directly in July 2005.[10] Other Iraqi informants from the Islamic Action Organization also think the information from the Western sources is not accurate.[11] Be that as it may, and while the exact details of the story have yet to be ascertained, it nonetheless appears that the Shiraziyyin were, so to speak, the subcontractors of the export of the revolution to the Gulf, more particularly in Bahrain and Saudi Arabia.

According to Ahmed al-Katib, the Shiraziyyin had since the beginning been determined to impose their agenda on the Iranian leadership, that is to push them to support their armed struggle against Saddam Husein.[12] Hence the accusation often formulated by their rivals that they caused the war between Iran and Iraq. Indeed, in the first stage of the revolution, the Iranian government intended to have normal diplomatic relations with Iraq and with its Gulf neighbours overall. The government was then led by Mehdi Bazargan, who pursued a policy of rapid transition from the revolutionary to the post-revolutionary stage.[13] For the Iranian leadership at

---

8   Marschall, (2003), p. 30.

9   Martin Kramer, "The Structure of Shiite Terrorism", quoted by Marvin Zonis and Daniel Brumberg, *Khomeini, the Islamic Republic of Iran and the Arab World*, Cambridge, Massachusetts: Center for Middle Eastern Studies, Harvard University, 1987, p. 34. A version of this paper appeared in Anat Kurz (ed.), *Contemporary Trends in World Terrorism*, New York: Praeger, 1987, but it does not provide this information; Michael Dunn, "When the Imam Comes: Iran Exports its Revolution", *Defense and Foreign Affairs*, vol. 15, July/August 1987, p. 46.

10   Personal interview, Iran, July 2005.

11   Personal interviews with Ja'far Mohammed, Syria, February 2005 and Ahmed al-Katib, London, July 2007.

12   Personal interview with Ahmed al-Katib, London, July 2007.

13   On the Bazargan period, *cf.* Bakhash (1985), pp. 52-70.

that time, Saddam Husein was considered less as a persecutor of the Shias in his country than as someone who had offered Ruhollah Khomeini asylum and had somehow supported his struggle against the Shah. The Iraqi opposition did not see things in this light of course. This was particularly so of the Shiraziyyin who were then the most active. Al-Da'wa cadres left Iraq massively only after the execution of Mohammed Baqer al-Sadr in April 1980. Because they had in some ways been supported by the Shah's regime at one stage, they also took time to decide what attitude to adopt vis-à-vis the new Islamic regime and when they decided unambiguously to embrace the cause of the revolution, they got close to different Iranian centres of power than the Shiraziyyin (cf. below). In the first year of the revolution, the Shiraziyyin were therefore the dominant force of the Iraqi Islamic opposition in Iran. In order to push Iran to support their project of overthrowing the Ba'th, they launched an active propaganda campaign in Iran, organizing anti-Saddam Husein demonstrations and distributing leaflets. Only one month after the revolution, they succeeded in establishing a radio in Abadan, a port town of Khuzistan close to the Iraqi frontier. The radio broadcast propaganda programmes in Arabic stigmatizing the Iraqi regime.[14] Soon, it also began to broadcast anti-Bahraini and anti-Saudi programmes. The Iranian central government was opposed to the project but could not prevent it. The Shiraziyyin had gained the support of chief figures of the Pasdaran who provided them with the means to operate it. They also gave them arms to organize attacks inside the Iraqi territory. It was only after the beginning of the Iran-Iraq war in September 1980, started by Iraq, that the Iranian central government began officially to support the Shiraziyyin and their Iranian allies in their project of escalation against Iraq and the Gulf regimes. The government had then passed into the control of the radical factions, following the attack against the American embassy in Tehran in November 1979 that had provoked the resignation of Mehdi Bazargan. The creation of the Office of the Liberation Movements in 1981 was the direct result of this. The first of a series of annual Conferences of the Liberation Movements gathering the cadres of revolutionary movements worldwide was organized in Tehran the following year.[15] The Shiraziyyin played a central organizational role in this.

Because they had a privileged point of access in the Arab countries, the Shiraziyyin were also occasionally involved in other realms of the Islamic Republic's early foreign policy in the Arab world. The Islamic Front for the

---

14   Ahmed al-Katib, our informant, was the manager of the programmes.

15   Robin Wright, *Sacred Rage. The Wrath of Militant Islam*, New York: Simon and Schuster, 1985, pp. 26-30.

Liberation of Bahrain, for example, forged good relations with some PLO cadres during the liberation movements' conferences. Its cadres helped the PLO to open their embassy in Tehran.[16] In turn, Yasir 'Arafat tried to intercede personally with the Bahraini Emir 'Isa bin Salman Al-Khalifa to release the IFLB activists imprisoned after the expulsion of Hadi al-Mudarrisi.[17] After the beginning of the Iran-Iraq war in September 1980, when the PLO publicly declared that it would adopt a neutral stance between the two belligerents, Murtadha Badr attempted to mediate between the Islamic Republic and the PLO: "Sh. Mohammed Montazeri called me and asked me to call Yasir 'Arafat to explain to him that his stance had irritated the leaders of the Iranian revolution and that he should reconsider it".[18]

Their close association with the Iranian regime offered many advantages to the Shiraziyyin. It provided them with a new legitimacy in the eyes of their detractors. They had been unable to impose themselves with the Najafi *marja'iyya*, but they had been recognized by Ruhollah Khomeini. They were also provided with material means to achieve their political goals: offices in Tehran, administrative facilities, arms to carry out their operations in Iraq and the Gulf. For a network whose domestic social bases were often rather limited, the Islamic revolution was a unique opportunity to have access to external resources to provoke the change they probably would have been unable to induce by themselves. For the Iraqi leaders of the IAO, the relocation of the bulk of the cadres to Iran had also the advantage of favouring the implementation of Mohammed Taqi al-Mudarrisi's project to create a genuine transnational political party organized around an integrated command structure placed under his supervision. The de-territorialization of the Gulf activists increased their dependence on their Iraqi leadership, who were the brokers of their relations with the Iranian regime. Cut off from their domestic base, the Gulf activists were indeed less in a position to act as independent national movements than if they had been able to

16   Murtadha Badr, *The Story of Political Islam in Bahrain*, n° 18, *Al-Watan* (Bahrain) 4 March 2006.

17   Personal interview, Bahrain, February 2006. One can surmise this move was not so much because of the personal relationship between activists of the IFLB and the PLO as a part of the effort by the PLO to convince the Gulf rulers that they had nothing to fear from the Islamic revolution, in order to create a wide anti-Israeli front. *Cf.* Chris P. Ioannides, "The PLO and the Islamic Revolution in Iran", Augustus Richard Norton and Martin H. Greenberg (eds), *The International Relations of the Palestine Liberation Organization*, Carbondale and Edwardsville: Southern Illinois University Press, 1989, p. 81.

18   *The Story of Political Islam in Bahrain*, n° 17, *Al-Watan* (Bahrain), 26 February 2006.

remain on their domestic territories and organize wide grassroots support there.

In the Midst of Iranian Factional Politics

But the high dependence on Iran was double-edged for the Shiraziyyin since it was also a threat to their autonomy. They were actually taking the risk of becoming a nationally controlled transnational network whose agenda would be constrained by the way the Iranian government defined its own priorities. This was all the more so since, like any exiled political organization,[19] the Shiraziyyin were in a fundamentally unequal relationship with the Iranian state. Moreover, Iran did not back the liberation movements simply out of ideological commitment. It pursued an agenda of its own, which fluctuated according to the unstable balance between its various power centres. These had different definitions of what exactly "exporting the revolution" meant. Would the revolution spread by the sole virtue of its exemplarity with merely the help of traditional propaganda means? Or was it necessary to provide operational facilities to the "liberation movements"? The "Islamic left", named as such because of its resemblance with other Third Worldist revolutionary currents, was clearly committed to the second option.[20] As mentioned previously, Husein Ali Montazeri was considered as the patron of the Islamic left's views. This faction also included a personality like S. Ali Akbar Mohtashami who, while he was ambassador to Syria in 1982-1983, played a critical role in creating the Hezbollah. Another important figure of the left faction was Mohammed Musavi Khoiniha, who had led the occupation of the American embassy in Tehran in 1979 and was then appointed Prosecutor General. One should add that at least one of Ruhollah Khomeini's sons, Ahmed, supported the Islamic left.[21] The "right" faction was more in favour of the construction of a strong central state power. For reasons of religious orthodoxy as well as economic pragmatism, it was attached to private property. On matters of foreign policy, the rightists advocated a pragmatic approach in which the armed export of the revolution found no place. They believed rather that Iran should try to export its model by being successful as a state,

---

19   Schain, (2005), p. 118.

20   Mehdi Moslem, *Factional Politics in Post-Khomeini Iran*, New York: Syracuse University Press, 2002, p. 48.

21   Said Amir Arjomand, "A Victory for the Pragmatists: The Islamic Fundamentalist Reaction in Iran", in James Piscatori (ed.), *Islamic Fundamentalisms and the Gulf Crisis*, The American Academy of Arts and Sciences, 1991, p. 55.

not by interfering in other states' internal affairs.[22] They envisaged foreign policy in a rather traditional way. They did not aim to destroy the inter-state system to establish an inclusive Islamic state but wished to make Iran a powerful actor within the system as it was. In other words, they favoured the international perspective over the transnational one. The right faction included powerful figures from the Qom religious seminaries, among others Sh. Ali-Akbar Hashemi-Rafsandjani (b. 1935) and S. Ali Khamene'i (b. 1939). Initially Speaker of the Parliament, the former was elected President of the Islamic Republic after Ruhollah Khomeini's death in 1989. The latter was elected President of the Islamic Republic in 1981 and succeeded Ruhollah Khomeini as the Supreme Guide.

The conflict between the two factions over the definition of Iran's foreign policy arose mainly because of Iran's growing isolation in the international community. Iran was caught in a war with Iraq it was unable to win and in which all its Gulf neighbours had sided with its enemy. It had broken diplomatic relations with the United States and had also to face the Soviet presence at its Afghan borders. In brief, Iran's aggressive foreign policy had led nowhere but to the weakening of the country's international position. This at least was what the conservatives thought. They reached the conclusion that Iran needed to adopt a more compromising stance, in particular towards its Gulf neighbours. The latter had interpreted the failed coup of December 1981 in Bahrain as an attack against all the Gulf monarchies. United since May 1981 in a defence pact named the Gulf Cooperation Council (GCC), they had collectively supported Iraq, which Saudi Arabia and Kuwait had provided with extensive financial aid, during the war. Moreover, the GCC countries had become the fulcrum of American security strategy in the Gulf. In brief, the attempt by the Shiraziyyin at exporting the revolution to Bahrain and Saudi Arabia had proved totally counter-productive seen from the point of view of Iran's interest as a state. As one Iranian diplomat with keen knowledge of Eastern Arabia once put it: "I always tell my Bahraini friends to be realistic: what is Iran's interest in supporting some 300,000 Shias in a small island?"[23] For the Iranian pragmatists, being reconciled with its Gulf neighbours was a strategic imperative, "the other face of [its] policy of Iraqi containment".[24] Those who

---

22 Except of course in Lebanon and Iraq.

23 Personal interview, December 2006.

24 R. K. Ramazani, "Iran's Foreign Policy: Both North and South", *The Middle East Journal*, vol. 46, n° 3, summer 1992, p. 399.

basically shared this view finally came to have the upper hand in Iran in the mid-1980s.[25]

In 1986, the Iran-Contra affair offered the golden opportunity they were waiting for to weaken the hardliners. Mehdi Hashemi, the head of the Office of the Liberation Movements, had leaked to the Lebanese newspaper *al-Shira'* (the Sail) the information that the United States had agreed to sell arms to Iran in exchange for the liberation of its hostages detained by Hezbollah in Lebanon. According to Fouad Ibrahim, the decision to leak the deal to the Lebanese media was taken during a meeting between Mehdi Hashemi and a leader of the Islamic Action Organization, whose name he does not mention.[26] The latter undertook the trip to Lebanon and provided *al-Shira'* with the whole story. In the article, Mehdi Hashemi was interviewed saying essentially that he refused to see the state's logic prevail over that of the revolution. Responding to Ali-Akbar Hashemi-Rafsandjani, who had clearly expressed the wish to disband the Office of the Liberation Movements, he explained blatantly: "this office is under my patronage. Its philosophy is different from yours. You are a state with relations that you must preserve. The Office is a revolution and it has relations of its own it must preserve".[27] By making the arms deal with the "Great Satan" public, Mehdi Hashemi hoped to discomfit Ali-Akbar Hashemi-Rafsandjani, then the Parliament's speaker and the main negotiator of the deal. This proved a miscalculation. Ali-Akbar Hashemi-Rafsandjani and his entourage remained untouched and got the full public support of Ruhollah Khomeini who, on the other hand, denounced Mehdi Hashemi's attitude as driven by "selfish ambitions" and as jeopardizing the unity of the Islamic Republic. He was arrested, forced to confess publicly to being a "deviant and plotter" and finally executed in September 1987.[28] This *de facto* ended the activities of the Office. The final stage of the fall of the proponents of the violent exportation of the revolution occurred in March 1989 with the dismissal of Husein Ali Montazeri from his status of heir apparent of Ruhollah Khomeini. A few months later in June, the death of Ruhollah Khomeini paved the way for the overall dominance of the pragmatic conservatives, with the

---

25   There have been many articles on the shift in Iranian foreign policy at this period. Christin Marschall (2003) offers a good overview of them and adds the results of her own investigations. See pp. 76-98.

26   Ibrahim (2006), p. 145.

27   Quoted by David Menashri, *Iran. A Decade of War and Revolution*, New York: Holmes & Meier, 1990, p. 379.

28   *Ibid.*, pp. 381-2.

advent of the Rafsandjani-Khamene'i tandem to the most powerful official positions of respectively President of the Republic and Supreme Guide.

The reorientation of Iran's foreign policy naturally constituted a severe set-back for the Shiraziyyin. The fact that they had consciously tied their political fate to the success of the exportation of the revolution through Iranian operational support had made them particularly vulnerable to the change in Iran's priorities. Initially a useful tool of Iran's foreign policy, they had now become a burdensome presence. Deprived of Iranian support, and cut off from the few remnants of their base in Karbala, the Iraqi wing quickly lost influence among the Iraqi opposition. Together with their estrangement from the Najafi *marja'iyya*, this largely explains why they have little influence in post-Saddam Husein Iraq, although they seem to have retained a good network of relations in Karbala. The predicament was no less difficult for the Gulf wings of the Shiraziyyin.

Because they had tended to put all their eggs in one basket and counted on Iranian help to overthrow the Al-Khalifa regime by military means, the Bahrainis suffered the most. As explained by Murtadha Badr, "Sh. Rafsandjani was a pragmatic man. First, he tried intelligently to improve Iran's relations with the neighbouring countries and the international community. The Gulf countries, and Bahrain in particular, stated as a condition the closure of the Front's office and the end of its activities. And this is exactly what happened."[29] The activists' personal facilities – houses, cars, etc. – provided by the Iranian regime were confiscated. Some activists were even arrested and imprisoned for a while. Many had to leave the country precipitately to Syria, Denmark, Sweden, Spain, any place where the right of asylum was generous. For the IFLB, the predicament was all the more difficult to overcome since they had had difficulties in retaining roots at home with, according to Mohammed al-'Alawi, no more than three hundred unorganized sympathizers left who proved unable to maintain their influence in the face of al-Da'wa's activists.[30]

The Conflict over Religious Authority

Another element contributed to the rupture between the Shiraziyyin and the Iranian regime: the challenge mounted to Ruhollah Khomeini's religious authority by Mohammed al-Shirazi. In the words of one of his Iraqi

---

29   *The Story of Political Islam in Bahrain*, n° 18, *al-Watan* (Bahrain), 4 March 2006.

30   Personal interview, Bahrain, December 2006.

followers: "Imam al-Shirazi has been fought by two states: Iraq and Iran".[31] Beyond the history of particular individuals, this conflict reveals how much the logic of the Islamic Republic, once it entered the post-revolutionary phase and began to act as a state moved by national interest and *raison d'Etat*, had difficulties adjusting to the intrinsic logic of the transnational networks of the *marja'iyya*. Iran pretended to embody the supreme Islamic religious authority worldwide and submit all religious scholars to the authority of its Supreme Guide. For their part, the bulk of the clerics strove to remain independent of any state and, as they succeeded in circumventing the Ba'thist regime in Iraq, also strove to keep out of the Islamic Republic's endeavour at absorbing them.

A recurring theme of the Shirazi discourse is that the Islamic Republic is indebted to them. They like to stress that at a time when most of the *mujtahid* of Najaf ignored Ruhollah Khomeini's struggle against the Shah, Mohammed al-Shirazi was issuing regular communiqués supporting him. When Ruhollah Khomeini established himself in Najaf in 1964, Mohammed al-Shirazi was the only one to organize a welcome ceremony for him. When Ruhollah Khomeini was asked to leave Iraq in 1978, Mohammed al-Shirazi tried to organize his stay in Kuwait. As we have seen, this is not to mention the operational aid the al-Mudarrisi brothers provided to the Iranian religious opposition. In his biography of Mohammed al-Shirazi, Ahmed al-Katib underlined the fact that Ruhollah Khomeini effectively felt indebted to Mohammed al-Shirazi. This was to the extent that after Mohammed al-Shirazi established in Qom six months after the revolution, he asked for a personal meeting with Ruhollah Khomeini to congratulate him for his great victory over the Shah, but "Khomeini refused because he wanted to pay him a visit first in his house. It was a way to welcome him to Qom and to respond to Mohammed al-Shirazi's support during the time of the Khordad uprising in 1963[32] and his warm reception in Karbala later on".[33]

The Shiraziyyin's insistence on their support for Ruhollah Khomeini before the revolution is not only a way to stress their proximity to the leader of the revolution and benefit from his legitimacy. It is also a way to

---

31   Personal interview, Iran, July 2005.

32   "Qiyam-e Khordad", the "June 1963 Uprising", when the 'Ashura processions turned into violent demonstrations against the Shah, pushing Khomeini to voice for the first time open criticism against the Iranian regime.

33   Ahmed al-Katib, *The Shia Marja'iyya and the Prospects for its Development. Imam Mohammed al-Shirazi as an Example* (in Arabic), Beirut: Arab Scientific Publishers, 2002, p. 127. Available in electronic version on Ahmed al-Katib's web site at www.alkatib.co.uk/shf.htm.

underline their ideological as well as material independence from Iran by presenting Mohammed al-Shirazi as a precursor of Ruhollah Khomeini. His followers stress that he formulated his theory on Islamic government long before Ruhollah Khomeini and began struggling against impious regimes long before Ruhollah Khomeini rose against the Shah. In brief, the Shiraziyyin, while making their ideological and political proximity with Ruhollah Khomeini a source of legitimacy simultaneously have striven to enhance their autonomy towards him. Moreover, a recurring theme of their discourse is the distinction they draw between supporting the Islamic revolution as a process meant to be global and pledging allegiance to Iran as a particular embodiment of this global process. For them, the revolution in Iran was a means towards something else and not an end in itself. This way of envisaging things corresponded to the official rhetoric of the Iranian leaders but, since the Shiraziyyin were not part of the Iranian leadership they did not have to care about the concrete modalities of government and were hence more prone to remain committed to universal principles that were soon dropped by the mainstream of the Iranian leaders.

Less interested in pan-Muslim revolution than his nephews, Mohammed al-Shirazi was however deeply committed to the worldwide diffusion of Islam and, more prosaically, to the increase of his own audience as a *marja'*. Only a few months after he established in Qom, he began to express reserves on some principles of Islamic government endorsed by Ruhollah Khomeini. While agreeing on the concept of clerical government, he was hostile to the idea of rule by a single *marja'*. Rather, he remained faithful to the traditional idea of a collective leadership of the *marja'* and his vision of clerical political rule was that of a college of *marja'*. It is at this period that he specified his idea of the government of the jurisprudent and renamed it the "*shurat al-fuqaha*" (the council of the jurists) or "*shurat al-maraji'*" (the council of the *marja'*). According to him, collective political leadership of the most learned of the *mujtahid* was the best means to prevent the alteration of the Islamic state into a dictatorship.

It was the practical consequence of Mohammed al-Shirazi's conceptions more than the doctrinal divergence as such that led to the conflict with Ruhollah Khomeini. In line with his commitment to the pluralistic and non-hierarchical character of the *marja'iyya*, Mohammed al-Shirazi intended to treat Ruhollah Khomeini as his peer: "despite the establishment of the Islamic Republic, al-Shirazi did not recognize the power of any *faqih* over another one or over the emulators of the other *fuqaha* [...]. [He] refused the rule of a *faqih* over the others, even inside one single country".[34] The

---

34   *Ibid.*, p. 103.

fact that Mohammed al-Shirazi considered himself as Ruhollah Khomeini's peer motivated his refusal to integrate into the Iranian state apparatus in a position that would *de facto* put him as the hierarchical inferior of Ruhollah Khomeini. According to Ahmed al-Katib, the latter indeed offered Mohammed al-Shirazi the position of prayer leader of the main mosque of Ahvaz, the capital of Khuzistan.[35] Mohammed al-Shirazi refused and rather chose to work to establish his position in the Qom *hawza* and from there in the Shia world overall.[36] With the expulsion of thousands of residents of Karbala of Persian stock to Iran, he had at his disposal a natural constituency to support his claim to religious authority. The patronage relations established at the time the al-Shirazi were in Karbala were reinforced by the situation of exile. Indeed, Mohammed al-Shirazi provided many services to the refugees who had, for the most part, come deprived of any means to survive in Iran. Mohammed al-Shirazi could provide education to those unable to integrate into the Iranian schooling system. He provided a work with a decent salary for others, occasional help at times of material hardship. At the symbolic level, he kept the Karbala identity vivid and contributed to maintaining a strong sense of community among the Karbala refugees. He soon appeared as the symbol of this identity. In order to mobilize his constituency, he established a network of *huseiniyya* in almost all the main cities of Iran. The *huseiniyya* were all named the *huseiniyya karbala'iyya*, literally the "Karbala *huseiniyya* ". In 1984, it is by using this network that he gathered a demonstration against Saddam Husein of some 10,000 people in Tehran, a true show of force. At the time of writing, his house in Qom was lying at the heart of a quarter mainly inhabited by Karbala people.

Of course, Mohammed al-Shirazi's attitude represented a clear challenge to Ruhollah Khomeini's monopoly over religious authority. As emphasized by Olivier Roy indeed, the Islamic Republic, far from having consecrated the traditional religious institution, undermined its foundations by systematically pushing aside all those whose religious standard and popular constituency could rival Ruhollah Khomeini's.[37] The plurality of the *marja'iyya* appeared as a threat to the process of Islamic state-building which necessitated a centralized management of religious affairs. So was the *marja'iyya*'s financial independence. Mohammed al-Shirazi soon became one of the many victims, like Mohammed Shariat-Madari and Husein Ali Montazeri among others, of the obliteration of the peripheral centres of religious

35   *Ibid.*, p. 127.

36   *Ibid.*

37   Olivier Roy, "The Crisis of Religious Legitimacy in Iran", *The Middle East Journal*, vol. 53, n° 2, spring 1999, p. 209.

powers. His estrangement from the Najafi *marja'iyya* further facilitated the things, since few among the established *mujtahid* in Najaf proved ready to take up his defence and activate their networks in Qom to alleviate somehow the pressure that was put on him.

According to most accounts, Mohammed al-Shirazi's position began to deteriorate noticeably in 1982, when he began to voice open criticism about the running of the war with Iraq. At the beginning of the war, Mohammed al-Shirazi was among those who thought that, in the face of the inability of the Iraqi people to rise up against Saddam Husein, the war was the best and quickest way to establish an Islamic state in Iraq. But as the war lasted with no clear winner emerging, he reached the conclusion that Iran was actually unable to win and began to revise his opinion, seeing the war as a major obstacle to an Islamic revolution in Iraq since it gave Iraqis the wrong image of Iran as an expansionist state.[38] This was particularly so in mid-1982 after the Iranian army succeeded in ousting the Iraqi army from Iranian land and in turn penetrated Iraqi territory. Like many others, Mohammed al-Shirazi felt that Iran, which had until then fought a defensive war against Iraq, was becoming the aggressor. Convinced that Iran could do nothing more than to needlessly prolong the battle, he thought best to stop it. This would not only spare many Muslim lives but would moreover put an end to the uncomfortable situation of the Iraqi Islamic opposition which, in the eyes of the Iraqis, had now become allied with a state aiming at occupying their country. As a matter of fact, few if any Iraqi soldiers went over to the Iranian camp and Shia solidarity did not operate as the motor for a genuine revolution in Iraq.

Mohammed al-Shirazi's position on the war was a major factor that contributed to his estrangement from the Iranian rulers. According to Ahmed al-Katib, the latter had initially considered him to lead the united front of the Iraqi opposition they were wishing to build. They finally changed their mind and chose instead S. Mohammed Baqer al-Hakim, a son of the late Muhsin al-Hakim who became head of the Supreme Assembly for the Islamic Revolution in Iraq (SAIRI), created in 1982.[39] From his house in Qom, Mohammed al-Shirazi continued to give lectures as well as to voice criticism over the deviation of the Islamic Republic from Islamic values, which was leading it more and more to resemble a dictatorship. He more particularly disapproved of the summary executions of so-called "anti-revolutionaries" as well as the massive confiscation of private properties. It is also at this period that he began to develop with particular insistence

---

38   Al-Katib, p. 135.

39   *Ibid.*

the concept of "non-violence" (*la 'unf*) which, with the *shurat al-fuqaha*, became the second cornerstone of his political thought. Drawing on the example of Gandhi, he considered it possible to achieve a genuine political revolution without firing one bullet. This again constituted an indirect critique of the Islamic revolution.

Mohammed al-Shirazi's dissociation with the Iranian regime led logically to tensions with his nephews Mohammed Taqi and Hadi al-Mudarrisi. Iraqi activists of the Islamic Action Organization accounted that while Mohammed Taqi al-Mudarrisi announced his *marja'iyya* publicly in the late 1990s, he had behaved as a *marja'* ever since the movement's relocation to Iran. This means that he did not take his orders from his uncle, who was anyway based in Qom while he was himself operating from Tehran. When Mohammed al-Shirazi reiterated his attachment to the principle of collegial rule by the *marja'*, Mohammed Taqi al-Mudarrisi remained faithful to the doctrine of *wilayat al-faqih* as formulated by Ruhollah Khomeini. It goes without saying that the armed option taken by the Islamic Action Organization, and in particular the suicide attacks it perpetrated against some leaders of the Iraqi regime, meant that they actually disregarded the authority of Mohammed al-Shirazi. Relations, however, were never broken, not least because they were based on strong and old family alliances. Moreover, after the al-Mudarrisi brothers' disgrace in the mid-1980s, the strain somehow ended. Nonetheless, the different al-Mudarrisi and al-Shirazi options towards the Iranian regime led to the appearance of two distinct although related currents. In many respects, the two currents corresponded to a split between the religious and the political domains of activity of the Shirazi group. Disappointed by the experience of the Islamic revolution, Mohammed al-Shirazi concentrated on his career as a *marja'* and his discourse underwent de-politicization. As for Mohammed Taqi and Hadi al-Mudarrisi, they went on with a political agenda of their own that increasingly came exclusively to concern Iraq and more marginally the Gulf monarchies. Both announced their *marja'iyya* in the 1990s, which permitted them to gain further autonomy since they were now religiously self-sufficient and needed no longer to refer to an external *marja'iyya* to legitimate their political choices. Despite this split however, it is still justified to speak about the Shiraziyyin as a single network. First, when I met them in 2005, Mohammed Taqi and Hadi al-Mudarrisi unambiguously claimed to be part of what they called the "Shirazi school" (*al-madrasa al-Shiraziyya*) so that Mohammed al-Shirazi is indisputably recognized as the eponym of a school of thought that remains united beyond the divergence of interpretation by particular individuals. As we shall see, a major factor that contributed to this was the political weakness of the al-Mudarrisi brothers who never recovered from the elimination of their Iranian supporters and became marginal political actors. In this context, they never had actually the means to found an autonomous network. Mohammed al-Shirazi, on the contrary, clearly succeeded in overcoming the crisis with the Islamic Republic and in benefiting from the globalization process to enhance his religious audience worldwide (*cf.* chapter 8). Second, as a direct consequence, the institutions emanating from either Mohammed al-Shirazi or his nephews are interconnected poles of the same constellation. Individuals circulate indifferently within the transnational web they constitute.

A third argument militating in favour of treating the Mohammed al-Shirazi and the al-Mudarrisi brothers as part of a single network is that they have been seen as such by the others. Indeed while, contrary to their uncle, the al-Mudarrisi brothers succeeded in maintaining rather good relations with the Iranian regime, they were marginalized as early as 1982 in the reorganization of the Iraqi opposition undertaken by the Iranian rulers. Hence, Mohammed Taqi al-Mudarrisi was integrated into SAIRI but not in the leadership position, which would have been congruent with his active role in the exportation of the revolution. Moreover, he was the only member of the IAO, which implied that the organization was given a single vote among fifteen representatives while, for example, al-Da'wa had five votes.[40] Clearly, as early as 1982, the Iranian authorities had chosen to favour other figures than the al-Mudarrisi brothers in their Iraqi policy. They had probably realized that the IAO base was too limited so that it was best to bet on more powerful opposition groups. But although al-Da'wa was better represented, nevertheless it did not have a voice equal to its political weight inside Iraq. The marginalization of both the IAO and al-Da'wa was further confirmed in the reshuffle of SAIRI's governing body in 1986. To protest, Mohammed Taqi al-Mudarrisi withdrew and asked his deputy Muhsin al-Huseini to replace him. While the 1986 reshuffle can be read as a reflection of the pragmatic turn of Iran's foreign policy, the fact that Mohammed Taqi al-Mudarrisi was not chosen as SAIRI's leader from its inception probably reflected the will of the Iranian rulers to favour lesser autonomous and therefore more controllable figures. Mohammed Baqer al-Hakim, the head of SAIRI, rose to prominence not because he possessed a genuine basis in Iraq but because of Iranian patronage. The relative marginalization of al-Da'wa only confirmed this, as the party always showed its willingness to retain an autonomous capacity of decision.

---

40   Abdul-Jabar (2003), p. 239.

The second act of the conflict between Mohammed al-Shirazi and the Iranian regime occurred after the death of Ruhollah Khomeini in June 1989, in the context of the Iranian regime's crisis of religious legitimacy and the subsequent intensification of the struggle for the *marja'iyya*. After the dismissal of Husein Ali Montazeri, Ruhollah Khomeini was aware that he could not appoint a successor chosen among the senior *mujtahid* of Qom, who were either openly opposed to the regime or kept aloof from it. In April 1989, he ordered the enactment of a new constitution that offered at least a formal solution to the succession problem. One of the main innovations concerned the qualifications of the Supreme Guide. He still had to be a *mujtahid* but needed not anymore to be a *marja'*. In line with declarations he had made in the previous months, Ruhollah Khomeini considered that the preservation of the Islamic Republic as a regime should prevail over the strict implementation of religious law. This implied that the political aptitudes of the Supreme Guide were more important than his competence in Islamic jurisprudence. This permitted the appointment of Ali Khamene'i as the new Guide. The latter had been the President of the Islamic Republic between 1981 and 1989, and had therefore solid political experience. But he had not even reached the level of *ijtihad* which, according to some, was apparently conferred on him by Ruhollah Khomeini on his death bed.[41]

Yet, the regime proved unwilling to implement one logical consequence of the de-linking between the world of state politics and the world of the *hawza*: the autonomization of the religious institution. In line with what Ruhollah Khomeini had himself unsuccessfully tried to achieve, Ali Khamene'i strove to accentuate the bureaucratization of Qom seminaries by bringing their administration under the authority of the state.[42] By injecting state money into the seminaries and reinforcing their surveillance, he transformed them into a quasi-governmental institution.[43] This attempt of course aroused strong resistance within the *hawza*. While trying to come to terms with the leading *mujtahid* of Qom, he simultaneously intimidated

---

41   Roy P. Mottahedeh, "Shi'ite Political Thought and the Destiny of the Iranian Revolution", in Jamal S. al-Suwaidi (ed.), *Iran and the Gulf. A Search for Stability*, Abu Dhabi: The Emirates Center for Strategic Studies and Research, 1996, p. 75.

42   Wilfried Buchta, *Who Rules Iran? The Structure of Power in the Islamic Republic*, The Washington Institute for Near East Policy and the Konrad Adenauer Stiftung, 2000, p. 94.

43   Mehdi Khalaji, *The Last Marja. Sistani and the End of the Traditional Religious Authority in Shiism*, The Washington Institute for Near East Policy, Policy Focus n° 59, September 2006, p. 31.

the most recalcitrant. He sent vigilante gangs to disturb their lectures, and incarcerated and tortured their relatives. This is what happened to Mohammed al-Shirazi. Cloistered in his house in Qom, he had long retreated from the Iranian political debate. Wilfried Buchta recounts that, in December 1995, Ali Khamene'i, trying to achieve a measure of compromise with Qom's scholars, visited Qom to meet them. Mohammed al-Shirazi was among those who refused to meet him. In retaliation, his two sons Mahdi and Murtadha al-Shirazi were incarcerated and tortured.[44] During the same period in 1996, Murtadha al-Shirazi published a provocative book entitled *Shurat al-Fuqaha* in which he exposed his father's theory of Islamic government. In the context of the debate over Ali Khamene'i's religious authority and legitimacy to rule, the mere theological discussion of the validity of the *wilayat al-faqih* doctrine had become a major way to position oneself politically.[45] The book therefore earned its author another stay in prison, after which he headed for the United States where he undertook medical treatment and founded the Imam Shirazi World Foundation in Washington. From there, he went on with disseminating the thought of his father worldwide. In the meantime, Mohammed al-Shirazi was himself put under house arrest in Qom and saw his activities severely restricted. Several of his close associates were imprisoned for a while, with many choosing to leave Iran either for Western countries or Lebanon and Syria.

The victory of S. Mohammed Khatami in the 1997 presidential elections and the subsequent arrival of the reformists to power entailed a loosening of the pressure on many dissident *'ulama* in Iran. Gradually, the Shiraziyyin resumed their activities rather freely. In 2005 when I visited their offices in Qom, they would avoid open friction with the regime and were content with ignoring it. All the clocks in the house were set at one hour behind the "regime's hour" (sic) which they deemed not "*shar'i*", i.e. not true to Islamic law. In return, they were able to publish books and had even a web site directly run from Qom, which of course implied official authorization. They also had *huseiniyya* in which they would gather freely. However, there remains a point of friction between the Shiraziyyin and the Islamic Republic: the personality cult his followers have built around Mohammed al-Shirazi, which draws on the very same mechanisms as the one organized by the Iranian regime around Ruhollah Khomeini.

While the personality cult was present since the inception of Mohammed al-Shirazi's struggle for the *marja'iyya*, his death in December 2001 marked an escalation in this respect. The Iranian authorities tried to prevent

---

44   *Ibid.*, p. 95.
45   Roy (1999), p. 203.

it at the funeral. Mohammed al-Shirazi had expressed a wish to be buried temporarily in the garden of his house in Qom, waiting for an eventual return to Karbala once the political conditions would allow it. According to the tradition, when a *mujtahid* dies in Qom, the cortège of mourners carries the corpse from his house to the shrine of Fatima and then to the place of burial. Fearing that Mohammed al-Shirazi's house would become a place of worship, the Iranian security forces prevented the corpse from leaving the shrine's walls. They seized it and, as is the tradition for religious scholars in Qom, buried it inside, in the hall of the shrine, next to his brother Hasan whose corpse had been brought to Qom after his assassination in Beirut. The move was intended to mark the unimportance of Mohammed al-Shirazi. Of course, he was buried in a place reserved for distinguished religious figures, but by having his grave overwhelmed with those of many other scholars, the Iranian authorities wanted to bring Mohammed al-Shirazi back to the rank of an ordinary cleric not deserving any particular treatment. Mohammed al-Shirazi's grave is indeed not distinguishable from the others, and one walks on it without noticing. The possibility of organizing mourning sessions on the grave is very limited, even more so since the particular corner where the tomb lies has been restricted to women only since July 2005. In August 2005, a small mourning session over the grave by women from the al-Shirazi family was quelled by the police. According to the family, the women were severely beaten and taken into custody for a few hours.

Nevertheless, the Iranian authorities' deeds did not prevent the personality cult from developing exponentially. The seizure of the corpse only served to reinforce the victimization pattern on which the Shiraziyyin had built their identity since the inception of the movement. The room where Mohammed al-Shirazi used to write and sleep in Qom was transformed into a memorial. Visitors are invited to visit and photograph what resembles a monk's cell. With no window, it contains only a simple mattress lying on the bare ground. Mohammed al-Shirazi's black turban is lying down on a small table. As with Ruhollah Khomeini, the title "Imam" was added to Mohammed al-Shirazi's name, a habit considered sacrilegious by most of the traditional clerics because it implies the tacit identification of the person with the Hidden Imam. It was also in this period that his followers began openly to present Mohammed al-Shirazi as the *mujaddid* of the current Hegirian century (*cf.* chapter 3).

Sayyida Zaynab: The Birth of a New Shia Hub

Following the breach with the Iranian regime, many Shiraziyyin chose to relocate to Syria, in the tiny city of Sayyida Zaynab. This was more particularly true of the political wing of the network, and more particularly of the clerics engaged in the Iraqi and Gulf movements under the leadership of Mohammed Taqi al-Mudarrisi. As for the lay cadres, they most often chose to resettle in Western Europe or the United States. The choice of Sayyida Zaynab was made for pragmatic reasons. First, the Shiraziyyin had an old base in the city thanks to the efforts of Hasan al-Shirazi. After he left Iraq in 1970, Mohammed al-Shirazi's brother resettled between Lebanon and Syria where he created several religious institutions. His main success was the *Hawza* Zaynabiyya in Sayyida Zaynab. At the time he arrived there in the early 1970s, the city was no more than a tiny suburb of Damascus. It hosted the tomb of Zaynab, the sister of Imam Husein, reputed for her courage during the battle of Karbala. Left abandoned and crumbling, the tomb was hardly a place of pilgrimage. In any case, it was not a religious centre, especially since the Syrian population counted among them very few Twelver Shias.[46] However, after the massive expulsion of foreign students of the Najaf seminaries in 1970, many of them had chosen to resettle in Sayyida Zaynab. This was particularly so of the Afghans, who were not ready to return home because their country was then hit by famine and the region of Hazarajat where the Shias are concentrated was regularly a battleground between the Shia Hazaras and Sunni Pashtos.[47] A community of Shia Afghan students and teachers was therefore in the process of formation in Sayyida Zaynab in the early 1970s so there was a population of potential students for a *hawza*.

Moreover, Hasan al-Shirazi had the idea of bringing about a rapprochement between the Twelver Shias and the 'Alawiyyin. The latter, forming around twelve per cent of the Syrian population, constituted a heterodox current of Shiism whose followers were initially clustered in the mountainous regions of northern Syria. When the Ba'th party seized power in the 1960s, and more particularly after the accession of Hafez al-Asad who was himself from the 'Alawi community to power in 1970, the 'Alawiyyin were mobilized in order to form a major pillar of the Syrian regime. Because the 'Alawiyyin were regularly denounced as pagans by the Muslim Brotherhood, who were the main opponents to the Ba'thist regime, Hafez al-Asad had been concerned to prove that they belonged to Islam. In 1973, he

---

46   0.5 per cent according to most estimates.

47   Personal interview with Sh. 'Abbas al-Nuri.

asked Musa al-Sadr, then the leading religious figure of Lebanese Shias, to issue a *fatwa* certifying that the 'Alawiyyin were Shias. Hasan al-Shirazi benefited from this context when he strove to establish contacts within the Syrian ruling circles. Like other Iraqi opponents, he naturally benefited from the antagonism between the two rival Ba'th regimes of Syria and Iraq, which gave Syria an obvious interest in supporting Iraqi opponents in general. The Shiraziyyin have many anecdotes about the way Hafez al-Asad, who allegedly received him several times, was struck by Hasan al-Shirazi's charisma and gave him *carte blanche* to develop Twelver Shia religious activities in Syria. While the rapprochement between the 'Alawiyyin and the Twelvers had only limited success, the Syrian regime's interest in the project helps explain the success of the *Hawza* Zaynabiyya and, overall, the rapid development of Sayyida Zaynab into a Shia learning centre as the pressure on Najaf seminaries increased over the years. Indeed, while Hasan al-Shirazi initiated the move in the mid-1970s, the transformation of Sayyida Zaynab accelerated considerably after the Gulf War and the quelling of the Shia uprising of March 1991, which pushed thousands of Iraqi Shias to resettle in Sayyida Zaynab. During the 1990s, the city therefore witnessed the creation of many other Shia religious schools. They were also staffed by students who considered Qom, which had risen as the main learning centre after the decline of Najaf, as too politicized as well as too much subjected to Iranian control. In the 1990s, undertaking religious education in Qom meant, in some countries, taking the risk of being suspected of serving as an agent of the exportation of the Islamic revolution. The development of Sayyida Zaynab as an alternative *hawza* to both Najaf and Qom did not mean that the Islamic Republic was absent from the local scene. The regime that pretended to lead the Shia world could not be absent. Not only did it open its own *hawza*, which was the biggest one after the *Hawza* Zaynabiyya in terms of numbers of students at the time of writing, but it played a decisive role in the transformation of Sayyida Zaynab into a major place of pilgrimage. It is with Iranian money that the shrine of Zaynab was restored, being, at the time of writing, a splendid place of worship with gold cupolas.[48]

The Shiraziyyin were the first to understand the potential of Sayyida Zaynab. Even before the conflict with the Iranian regime, the Saudis had established a *hawza* there in 1983, which was run jointly with Iraqis. Since

---

48   For further details on the transformation of Sayyida Zaynab, see Sabrina Mervin, "Sayyida Zaynab: banlieue de Damas ou nouvelle ville sainte chiite?" *Cahiers d'études sur la Méditerranée et le monde turco-iranien (CEMOTI)*, n° 22, July-December 1996.

so many Saudis visited Syria during summertime and visited the shrine of Fatima, the country was indeed a useful place to recruit new activists and sympathizers. Mohammed Taqi and Hadi al-Mudarrisi established institutions there at the end of the 1980s and were progressively joined by many Saudis and Bahrainis. Hasan al-Saffar, for example, established his headquarters there until 1993. The place was all the more practical since it was easily accessible from Saudi Arabia. It was in Sayyida Zaynab that Mohammed al-Shirazi created his first web site in 1998, thanks to the skills of one of his young followers trained in computer sciences whom he explicitly sent to Syria with the task of establishing the site. The site gave information on the life and thought of Mohammed al-Shirazi, releasing his communiqués on various matters, making available some of his books and offering a mail box to ask him questions. In other words, even cloistered in his house in Qom, Mohammed al-Shirazi was skilful in resorting to modern means of communication to maintain the link with his followers and make the world know about his situation in Qom.

FROM AL-DAʿWA TO HEZBOLLAH

Like the Shiraziyyin, the Gulf activists of al-Daʿwa felt enthusiastic about the Islamic revolution and did not conceal their admiration for what Ruhollah Khomeini had achieved. They organized ceremonies to celebrate the advent of the new regime, sent supportive messages and delegations to congratulate the Supreme Guide directly. However, they always took care not to be absorbed by the Iranian state apparatus and to retain their autonomy. Yet it was from al-Daʿwa that the so-called "Hezbollah" pro-Iranian network was born. How do we explain this?

An Assortment of Autonomous National Movements

Since their inception, a sharp difference had existed between the way the Shiraziyyin and al-Daʿwa conceived the nature of the transnational tie. Unlike Mohammed Taqi al-Mudarrisi, the Iraqi leaders of al-Daʿwa did not wish to head a transnational political party. They had established networks of interpersonal relations in several Gulf monarchies and had disseminated their ideas, but then did not really care about what local activists would do with them, and more particularly what conclusion they would draw from them in terms of concrete action on the domestic political scenes. What is certain, is that the Iraqi activists of al-Daʿwa did not care about overthrowing the Bahraini Emir, and even less the Kuwaiti one. If they instrumentalized some Kuwaiti activists, it was, as shown previously, with the aim of pressuring the Kuwaiti regime so that it would renounce its support of Iraq in its war against Iran. Beyond the ideological sympathy al-Da'wa felt towards Iran, it wanted Iran to win the war against Iraq because it was the only means to size power after the destruction of virtually all its cells inside Iraq. In other words, al-Da'wa used its transnational connections in order to better serve what remained its first priority: overthrowing Saddam Husein. Transnational ties were a resource for a national political struggle and, consequently, the transnational network was a loose collection of autonomous national movements, a constellation of interconnected poles. The Iraqis did not strive to oversee the actions of the Gulf activists, asking them to conform to any kind of grand worldwide project. Like the Iraqi al-Da'wa, the Gulf al-Da'wa were national parties, each developing its own political strategy in accordance with the distinctive features of its domestic environment. Therefore, contrary to what many Bahrainis and Kuwaitis say, al-Da'wa in Bahrain and Kuwait never, strictly speaking, constituted "branches" of Iraqi al-Da'wa. They were only part of a same intellectual and political current sustained by a web of interpersonal ties.

This initial configuration became accentuated over the years, especially after Iraqi al-Da'wa underwent splits and internal dissensions during the time its leaders were in exile in Iran. These entailed the progressive secularization of the party by the marginalization, and final disappearance, of the clerical element within the effective leadership. The split of 1988 was decisive in this respect. The clerical cadres of the party, gathered in a self-appointed Council of the Clerics (*Majlis Fiqhi*) supposed to guarantee the religious validity of the decisions taken by the elected leadership, strove to take a direct role in the party's decision making. Indeed, while the internal status of the party recognized the role of the Council of the Clerics, the lay cadres of the party were the real decision makers and rarely referred to the clerics. In order to reassert their decision-making role, the clerics called upon the doctrine of *wilayat al-faqih*. Some even contacted Ahmed Khomeini in order to reflect on the best way to link the party organizationally to the office of his father, the Iranian Supreme Guide, in whom the clerics of al-Da'wa recognized the supreme religious authority.[49] This provoked a general outcry among the lay cadres, who were attached to maintaining the autonomy of the party towards Iran and were in favour of a strict internal decision-making process. For them, al-Da'wa was an Iraqi national party in exile, not an Iranian proxy. Finally, the head of the Council of the Clerics, S. Kadhem al-Ha'iri, himself a proponent of the *wilayat al-faqih*, was obliged to retreat and to follow the lay cadres on the

---

49   Ra'uf (2000), p. 225.

idea of an internal source of authority. The clerical cadres were entitled to play a role in their capacity as members of the party and not because they were mandated to do so by Ruhollah Khomeini. However, the crisis led to a quasi split inside Iraqi al-Da'wa, with the Council of the Clerics starting to issue independent communiqués. In 1992, some lay cadres began doing the same, releasing communiqués signed "Cadres of al-Da'wa Party" (*Kawadir Hezb al-Da'wa*).[50] Al-Da'wa was still formally existing but had a *de facto* split leadership between the clerics and the laymen. To counter Iranian hegemonic pretensions, some lay cadres sought to substantiate their position within the party by a religious sanction, and came closer to Mohammed Husein Fadlallah who, in 1995, openly challenged the doctrine of *wilayat al-faqih* and the authority of Ali Khamene'i by announcing his *marja'iyya*.[51] The break up between the clerical and lay cadres of al-Da'wa was completed in 2000 when Mohammed Mahdi al-Asefi, then the official spokesman of al-Da'wa for two decades, quit because the lay cadres refused to include a representative of Ali Khamene'i in the governing body of the party.[52] He was already well known for promoting the *wilayat al-faqih* from the early 1980s, but his decision to quit was a way to take a clear position in this respect for the first time. Since then, he has become very close to the Iranian Supreme Guide. At the time of writing, he was still living mainly in Qom, although coming back regularly to Iraq since the fall of Saddam Husein. There, he is among the leaders of the World Academy of the Family of the Prophet (*Jami'at Al-Bayt al-'Alamiyya*), an Iranian institution aimed at propagating the Shia doctrine worldwide and, more narrowly, to support the *marja'iyya* of Ali Khamene'i. Like 'Ali al-Kurani, Mohammed Mahdi al-Asefi has kept close ties to his ex-pupils in Kuwait and is among the personalities regularly invited to give lectures in the emirate, where he is very popular.

The progressive retreat of the clerical cadres from Iraqi al-Da'wa led to an accentuation of the national trend within the party and therefore to the loosening of the links between the Iraqi and the Gulf activists. Indeed, the clerics were the carriers of the transnational ideology and the links between the Iraqis and the Gulf activists. As individuals, the clerics of the Iraqi party remained in touch with the clerics in the Gulf. They continued to form a network of colleagues sharing the same ideas, in particular on the matter of *wilayat al-faqih*, which most of the clerical leaders of al-Da'wa in Kuwait

50   Abdul-Jabar (2003), pp. 258-9.

51   Jamal Sankari, *Fadlallah. The Making of a Radical Shi'ite Leader*, London: Saqi Books, 2005, p. 256.

52   Ra'uf (2003), pp. 65-6.

and Bahrain embraced after the Islamic revolution. Significantly however, unlike their Iraqi counterparts, the endorsement of the *wilayat al-faqih* did not lead the Kuwaiti and Bahraini clerics to wish to tie their movements organizationally to the Iranian Supreme Guide. The main reason was that the Kuwaiti and Bahraini movements were entirely autonomous from Iran in terms of finances, political leverage and social base. This is why, unlike the Shiraziyyin who came to depend on the operational facilities provided by the Islamic Republic to exist politically on the domestic scene, the leadership of the Kuwaiti and Bahraini al-Daʿwa never relocated to Iran, and the geographic distance no doubt helped to maintain autonomy in the framework of doctrinal sympathy. The Kuwaiti and Bahraini cadres of al-Daʿwa did not have to be exiled to Iran because they represented the Shia political mainstream in their countries, which was entrusted with the old legitimacy of the Najafi institution and, in Bahrain, was embodied by key figures of the local religious establishment. Enjoying a wider social base than the Shiraziyyin, they had the means to achieve significant domestic gains merely by exercising their *de facto* bargaining power with the regime. All the more so since their aims were much less radical than those of the Shiraziyyin. While they endorsed the idea of an Islamic state in principle, they had remained attached to the gradualist conception of action which was that of Iraqi al-Daʿwa before its leaders decided to take short cuts. Extracting concessions from the governments was far enough for them. They fought for more democracy and power sharing rather than for a radical overthrow of the established orders.

This explains why the Gulf al-Daʿwa movements had, since their inception, a different comprehension of the concept of "exportation of the revolution" than the Shiraziyyin, which *in fine* better corresponded with the way the pragmatic wing of the Islamic regime understood it. They were ready to promote the *wilayat al-faqih* and the good image of the Islamic Republic in general. They were also ready to act to defend the legitimacy of Ali Khameneʾi among their constituency and support his claim to be the supreme religious authority worldwide. While this would need further confirmation, it is also very probable that al-Daʿwa was from its inception closer to the pragmatic right than to the leftist faction. Contrary to the Shiraziyyin who were essentially close to the group of Ali Husein Montazeri and the Pasdaran, their connections were first and foremost among the office of the Prime Minister until 1989 when the function was abrogated, and the intelligence services in general. In other words, they were closer to the central state institution while the Shiraziyyin were well connected with the periphery, among the groups which often operated without the central institution's knowledge.

Al-Da'wa was best positioned to act on behalf of Iranian 'soft' power because it remained present at home even during the darkest years of the repression. In Bahrain, al-Da'wa ended its existence as an organized politi-cal group in 1984 when some of its cadres were arrested and its leaders were asked to sign a written engagement to disband the party. Despite the strong pressure put on them by Bahraini authorities, the key figures of al-Da'wa stayed in the country, most notably 'Isa Qasem and 'Abd al-Amir al-Jamri. The latter agreed to officiate as a religious judge (*qadhi*) in the ministry of Justice and Islamic Affairs between 1983 and 1988. True, 'Isa Qasem left for Iran in 1991 but he did it at a time when this no longer constituted an act of provocation for the regime, after the Gulf War had allowed the con-siderable easing of diplomatic relations between Iran and Bahrain (*cf.* chap 7). After his departure from the United Arab Emirates in 1989, 'Abdallah al-Ghurayfi established himself in Syria not because he planned to oppose the Bahraini regime from abroad but because he was offered an important function as the head of the *hawza* of Mohammed Husein Fadlallah. As for 'Abd al-Amir al-Jamri, he stayed in Bahrain all the time, even at the peak of the dark years in 1994-1998 when the Al-Khalifa regime suppressed a spontaneous uprising by the Shia youth.

Those who wished to continue open organized political action did not take a plane to Iran but chose to establish themselves in London, where a handful of lay leaders of al-Da'wa, among whom were Sa'id al-Shihabi and Mansur al-Jamri – one of the sons of 'Abd al-Amir al-Jamri – created the Islamic Bahrain Freedom Movement (IBFM) (*Harakat Ahrar al-Bahrain al-Islamiyya*) in 1982. The choice was strategic. Rather than becoming as-sociated with an isolated regime castigated by almost the entire interna-tional community, including the heavyweights of the Arab world like Saudi Arabia and Egypt, al-Da'wa chose to settle in a place where it could best strive to make its struggle internationally legitimate. In London, the cadres released various publications including, from the mid-1990s, a very active web site in both Arabic and English named "Voice of Bahrain" (*Sawt al-Bahrain*), where to this day they publish regular reports on the abuses per-petrated by the Bahraini government.[53] They set up contacts with Human Rights NGOs like Amnesty International and tried to lobby the United Nations. They also had regular meetings with British deputies whose sym-pathy they tried to catch, hoping they would pressure their government to advise its Bahraini ally to adopt a more compromising stance towards

---

53   www.vob.org

its opposition. In order to better present their case to Westerners, they portrayed their struggle as one for democracy in general, explaining that their main objective was the reinstatement of the disbanded Parliament and not the implementation of Islamic law. They of course avoided using Iranian-like rhetoric, which they reserved for Bahrainis. They even dropped the word "Islamic" in the English translation of their movement's name, which became the Bahrain Freedom Movement in the English version of their web site. They were also past masters in playing with the ambiguity of the Arabic term "*ahrar*" both meaning "independent" and "liberal" in the political sense. Particularly since the recent appearance of a new political category named "islamo-liberals" in the Gulf countries,[54] many of the movement's cadres like to depict themselves as "*ahrar ya'ni liberaliyyin*", that is "*ahrar* in the sense of liberals".

Despite its physical removal from Bahrain, the IBFM succeeded in keeping in constant contact with the opposition at home. This was another of its achievements: contrary to many exiled movements, including the Islamic Front for the Liberation of Bahrain, the Islamic Bahrain Freedom Movement succeeded in continuing to be legitimate in the eyes of opponents who remained at home and in co-ordinating with them.[55] The task was especially difficult because charismatic leaders were among the insiders who had remained in Bahrain. The fact that the IBFM enjoyed a family link to the insiders probably facilitated the maintenance of the political tie. The IBFM's ability to keep roots at home was best manifested in its role during the 1994-1998 *intifada*. The uprising began as a spontaneous popular revolt by the Shia youth in the context of a worsening economic crisis and was in no way the result of a concerted action by the domestic or the exiled opposition. The main figure of the movement soon appeared to be a young cleric, Sh. 'Ali Salman (b. 1965), with no previous activist experience with either al-Da'wa or the Shiraziyyin. Although he had studied in Qom in the early 1990s, he was not a proponent of Ali Khamene'i's *marja'iyya* but an emulator of the quietist Abu al-Qasem al-Khu'i. When he was compelled to leave Bahrain by the authorities in 1995 he did not fly back to Qom but headed London, where he did not engage formally in the IFBM but nonetheless closely associated with its structure. Together, they tried to give a political meaning to the hazy spontaneous upsurge of anger of their

---

54   Stéphane Lacroix, "Between Islamists and Liberals; Saudi Arabia's New "Islamo-Liberal" Reformists", *The Middle East Journal*, vol. 58, n° 3, summer 2004.

55   As shown by Yossi Schain, the capacity to retain roots at home is of major importance for the exiled opposition. *Cf.* Schain (2005), pp. 77-81.

co-religionists, mainly by releasing regular communiqués distributed in Bahrain in which they demanded the reinstatement of the Parliament.

In Kuwait, despite the general suspicion of the Shias that marked the 1980s, the cadres of al-Da'wa also never exiled abroad and were even able to pursue successful political careers. They won three seats in the 1981 elections: that of 'Adnan 'Abd al-Samad, 'Abd al-Muhsin Jamal and Naser Sarkhu. Although the regime used tricky measures to counter their influence, for example through the definition of the constituencies and support to non-oppositionist Shia leaders in the 1985 elections, none of the al-Da'wa leaders was ever arrested and imprisoned. They formed a legal opposition fighting the government not in order to change the established regime radically but to re-establish the balance between the ruling family and the elected assembly. In that, their role hardly differed from that previously played by the old Sunni merchant oligarchy.

What is Hezbollah?

It is from the milieu of al-Da'wa activists that, in the course of the 1990s, emerged what is colloquially designated as the "Hezbollah Line" (khatt Hezbollah) by Shia Islamic activists. "Hezbollah" is initially a Quranic term meaning the "party of God". After the revolution, it became a recurring concept of Ruhollah Khomeini's speeches to designate those truly committed to the defence of Islam and the Islamic revolution. The term was then appropriated by vigilante groups constituting a loose network of volunteers supported by some individual figures of the regime and claiming to act in order to safeguard the revolution against its enemies.[56] While, in Iranian parlance, the word "Hezbollah" designates the hardliners in general, it can also refer to structured pressure groups, often used by the regime to intimidate or even assassinate this or that recalcitrant person.[57] While many self-describe as "Hezbollah", many others often prefer to speak about them as partisans of the "Imam's Line", that is those who keep faithful to the heritage of so-called "Imam Khomeini". This is the case, for example, of those who perpetrated the attack on the American embassy in Tehran in November 1979. Over the years, the label "Imam's Line" has been preferred by the vigilantes because "Hezbollah" came to have a pejorative connotation in an

---

56   Farhad Khosrokhavar and Olivier Roy, *Comment sortir d'une révolution religieuse*, Paris: Seuil, 1999, p. 28.

57   Rubin (2001), pp. 45–87.

Iranian society weary of revolutionary language and favourable to a more relaxed implementation of the Islamic ethic.[58]

Outside Iran, the word "Hezbollah" mainly refers to the famous pro-Iranian Lebanese militia created in 1982 under the direct supervision of a detachment of Pasdaran sent to Lebanon to support the PLO's fight against Israel. A proxy of Iran in the Israeli-Palestinian conflict and therefore a means to enhance Iran's credentias in the Arab world, Hezbollah was also meant to be the main vehicle of Iranian influence among Lebanese Shias. Contrary to the Movement of the Deprived (henceforth Amal) created in 1973 by Musa al-Sadr, Hezbollah was a partisan of the abolition of the sectarian political system it wished to replace by an Islamic Republic. As the fight over the *marja'iyya* deepened after the death of Ruhollah Khomeini, Hezbollah became of course an active promoter of Ali Khamenei's religious leadership. As a matter of fact, the growing prestige of Hezbollah in Lebanon and the Arab world greatly contributed to enhancing Ali Khamene'i's credentials to the point that, at the time of writing, some say he may be the most emulated *marja'* in Lebanon.

Colloquial reference to "Hezbollah" is also widespread in the Gulf countries to designate the pro-Iranian Shia political currents. Unlike Lebanon however, the label "Hezbollah" does not always refer to the existence of organized political formations, so that its usage sometimes comes closer to the Iranian than to the Lebanese one. In the words of Sh. Ibrahim al-Ansari, one of the figures of Hezbollah in Bahrain, "Hezbollah is a concept (*mafhum*) in Bahrain and an organization (*tanzim*) in Kuwait and Saudi Arabia".[59] From a phenomenal point of view, Bahrain is the place in the Gulf where the presence of Hezbollah is the most obvious since the arrival of the new Emir in 1999 and the liberalization of political life. People do not hesitate to raise the yellow flag of the Lebanese Hezbollah during the many demonstrations that punctuate the life of the country. During Muharram days, the streets are covered with portraits of Ruhollah Khomeini and Ali Khamene'i. Yet, informants all agree with Ibrahim al-Ansari that Hezbollah in Bahrain does not refer to a structured political organization but rather to an informal current revolving around individuals. The idea of a structured political group named Bahraini Hezbollah, they often say, is a mere fantasy of the Bahraini government in order to deny the popular legitimacy of the mid-1990s uprising[60] by portraying it as yet another Iranian

---

58   *Ibid.*

59   Personal interview, Iran, July 2005.

60   See the next chapter for more details on the mid-1990s uprising.

attempt to export its revolution to Bahrain. Indeed, in 1996, the Bahraini government claimed it had uncovered a plot by the "Bahraini Hezbollah", which it said was responsible for a series of bomb explosions. A handful of presumed members of this Hezbollah were arrested, and forced to confess publicly. They acknowledged having been trained in Iran by the Pasdaran and in Lebanon by the Lebanese Hezbollah. The foreign press that recounted the event remained as sceptical as Bahrainis themselves about the real existence of the Bahraini Hezbollah.[61]

It remains that the average Shia Islamic activist is often very much able to say who is and who is not from Hezbollah. The names mentioned reveal two main channels of affiliation. First, one finds people who used to be well-known members of al-Da'wa. Among them is for example 'Abd al-Wahhab Husein. He was not among the leadership of the Islamic Enlightenment Society but was socialized politically among al-Da'wa activists in Kuwait. According to some informants, he was particularly close to Mohammed Mahdi al-Asefi. He came back to Bahrain after the Islamic revolution where he became a fierce opponent of the regime, and played a leading role during the mid-1990s uprising. Seen as a radical by the Bahraini authorities, he was the last of the political prisoners released in 2001, after the general amnesty declared by the new Emir Hamad bin 'Isa Al-Khalifa. Considered a hero of the uprising, he became the head of the Islamic Enlightenment Society when it was reopened in 2001.

Another name is also often mentioned by informants as being "from Hezbollah": 'Isa Qasem. 'Isa Qasem's political identity is a matter of debate because he himself never expounded publicly on that matter and, people say, would probably deny any political affiliation as he wants to be a religious leader unrelated to any particular faction. In 1996, during the affair of the alleged Hezbollah plot, the Bahraini authorities designated 'Isa Qasem, in Qom since 1991, as the mastermind behind the plot.[62] While Bahraini Shias denied he was ever involved in any kind of plot, they generally agree that 'Isa Qasem is from Hezbollah because he calls people to emulate Ali Khamenei's *marja'iyya* and allegedly agrees with the doctrine of *wilayat al-faqih*. This folk conviction is reflected in the popular iconog-

---

61   On the 1996 so-called "Hezbollah coup", see Fuller and Francke (2001), p. 135; Kathy Evans, "Bahrainis Implicate Iran in TV 'coup' confession", *The Guardian*, 6 June 1996; John Lancaster, "Bahrain Sentences 15 As Plotters Aided By Iran", *Herald Tribune*, 27 March 1997; Joe Stork, "Bahreïn en lutte pour la démocratie", *Le Monde Diplomatique*, July 1996; David Gardner, "Le pays dont l'explosion risque de déstabiliser le Golfe", *Courrier International*, 25 April 1996 (translated from the *Financial Times*).

62   *The Guardian*, 13 June 1996, Kathy Evans, "Bahrain Plot 'Is Led from Qom'".

raphy one can observe in the streets of the Shia localities. For example, during 'Ashura 2006, a big portrait of 'Isa Qasem was put in parallel with that of Ali Khamenei's in Manama's old Shia quarter. This was a way of signifying the relation of religious allegiance between the two men. Another big poster covering the wall of a house in the same area showed 'Isa Qasem together with Ruhollah Khomeini, Ali Khamene'i, Mohammed Baqer al-Hakim – the head of SAIRI – and Hasan Nasrallah – the general secretary of the Lebanese Hezbollah. He was therefore put in a line of prominent figures belonging to the "Imam's Line". The caption of the poster, a quotation by 'Isa Qasem himself, was eloquent in that respect: "keep the way of Khomeini until the arrival of the Mahdi [i.e. the Hidden Imam]".

A second category of persons mentioned by informants forms what can be called the "generation of the Islamic revolution", that is those who did not live the early period of activity of the Shia Islamic movements and were socialized politically after the Islamic revolution. They are usually younger than the ex-activists of al-Da'wa. At the time of writing, the clerics among them were usually not beyond their early fifties. Either they were too young to be activists of al-Da'wa in the 1970s and 1980s, or they had left Bahrain to undertake religious studies. Most of them were politicized in Iran during their religious education in one of Qom seminaries. This is the case for the above-mentioned Ibrahim al-Ansari. He openly admitted to being "Hezbollah" when I met him, adding, as is often the case, "but we are all from Hezbollah". This is a common way to evade the question of affiliation to Hezbollah, playing on the polysemy of the word by attributing to it the basic meaning of "partisans of God". Born in the mid-1950s in a modest Bahraini family of Iranian descent, Ibrahim al-Ansari left Bahrain in 1974 to undertake religious training in Najaf. There, he attended lessons by Mohammed Baqer al-Sadr but was mainly a student of quietist *mujtahid*, including 'Ali al-Sistani among others. This was the case with most of the foreign students in the 1970s, because they were closely monitored by the Iraqi authorities and because Mohammed Baqer al-Sadr himself was under surveillance. Ibrahim al-Ansari frequented the Iranian exiles around Ruhollah Khomeini, with whom his command of Persian allowed him to communicate easily, more than the Iraqi Shia opposition. In particular, he developed a regular relationship with the entourage of S. Mostafa Khomeini, the other son of Ruhollah Khomeini, who died in Najaf before the revolution. It is this close relationship to the Iranian activists that probably aroused the suspicion of the Iraqi authorities, who jailed him for three months in 1979, and then expelled him. He then reached Qom where he completed his religious studies and also officiated as predicator among the

Arab minority in Khuzistan. After the end of the Iraq-Iran war, he tried to return to Bahrain but was informed that he was *persona non grata* there, which he was still at the time of writing. He was working at the Imam Reza shrine in Mashhad, where he participated in the management of the thousands of Arab pilgrims who come each year to visit the sanctuary.

Another prominent figure of Hezbollah whose profile is revealing is Sh. Husein al-Akraf. Born in 1972 in Diraz, he is the most famous *radud* of Bahrain. A *radud* is an eulogist who chants religious poems about the family of the Prophet during the celebration of the birth and death of each one of them. His role is particularly central in accompanying the 'Ashura processions. His task is to set the verses to melody without transforming them into mere profane music. Husein al-Akraf is not only popular because he has a beautiful voice and an artistic talent to invent new melodies, but also because of his eminent role during the mid-1990s *intifada*. He then led the biggest 'Ashura cortège, that of *Ma'tam* bin Sallum in Manama, which was also the most politicized with the *Ma'tam* al-Qassab of the Shiraziyyin. He not only chanted classical poems but composed new ones in which he connected the drama of Karbala and that of the Bahraini martyrs, Husein's fight against Yazid and the Bahrainis' fight against the Al-Khalifa. For that, he was imprisoned five years in the second half of the 1990s, which only added to his popularity after the general amnesty of 2001. Too young to have been among al-Da'wa activists before 1984, he nonetheless studied with 'Abd al-Amir al-Jamri in Bahrain, before going to Qom between 1991 and 1995 where he joined 'Isa Qasem. During his interview, he was particularly keen to stress that he belonged to the Imam's Line, i.e. believing in the absolute validity of the concept of *wilayat al-faqih* and vowing allegiance to Ali Khamene'i.[63]

The two channels of affiliation are confirmed in the Kuwaiti case where one finds the Hezbollah activists have similar careers. A major difference with Bahrain is that the Hezbollah current in Kuwait does exist as a structured political group, named the Islamic National Alliance (*Al-Tahaluf al-Islami al-Watani*). It was created in 1998 after the breakdown of a front gathering all the Shia currents in Kuwait which had been created in the aftermath of the 1991 Gulf War. Among its leaders one finds old activists of al-Da'wa (i.e. the Social Society for Culture) like 'Adnan 'Abd al-Samad and 'Abd al-Muhsin Jamal. But the general secretary of the group from the outset, Sh. Husein al-Ma'tuk, is from a younger generation. Born in 1969, he was educated in the National Ja'fari School at the time when several of its teachers were Iraqi al-Da'wa exiles. The strong relationship he developed

---

63   Personal interview, Bahrain, November 2002.

with these teachers, most particularly ʿAzz al-Din al-Salim and Sh. ʿAdel al-Khazraji, had a great influence on him so that when the Islamic revolution erupted, he was aware of the importance of the event which he followed cautiously. In 1982, aged only thirteen, he decided to go to Qom to undertake religious education. He stayed there ten years. He came back to Kuwait after the Iraqi invasion and the liberation in 1991. There, he began to teach and write, participating in the opening of a *hawza* in 1996. He also engaged in political activities and, in 1998, became the general secretary of the Islamic National Alliance.

Because al-Daʿwa never really anchored in Saudi Arabia, al-Daʿwa activists have not been involved in the creation of the Saudi Hezbollah. In a country where the Shiraziyyin dominate the field of political Shiism, Hezbollah does not enjoy a wide popular basis. However, the Saudi Hezbollah, as in Kuwait, does have a structured existence, although it is reduced to a small group. Unlike its Kuwaiti counterpart, it is not afraid to name itself "Hezbollah". Its official name is the Hijazi Hezbollah (*Hezbollah al-Hijaz*) and its emblem looks very much like that of the Lebanese Hezbollah: a Kalashnikov raised by a vengeful fist emerges in between a dome and the Kaʿba, evoking Jerusalem's Dome of the Rock, and the Kaʿba of Mecca. The slogan below says unambiguously: "Hezbollah: The Islamic Revolution in the Hijaz". Like the Saudi Shiraziyyin, who claimed their objective was to set free the "Arabian peninsula" although their actual target was the Saudi state, the group refused to refer to any state entity named Saudi Arabia. It chose its name following a recurrent habit of Ruhollah Khomeini himself, who often preferred to refer to the "Hijaz" rather than to "Saudi Arabia". For him, it was a way to point out the illegitimacy of the al-Saʿud family, whom he considered as mere occupiers of the holy land of the Hijaz, where the two holy cities of Mecca and Medina lay. Referring to Saudi Arabia as the Hijaz was therefore also a way to substitute a religious geography for a political one: the whole territory of the Saudi state should be set free because it was an extension of the holy Hijaz. For the Saudi Hezbollah therefore, calling itself "Hijazi Hezbollah" does not indicate a pattern of regional recruitment and even less a regionalist claim. Its leaders are all from Qatif and Hasa. None of them is from the Shia community of Medina.

The birth of the Hijazi Hezbollah has been the object of contradictory accounts, with several dates of creation being put forward.[64] S. Hashem

---

64 The report by International Crisis Group (ICG), whose authors are well informed and did fieldwork in Saudi Arabia, considered it was created in 1987: *The Shiite Question in Saudi Arabia*, Middle East Report n° 45, 19 September 2005, p. 6. An article by Sabah al-Musawi, fragments of which have been re-

al-Shukhus (b. 1957), who is often mentioned as the leader and main founder of the Hijazi Hezbollah, explained to me that his group began its formal existence earlier around 1983 while he was studying in Qom with other Saudi students.[65] It was named the Assembly of the Hijazi 'Ulama (*Tajammu' 'Ulama al-Hijaz*) and published various religious and political material. In the late 1980s, it began releasing a monthly called the *Letter of the Two Holy Mosques* (*Risalat al-Haramayn*). Since its inception, the group was colloquially referred to as the "Qom group" by contrast with the "Tehran group", i.e. the Shiraziyyin gathered in the Organization for the Islamic Revolution in the Arabian Peninsula and whose meeting point was in Tehran. The two groups were clearly unrelated. Hashem al-Shukhus himself was born in a small village of the Hasa oasis where the *intifada* of Muharram 1400 did not spread. He therefore did not participate in this founding event fostered by the Shirazi activists. His father was a religious scholar who had studied in Najaf and had taught his son the basis of religious sciences. In 1972, he left for the religious seminaries of Najaf where he followed some lessons by Mohammed Baqer al-Sadr but, like Ibrahim al-Ansari, did not become an activist of al-Da'wa. However, he already felt a deep admiration for Ruhollah Khomeini so he often assisted at his Friday prayer in Najaf. Hashem al-Shukhus came back to Saudi Arabia after the Islamic revolution and did not wait long before going to Iran where he began to be politically active in the context of the war effort against Iraq, castigating the support his country gave to Saddam Husein.

Understandably, Hashem al-Shukhus denied any implication in the several acts of political violence the Hijazi Hezbollah claimed responsibility for, so that it is still not clear when the Assembly of the Hijazi Scholars mutated into an armed group. What is certain is that one began to hear about the Hijazi Hezbollah at the end of the 1980s when it claimed responsibility for a series of attacks on oil infrastructures as well as the assassination of Saudi diplomats abroad.[66] Fouad Ibrahim mentions that Hezbollah's first armed operation was in retaliation for the death of several hundred Iranian

---

produced on various Arabic web sites, mentioned that the Hijazi Hezbollah was created in 1992. But it does not appear very well informed as it puts the Shirazi groups as stemming from the same origin as Hezbollah. Moreover, it has totally inaccurate information on Kuwaiti Hezbollah. *Cf.* "What is between the Saudi Movement and the Sunnite School" (in Arabic), *Elaph.com*, 8 April 2005 (www.elaph.com).

65   Personal interview, Saudi Arabia, October 2004.

66   Joshua Teitelbaum, "Saudi Arabia's Shi'i Opposition: Background and Analysis", The Washington Institute for Near East Policy, Policy Watch n° 225, 14 November 1996, p. 1.

pilgrims at the hands of the Saudi security forces during the 1987 pilgrimage to Mecca.[67] In 1996, it was suspected of having perpetrated the attack against the American military camp of al-Khobar in the Eastern Province, although there are still doubts about who is really to blame for this operation.[68]

Hezbollah in the Iranian Politics of Influence

The conclusion that can be drawn from the examination of the Hezbollah current in the Gulf is that it is the manifestation of the pragmatic turn of Iranian foreign policy. This is so in two ways. First, Hezbollah is clearly the product of the Iranian government's endeavour to assert its control over the foreign movements that proclaimed their commitment to Ruhollah Khomeini's path. Indeed, the problem of the Shiraziyyin was that they always attempted to retain a measure of independence that rendered them too difficult to manage for a state that had decided to promote its own interests independently of any hazy Islamic cause. The same could be said of al-Da'wa in Iraq. If most of the clerical cadres of al-Da'wa pledged allegiance to Ruhollah Khomeini and the Islamic Republic, the lay cadres for their part showed far more restrain in their engagement with the Iranian state. Creating their own variety of revolutionary organization is a typical means by which host states try to avoid the inevitable strain created by the presence of revolutionary foreign movements on their soil.[69] The creation of the Supreme Assembly for the Islamic Revolution in Iraq (SAIRI) was nothing more than an example of that. While it was initially an umbrella organization, SAIRI quickly became a movement in its own right, which most al-Da'wa and Shirazi activists left. It was the archetype of the pro-Iranian organization. The birth of Hezbollah in the Gulf is part of the same attempt by Iran to control the revolutionary zeal of Gulf Shias so that it does not endanger its diplomatic relations with its neighbours but can also be a useful tool of pressure if needed. But why then, choose to lean on al-Da'wa? As shown above, because they had maintained a strong presence in their home country and were only marginally exiled abroad and in particular to Iran, al-Da'wa groups in the Gulf were even more autonomous towards Iran than their Iraqi counterpart. For that reason, and while their

---

67 Ibrahim (2006), p. 142.

68 Joshua Teitelbaum, *Holier than Thou. Saudi Arabia Islamic Opposition*, Washington Institute for Near East Policy, Washington: 2000, pp. 83-98.

69 John Bowyer Bell, "Contemporary Revolutionary Organizations", in Robert O. Keohane and Joseph S. Nye Jr (eds), *Transnational Relations and World Politics*, Cambridge, Massachusetts: Harvard University Press, 1972, p. 166.

sympathy with the Islamic Republic was not in question, they hardly fitted the definition of easily controllable movements.

We touch here the second aspect of Iran's pragmatic approach to foreign policy. It wanted to have easily mobilizable tools but, maybe more, it wanted to have influence on the main political players in the Shia world. A small structure like the Hijazi Hezbollah was of course useful to convey direct threat to the Saudi regime and let it know that it could be hit at the heart of its sovereign territory. But having good relations with al-Da'wa in Bahrain and Kuwait meant that it was in touch with people having a fair share of influence on the local political scene. In Bahrain, this even meant that, considering the fact that the Shias were the majority, it would be on good terms with those likely to seize power one day. Supporting those likely to rule a country rather than a vanguard elite with a vague project and little popular base is indeed the most sensible attitude for a state supporting opposition movements.[70] Another reason why Iran chose to support al-Da'wa was that it was useful to reinforce the contested legitimacy of the Supreme Guide Ali Khamene'i inside Iran. As once explained by a proponent of the Imam's Line in the Gulf: "Hezbollah does not follow the Islamic Republic, it follows the *wali al-faqih*. It does not follow the President, it follows the Supreme Guide."[71] As a matter of fact, in Bahrain during 'Ashura, Hezbollah's followers cover the old quarter of Manama with portraits of Ruhollah Khomeini and Ali Khamene'i, not of Mohammed Khatami or Mahmud Ahmadinejad, the president since 2005. For Ali Khamene'i, such manifestations of allegiance sustain his claim to the *marja'iyya* in the face of his detractors. Indeed, as shown previously, being a *marja'* is as much a matter of religious knowledge as of concrete social power.

As we shall see, the reliance on either one or the other of these two aspects of Iranian foreign policy after the pragmatic turn is of course very much linked to the specific definition of Iran's national interests at a particular moment in time but also to the actual domestic contexts. In brief, the relation between Iran and its friends is not unilateral and greatly depends on the agenda of the very friends, which in turn is shaped by their local room for manoeuvre in a changing local political context. The more the movements that endorse Iran's official ideology have audience at home, the less they are likely to respond to an Iranian solicitation which would contradict their domestic interests, and the more they are likely to use Iran in their own local game rather than being used by it. In brief, the relation

---

70   Schain (2005), p. 79.

71   Personal interview, Bahrain, November 2002.

between Iran and its proxies is based on permanent negotiation and not on unilateral instrumentalization.

The Reinterpreting of Factionalism

In the Gulf, the conflict between the Shiraziyyin and the Iranian regime, and the subsequent mutation of al-Da'wa into Hezbollah, entailed a process of reinterpreting of the initial quarrel between al-Da'wa and the Shiraziyyin. It shifted from a quarrel formulated in terms of Najaf against Karbala, al-Da'wa against the Islamic Action Organization or the traditionalist *marja'* against the modern *marja'*. It became a dispute between the pro- and the anti-Iranians. The reinterpretation process also corresponded to a generational jump, from the generation of those socialized politically in the 1970s to those who engaged in politics after the Islamic revolution. For the latter indeed, the Islamic republic was the main model of reference and the initial dispute between Mohammed al-Shirazi and the *marja'iyya* in Najaf did not make much sense. Many had only a vague idea of the roots of the conflict and rather focused on the idea that, in general, "the Shiraziyyin were against Iran".

As before, the quarrel has both a political and a religious content. On the one hand, the dispute is formulated in the same terms as in Iran. It is a debate about a certain model of Islamic political system: that summarized in the doctrine of *wilayat al-faqih*. However, those who identify themselves as proponents of Iran and *wilayat al-faqih* are far from always endorsing all aspects of the Iranian regime's practice and recognize that there are errors. They distinguish between the principle of Islamic government outlined by the *wilayat al-faqih* and the concrete modalities of its application. Some advance pragmatic arguments to justify their support of Iran as a state despite its mistakes: the Islamic Republic must be supported because it is the only Shia state – the only Islamic state many say – a state that succeeds in maintaining itself in the face of general international hostility. For them, weakening Iran amounts to weakening the Shias overall in front of their many enemies. Therefore, through the campaign they launched against the Islamic Republic, the Shiraziyyin are accused of actually weakening the Shias because they show to the others that the Shias are divided. As one Bahraini figure of the Imam's Line said:

"We don't ask them to support the Imam [Khomeini] or Iran but I personally always say that if I disagree with my brother it's OK. But I must not go and explain to people that I disagree with my brother. Because for people who come from outside the sect, they realize that this group disagrees with this group."[72]

On the other hand, despite its reinterpretation, the quarrel retains the very traditional aspect of a conflict between the partisans of two competitors for the supreme religious authority: Mohammed al-Shirazi and Ruhollah Khomeini, and even more his successor Ali Khamene'i. For many people for whom this aspect is more important than the quarrel over the political model embodied by the Islamic Republic, what is important is to be loyal to the heritage of Ruhollah Khomeini through the successor he himself designated. They make a clear distinction between the regime itself and the Supreme Guide, between the institutions and the revolution as a process of overthrowing the oppressive political order of the Shah.

The discourse of the Shiraziyyin about the Imam's Line is also a mixture of different arguments. One aspect of their criticism is that their adversaries are late comers in the Imam's Line. They are opportunists who began to support the revolution belatedly, when they understood that they could use Iranian support to advance their interests. It was not an adhesion of principle. It was dictated by opportunistic concerns. Like their adversaries, they make a distinction between adhering to the Iranian regime and adhering to the revolution, saying that even if they criticize the errors of the Islamic Republic, they were actually the only genuine and sincere partisans of the revolution. In the course of the years 2005 and 2006 in Bahrain, the Shiraziyyin did not hesitate to make their arguments public in the press. 'Abd al-'Athim al-Muhtadi al-Bahrani and Ja'far al-'Alawi explained their disappointment in the way the Shiraziyyin were treated by the Islamic Republic and the way the affair was instrumentalized to sideline them on the domestic religious and political scene.

Here is the way 'Abd al-'Athim al-Muhtadi al-Bahrani presented things:

"After the campaign of arrests and executions of Shias in Iraq, many Iraqi *'ulama* went to Iran. The Islamic Republic integrated many of them [...] But unfortunately, this led to an unfair competition between, on the one hand, these late supporters of the Imam's Line, most of whom were not very politicized and came merely to have a salary to live, and on the other hand, its old allies from the group of S. al-Shirazi. The late comers of al-Da'wa and Najaf succeeded in discrediting S. al-Shirazi in the eyes of the Iranians in order to prevent him from leading the Arabs. And the Iranians were influenced by the campaign against S. al-Shirazi. This campaign was very active and constituted a strong attack against the Sayyid and his group, even after all these sacrifices they made for Imam Khomeini and his movement during

---

72   Personal interview, Bahrain, October 2002.

the time of exile, hardship and need. Personally, this led me to lose confidence into the Iranian leadership. I considered they were not loyal to their true allies."[73]

Ja'far al-'Alawi presented his argument in a very similar way:

"Today, I am surprised to hear some say despicable words against us concerning the revolution, when we were with the revolution during hard and dangerous times. And at this time, some people belonging to some Islamic currents had taken a negative stance towards the revolution. And we have tape-recorded words of some people from these currents, and we remember some actions by these parties that at the end rallied to the revolution, after its victory. Is it the same thing to have been zealous during hard times, during those fifteen years when the Message Movement stood with the revolution, while it was the darkest times? Is it the same thing as to have rallied to the revolution after it won?! We, as a movement, we were a part of the Arab revolution in Iran."[74]

Another salient aspect of the Shirazi language beyond the doctrinal arguments about *wilayat al-faqih* is the dismissal of the religious credentials of Ali Khamene'i. As we have seen, they are in consensus with many scholars. A favourite way to put the Supreme Guide's religious authority publicly into question is the performance during 'Ashura days of the *tatbir*, that is the ritual of incising the forehead and hitting it to make the blood flow. Indeed, in 1994, Ali Khamene'i issued a *fatwa* demanding that the Shias stop practicing this ritual and instead give their blood to the hospitals. His argument was not religious. He did not declare the *tatbir* "*haram*", forbidden religiously, but explained that it contributed to giving the wrong image of the Shias as violent and bloodthirsty people. Moreover he said, instead of letting blood flow down on the earth and be wasted, the Shias should rather give it to help cure ill people. Since the days of Karbala, the Shiraziyyin were known to be the fervent partisans of the *tatbir*, which the Najafi establishment generally considered with disdain as an expression of inappropriate popular piety. Therefore, they could not miss this opportunity to reaffirm their attachment to the *tatbir*, which they transformed into the dramatized expression of their opposition to Ali Khamene'i. Significantly, the Shiraziyyin's persistence in performing the *tatbir* is the most often mentioned element of irritation in the interviews with partisans of the Imam's Line. This is particularly so in Bahrain, where there is entire freedom of practice for even the most bloody Shia rituals, which is not the case in the other Gulf monarchies. The *Ma'tam* al-Qassab is therefore well known for being a major point of convergence, in the Gulf, for people

---

73   *The Story of Political Islam in Bahrain*, n° 5, *al-Watan* (Bahrain), 21 December 2005.

74   *The Story of Political Islam in Bahrain*, n° 23, al-Watan (Bahrain), 2 June 2006.

performing the *tatbir*. In 2006, the Bahraini Shirazyyin were particularly proud because dozens of Kuwaitis had come to Bahrain for 'Ashura to increase the number of the penitents practising the *tatbir*. One of Hadi al-Mudarrisi's brother, S. Mohammed Baqer al-Mudarrisi, had even come in support and joined the bloody procession. For the Imam's Line, this was taken as a real provocation. As one of them said, the *tatbir* is really a serious bone of contention:

"The difference between the two schools of thought is not very big after all. [...] But for me personally, there is something that really created a dispute with them. It is the *tatbir*. When I was younger, I did the *tatbir* sometimes. I was young and I did not know why I did it. Something pushed me to do it. But when S. Khamene'i judged about the question of *tatbir*, we all thought that his arguments were really convincing. [...] But they, those who belong to the other school, they said: 'no, we are not convinced by these words'. And then there have been arguments, etc.! Basim al-Karbala'i[75] for example, he said 'O you who said that the *tatbir* causes backwardness within the *umma*, it is you who should be more developed'. In other words, he said to S. Khameine'i: 'why do you say that'? He is answering to S. Khamene'i! But Khamene'i is a *faqih* in our eyes and you, Basim, you are not. [...] Unfortunately, they want to distinguish themselves. If they would drop the *tatbir* for example, that is harming not only us but all the Muslims in the world, then there would be a possibility of encounter between us."[76]

The other privileged moment of expression of the conflict is the elections. Kuwait is the most illustrative case as it possesses the most institutionalized and open political space of the three countries under study. Moreover, unlike Bahrain where Shia factions have succeeded in uniting in one single big Shia front after 2001, the unification of the various Shia political forces in the aftermath of the Gulf War misfired (*cf.* chapter 7), leaving a particularly fragmented landscape with as many as six Shia politico-religious groups at the time of writing. The 2003 elections however, witnessed the birth of an alliance between the Shiraziyyin and a handful of people who had remained faithful to the initial al-Da'wa line and referred to the *marja'iyya* of Mohammed Husein Fadlallah. They were gathered around a religious centre and *huseiniyya* named Dar al-Zahra (the House of Zahra), organ-

---

75   Basim al-Karbala'i is probably the most popular of the *radud* in the Shia world. He was born in Karbala in 1967 and, because he was of Iranian stock, was expelled from Iraq with all his family in 1980. He resettled in Qom where he became a part of the entourage of Mohammed al-Shirazi. He resettled in Kuwait in 1993, where he established a little enterprise distributing his audio and video tapes. He is very well known to be a major proponent of the Line of Shirazi. His popularity enrages the partisans of the Imam's Line.

76   Personal interview, Bahrain, October 2002.

izing religious lectures and activities.[77] The two groups decided to support each other's candidates in the first constituency comprising the historical places of Shia settlement in Kuwait (Dasma, Bneid al-Gar). Yusef al-Zilzila for al-Da'wa and Saleh 'Ashur for the Shiraziyyin, succeeded in defeating 'Adnan 'Abd al-Samad and Ahmed Lari, the two candidates of the Islamic National Coalition, the organizational expression of Hezbollah in Kuwait since 1998. The Shiraziyyin had however bigger ambitions than an occasional alliance in one constituency. They wanted to constitute a broad front of anti-Hezbollah Shia societies. In 2004, they announced blatantly in the Kuwaiti press that they had formed a "front" (*jabha*) named the Front for Justice and Peace. One of its aims would be "to fight the political and social role of Kuwaiti Hezbollah".[78] They proclaimed that the front would be an umbrella organization including several Shia societies. However, they were refuted the following day by a representative of one of these societies. Apparently, the Shiraziyyin had overcommitted themselves and, in the end, it was announced that the famous front was actually not an umbrella organization but only a Shirazi organization. In 2006 however, on the eve of the elections, an umbrella organization of five Shia societies effectively emerged, named the Coalition of the National Assemblies (*I'tilaf al-Tajammu'at al-Wataniyya*). While the members abstained from any heated commentaries about the aims of the Coalition, which were put as being "to promote equality in the framework of the nation", it actually included all the Shia societies with the exception of the Islamic National Alliance. The Shiraziyyin, who were the driving force behind the unification of the five groups, argued that the latter had been invited to join but had refused "because they are too close to Iran and want to dominate the whole Shia scene".[79] Actually, it was said by others that nothing was done to make them a place.

Two conclusions can be drawn from the reinterpretation of the quarrel between Mohammed al-Shirazi and the central religious authority. First, there is a striking permanency of the fault lines structuring the Shia Islamic political scene in the Gulf monarchies. At the time of writing, despite the considerable evolution entailed by the Islamic revolution, the renewal of the activist generations and, as we shall see in the following chapters, the

---

77   Zahra is the nickname of Fatima, the daughter of Prophet Mohammed and wife of Imam 'Ali. Fatima al-Zahra can be translated by "Fatima the Pure".

78   *Al-Siyasa* (Kuwait), 30 December 2004, Samih Shams al-Din, "A New Shiite Front to Fight Kuwaiti Hezbollah" (in Arabic).

79   Personal interview with 'Abd al-Husein al-Sultan, secretary general of the Shirazi society The Front for Justice and Peace, Kuwait, May 2006.

autonomization of the Shia Islamic movements from the *marja'iyya*, there were still many domestic political rivalries that could not be understood if the genealogy of the quarrel were to be ignored.

The second conclusion is that the Islamic republic of Iran is not anymore a consensual model within the Shia Islamic movements. Far from this, it is now a fault line. Before the conflict between the Shiraziyyin and the Iranian regime, opposition to *wilayat al-faqih* was confined to the traditional clerical circles and was hence mainly expressed in the terms of a scholarly dispute. But, like other such disputes that traditionally punctuated the life of the religious seminars, its resonance in political life was limited in scope. Indeed, while in Iran those scholars who dared to oppose to the state doctrine were considered as political opponents and treated as such, they never managed nor endeavoured to create political organizations. Their main aim was to keep the autonomy of the religious institution from the encroachment of the state, not to create organized political contest. In many respects, Mohammed al-Shirazi also behaved as a typical religious scholar since, when he entered into dissent with the Islamic republic, he abstained from any attempt at setting up a political organization to promote his alternative vision of what the Islamic political institutions should be. Instead, he retreated into the religious field. But because he was already the eponymous figure of several political movements, his religious positioning could not but have direct consequences in the political field. This is why his dispute with S. Ruhollah Khomeini spilled over into the political arena. It did this, however, not in Iran or in Iraq but in the Gulf monarchies, because they were the only place where Mohammed al-Shirazi's *marja'iyya* translated into significant, and sometimes powerful, political movements.

This bipolarization of the Shia Islamic scene has important consequences for the analysis of Iran's political influence outside of its borders. Indeed, the time is over when the Islamic republic could claim unconditional allegiance from all the Shia Islamic movements. Hence, the time is over when one could analyse them as mere proxies of Iranian foreign policy. In retrospect, when one looks at the whole history of the Shia Islamic movements in the Gulf, the period of fusion with Iran lasted rather a short time. Already in the mid-1980s elements of Iraqi al-Da'wa – the cadres of al-Da'wa – and the Shiraziyyin – both Mohammed al-Shirazi and his nephews Mohammed Taqi and Hadi al-Mudarrisi – were in a process of distancing themselves, although for different reasons as we have seen. The illusion of a fusional relation remained for the outside world because, be it in Iraq or in the Gulf, the impossibility for these movements to exist at home as legitimate organizations made Iran their natural territorial sanctuary and, apparently, the Islamic republic their natural protector. Today however, the fracture line is coming to light and, in some cases, is even part of the public political debate as is the case in Kuwait.

PART IV

THE AUTONOMIZATION OF POLITICS

Writing in the mid-1970s, John Bowyer Bell noted that, in the post-colonial period, national liberation movements tend to resort to transnational ideologies to legitimate their domestic fight. By contrast with the anti-colonial movements, nationalism lost its legitimacy in their eyes if not accompanied by a universalistic rhetoric committed to the liberation of mankind overall. Therefore, while most often engaged in strictly domestic struggle against particular regimes, a struggle in the service of which they mobilize the nationalist register, they simultaneously claim to work for "the destruction of the entire nation-state system, considered as a passing phase of history".[1] The previous chapter clearly showed that the Shia Islamic movements fit this model: since their inception, they targeted a particular nation-state despite their transnational pledge.

Because the balance between the lay and the clerical cadres finally proved favourable to the former within the Iraqi mother party, the various chapters of al-Daʿwa were better prepared to deal with the very notion of the nation-state. After they cut ties with the *marjaʿiyya*, the Iraqi lay cadres easily came to terms with their identity as an Iraqi national party, leaving the transnational dream to the clerics. In the Gulf, the clerics continued to dominate al-Daʿwa movements but, since they were tied with a *marjaʿiyya*, that of Abu al-Qasem al-Khuʾi, that did not endeavour to transform its transnational networks into a political movement, they had a total autonomy of political decision making. Even after their rapprochement with the Islamic Republic of Iran, they were careful to keep their independence and never made the confusion between ideologically and religiously supporting the Islamic Republic and becoming its satellite. As for the Shiraziyyin, they were the repositories of the anti-national transnational ideology. In

1   Bowyer Bell (1972), p. 153.

their case, transnationalism does not mean merely having networks of interpersonal relations cutting across national frontiers but, on the one hand, striving to abolish national states within the *dar al-Islam* and, on the other hand, establishing a transnational integrated structure command, that exists as a genuine transnational political movement. The fact that the clerics always retained ultimate power among the Iraqi leadership greatly contributed to the persistence of the transnational commitment. Indeed, it is the Iraqi mother organization that strove to maintain the partisan structure within the by nature transnational framework of the *marja'iyya*. For them, the *marja'* was to be obeyed both as a religious and a political authority. Therefore, the Shiraziyyin's relationship to the existing nation-states was essentially instrumental. In the Gulf, they established good relations with the ruling circles in order to circumvent the local religious establishment linked to the Najafi *marja'iyya*. In Iran, their commitment was not to Iran as a state but to the revolution as a process meant to end only after the establishment of an Islamic state on the entire territory of Islam. This explains why they felt at home in the early years of the revolution but were estranged in the post-revolutionary era, when Iranian foreign policy shifted to that of a traditional nation-state.

The practical implementation of the transnational ideology was however never really achieved by the Shiraziyyin. It is true that Mohammed Taqi al-Mudarrisi clearly succeeded in bringing under his authority a network of activists of various national belongings. But the fact remains that the activists from the Gulf monarchies had their respective political organizations distinct from the Iraqi one. While the leaders of those national organizations were supposed to refer directly to Mohammed Taqi al-Mudarrisi, they actually retained a distinct existence. They acted in unison with the Iraqi mother organization as far as their analysis of the situation, of the aims of the struggle and the means to achieve them, was the same. During the period of exile in Iran moreover, the Gulf activists were in a relation of material dependence on the Iraqis and their supporters within the Iranian regime. But the will of the Gulf activists to have organizations of their own shows that national idiosyncrasies were actually never dissolved within the overall Islamic fight. Even at the peak of revolutionary fervour in the early 1980s, and despite their feeling that the Bahraini and Saudi states were illegitimate territorial entities, the Bahraini and Saudi activists never renounced referring to these entities as the target of their fight. The Bahrainis named their organization the "Islamic Front for the Liberation of Bahrain". The Saudis, while refusing to use the term "Saudi", nonetheless claimed to fight for the Islamic revolution within a territory that was actually confined to the frontiers of the Saudi state. They named their movement the "Organization for the Islamic Revolution in the Arabian Peninsula". "Arabian Peninsula" here did not refer to the traditional geographic entity extending south of Syria to Yemen but to the territory conquered and unified by the Al-Sa'ud. Although they collaborated with the Bahrainis, including during the 1981 coup, they never claimed to substitute themselves to the national Bahraini activist framework. Relations between the various national chapters of the Shirazi network were, *in fine*, very much looking like traditional international – as opposed to transnational – relations. They were allies and not the elements of an integrated transnational movement.[2]

As we shall now see, the 1990s and the 2000s witnessed a dramatic accentuation of this tendency, being actually a period that could be described as that of the failure of the transnational project and the triumph of the states. What we observe about the Shia Islamic movements is therefore totally at odds with what I would call a diffuse "transnationalist vulgate" that tends to pervade the analysis of international relations and underlines the fading of states in the face of so-called "transnational threats". From the case of the Shia Islamic movements, important lessons can be drawn about the resilience of the state and, concomitantly, the practice of politics in the transnational space.

---

2   Something that was also well noted by John Bowyer Bell for the movements he studied, *ibid.*, p. 154.

7

POLITICS IS DOMESTIC

Throughout their history, the various Shia Islamic movements under scrutiny here proved essentially reactive to the states' initiatives. They adapted to the states' policies and were rarely able to impose an agenda of their own on them. This explains why the Shia Islamic movements have been particularly sensitive to the transformation of the regional inter-state system that occurred in the 1990s and 2000s. The transformation of the geopolitical context at various levels, and the consequences it had on the internal political equilibrium of the Gulf monarchies, brought about sweeping changes in the Shia movements' political strategies and ideological conceptions. The political liberalization implemented in the context of a general détente of diplomatic relations as well as the sharp crisis of the welfare state, entailed a redefinition of the states' policies towards their opponents, and hence led to the opening of new political opportunities for the Shia movements. The latter hence underwent a process of "domestification": ceasing to be anti-system forces, they integrated into the institutional channels of conflict regulation established by the states and relinquished their transnational ideology. Overall, they have endeavoured to redefine their relations with the respective regimes, sometimes to the point of openly embracing values and conceptions they were previously profoundly at odds with.

NEW POLITICAL OPPORTUNITIES

The 1991 Gulf War was the point of departure of a new dynamic in diplomatic relations between Iran and its Arab neighbours of the Gulf. In Iran, it helped to consolidate the pragmatic turn engaged in the mid-1980s and, in particular, to finally achieve reconciliation with Saudi Arabia.[1] Despite

---

1   For the evolution of the relations between Iran and its Gulf neighbours, see
     Marschall (2003) and K. L. Afrasiabi, *After Khomeini. New Directions in Iran's*

its long-stated doctrine of no involvement by foreign actors in Gulf affairs, Iran supported the United Nation's resolution giving the mainly Western coalition a mandate to liberate Kuwait from Iraqi occupation and offered its full support to the Gulf states.

Political Liberalization

The reshaping of the geopolitical map had a direct impact on the internal political spaces of each of the three countries under scrutiny. The Gulf War indeed exposed the structural fragility of the Gulf regimes which, despite huge expenses for the purchase of often sophisticated armaments, proved unable even to try to resist Saddam Husein's military offensive. More than ever, the Gulf monarchies appeared as economically wealthy but militarily weak countries, structurally dependant on Western powers for their external security. The strain put on the regimes' legitimacy only added to previous economic problems caused by the severe drop of the oil prices since the mid-1980s. With a barrel of oil occasionally falling as low as four dollars at the peak of the crisis in 1986-1988,[2] the Gulf monarchies' budget was severely affected, and so was their capacity for redistribution. The problem would have remained politically manageable had the population not witnessed spectacular growth, fostered by the natalist policies implemented since the 1970s.[3]

The 1990s hence opened with an ever-increasing imbalance between the available resources and the number of those claiming their share of the wealth, in a context where the oil boom had habituated the population to particularly generous policies of "patronage and largesse",[4] the essence of the Gulf welfare state.[5] In such a system, oil wealth is redistributed through various forms of social advantages. This consists in subsidized or even sometimes free basic services – electricity, water, housing, telephone,

---

Foreign Policy, Boulder: Westview Press, 1994, chapter 3 pp. 85-115.

2   For an appraisal of the oil price crisis of the mid-1980s, see Robert Mabro (ed.), *The 1986 Oil Price Crisis: Economic Effects and Policy Responses*, Oxford: Oxford University Press, 1988. See in particular the introduction by Robert Mabro, pp. 1-14.

3   Onn Winckler, *Arab Political Demography. Volume 1: Population Growth and Natalist Policies*, Brighton: Portland, 2005, pp. 46 and 54.

4   Daryl Champion, *The Paradoxical Kingdom. Saudi Arabia and the Momentum of Reform*, London: Hurst, 2003.

5   Hazem Beblawi, "The Rentier State in the Arab World", in Hazem Beblawi and Giacomo Luciani (eds), *The Rentier State*, London: Croom Helm, 1987, pp. 53-9.

health care – but, more importantly, the guarantee of a correctly paid and not too demanding employment in the public administration. Often criticized for its bureaucratic inefficiency, the plethoric Gulf bureaucracy had the invaluable advantage, for the rulers, of transforming virtually all their citizens into civil servants depending on the state for their very subsistence. Entitled with extensive social rights, the citizens of the Gulf were expected to refrain on political demands.[6]

Because the redistributive capacity was a central element of the states' political legitimacy, its weakening had direct consequences on their ability to generate political consent among the population and could not but involve important political adjustments. These mainly took the form of political liberalization policies which, although with sharp differences according to the particular national context, redefined the structure of political opportunities for the opposition movements of all persuasions, including the Shia ones.

The Return to Ante-Revolution Situation in Kuwait

Among the three countries under scrutiny there, Kuwait was the first to react to the new context described above. During the 1980s, the country had witnessed a marked return of authoritarianism, the main manifestation of which was the disbanding of Parliament in 1986. Shortly before the Iraqi invasion, a popular movement had emerged demanding its reinstatement but had been brutally rebuffed. In 1990, instead of restoring the Parliament, the Emir established a new assembly that was deprived of any legislative power and, moreover, only partially elected. It is the Iraqi invasion and the subsequent weakening of the regime that helped to unblock the situation. While the Al-Sabah were in exile in Ta'if in Saudi Arabia during the seven months of the occupation, those who were physically confronted with the Iraqi army constituted into networks of solidarity from which new political leaders emerged in the post-war period. Most of them belonged to the middle and lower classes and had never exercised political or institutional responsibilities. Their experience of the occupation brought about a genuine "transformation of consciousness",[7] as they learned to rely on themselves rather than on the provisions of the welfare state. They took

---

6 Anh Nga Longva, "Citizenship in the Gulf States: Conceptualization and Practice", in Nils Butenschon, Uri Davis and Manuel Hassassian (eds), *Citizenship and the State in the Middle East. Approaches and Applications*, Syracuse (New York): Syracuse University Press, 2000; Abdulhadi Khalaf, "What the Gulf Ruling Families Do when they Rule", *Orient*, vol. 44, n° 3, 2003.

7 Tétreault (2000), p. 87.

charge of the distribution of basic foodstuffs to the population and some even organized an embryonic armed resistance. Overall, they went out of the war with the feeling of having been the custodians of national pride in times of hardship.[8] In March 1991, they joined forces with older political activists and intellectuals to present a petition to the Emir entitled "Vision for the Future of Kuwait", which demanded the reinstatement of the Parliament according to the provision of the 1962 constitution.

It is in the context of this overall empowerment of the opposition that the Shia movements achieved their re-integration into the political arena. More than other political forces, the Shia movements capitalized on their role in the so-called "resistance" in order to renegotiate their position within the political imbalance. Indeed, it is a commonly held opinion in Kuwait, among the Shias but also among many Sunnis, that Shias were overrepresented in the ranks of those who stayed during the occupation. Many Shias even say that at that time, they constituted the majority of the population present in Kuwait. Politically minded Shias do not hesitate to put forward the explanation that the Shias stayed because they are particularly patriotic and eager to defend Kuwait. Less impassioned and interested opinions underline that the Shias being among the relatively less privileged segments of the population, many do not have the financial means to leave Kuwait during the entire summer season. Therefore, in the heat of August when the Iraqi soldiers crossed the border and when most affluent Kuwaitis were away on vacation in more hospitable climates, the Shias were there. Be that as it may, what is sure is that prominent Shia figures were in Kuwait at the time of the invasion. The most well-known case is that of 'Abd al-Wahhab al-Wazzan, a well-known merchant who, before the war, used to be active in the Social Society for Culture that was the legal front of al-Da'wa. He played a key role in organizing the supplying of foodstuffs to the population and, together with Ahmed al-Baqir, a Sunni Islamic activist, he took the lead of a popular government within Kuwait which coordinated with the government in exile in Ta'if. In 1999, he was appointed Minister of Industry and of Labour and Social Affairs.

The leading role played by Shia figures during the occupation permitted the Shias overall, and the Islamic movements in particular, to go out of the war with a new legitimacy. They had been suspected of disloyalty to the Kuwaiti nation in favour of an atavistic leaning to Iran: however, they had proven by their deeds that they were even more committed than many

---

8   Neil Hicks and Ghanim al-Najjar, "The Utility of Tradition: Civil Society in Kuwait", in Augustus Richard Norton (ed.), *Civil Society in the Middle East*, Leiden: Brill, 1995, pp. 200-2.

Sunnis to preserving the independence of Kuwait. Hence the page of the 1980s was turned and the Shia political movements regained their status as legitimate components of the Kuwaiti political spectrum. They joined with the other political groups to sign the Vision for the Future of Kuwait. In April 1992, very much in the same mood that animated the "young men" in the mid-1970s, Shia political groups as well as independent personalities united in the framework of a broad front named the National Islamic Coalition (al-I'tilaf al-Islami al-Watani), aiming at increasing the representation of Shias in the Parliament, whatever the political outlook of those elected. The main figures of the Coalition were 'Abd al-Wahhab al-Wazzan, 'Adnan 'Abd al-Samad and Naser Sarkhu.[9] The two latter were elected in the subsequent elections. The Coalition also supported 'Ali al-Baghli, a Shia of liberal[10] persuasion who was elected and subsequently appointed Minister of Oil. The Shiraziyyin, who did not represent much political weight at that time, did not formally join the coalition. Nonetheless, at least one of the men they had supported in the past was elected thanks to the support of the National Islamic Coalition: Ya'qub Hayati. The latter was an independent deputy considered pro-government by those being in the orbit of the Social Society for Culture. Indeed, he had been supported by the government in the 1985 elections, which were marked by massive fraud organized by the rulers. Although he never defined himself as a Shirazi, he was their main political intermediary at the parliamentary level before 1999, when Saleh 'Ashur was first elected.

The Nationalist Bent of the Shiraziyyin in Saudi Arabia

In Saudi Arabia, the regime's inability to defend the sacred land other than by resorting to a non-Muslim army not only harmed its religious credentials: it also weakened its military credibility. Moreover, the plummeting of oil prices and the subsequent curtailing of state expenses directly damaged its redistributive capacity. This conjunction of factors contributed to the transformation of what used to be an occasional and easily manageable opposition into an increasingly organized movement whose core was constituted by Sunni religious scholars influenced by the ideas of the Muslim Brotherhood. The children of the Al-Sa'ud's massive financing of Islamic learning, many of them originated from Najd, the cradle of Wahhabism and the region most favoured by the regime. Many were working in the

9   Al-Khaldi (1999), p. 125; al-Mdayris (1999), p. 40.

10   In the Arab world, "liberal" is a rather vague denomination meaning basically "non-Islamic".

religious bureaucracy as teachers, prayer leaders, religious judges and so forth.[11] A few weeks after the liberation of Kuwait, fifty of them presented the King with a "Letter of Demands". Among the signatories were younger Sunni clerics like Sh. Salman al-'Awda and Sh. Safar al-Hawalli, but also senior *'ulama* close to the ruling dynasty, most notably Sh. 'Abd al-'Aziz ibn Baz, the kingdom's *mufti*[12] who had agreed to provide the Al-Sa'ud with a *fatwa* authorizing the resort to the international coalition. Criticizing the regime's lack of true commitment to Islamic values, the signatories demanded concrete steps to balance the absolute power of the rulers. A year later in summer 1992, one hundred well known Sunni religious figures submitted to the government the "Memorandum of Advice", a petition consisting of respectful, but firm, advice for the Al-Sa'ud to undertake a set of reforms in order to stick better to Islamic commandments. Through a general critique of the lack of commitment to religious law, they broached very concrete issues such as foreign policy, which they deemed too subservient to states hostile to the Muslims like the United States, the condition of the army, and also the situation of the welfare state.[13]

The response of the Saudi regime to this unprecedented upsurge of political contention was multi-faceted. Perfectly aware that the changing geopolitical and socio-economic conditions necessitated a more consistent answer than the traditional arsenal of intimidation and repression, it enacted three reforms that partially met the demands of the opposition. Most importantly, the new laws decided the establishment of a Consultative Council composed of sixty members appointed by the King whose task was, when explicitly asked by the ruler, to express opinions on policy matters. A law regulating the administration of provinces was also enacted that established local councils, also appointed by the King. The scope of these reforms was rather modest because they did not really challenge the Al-Sa'ud's rule. Even more so since, while striving to widen the basis of

11   Gwenn Okruhlik, "Networks of Dissent: Islamism and Reform in Saudi Arabia", *Social Sciences Research Council*, www.ssrc.org/sept11/essays/okruhlik.htm (published in *Current History*, vol. 100, n° 651, January 2002), p. 3.

12   Literally the one who is legitimately entitled to issue *fatwa*. In the Sunni world, the *mufti* is the supreme religious authority, most often designated as such by the state.

13   R. Hrair Dekmejian, "The Rise of Political Islamism in Saudi Arabia", *The Middle East Journal*, vol. 48, n° 4, autumn 1994, pp. 633-4. For an overall review of the ideology and claims of the Sunni Islamic opposition in Saudi Arabia, see Fandy (1999).

their support, the rulers also consolidated dynastic rule by further formalizing and clarifying the modality of succession.[14]

In parallel to these institutional adjustments, the Saudi regime undertook to tackle the long-neglected question of national identity. At the head of a kingdom unified by military coercion, the Al-Sa'ud never really bothered to diffuse a national narrative underlining a common history and identity to the various regions under their control. Added to the dynasty's rather narrow regional and religious base, the lack of endeavour at nation-building resulted in the various regions maintaining separate historical and identity narratives, often reinforced by the fact that they belonged to different currents of Islam, as is the case, for example, in Hijaz and Hasa.[15] Because for the first time it brought a common value to virtually all Saudi nationals, the establishment of the welfare state in the mid-1970s was central in linking together the different segments of the population. Even if the redistribution of wealth was far from being egalitarian, the marginalized sectors nonetheless benefited from the spectacular upsurge of riches. In this context, the collapse of the welfare state, officially announced by the then Prince regent 'Abdallah in 1998,[16] was also the end of a central pillar of national cohesion. This explains why when announcing the above mentioned institutional reforms, King Fahd preceded his speech by a long narrative recounting the history of the kingdom and stressing the importance of commitment to the nation.[17] Clearly, the regime was attempting to develop a new kind of social engineering. The new state nationalism it promoted was an attempt at changing its social structure and, more precisely, the rulers-ruled relation, in order so survive. Now, the rulers were to be obeyed not so much because they redistributed their wealth or were the custodians of the holy land but because they embodied the unity of the nation.

As in Kuwait, it is in the light of the new imbalance between the regime and the opposition that one should understand the dramatic shift of the

---

14   Joseph A. Kechichian, *Succession in Saudi Arabia*, New York: Palgrave, 2001.

15   Christine Moss Helms, *The Cohesion of Saudi Arabia: Evolution of Political Identity*, London: Croom Helm, 1981. On the case of Hijaz, see Mai Yamani, *Cradle of Islam: The Hijaz and the Quest for an Arabian Identity*, London: I. B. Tauris, 2004.

16   Fatiha Dazi-Héni, *Monarchies et sociétés d'Arabie. Le temps des confrontations*, Paris: Presses de Sciences Po, 2006, p. 28. 'Abdallah was prince regent between 1995 and 2005, when King Fahd was incapable of governing after a stroke. 'Abdallah was officially crowned king in 2005, after the death of Fahd.

17   Madawi al-Rasheed, "God, the King and the Nation: Political Rhetoric in Saudi Arabia in the 1990s", *The Middle East Journal*, vol. 50, n° 3, summer 1996, pp. 359-71.

Saudi Shiraziyyin. Very significantly, they began by altering their language. Renouncing transnational rhetoric, they began to espouse the nationalist discourse of the regime, suggesting that, before being Shias, they were loyal citizens attached to the well-being of their country and ready to support the ruling dynasty. Compared with the Sunni Islamic opposition who remained rather wary about the new Saudi nationalism, the Shiraziyyin displayed an amazing willingness to embrace the Al-Sa'ud's new nationalist rationale. The fact that, compared with their Bahraini and Kuwaiti counterparts, they counted in their ranks several activists of great intellectual standard, with an influence even beyond the borders of their organization and country, greatly helped to materialize the ideological shift. The first person responsible for it was Hasan al-Saffar himself, the leader of the Organization for the Islamic Revolution in the Arabian Peninsula. A true political intellectual with his own original vision and worldview, he was intellectually independent from the doctrine articulated by Mohammed al-Shirazi and Mohammed Taqi al-Mudarrisi, not the least because he had been trained within a wide array of seminaries in Najaf and Qom.

The change in the Saudi regime's language only helped him to materialize a vision he had began to articulate some time before the Gulf War, as early as the mid-1980s, in the context of the weakening and final marginalization of the Shiraziyyin in Iran. Fouad Ibrahim recounts that, in 1985, Hasan al-Saffar suggested that the name of the OIRAP be changed for a more "moderate" one, less evocative of Iranian linkage.[18] The project did not materialize out of fear that the movement's base in Saudi Arabia was not yet ready for it, but also because it would have provoked the ire of Mohammed Taqi al-Mudarrisi. Ja'far al-Shayeb, another cadre of the movement, mentioned that the Saudi activists were feeling more and more at odds with the Iraqi leadership and were willing to achieve independence.[19] The Saudis made up almost 80 per cent of the students of the *Hawzat* al-Qa'im in Tehran, which was a major institution in the training and recruiting of Shirazi activists at the time. Yet, Saudis were not involved in decision making at the transnational level, which fell almost entirely in the hands of Mohammed Taqi al-Mudarrisi. There was the feeling that Iraqis monopolized positions of power and tended to consider the Saudis, and the Gulf activists overall, as henchmen. Saudis felt that they had contributed a lot to making the Shirazi current known in the Gulf but that their contribution had not been recognized. Finally, they had the feeling that the transna-

---

18   Ibrahim (2006), p. 141.

19   Personal interview, Saudi Arabia, September 2004.

tional ideology carried by Mohammed Taqi al-Mudarrisi was failing to formulate a more refined diagnosis of their particular national situation.

In 1987, the execution of Mehdi Hashemi and the general crisis of confidence between the Islamic Republic and the Shirazyyin gave the Saudis the opportunity to implement their own vision. The shift was clear at the rhetorical level as Hasan al-Saffar began to depart from his previous revolutionary language in his publications, shifting to new themes of reflection such as human rights, freedom, political and religious pluralism. The first landmark in that respect was the publication in 1990 of *Pluralism and Freedom in Islam* (*Al-Ta'adudiyya wa al-Huriyya fi al-Islam*).[20] Instead of referring to Mohammed Taqi al-Mudarrisi's conception of revolutionary action which had been the doctrine of the OIRAP in the previous years, Hasan al-Saffar rather elaborated on the conceptions developed by Mohammed al-Shirazi after his conflict with Ruhollah Khomeini, that were characterized by a committment to political pluralism and non-violence. The Gulf War helped to further materialize the shift of strategy, as well as the dissociation with the Iraqi leadership. Indeed, with the prospect of Saddam Husein being deposed by the coalition, Mohammed Taqi al-Mudarrisi naturally refocused on Iraq, trying to figure out the concrete modality of a return home after the regime change. In this respect, he calculated that his constituencies in the Gulf monarchies could be useful to placate the possible hostility of Iraq's Arab neighbours to the prospect of a Shia-governed Iraq. This was particularly so of Saudi Arabia, the support of which he considered decisive. He therefore explicitly enjoined Hasan al-Saffar and his followers to strive to send positive signs to the Al-Sa'ud.

For Hasan al-Saffar and his companions, this was a unique opportunity to achieve independence and complete the reformist shift without alienating their Iraqi companions. In early 1991, they decided to cut their organizational ties with the Iraqis and to rename their organization the Reform Movement (*al-Haraka al-Islahiyya*). The publication of their main mouthpiece, the Islamic Revolution (*al-Thawra al-Islamiyya*), was stopped in favour of a new organ named the *Arabian Peninsula* (*al-Jazira al-'Arabiyya*). Its content had nothing to compare with the previous journal. One found no call to overthrowing the Saudi regime but rather an attempt to write down the history of the Shias of Saudi Arabia in order to give them the historic and symbolic material to remain committed to their cultural specificity.[21]

For Hasan al-Saffar, this was clearly a way to send signs to the Al-Sa'ud that he wanted to open negotiations. To increase the pressure, he simulta-

20   Fandy (1999), p. 199.
21   Al-Rasheed (1998).

neously made contacts with the Sunni Islamic opposition based in London, therefore implicitly threatening the regime with a sacred union of Sunni and Shia opponents. These efforts were rewarded and, in October 1993, the Reform Movement signed an agreement with King Fahd by which all the activists were granted amnesty and the right to return home.[22] Most of them actually returned to the Eastern Province, including Hasan al-Saffar. Among those who used to write inflammatory articles in the Reform Movement's various publications, several were offered positions as journalists in the highly controlled local media. The activists' reimplantation, however, did not pass without problems. In the face of huge expectations that the accord had raised among the Shia population, the lack of implementation of promises by the Saudi authorities created disappointment as well as divisions within the ranks of the Reform Movement, pushing some to leave Saudi Arabia once more. This was the case of Tawfiq al-Seif and Hamza al-Hasan, who stayed in London and thereafter launched *Saudi Affairs (Shu'un Sa'udiyya)*, a journal in both hard and electronic[23] versions dealing with Saudi political affairs and whose tone remained critical.

Those who chose to stay home, while striving to forge comprehensive relations with various sectors of Saudi society and the political spectrum, including the leftists and some Sunni Islamic activists, went on with their effort to stick to the regime's own language. In 1996, Hasan al-Saffar published a little booklet entitled *Nation and Nationality. Rights and Duties (Al-Watan wa al-Muwatana. Al- Huquq wa al-Wajibat)*, which completed the doctrinal turn of the Saudi Shiraziyyin. In the book, Hasan al-Saffar did not talk so much about political pluralism and freedom as he had previously, but insisted on the idea that "there is a solid link between religion and love of one's homeland (*watan*)".[24] While deploring the division of the "Islamic homeland" into fifty states with boundaries difficult to cross, he enjoined Muslims to assume their responsibilities as citizens of one particular state. Indeed, he wrote, people belong to three circles of identity – the Islamic *umma*, the nation-state (*watan*) and the villages or towns where they are born (*watan 'urfi*) – which do not contradict but rather complete one another. Those who thought otherwise were foolish radicals. Therefore, while the realization of the unity of the Islamic *umma* should remain a horizon, "a beautiful memory of the past and a dream for the future", it was the duty of each Muslim to defend his nation-state as well as to co-operate

---

22   For details on the accord, see Ibrahim (2006), pp. 178-208.

23   www.saudiaffairs.net

24   Hasan al-Saffar, *Nation and Nationality. Rights and Duties* (in Arabic), Beirut: Dar al-Safwa, 1996, p. 27.

with his fellow-citizens having other religions and convictions. In a clear rupture with his own past experience, with the doctrine of Mohammed al-Shirazi and Mohammed Taqi al-Mudarrisi, he felt compelled to specify that "it is true that Muslims have the duty to spread Islam worldwide, but they must begin with the place which is closest to them".[25] In other words: do not meddle in the others' business, care for your country first before thinking about the world.

A Popular Uprising in Bahrain

Bahraini rulers were less affected than their Saudi and Kuwaiti counterparts by the Gulf War, so the liberalization process took time to materialize and witnessed a severe setback in the mid-1990s. Indeed, Bahrain was not directly threatened by the Iraqi army as were Kuwait and Saudi Arabia. Moreover, having no complex about their alliance with the United States, the Al-Khalifa saw the war as an occasion to reinforce their strategic alliance with them and, contrary to the Al-Sa'ud, considered the installation of US troops (the Navy's Fifth Fleet) in their territory as an opportunity more than a constraint. Rather than the altering of the geopolitical balance, the most worrying for the Bahraini rulers was the severe deterioration of the population's socio-economic situation. By that time already, Bahrain had witnessed a quasi-complete depletion of its hydrocarbon resources and, among the GCC countries, was the most affected by the crisis of the welfare state and the political model it was sustaining. To tackle the crisis, the Bahraini government had striven to diversify its economy as soon as the 1970s, developing new industrial activities (aluminium), offshore banking and tourism. But it had nonetheless remained highly vulnerable to the fluctuation of oil prices because oil related activities, like refining and petrochemicals, accounted for the bulk of its budget. By the same token, its banking economy was highly dependant on petrodollars.

An aggravating factor of the Bahraini socio-economic crisis was the country's huge population growth, which had made it the second most densely populated country worldwide after Singapore. In the context of saturation of the public sector, the arrival of increasingly bigger amounts of young Bahrainis on the labour market provoked the crisis of the redistribution mechanism. Bahrainis were now more and more obliged to seek employment in the private sector where, like in the other Gulf countries, companies relied on cheap foreign labour and were very reluctant to hire nationals, reputed badly trained and lazy. Therefore, while unemployment

---

25   *Ibid.*, p. 41.

was about to reach a mass scale, the Bahrainis who nonetheless succeeded in finding a job in a private company were suffering from low wages and often mediocre working conditions by the usual standards of the Gulf.[26]

The worsening of the socio-economic situation was the main incentive that pushed the Bahraini rulers to engage in a liberalization policy – although timid – inspired by the initiatives of their neighbours. They hence allowed several opponents to return from exile and released several others from prison.[27] The Bahraini opposition movements reached the conclusion that the time was ripe to make precise demands to the government and, in particular, to insist that Parliament be reinstated. They were worried by rumours talking about the creation of a Consultative Council appointed by the Emir and, on the Saudi model, only vested with an advisory status. Hence in November 1992, a coalition of opponents of various ideological backgrounds – from leftists to both Sunni and Shia religious – presented the Emir with the "Elites' Petition", the main demand of which was the restoration of the Parliament disbanded in 1975. The government, however, chose to ignore the petition and instead established a Consultative Council of thirty members, equally divided into Sunni and Shia notables and professionals.[28]

While liberation of some opponents and the creation of the Consultative Council no doubt represented a positive move as compared with the previous years, it was far from the kind of political freedom the country had enjoyed in the 1970s. In this respect, the liberalization constituted a step back. Actually, the real watershed in Bahraini political history occurred two years later when the combination of social strain and political frustration degenerated into a popular uprising that lasted four years (1994-1998). The starting point of the uprising is often described as having been a charity marathon organized in November 1994 by several foreign companies.

---

26   I developed the Bahraini context in more details in Laurence Louër, "The Political Impact of Labor Migration in Bahrain", *City and Society*, vol. 20, n° 1, 2008, as well as in "Démocratisation des régimes dynastiques: le modèle bahreïnien en question", in Rémy Leveau et Frédéric Charillon (eds), *Monarchies du Golfe. Les micro-Etats de la péninsule arabique*, Paris: La Documentation Française, 2005, pp. 111-26. See also Louay Bahry, "The Socioeconomic Foundations of the Shiite Opposition in Bahrain", *Mediterranean Quarterly*, vol. 11, n° 3, summer 2000; Louay Bahry, "The Opposition in Bahrain: A Bellwether for the Gulf?", *Middle East Policy*, vol. 5, n° 2, May 1997.

27   Abdulhadi Khalaf, "Contentious Politics in Bahrain. From Ethnic to National and Vice Versa", *The Fourth Nordic Conference on Middle Eastern Studies: The Middle East in a Globalizing World*, Oslo, 13-16 August 1998, www.hf.uib.no/smi/pao/khalaf.html

28   Fuller and Francke (2001), pp. 127-30.

As the marathon runners, both men and women dressed in shorts and tee-shirts, entered some Shia villages, groups of villagers headed by activist clerics tried to stop them, considering that running among them in such light clothing was a direct insult to the their religious and moral values. Things disintegrated into fist-fighting and stone throwing. The same night, the security forces arrested several of the protesters, including their leader, Sh. 'Ali Salman (b. 1965). He was then a rather obscure young cleric who had studied in Qom between 1987 and 1992 and then assiduously frequented the learning circles of 'Abd al-Amir al-Jamri. His arrest sparked a cycle of mass-demonstrations and repression that led to the death of a dozen demonstrators and the incarceration of hundreds of others, without mentioning the widespread practice of torture by the security forces.[29]

But bringing out the marathon episode as the main cause of the uprising amounts to favouring an analysis of the events as having been driven by religious motives. Rather, many Bahraini informants mention that the uprising was caused by the quelling of a series of demonstrations by unemployed people, usually in front of the Ministry of Labour and Social Affairs. The fact that 'Ali Salman, who led several of these demonstrations, engaged villagers to organize a protest against a marathon organized by foreign private companies was probably not a coincidence, since it was precisely the foreign companies that were accused by the population of being responsible for the unemployment problem by their refusal to hire Bahrainis. A further indication that the marathon only catalyzed a previously existing social strain and was not as such a cause of the uprising is that, for a period of four years, the unrest did not only consist of street battles between the demonstrators and the security forces but included several episodes of violence against Asian workers, the cheap labour favoured by the private companies' recruitment policy.

Be that as it may, the unrest was only appeased after the death of the old Emir and the accession to power of his son in March 1999. The succession marked a real watershed in Bahraini liberalization policy, as well as in the organisation of the Shia Islamic scene. Indeed, in order to bring back

---

29   On these events, see Munira A. Fakhro, "The Uprising in Bahrain: An Assessment", in Lawrence G. Potter and Gary Sick (eds), *The Persian Gulf at the Millennium: Essays in Politics, Economy, Security and Religion*, New York: St Martin's Press, 1997, pp.167-88; Fred H. Lawson, "Repertoires of Contention in Contemporary Bahrain", in Quintan Wiktorowicz (ed.), *Islamic Activism: A Social Movement Theory Approach*, Bloomington: Indiana University Press, 2004, pp. 89-111; J. E. Peterson, "Bahrain: The 1994-1999 Uprising", *Arabian Peninsula Background* Note, n° APBN-002, published on www.JEPeterson. net, January 2004.

peace and order, the new Emir announced his intention to effect what he presented as a genuine regime change, the pillar of which would be the transformation of Bahrain into a constitutional monarchy. He submitted his project to a popular referendum in 2001, gaining more than 98 per cent approval from the voters who had come out *en masse* to participate in the ballot, therefore giving the new ruler a legitimacy which his predecessors never enjoyed. Feeling confident, the then King Hamad bin 'Isa Al-Khalifa decided on a general amnesty towards his opponents and announced the holding of free municipal and legislative elections for 2002. It is in this context that the exiles all came back to Bahrain and all the political prisoners were released. A notable exception in this respect was Hadi al-Mudarrisi, who was still *persona non grata* in Bahrain at the time of writing and did not regain, nor ask for, his Bahraini citizenship. The old political groups were dissolved but were authorized to reconstitute under new names. This was in particular the case of the Islamic Front for the Liberation of Bahrain, which became the Islamic Action Society (*Jama'iyyat al-'Amal al-Islami*). Al-Da'wa did not resume an organized autonomous existence but many of its activists joined al-Wifaq (the Concord), a new party created by 'Ali Salman with the aim of gathering all the Shia Islamic currents under one banner. The young leader succeeded the feat of strength of accommodating al-Da'wa and Hezbollah with the Shiraziyyin, who accepted joining al-Wifaq while retaining in parallel their own autonomous organisation.

The creation of al-Wifaq was very much symptomatic of the new trends at work among the Shia Islamic activists. Indeed, the "patriarchs" of al-Da'wa, most importantly 'Isa Qasem, 'Abdallah al-Ghurayfi and 'Abd al-Amir al-Jamri, did not assume formal responsibilities in the new movement, leaving the floor to activists who had made their reputation thanks to their role in the *intifada*, an event during which 'Isa Qasem and 'Abdallah al-Ghurayfi were out of the country[30] and therefore in which they played no role. 'Abd al-Amir al-Jamri, who stayed in Bahrain throughout the uprising and was even arrested, had retired from political life when al-Wifaq was created, due to a serious illness that finally killed him in 2006. The historic figures of al-Da'wa did not disappear however and still benefited from considerable social power, even being considered as the spiritual leaders of al-Wifaq. We will broach in the next chapter the issue of the scope of their effective influence on the movement's internal decision-making process. At this level of the analysis, what one must essentially bear in mind is that, in the 2000s, involvement in the *intifada* was really the main yardstick of political legitimacy among the Shia population. This was to the extent that the

---

30   'Isa Qasem was in Iran and 'Abdallah al-Ghurayfi was in Syria (*cf.* chapter 6).

old factional quarrels, while still potent at some levels, were overwhelmed by a common agenda defined on the basis of strictly domestic issues. The Shiraziyyin, al-Da'wa and Hezbollah agreed that the struggle using democratic means in order to achieve the reinstatement of the Parliament was the best agenda. The issue of the relationship to the *marja'iyya* and Iran was no longer relevant in this realm, and was only reactivated in the form not of different political choices but of competition for social power.

While the Shia Islamic arena was redrawing itself however, the King unilaterally enacted a new constitution, in 2002. Compared with that voted for by Parliament in 1973, it was far less liberal, in particular because it greatly limited the legislative power of the elected assembly by putting it under the control of a body appointed by the King. Hence, liberalization did certainly mean something in terms of freedom of speech and political association but, at the institutional level, it was also a way for the rulers to reinforce their grip on power. This is not to mention the iniquitous apportionment of the electoral constituencies, that were shaped so as to limit the opposition's chance to control the elected chamber, with little-populated Sunni areas being granted similar representation to heavily-populated Shia ones. To add to the discontent of the Shia population, the government massively naturalized hundreds of Sunni expatriates, most of them working in the security services. Contrary to customs in the other Gulf monarchies where military and naturalized citizens cannot vote, the latter were granted full political rights. This explains why while all the political groups participated in the municipal elections, four of them decided to boycott the legislative elections of October 2002. Two were of liberal persuasion, regrouping ancient leftist and Arab nationalist activists, the other two were al-Wifaq and the Islamic Action Society. Their aim was the invalidation of the 2002 constitution and a return to the 1973 one. [31]

How Can Shias Be Nationalists?

In all three countries, and although in different ways as well as at different levels of intensity, the 1990s and early 2000s have witnessed the establishment of compromise between the regimes and the Shia Islamic movements. Once the possibility was broached, this even led to the latter's integration into official political institutions, at the national level in Kuwait, or at the municipal level in Saudi Arabia and Bahrain. In some cases, this move was

---

31   Laurence Louër, "Les aléas du compromis des élites au Bahreïn", *Maghreb-Machrek*, n° 177, 2003.

accompanied by a marked shift in political language, the most spectacular in this respect being the case of the Saudi Shiraziyyin, who openly embraced the nationalist ideology promoted by the Al-Sa'ud and seemed to have totally forgotten the pan-Islamic pledge of their Iraqi spiritual fathers. Kuwaitis from all the Shia Islamic currents also emerged from the Gulf war with a political strategy clearly oriented to the ostentatious displaying of nationalist feelings in a particular historical context where, more than ever, commitment to the nation was the inescapable element of political legitimacy. Even in Bahrain where the Shias' capacity for identification with the official national narrative promoted by the state is particularly problematic, the Shia Islamic activists claimed to act for the nation's sake. While the Shia communal language is a central element of their political identity, in public the main themes articulated by the leaders are those of democracy and national belonging.

But what lies behind these nationalist discourses in terms of actual social processes? Are they a sign that, in countries like Saudi Arabia and Bahrain, the predicament of nation-building is about to be overcome so that Shias can share with their Sunni fellow-citizens a sense of national citizenship? These questions are of course too large and complex to be addressed merely in a few pages but, for the sake of this study about Shia transnationalism, it is worth providing at least some hypotheses and threads of analysis.

The issue of national belonging is a theme I had the occasion to broach very often with my informants in the course of this research. In September 2004, a conversation I had with a group of Saudi Shia businessmen gave me much food for thought about it. At one point in the conversation, we engaged in a heated debate about "nation" (*watan*), "citizenship" (*muwatana*) and "patriotism" (*wataniyya*), discussing whether the Shias could be really part of the Saudi nation. Pressed by my interlocutors to express, as a supposed expert on the matter, my point of view about this issue, I finally said I had the feeling that many Shias had no attachment to the nation and that, at the end of the day, maybe the main problem was precisely that there was no Saudi nation for the Shias to be Saudi patriots in any way. My words aroused fiery protestation among my interlocutors. One of them told me that "the Shias love their *watan*", the best proof being their attitude during the Gulf War. While the Sunnis fled the Eastern Province *en masse* after the incursion of the Iraqi army, the Shias stayed to defend their *watan*. He ended: "we are *muwatinin* of this country, yes we are! We were *muwatinin* before the Al-Sa'ud came and we will be after they leave!" I suddenly realized that when using the Arabic words "*watan*", "*muwatana*" and "*muwatin*", my interlocutors and I meant different realities. While I was talking about modern citizenship linked to the establishment of the nation-state, they talked about belonging to and love of a homeland. They were not saying to me that they were feeling a part of something like a Saudi nation, they were just telling me that they were the original inhabitants of the land of Qatif and Hasa, a land they had no intention of leaving and were ready to defend it by arms. This clearly reflected the gap between the intellectual discourse of Hasan al-Saffar and his entourage on the one hand, and the average Shia on the other hand. While using the same words, they actually meant totally different things.

Hence a first remark: while the previous period was characterized by the Shia movements' tendency to hide their national dimension behind the transnational Islamic rhetoric, the current period is characterized by the opposite tendency to hide the gap between the Shias' representation of the collective self and that endorsed by the states. In other words, with the notable exception of Kuwait, nationalism in the mouth of the Shia Islamic activists is first and foremost a way to express their allegiance to the ruling dynasties. It is only in Kuwait where, for the reasons explained before and that are linked to the peculiar state formation process (*cf.* chapter 2), the nationalism of the Shias can be understood as a sincere form of patriotism expressing the Shias' ability to identify with the Kuwaiti founding myths. By contrast, Saudi and Bahraini nationalist language, be it in the mouth of the rulers or in that of Hasan al-Saffar, is a "nationalism without a nation",[32] a state ideology expressing a rather bashful endeavour at national integration, the realization of which was not even at the embryonic stage at the time of writing.

This leads us to a second conclusion: in Bahrain and Saudi Arabia, one must distinguish between what I would call the "domestification" of the Shia movements and their "nationalization", that is between the absorption into the arena of the state – the state's capacity of attraction – and the sharing of a common sense of nationality. By making this remark, I do not wish to articulate an approach in terms of cynical political tactics. Indeed, I think that most of the Shia activists I met in Saudi Arabia and Bahrain were sincere in their nationalist language in the sense that they really hoped that Shias and Sunnis could feel part of the same people and share the same national identity. Moreover, it is certain that while it has profound resonance in the Shia collective memory, the myth of Ancient Bahrain and of the Bahrani people has not resulted, for the moment, in the development

---

32   G. Aloysius, *Nationalism without a Nation in India*, Oxford University Press, 1998; Christophe Jaffrelot (ed.), *Pakistan. Nationalism without a Nation?*, New Delhi: Manohar, 2002.

of a socially deeply-rooted nationalist ideology alternative to state nationalism. In other words, the Shias do not bear an alternative nationalist project although their history offers all the material likely to help it materialize one day, in different historical circumstances. Shia religious communalism rather than alternative nationalism is the ideology most likely to put into question the state's nationalist social engineering. In a country like Saudi Arabia however, if well handled by the state, Shia communalism could also be part of a differential mode of political integration, whereby marginalized minorities could succeed in securing their presence within the structure of power by institutionalizing themselves as a legitimate interest group. This type of political integration could not be implemented in Bahrain where, considering their status as the demographic majority and the native inhabitants of the country, Shias contest their very status as a political minority.

By contrast with nationalization which would imply that, at the time of writing, the states' social engineering had been able to induce actual societal effects, domestification means that the state, as a territorialized bureaucratic apparatus penetrating society, has finally succeeded in imposing itself as the hegemonic frame of reference and the final target of political struggle. First, it has succeeded in defining the boundaries of the concrete society which constitutes the territorial field of the struggle. Second, it has imposed itself as the desirable end of the struggle in the sense that people fight to conquer it or to be in it, not to dissolve it in favour of another state form. Third, the state is asked by the Shia movements to implement new laws and regulations in order to improve the Shias' lot as citizens. Hence, the state is seen as the main agency likely to improve their situation.

This capacity of attraction could well be the result of a phenomenon clearly underlined by scientists working in different fields of the social sciences: contention in its various forms often results in the struggling parties looking like each other, and reaching an agreement on the grounds of the conflict through a process by which the contenders are acculturated to the language and the worldview of the contested. This is what Alain Touraine showed while studying the labour social movements, stressing that a major element defining a lasting social movement is its ability to share with its enemy what he calls a "historical system of action",[33] a single sphere created by the conflict seting them in opposition. They struggle in the name of the same values and for the sake of ther same concrete society. In his analysis of ethnicity, Fredrik Barth arrived at the same conclusion: ethnic groups, especially when they are politicized and generate political organizations

---

33   Alain Touraine, *Production de la société*, Paris: Biblio, 1993 (first edition Seuil 1973), pp. 323 and following.

which engage in identity politics, tend to become similar in structure and values so that their objective difference is reduced to a small set of diacritical signs.[34] Another example of this phenomenon is the stigmatized populations studied by Erving Goffman, who end up expressing their contention in the language of the people who reject them.[35] A major conclusion of these different works is that the dominant group, the one which is the object of the contention, most often succeeds in imposing its worldview on its opponents and that political change is the result of this dialectical relation. A major attribute of the dominant group's power is to impose its frame of reference on the dominated. In our case, the frame of reference is the territorial limits of the struggle but also its final objective, that is the state as it is: conquering it as a whole or having a say in its policy. In brief, the nation state appears as the impassable horizon of politics.

THE FALL OF THE BA'TH IN IRAQ:
BACK TO SHIA TRANSNATIONALISM?

Following the attacks of 11 September 2001 in New York, the American administration led by George W. Bush decided on a new foreign policy aimed at reshaping the Middle East on a democratic basis in order to eradicate the terrorist threat. A major chapter of this plan, the deposition of Saddam Husein in Iraq has been rightly considered as a major historical rupture that set in motion new geopolitical dynamics in the Middle East. One of the most often pointed out aspects of this shift has been the modification of the Shias' overall status as political actors, with a marked tendency to depict them as the object of a broad revival rendering them more assertive, but also more cohesive within the nation states and, more importantly, beyond them. In brief, one could witness the return of Shia transnationalism, bolstered by the arrival to power of the Shia movements in Baghdad and the empowerment of Iran.

The "Shia Revival"

In December 2004, in a henceforth famous interview published in the *Washington Post*, King 'Abdallah II of Jordan expressed deep concern about what he perceived as the overall empowerment of the Shias following the

---

34   Fredrik Barth, "Introduction", in Fredrik Barth (ed.), *Ethnic Groups and Boundaries. The Social Organization of Culture Difference*, Oslo, Universitetsforlaget/ Boston, Little, Brown and Company, 1969, p. 35.

35   Erving Goffman, *Stigma. Notes on the Management of Spoiled Identity*, Old Tappan, New Jersey: Touchstone Books, 1986, p. 114.

accession to power in Baghdad of the Shia Islamic movements.[36] While explaining why he was so concerned, he formulated a concept that hit the bull's-eye and thus became a central theme of the media debate about the new regional order: the "Shia crescent". The success of the concept no doubt lay in its ability to sum up in a short formula the spontaneous perception of the Shias by the majority of the Sunnis: people united by a corporate solidarity beyond national borders and subservient to Iranian expansionism. Indeed, in the mind of the Jordanian ruler, the Shia crescent referred to the formation of a broad alliance between all Shias, at the centre of which was the Islamic Republic.

In the media, King 'Abdallah's interview marked the departure for an all-out analysis which gave substance to what was initially a rather vague notion, by drawing the outlines of an apparently coherent Shia collective dynamic transcending the borders of the various states. In other words, facts and events involving Shias in different places in the Middle East were increasingly analyzed from the *a priori* assumption that they were linked together or at least had a reciprocal influence. The empowerment of Iran as the result of the elimination of the Taliban in Afghanistan, the fall of Saddam Husein in Iraq, the direct presence of the USA in Iraq which has put them within shooting range of Iranian nuisance capacity and the very likely possibility that Iran is pursuing a military nuclear programme, has been seen as a major cause of Shia emboldening. Hence, while Iraq was described more and more as having become an Iranian satellite, in Lebanon, the initiatives of Hezbollah were seen as the result of the Shias' overall confidence and, moreover, as the direct consequence of Iranian foreign policy. The Gulf did not escape this type of analysis. Analysts pointed out the new self-assurance of Saudi Shias since the fall of Saddam Husein and, conversely, every episode of the traditionally agitated Bahraini political life was now seen in the light of the overall Shia empowerment, as a spill-over effect of Iraqi developments or the new Iranian confidence. In 2006, a book by Vali Nasr, *The Shia Revival*, systematized this type of approach. While he does not believe that the Shias are docile tools in Iranian hands, the author insisted that the general empowerment of the Shias was one of the major consequences of the Bush administration's new Middle Eastern policy and warned that it could create a general and violent rift between Sunnis and Shias all over the region. But his analysis remained in many respects undecided between the proposal that the Shia revival was a mere

---

36   Robin Wright and Peter Baker, "Iraq, Jordan See Threat to Elections from Iran", *Washington Post*, Wednesday, December 8, 2004.

casual conjunction of events and the idea that it was the product of the reciprocal influences the various national situations exerted on one another.

The Gulf is a particularly interesting case study to broach the issue of the consequences of the geopolitical upheaval brought by the new American policy in the Middle East. Among the region's countries indeed, the Gulf monarchies have probably been the most worried by the empowerment of Iran, a country to whom they are neighbours and with whom they have had painful relations in the recent past. The new regional deal has changed their threat perception. In the 1990s as we have just seen, with the notable exception of Bahrain, they first and foremost were afraid of Sunni Islamic contestation and had changed their perception of their Shia opponents. Now, very much as in the 1980s in the aftermath of the Islamic revolution, they fear their own Shia populations will be emboldened. The election of Mahmud Ahmadinejad to the Iranian presidency in 2005 aggravated this reading of the situation since, although they have not been directly targeted by his aggressive rhetoric, the change of tone of Iranian foreign policy has reminded them of the early days of the revolution. Hence, among Gulf policy-makers and analysts, the idea is widespread that Iran is resuming with the exportation of the revolution. Wrong or right, this perception has had far reaching implications for the position of the Shia movements within the domestic political arenas of the three countries under scrutiny. As we shall see, more than the Shias' own initiatives, which proved strikingly similar to the options taken during the previous decade, it is mainly the rulers' changing threat perception that explains the changes we will now analyse and, therefore, that is the main common denominator of the various phenomenons composing the so-called "Shia revival".

A Policy of Relative Religious Recognition in Saudi Arabia

Among the Gulf monarchies, Saudi Arabia has no doubt been the country most affected by the dynamics set in motion by the new American policy, including when one looks at the situation of the Shias. Indeed, the kingdom was among the main targets of the United States, after the investigation had shown that the majority of the terrorists of the 9/11 attacks were Saudi citizens and the American authorities reached the conclusion that it was the very ideology of the Saudi regime that had paved the way for the radical interpretations of Islam nourishing terrorism. As in 1991, the strain put on the Saudi regime resulted in a wave of liberalization when the regime's opponents took the opportunity of resuming their demands for reform. In the course of 2003, the latter launched a series of petitions, the main one entitled "Vision for the Present and Future of the Country". In a marked difference with the 1990s petitions, the group of signatories was heterogeneous in terms of ideology and religious affiliation, comprising both liberal and Islamic activists, Sunnis and Shias alike.[37] In other words, the opposition had apparently succeeded in transcending their divergences, imposing a generally similar diagnosis on the kingdom's situation.

Among the initiatives taken by the rulers to tackle this new upsurge of contestation, a series of conferences of "National Dialogue" was established under the patronage of Crown Prince 'Abdallah, with the aim to formulate recommendations for reform. Among the other measures taken by the rulers was the relative liberalization of the debate in the media and the holding of municipal elections in the course of the year 2005. Half of the councils' members were actually elected by the male citizens, while the other half were appointed by the government, including the president. The prerogatives of the council were rather limited and the ballot stirred little interest from the population, with only fifteen per cent of the eligible electors registering on the lists.[38] However, in a country where politics had been taboo for so many years, the move represented a significant step.

To date, the Shia Islamic opposition has probably been the main beneficiary of the new set of reforms. While they joined forces with the other sectors of the political spectrum, Hasan al-Saffar and his companions set in motion a specifically Shia agenda capitalizing on the Saudi rulers' new threat perception to renegotiate their position. Indeed, in organizing pressure on the Saudis, the Americans resorted, among other things, to the fears generated by the perceived Shia empowerment and distilled rumours about a project to create a new Shia state in the Gulf from the partition of the Eastern Province and its union with Bahrain (cf. chapter 1). The rumour culminated in the weeks preceding the American invasion of Iraq and was cleverly used by the Shiraziyyin to show the rulers that improving the lot of their Shia citizens was not only a matter of justice but a strategic choice for the kingdom's security. It was time for the Al-Sa'ud to take positive steps to convince the Shias that they had no interest in playing the game of foreign powers, in this case not so much Iran as the US. Therefore, while some Shirazi figures publicly suggested that they envis-

---

37   On the 2003 petitions, see International Crisis Group (ICG), *Can Saudi Arabia Reform Itself?*, Middle East Report n° 28, 14 July 2004, pp. 13-15.

38   On the 2005 elections, see Pascal Ménoret, "Le cheikh, l'électeur et le SMS. Logiques électorales et mobilisation islamique en Arabie Saoudite", *Transcontinentales*, n° 1. *Réformes et « Grand Moyen-Orient »*, 2005 (available on Pascal Ménoret's blog, http://pascal-menoret.over-blog.com).

aged the partition as a possible solution for their co-religionists' predicament, Hasan al-Saffar for his part made unprecedented declarations about his commitment to the Saudi monarchy. The most significant episode was that of the 2004 American State Secretary report on religious freedom in Saudi Arabia, which denounced the treatment of the Shia minority but which Hasan al-Saffar, through an official *communiqué*, nonetheless stigmatized as an inadmissible intrusion in Saudi Arabia's internal affairs. While Hasan al-Saffar's position was the object of fierce debate among the Shiraziyyin, many of whom considered that he had exaggerated his legitimist positioning and should have kept silent, it was particularly revealing of his strategy. The latter, actually, was the same as defined in the previous period: to pressure while displaying overt, and what some considered immoderate and indiscriminate allegiance,[39] to the ruling dynasty and in particular Prince 'Abdallah. In no way did the new regional deal lead him to resume any form of transnational revolutionary project.

The first step in this respect was the presentation, in April 2003, of a petition to Prince 'Abdallah. It was eloquently entitled "Partners of the Nation" (*Shuraka fi al-Watan*) and signed by some four hundreds and fifty Shia personalities. The signatories, a heterogeneous group of persons with various regional,[40] professional and ideological backgrounds beyond their common social identity as Shias, pledged full allegiance to the Al-Sa'ud. In exchange, they demanded that the Shias be recognized officially as a fully-fledged and legitimate Islamic school of thought (*madhhab*), at the same level than the four Sunni ones. They also demanded equal social rights. The petitioners were received by Prince 'Abdallah, who agreed to be photographed beside fully-turbaned clerics and showed particular goodwill in listening to their complaints. A few weeks later in June 2003, he initiated the first conference of national dialogue, dedicated to an unprecedented public debate between representatives of the various religious components of the country. Shias, but also Sufis and representatives of the other schools of thought of Sunni Islam than the official one, sat together with figures from the Wahhabi establishment as well as with personalities from the Sunni Islamic opposition.[41]

---

39   Toby Jones, "The Iraq Effect in Saudi Arabia", *Middle East Report* n° 237, winter 2005, p. 3.

40   Something unprecedented was that Shias from Medina, who have only marginally enrolled in political activities, agreed to sign the petition.

41   Salman al-'Awda in particular, a leading figure from the Sahwa, the Sunni Islamic opposition inspired by the ideas of the Muslim Brotherhood.

Another step in Hasan al-Saffar's strategy was the show of strength that was organized at the occasion of the 2005 municipal elections in the Eastern Province. Indeed, as compared with the other provinces of the kingdom, Qatif and Hasa witnessed a rather high participation rate which was fostered by the Shiraziyyin's ability to mobilize their constituency, with the mosques and the *huseiniyya* serving as meeting places. Obviously, they succeeded in convincing the population that, despite the limited competences of the councils, these elections constituted a real opportunity for the Shias to influence the management of their region's local affairs and, overall, to show, by their mobilization, the extent of their power. As a result, the Shiraziyyin won almost all the seats submitted to the ballot and Ja'far al-Shayeb, a close associate of Hasan al-Saffar and a leading cadre of the Reform Movement, was finally appointed mayor of Qatif.

What have been the concrete outcomes of the Shirazyyin's strategy, in terms of the improvement of the Shias' lot that is their main declared aim? To date, it is mainly in the domain of religious freedom that progress has been made, because the regime's policy towards the Shias has mainly been one of religious recognition. In other words, the line is going in the direction of a – very – relative religious equalization and not in that of democratic rights or anti-discrimination policy in the social realm. Hence today, in the localities where the Shias constitute the overwhelming majority in the region of Qatif, they openly celebrate the most ostentatious and, in the eyes of the orthodox Sunnis, provocative rituals. People stick up posters with Shia religious slogans and iconography on the walls. They assemble in the squares of their villages to perform theatre plays retracing the life of the Imams. They form cortèges of penitents in the streets, with the police – composed of Sunnis – helping their progression by rerouting the traffic. In a related domain, one has noted a significant increase in the number of Shia mosques built in the Eastern Province, thanks to the end of the hindrance of construction permits.

Another aspect of the regime's policy of relative religious recognition was the reform of the Shia religious courts. In 2003, Hasan al-Saffar and his entourage submitted to the rulers a complete project to improve the courts' calamitous situation. In 1913 when King 'Abd al-'Aziz conquered the Eastern Province, the Shias were granted the right to have a separate judiciary for matters pertaining to religious and family affairs. Two religious judges were officially recognized, one in Qatif and one in Hasa, but the situation of the courts had never been reappraised since that period, with the two judges officiating for a population maybe reaching two million in the whole kingdom, in particularly tumbledown offices, with almost no administrative staff. The reform of the Shia judiciary had been an old demand from the Saudi opposition and the clerical establishment in general. It is significant that it is in the particular context described above that the rulers decided to answer favourably. In 2005, two Shia religious judges were appointed in the courts of Qatif and Hasa, plus three in a new appeal court created in Qatif, adding up to a total of seven judges. One should mention that the appointment of the Shia judges was the occasion of strategic co-optation for the government, which tried to engage the more reluctant and potentially dangerous sectors of the population. In 2006, it appointed Ghalib al-Hammad, a well-known figure of the Hezbollah trend, as the chief of the Shia supreme court of Qatif. Only time will tell whether this will effectively placate the militants of the Hijazi Hezbollah.

The reform of the Shia judiciary was no doubt a good step towards the improvement of the status of the Shia population in Saudi Arabia. But one should note that many Shias look at it with some indifference. For them, improvement of religious freedom is of course important but they wait above all for progress in the social realm. In a country where the unemployment rate reaches thirty per cent, the major concern is that of professional discrimination, especially among the younger generation. Lots of Shias have countless stories to tell about this or that brilliant student who got the best possible marks in his high school diploma but was refused registration at the university in profit of a Sunni mediocre student. The phenomenon appears to be particularly widespread among girls. Shias are also very angry about the ARAMCO recruitment policy, a company that provided so many jobs to them until the 1970s and contributed so much to the improvement of their socio-economic situation. Shias, they say, have been replaced by people coming from other parts of the country. They are particularly resentful of the Ghamid people, that is members of the Ghamid large tribe from south west Saudi Arabia who moved massively to the Eastern Province after the oil boom and were employed in ARAMCO to, say the Shias, replace the Shia employees. Shias often joke bitterly about this, saying that ARAMCO should be renamed "GHAMIDCO" to better reflect its staff's social composition. The employment problem is all the more important since the Shias have not developed any form of independent economy. In other words, private entrepreneurship is under-developed, and Shia businessmen cannot match the activities of their Sunni counterparts. In an economy where cronyism is the rule,[42] Shias again suffer from their lack of social capital and access to information. The few wealthy Shia

---

42   Champion (2003).

businessmen built their fortune because they managed to gain the trust of Al-Sa'ud princes.

Changing this state of affairs is another story to letting the Shias grieve Imam Husein in public or Hasan al-Saffar embracing King 'Abdallah. Provided they get it one day, the Shias' official recognition as a fully-fledged Islamic school of thought is unlikely to result in concrete progress in the field of social discrimination. For while social discrimination against the Shias has of course religious roots it is also grounded in general social practices that cannot be removed from one day to another. Hence, getting a good job in Saudi Arabia, as by the way in many other Arab countries, is a matter of "*wasta*", string-pulling. The problem is that being at the bottom of the social hierarchy, Shias have in general less social capital than their Sunni fellow-citizens, and therefore less access to various types of resources. Particularly, and this is the second reason why Shias' problems are difficult to solve by a mere decision from the top, when Saudi Arabia has entered an era of rarefaction of resources when competition is becoming even harder to sustain. Sunnis as such are not a privileged population and also suffer from the retrenchment of the welfare state. In this context, maintaining the religious stigma on the Shias can be seen as an efficient way to make sure they remain outside of the most rewarding social networks.

The Bipolarization of the Shia Political Arena in Kuwait

Viewed from the Shias' perspective, the way the new regional order impacted on Kuwait displays some strikingly similar elements with the way it impacted on Saudi Arabia. Indeed, it is no doubt that the Kuwaiti rulers' perception that the Shias' accession to power in Baghdad had proved that discriminating against the Shias could lead to dramatic developments pushed them to accede to old demands pertaining to religious equality. Like in Saudi Arabia also, the anti-discriminatory policy was implemented exclusively in the religious and not the political domain.

Compared with the other currents of political Shiism, the Shirazyyin in Kuwait were the most active in pushing for this policy of religious equalization. Two demands were essential for them in this respect. The first was the creation of a special Shia department at the Ministry of Religious Endowments. Up to 2004 indeed, the Shia religious endowments (*waqf*) were administered by the ministry in, theoretically, the same way as the Sunni ones. But the Shias were complaining that as the Ministry of Religious Endowments always fell into the hands of the Sunni Islamic movements unsympathetic to the Shias, their interests were not well represented. Hence the demand for a Shia department within the ministry, that would be administered by Shias. The second demand was, as in Saudi Arabia, pertaining to the reform of the Shia religious legal system. The Shiraziyyin demanded the creation of a court of appeal. The two issues were among the main themes of the campaign of Saleh 'Ashur when he first won his seat in Parliament in 1999. Significantly however, it is only in 2004 that he finally obtained satisfaction. He himself attributed the unblocking of the situation to the new regional context, that had made Kuwaiti rulers realize that, after all, they could satisfy their Shia citizens by taking rather simple measures and hence placate any attempt at using real or perceived discrimination for political purposes. By the way, these measures were paralleled by others, all moving in the direction of a better representation of Shias in the Kuwaiti public life. Hence since 2004, the Kuwaiti television displays programs about Shiism during 'Ashura in which Shia clerics explain the significance of this or that doctrine. Moreover, the performance of Shia religious rituals in public, which used to be forbidden because it was considered a perturbation of public order, is now authorized. This is so, in particular, of the traditional theatre plays recounting the martyrdom of Imam Husein in Karbala.

In the political space, the impact of the new regional situation has been rather limited, in particular when one looks at the redrawing of the Shia political map that occurred in the 2000s. As compared with the 1990s which witnessed an attempt at unifying the various Shia Islamic groups under the umbrella of the National Islamic Coalition, the 2000s witnessed the proliferation of new Shia political societies, in part under the influence of the liberalization of the right to form associations and in part because of the internal dynamics of the Kuwaiti political space itself.

The National Islamic Coalition collapsed immediately after the 1992 elections, leaving the floor to so-called "independent" figures. By the end of the 1990s, informal centres of social power among Shia society began to institutionalize. The first move occurred in 1998 when, in the prospect of parliamentary elections scheduled for the following year, the followers of the Imam's Line founded the Islamic National Alliance (*al-Tahaluf al-Islami al-Watani*). It included old activists of the Social Society for Culture like 'Adnan 'Abd al-Samad and 'Abd al-Muhsin Jamal, as well as new, younger activists politicized after the Islamic revolution, like the secretary general of the group, Husein al-Ma'tuk (*cf.* chapter 6). In 2003, the Islamic National Alliance split after quarrels over the candidacies, leading to the creation of the Islamic National Understanding (*al-Tawafuq al-Islami al-Watani*), headed by 'Abd al-Wahhab al-Wazzan and his wife Khadija

Mahmid. With only a small social base the two were said to be ideologically closer to the Iranian reformists clustered around then president Moham- med Khatami, while those who remained in the Islamic National Alliance were more identified with the conservative right and the Supreme Guide Ali Khamene'i. The same year, the Shiraziyyin officially announced the creation of a third Shia Islamic group named the Assembly for Justice and Peace (*Tajammuʿ al-ʿAdala wa al-Salam*). The following year in 2005, a fourth Shia group was created, named al-Mithaq (the Pact). Its general secretary was ʿAbd al-Hadi Saleh, the ex-vice president of the Social Society for Culture at the end of the 1980s who, in contrast with the bulk of the Society's members who shifted to the Hezbollah line, had remained faith- ful to the initial line of al-Daʿwa.

In addition to these four political societies, there are two other associa- tions worth mentioning. In 2001, S. Mohammed Baqer al-Muhri founded the Assembly of the Shia Religious Scholars (*Tajammuʿ al-ʿUlama al-Shiʿa*). Modelled on the Combatant Clergy Association in Iran, its aim was to gather the Shia clerics of Kuwait in order to transform them into a genuine pressure group. Since then, the Assembly has issued regular communiqués on important local and international matters. It was particularly active dur- ing the 2003 war in Iraq and in its aftermath. While it is not a political movement as such, the aim of the group is to influence the government and political actors so that the Shias' interests are better advanced. Mohammed Baqer al-Muhri himself came from a family of science[43] and was born in Najaf where he stayed until 1980, when the repression pushed him to reset- tle in Iran. He reached Kuwait only in the mid-1980s. He became known as a vocal opponent to Saddam Husein's regime, of which Kuwait was by then a principal supporter. This earned him arrest and prison. Because he was long absent from Kuwait, Mohammed Baqer al-Muhri was not social- ized politically in either one or the other rival lines born in the 1970s. He began only to emerge as an important figure in the aftermath of the liberation, but not in the framework of any constituted group or current. A free electron, the Assembly of the Shia Religious Scholars was for him the means to forge an autonomous centre of power by trying to constitute himself as the main spokesperson of the Shia community. While the As- sembly did not succeed in bringing together all the Shia scholars of Kuwait and in particular the most influential ones,[44] the group distinguishes itself by its rhetorical activism, systematically issuing communiqués on subjects

---

43   On the al-Muhri families, *cf.* chapter 2.

44   For example S. Husein al-Qallaf, an independent cleric who was elected three times to Parliament between 1996 and 2003.

as different as the coalition's intervention in Iraq in 2003 or the affair of the publication in a Danish newspaper of caricatures of Mohammed in 2006. Since the fall of Saddam Husein, Mohammed Baqer al-Muhri has been the main representative of 'Ali al-Sistani in Kuwait to whom he sometimes attributes contested declarations.

The last of the Shia political or semi-political groups is the Assembly of the Human Message (*Tajammu' al-Risala al-Insaniyya*). Created in 2006, it emanated from the Sheikhi community which, in the context of the liberalization of the right to form associations, for the first time took the step of constituting its own formal instrument of representation.

Beyond the apparent fragmentation, the Shia political scene witnessed a process of bipolarization around two blocs roughly espousing the outlines of the initial quarrel between the pro- and anti-Iranians. The Shiraziyyin were the main force that pushed for the formation of the National Coalition of the Assemblies (*I'tilaf al-Tajammu'at al-Watani*) in 2006, which included all the above mentioned societies with the exception of the Islamic National Alliance. Being unable to defeat their rivals alone, the Shiraziyyin opted for a strategy of alliance with all the other forces of the Shia political spectrum in an attempt to isolate the Islamic National Alliance. Not all the societies that integrated into the National Coalition of the Assemblies are as pathologically hostile to the Islamic National Alliance as are the Shiraziyyin. Being close to 'Ali al-Sistani, Mohammed Baqer al-Muhri is indeed not among the denigrators of Ali Khamene'i, about whom he speaks as a *marja'* and the *wali amr al-muslimin*, that is the political leader of all the Muslims worldwide.[45] In 2004, at the moment of the first attempt by the Shiraziyyin to establish a Shia front against the Islamic National Alliance (*cf.* chapter 6), he was probably the one who ruined the project. This explains why the Shiraziyyin refrained from making public anti-Hezbollah declarations in 2006, although they go on doing so in private by saying that these people are definitely too pro-Iranian to be worth working with.

Therefore, if the National Coalition of the Assemblies is not strictly speaking an anti-Hezbollah formation as the Shiraziyyin wished it to be, the fact remains that most of its constituents belong to political and religious currents that have been critical of the Iranian model in one way or another, while the Islamic National Alliance remains unambiguously on a line supporting the *wilayat al-faqih* and the conservative right in Tehran.

But the position towards Iran is certainly not the only determining factor explaining the bipolarization of the Kuwaiti political scene. Again, the

---

45   Personal interview, Kuwait, June 2003.

configuration would not last long if it was not anchored in strictly local cleavages and, in particular, the position towards the government and the ruling dynasty in general. The societies gathered in the National Coalition of the Assemblies are close to the government, the support of which they count on to get their candidates elected. The Shiraziyyin, who are the most active element within it, are essentially focused on communal objectives pertaining to the improvement of the situation of the Shias as a communal whole. In contrast, the Islamic National Alliance defines itself as an opposition movement and has much more ideological positions. The most recent example of that is the May 2006 crisis pertaining to the reshaping of the constituencies in prospect of elections that were to be held a few weeks later. In the parliamentary debates about the opportunity to reduce the number of constituencies in order to politicize the elections, fight clientelism and better prevent the government's intervention in the ballots, a group of twenty-nine deputies emerged that pressured the government to reduce the constituencies from twenty-five to five. Among the twenty-nine, the bulk were opponents to the government long known for demanding enhanced power for the Parliament. Those opposed to the reduction of the constituencies were known for being pro-government. In fact, the government was hostile to the five constituencies. Significantly, Saleh 'Ashur and Yusef al-Zilzila, the two deputies belonging to societies included in the National Coalition of the Assemblies, positioned themselves against the reduction to five constituencies, while the deputies of the Islamic National Alliance joined those in favour of it. The crisis was so severe that the government decided to dissolve Parliament and to hold new elections early, therefore postponing the debate to the next legislature.

At the time of writing, it was too early to make a clear evaluation of the success of the Shiraziyyin's attempt at weakening the pro-Iranian influence. Let us nonetheless mention that the results of the 2006 elections showed that this is far from being accomplished. If Saleh 'Ashur was re-elected for the third time in the first constituency, Yusef al-Zilzila, his ally in 2003 who integrated the al-Mithaq society, lost against Ahmed Lari, a member of the Islamic National Alliance. As for 'Adnan 'Abd al-Samad, he regained the seat he had lost in 2003. Hasan Jawhar, who is not formally in the Islamic National Alliance but is well known for being very close to it, was re-elected for the fourth time. In brief, only one candidate of the Coalition of the National Assemblies was elected against three for its rival. But, here again, one should be wary not to interpret the victory of the pro-Iranian current as an effect of the empowerment of Iran as a state. Indeed, it was the result of strictly domestic developments. The Islamic National Alliance benefited from the dynamics created by the opposition in the entire Kuwaiti society and not from what Iran did and said. This is the final argument showing that, in Kuwait, the political positioning of the Shias is the result of their participation in the main fracture lines organizing general political life.

Bahrain at a Dead End

In Bahrain, as in Saudi Arabia and Kuwait, the reframing of the geopolitical order has mainly had the effect of accelerating previously engaged dynamics rather that setting up new ones. By contrast with its neighbour however, the effect has essentially been negative, contributing to the further deterioration of the pre-2003 situation. This is mainly due to the fact that, because Shias suffer little religious discrimination and represent the demographic majority, a politics merely of religious recognition cannot substitute for a genuine democratization policy.

The boycott of the 2002 legislative elections marked the beginning of a new period of tension to the extent that the democratization process had come to a stalemate at the time of writing. If 2003 was characterized by a wait and see attitude on the part of both the opposition and the government, 2004 and the following years were marked by the rulers' systematic attempts to hinder the opposition's endeavour to mobilize the population and the international community in favour of the reinstatement of the 1973 constitution and the abolition of the 2002 one. Among the most serious breaches of political freedom have been the detention and maybe torture of opposition and human rights activists, the closure of societies, the banning of journals and web sites, the quelling of demonstrations and the restriction of political organisations' activities through the enactment of a new, restrictive, regulation. The result was that during the four years of Parliament's term, the boycotters overall and the Shia movements in particular were unable to achieve any significant progress in their agenda.[46]

As the legislature was coming to an end, most of the leaders of al-Wifaq reached the conclusion that it was worth trying another way and began to launch an intense campaign, among their base and in the population, in favour of participation in the 2006 elections. This decision provoked a split within al-Wifaq, when a handful of cadres, among whom were very

---

46   On this period, see Katja Niethammer, *Voices in Parliament, Debates in Majalis, and Banners on the Streets. Avenues of Political Participation in Bahrain*, EUI Working Papers RSCAS n° 2006/27, The European University Institute, Robert Schuman Centre for Advanced Studies, Mediterranean Programme Series, Florence, 2006 (www.iue.it/RSCAS/WP-Texts/06_27.pdf).

popular figures like 'Abd al-Wahhab Husein or Hasan Msheima who were heroes of the *intifada*, quit to found another movement named al-Haqq (the Right), which engaged in an active campaign in favour of the boycott. In an endeavour at internationalizing the Bahraini political debate, it chose to launch a petition that it intended to present to the United Nations, in which it demanded that the UN should sponsor a popular referendum on the 2002 constitution. As for the al-Wifaq leadership, its open aim was to win the majority of seats and hence the presidency of Parliament. For its part, the government used the same strategies as in 2002 to reduce the opposition's chances of winning the ballot. Hence, it naturalized hundreds of Sunni expatriates during the weeks preceding the vote. The issue was even more explosive this time since it turned into the so-called "Bandar gate" affair. In September 2006, Saleh al-Bandar, an English citizen of Sudanese origin working within the Bahraini public administration, published a disturbingly well-documented report revealing a conspiracy engineered by members of the Al-Khalifa dynasty to alter the sectarian balance of the country. He was expelled from the country but the report put a shadow over the entire electoral process, further infuriating the opposition and convincing the Shias that they had nothing to gain from it.

Nevertheless, by contrast with 2002, al-Wifaq maintained its decision to participate and succeeded in convincing its constituency that it was the lesser evil considering the situation. Actually, the turnout was high, reaching 72 per cent. However, al-Wifaq was unable to fulfil its expectations as it did not obtain an absolute majority. While it won all the constituencies it had targeted, most of its liberal allies were defeated, probably following fraud organized by the government. Most of the liberals were Sunnis denouncing the practice of the government as the main cause of sectarian tensions. They accused the government of having let al-Wifaq win in the Shia constituencies because it knew it could do nothing and instead focusing on defeating the liberal candidates, not only because they were allied to al-Wifaq but because it could not accept the idea that Sunnis would join Shias to fight the regime. Its best weapon, they said, was to make people continue to believe that only the Shias oppose the regime, for purely sectarian reasons. It is of course difficult to verify systematically all the opposition's affirmations about fraud and plots to change the demographic structure of Bahrain. Not least because the regime ousted the organizations that had played a useful monitoring role during the 2002 elections. The National Democratic Institute was requested to leave Bahrain in 2005 and even a trip to Bahrain by its patron, Madeleine Albright, could not make the King change his mind about it. By the same token, the local head of

Transparency International was harassed for alleged corruption, and the organization's offices closed. One can at least surmise that the closure of all these institutions would not have been necessary if the Bahraini government had nothing to hide.

On top of the manipulation of the electoral process, the Bahraini government resumed another of its preferred strategies to discredit the Shia Islamic opposition, that of accusing it of being the Trojan horse of Iranian destabilization policy. The December 2005 affair of the arrest of a certain Sh. Mohammed al-Sanad was typical in this respect. The sheikh, a Shia cleric educated in Qom and living for years between Bahrain and Iran as was the case for dozens of his colleagues, was arrested at the airport upon one of his trips back to Bahrain from Iran because he had, according to the authorities, incited against the government. As the news of his arrest crossed the country, some three hundred people rushed to the airport to protest and things degenerated into a mini-riot. A handful of young men were then arrested and condemned to several years in prison. As for Mohammed al-Sanad, he was himself soon released and engaged not to threaten public order anymore. The affair, which was given considerable local media coverage, was presented in the official media as an example of the harmful role played by Iranian agents in Bahrain. Some foreign embassies were even told that Mohammed al-Sanad had actually promoted the idea of a popular referendum in which Bahrainis would be asked to give their opinion on the possible uniting of Bahrain with Iran.

Put in the overall Bahraini internal context and restored in its truth, the affair however appears banal. First, one should note that Mohammed al-Sanad was barely known by the Bahraini public before this incident, precisely because he was living in Iran most of the time and did not meddle in Bahraini religious or political affairs. Second, in Qom, where he lived most of the time, he had worked for a long period in the office of Mohammed al-Shirazi who, as shown previously, was anything but a supporter of the Iranian regime. Third, at the time he was arrested, he had left the Shiraziyyin for years and had joined the office of Sh. Jawad Tabrizi (d. 2006), a leading Iranian *marja'* of Qom with quite a good following in the Gulf monarchies. While not an opponent of the Iranian regime, the latter was known for his reluctance towards the doctrine of *wilayat al-faqih* and for his quietist political stance. In terms of financing moreover, he was totally independent from the Iranian state. Finally, Mohammed al-Sanad had actually never asked for the holding of a referendum on Bahrain's uniting with Iran. He had simply signed the petition launched by al-Haqq to demand that the UN organize a referendum on the legitimacy of the 2002 constitution. In brief, Mohammed al-Sanad did not have the profile of an Iranian agent and, in the crisis hitting Bahrain since 2002, had simply taken sides in the political debate. Nothing less, but nothing more.

At the time of writing, violent incidents in Bahrain were following one after another and rumours of all sorts were spreading so that the country was no doubt in a state of worsening crisis. But this was in no way the result of any kind of spill-over effect from the civil war in Iraq, and even less of an Iranian grand strategy to overthrow the Al-Khalifa regime. In the short run, what can be witnessed in Bahrain is rather just the continuation of the dynamics engaged in 2002. In the longer run, it is simply another manifestation of the inability of the ruling dynasty to bridge the gap with the major part of its Shia population. The difference with Saudi Arabia here is striking. As in Saudi Arabia, the Bahraini rulers have felt particularly threatened by the shift of the geopolitical situation but reacted the other way round, that is by stepping back rather than going further in the liberalization process. The peculiarity of Bahrain's demographic imbalance no doubt played a role in this choice and the radical implications of the democratization of Iraq, with the demographic majority acceding to power and taking its revenge, giving Bahraini leaders food for thought about their possible future. But here again, it is through the representation that it aroused in the Sunni psyche and not through the modification of the Shia agenda that the regional context played a role in moving the Sunni/Shia relation. For the Shias, the new context only adds to the tools at their disposal to continue with their previous strategy. It is the Sunnis who now feel under siege.

The Decrease of Relational Modes of Diffusion

The cases of Saudi Arabia, Bahrain and Kuwait have shown that, far from having constituted a rupture, the fall of Saddam Husein and the regional dynamics it set in motion did not engender a new Shia political paradigm but have rather reinforced the progressive evolution of the Shia Islamic movements since the second half of the 1980s. Hence at the time of writing, these movements were more and more becoming traditional national political movements the agendas of which were defined essentially according to the structure of domestic political opportunities. This is not to say that the links between the various Shia movements have been destroyed. Neither is this the case of their relations to their religious authorities of reference. Far from it: the Shia transnational networks are still vivid because the interpersonal relations woven throughout the past years still provide an efficient infrastructure for communication, mutual support and general circulation of persons. However, in the framework of the domestification process, these links have ceased to play a leading role in shaping the concrete political actions of the Shia movements.

It is possible to reach another general conclusion from the most recent domestic developments in the three Gulf countries under scrutiny here: today, the relational mode of diffusion of ideas and patterns of action is playing a marginal role in favour of more volatile and fragile processes of emulation. A particularly telling example of this is the weak capacity for transnational networking of the new Iraqi Shia movements. While we still lack the necessary temporal distance to draw definitive conclusions in this respect, the fact remains that they had not spread outside of the borders of Iraq at the time of writing. In my eyes, this is not a coincidence and rather reveals the fact that the Iraqi movements have definitely also been absorbed by the domestic sphere, which makes them rather indifferent to what is happening to their co-religionists elsewhere. The best example in this regard is that of the so-called "Sadriyyin", the followers of S. Muqtada al-Sadr (b. 1973), who have constituted into a loose political group in the aftermath of Saddam Husein's fall.

As a politico-religious phenomenon, the Sadriyyin are reminiscent of the Shiraziyyin in several aspects. First, it is a movement constituted around a religious figure who uses his prestigious family ascendancy to grasp political power. In contrast to Mohammed al-Shirazi in his time, Muqtada al-Sadr never claimed the *marja'iyya* but claims religious legitimacy by reference to his father, S. Mohammed Sadiq al-Sadr (1943-1999) and, more generally, because of belonging to a famous lineage of clerics. His father was a cousin – and a student – of Mohammed Baqer al-Sadr, the founder and spiritual leader of al-Da'wa, whose daughter Muqtada al-Sadr himself married. Mohammed Mohammed Sadiq al-Sadr – more known as Mohammed Sadiq al-Sadr – emerged as a *marja'* after the death of Abu al-Qasem al-Khu'i in 1992, thanks to the support of the Ba'thist regime, who backed his claim to supreme religious authority because it wished to promote, after years of dominance of the Iranian *mujtahid*, what it deemed an authentic Arab and Iraqi *marja'* likely to constitute a more amenable interlocutor.[47] But the attempt ended in stalemate for the regime, as the *marja'* soon decided to follow another path and began establishing himself as a charismatic figure, in particular through his attempts at restoring the practice of the Friday

---

47   On the life of Mohammed Sadiq al-Sadr, see 'Adel Ra'uf, *Mohammed Mohammed Sadiq al-Sadr, the Popular Marja'. His Project of Change and Facts about his Assassination* (in Arabic), Damascus: Al-Markaz al-'Iraqi li al-I'lam wa al-Dirasat, 1999, pp. 73-97.

prayer sermon in the Shia mosques. Fearing the emergence of a new Shia contestation movement, the regime eventually opted for a radical solution: Mohammed Sadiq al-Sadr was assassinated in 1999 with two of his sons, with Muqtada the only remaining living son of the *marja'*.

A second point of resemblance between the Sadriyyin and the Shirazi-yyin is their anti-establishment outlook. Like Mohammed al-Shirazi, Mohammed Sadiq al-Sadr, and henceforth his son Muqtada, challenged the *marja'iyya* for being a sclerotic institution unable to answer the problem of its time. In the direct aftermath of Saddam Husein's fall, Muqtada al-Sadr was particularly vocal about the political apathy of the *marja'iyya* during the Ba'th rule, accusing the *mujtahid* of having let his father be assassinated without saying a word. He took up the language forged by his father, stigmatizing Abu al-Qasem al-Khu'i and 'Ali al-Sistani as the "silent *marja'iyya*" (*al-marja'iyya al-samita*) by contrast with the "speaking *marja'iyya*" (*al-marja'iyya al-natiqa*). A third point of resemblance with the Shiraziyyin is that Muqtada al-Sadr specialized in mobilizing the poorer segment of society by providing them with social services and articulating simple slogans.

There is however a major point of divergence between the two phenomena. Contrary to the Sadriyyin, Mohammed al-Shirazi and his followers were true cosmopolitans. They were socially, ideologically and structurally transnational. By contrast, Mohammed Sadiq al-Sadr and his son look like inward nationalists with little, if any, capacity of transnational networking. Indeed, when attacking 'Ali al-Sistani, Muqtada al-Sadr did not only flay those who, in his view, had coexisted with the Ba'thist regime and endorsed its practices by their silence. He also castigated them as elements alien to the Iraqi nation and therefore, in his view, illegitimate to exercise any kind of religious or political authority over Iraqi Shias. Like his mentor Abu al-Qasem al-Khu'i, and although he had lived in Najaf for more than half a century at the time of writing, 'Ali al-Sistani was indeed an Iranian born cleric who had never relinquished his Iranian nationality. By denouncing the influence of the Iranian and other foreign clerics over Najaf, Muqtada al-Sadr strove to extract the holy city from its transnational religious geography to bring it into the strict framework of the Iraqi nation state. Actually, whether he was aware of it or not, he aimed at nationalizing an institution that, for decades, had tried to escape all national boundaries. Mobilizing references strikingly reminiscent of the Ba'th rhetoric, Muqtada al-Sadr furthermore insisted that any legitimate Shia religious authority in Iraq should be of Arab stock. He therefore shifted, as the Ba'th used to, from Iraqi territorial nationalism to Arab ethno-nationalism, implying that even after possible naturalization, 'Ali al-Sistani would remain intrinsically foreign because a true Iraqi ought to be an Arab. Another element of Muqtada al-Sadr's language that inscribed him further in the nationalist paradigm was his insistence on the territorial integrity of Iraq, and his corollary hostility to the idea of federalism favoured by the other big Shia political players, namely al-Da'wa and SAIRI. In the name of Iraqi national identity, he furthermore called for Shia-Sunni union against the American occupation. In brief, at the ideological level, the Sadriyyin really appeared as a product of Iraqi nationalism, as one manifestation of the fact that, at the end of the day, the Ba'th dictatorship had succeeded in making sense of the often-labelled "artificial" frontiers of Iraq, even from among a prestigious Shia clerical family who had paid a particularly heavy tribute to the enforced Iraqi nation-building process.

A further proof of the essentially national inscription of the Sadriyyin is the fact that while Mohammed Sadiq al-Sadr built his popularity in the 1990s, it was only after the fall of Saddam Husein that the Shia world discovered him and realized the scope of his influence in Iraq. In other words, Mohammed Sadiq al-Sadr's *marja'iyya*, built during the years of embargo in a country isolated from its environment, was a national *marja'iyya* that did not spread outside of Iraq. Significantly, now that the country has re-opened and particularly now that many Shias from the neighbouring countries, and the Gulf monarchies in particular, have begun to return to Najaf and Karbala to perform pilgrimage but also provide charitable aid to their co-religionists, Muqtada al-Sadr has not developed networks in the Gulf monarchies.

In May 2004, the Shia community in Kuwait was shaken by heated debates when it appeared that several meetings had taken place at the Iranian embassy with some prominent members of the Islamic National Alliance, followers of the Imam's Line. According to the Shiraziyyin, who leaked the information to the press, the aim of the meeting was to examine the best way to organize political support for Muqtada al-Sadr in Kuwait.[48] The attempt by Iran to use the Iraqi Shia movements in its politics of influence is nothing new. What is significant here, it that the attempt at exporting Muqtada al-Sadr to Kuwait was a failure and that Iranian patronage could not compensate for the latter's intrinsic lack of transnational networking capacity. The attempts could have been more successful in Bahrain, where one can surmise that a figure of his type would be appealing to the young,

---

48   *Al-Qabas* (Kuwait), "Jarallah to the Iranian Chargé d'Affaires: Kuwait Protests and is Worrying about the Meetings at the Iranian Embassy" (in Arabic), 10 May 2004.

poor Shias hit by the economic crisis and struggling against an authoritarian regime manipulating sectarian identities. If he cannot be referred to as a religious authority like Mohammed al-Shirazi in his time, he could at least be emulated as a model of a radical political hero. The fact is that he is not. The walls of Bahraini cities and villages do not display his photo. Neither do Bahrainis put his face on the tables of their living room. In other words, Muqtada al-Sadr is not offered the treatment of other Shia figures who have been turned into transnational heroes thanks to their perceived contribution to the Shia cause, either because they have been martyred – like Mohammed Baqer al-Hakim – or because they are heroes of the fight against Israel – like Hasan Nasrallah. When asked why they do not judge Muqtada al-Sadr worthy to be placed on the walls and in their houses, my informants were generally surprised by the question and often took time to answer, as if the question was irrelevant and the answer evident. A recurring reply was that Muqtada al-Sadr is not a *marja'*, and therefore has no reason to be emulated. In other words, the only valid transnational authority is that of the *marja'*. For the emulators of 'Ali al-Sistani or for those who emulate other *marja'* but express respect for the Najafi *marja'iyya*, Muqtada al-Sadr was stigmatized as being a young ignorant illegitimately antagonizing the *marja'iyya*. Others stated that while Muqtada al-Sadr's fight against American occupation was certainly worthy of respect, he did not constitute a relevant model to emulate since his actions were a response to the Iraqi situation and not an absolute model of action transposable elsewhere. They added that, anyway, Muqtada al-Sadr does not have a universal political agenda to project outside of Iraq.[49] As for the followers of Muqtada al-Sadr themselves, interviewed during a stay in Sayyida Zaynab in February 2005, they found the question of why their leader does not create emulators abroad as irrelevant as the Gulf interviewees. They answered, with disdain, that these Gulf people were obviously spoiled children of oil wealth perverted by American influence, too afraid to endorse the flag of such a courageous man as Muqtada al-Sadr.

The Sadriyyin's absence of transnational networking capacity does not mean that what they do or will do in Iraq will not have repercussions at all in the Gulf monarchies or elsewhere. It simply means that these possible effects will not be primarily mediated by inter-personal networks of activists but by the impersonal vehicle of the media. Hence, a particularly important event in Iraq can spark anger and expressions of solidarity in the Gulf monarchies and the Shia world overall. For example, the destruction

---

49   These conclusions are the result of several personal interviews made in Saudi Arabia, Bahrain and Kuwait between June 2003 and December 2006.

of the Samarra mosque in February 2006 aroused popular demonstrations in Bahrain, as do other events unconnected to strictly Shia stakes. In Bahrain for example, the Shias feel very much concerned by the situation in the Palestinian territories and regularly take to the streets to say so. However, as by the way with Palestinian developments, Iraqi events do not exercise a determining influence on the way the Shia movements envisage their political positioning in the domestic political realm.

8

THE SECULARIZATION OF
POLITICAL PRACTICES

The prevalence of the dynamics of domestification in the political domain does not mean that the transnational networks woven around the *marja'iyya* have vanished. Far from it, the interpersonal relations built throughout the past years still provide an efficient infrastructure for communication, mutual support and overall circulation of persons. Moreover, the *marja'* have witnessed an unprecedented increase of their networks' geographical scope. Because of the domestification process however, the transnational links, be they between the movements themselves or between the movements and their religious authorities of reference, have ceased to play the foremost role in shaping the concrete political actions of the various Shia movements. Hence, one can speak about a genuine process of autonomization of these movements from the traditional centres of religious reference in Iraq and Iran. As we shall now argue in this final chapter, this implies an almost complete de-linking between politics as the concrete practice of decision-making and religious authority. This in turn means that a process of secularization, while often disguised in the clothing of religion, is at work among the various Shia Islamic movements. Hence behind the apparent domination of the clerics in the leadership apparatus of these movements, clerical hegemony over political affairs is put into question.

THE EXPANSION OF THE *MARJA'IYYA'S*
TRANSNATIONAL NETWORKS

In contrast to the political movements, the *marja'iyya* has not experienced any process of domestification. On the contrary, it even witnessed an unprecedented geographic extension of its networks and, by the same token, of its capacity to project its authority transnationally.

From the Transnational to the Global

In many respects, the geographic enlargement of the clerical networks appears as the mere continuation of the centralization process that was engaged in the nineteenth century. Under the successive patronage of Abu al-Qasem al-Khu'i and 'Ali al-Sistani, the Najafi *marja'iyya* succeeded in extending its networks to further areas of the Shia world. The central institution's challengers, the Shiraziyyin, also dramatically developed their realm of action, sending representatives and opening institutions in Pakistan, India, Azerbaijan, Eastern Africa, etc.[1] A new phenomenon that developed in the 1990s was the spreading of the networks beyond the traditional borders of the Shia world, up to the West. This was mainly the reflection of the massive flow of Shia populations to Western countries. Iraqis in particular, escaping the political repression and the deteriorating socio-economic conditions in their country, constituted a fully-fledged diaspora and were a major vehicle of the diffusion of the *marja'iyya* networks in the West. This is how, for example, London became a foremost centre of Shia activity. This was actualized in the opening of the Khu'i Foundation in 1992, placed under the patronage of Abu al-Qasem al-Khu'i. Administered by the sons of the *marja'*, it was, at the time of writing, providing religious services of various sorts to Shia expatriates, including running a network of Islamic private schools. Although to a lesser extent, the Shiraziyyin also established institutions in London. They opened a *huseiniyya* which, at the time of writing, was administered by a long-standing Bahraini expatriate to London. It is from this centre that the Shiraziyyin were organizing the translation into English of dozens of books by and about Mohammed al-Shirazi. The United States also witnessed a dramatic increase of Shia activities of all sorts. The Khu'i Foundation has a branch in Washington, and it is also there that Murtadha al-Shirazi chose to establish the Imam al-Shirazi World Foundation in the mid-1990s, after he fled from Iran (*cf.* chapter 6). Canada and Australia, where many Iraqi Shias established themselves are two other important loci of Shia activities in the West.

The Shiraziyyin have also extended their realm of action to the little city of Dearborn in the suburbs of Detroit, where lies to date the biggest Shia

---

1 As was the case for other *marja'* either based in Iraq or Iran, but we shall here concentrate on the networks most active in the Gulf.

community of the United States.[2] Since 1997, the imam of Dearborn's most important Shia community centre has been S. Hasan al-Qazwini. The latter is a son of Murtadha al-Qazwini, one of the first and most faithful companions of Mohammed al-Shirazi (*cf.* chapters 4 and 5). Hasan al-Qazwini is also married to a daughter of Mohammed al-Shirazi. The career of Hasan al-Qazwini in the US is rich in teachings on the way the Shiraziyyin extended their networks geographically and on the personal evolution of some of its figures. Indeed, despite his strong family link to the al-Shirazi family, and the overall respect he feels for his father in law, Hasan al-Qazwini is not a Shirazi propagandist and even carefully avoids appearing as such among his constituency, mostly made up of Shias of Lebanese origin. Not even a single book by Mohammed al-Shirazi or any other figures of the Shirazi current can be found in his centre's library. This is because Hasan al-Qazwini is not himself an emulator of his father in law as a *marja'*. First, he does not consider him as the most knowledgeable and, second, he is perfectly aware that pushing forward his ties to the Shiraziyyin would have been an impediment to his career as a community leader who, by nature, must hold consensual views in order to grasp the allegiance of the majority.[3] Hence Hasan al-Qazwini is part of the Shirazi network in the sense that he is well inserted in the Shirazi family and religious infrastructure but he is not a member of the Shirazi faction in the sense that he is well inserted in the mainstream of the religious institution. In this case, the successful extension of the network implied the dropping of the factional identity. As we shall see, this type of disjunction is more and more frequent.

But the geographical enlargement of the Shia clerical networks is not only a modality of the old process of centralization. It is also revealing of the way the clerical institution was able to espouse the path of globalization, that is the process of increasing interdependence at a world level through dense flows of persons, goods, capital and ideas. Up to this stage of the analysis, there has been no need to refer to globalization as an explanatory concept for Shia transnational practices. Actually, it is only in the 1990s that the dynamics proper to globalization began to mark the transnational

---

2   On the history of the Shia community of Dearborn, see Linda S. Walbridge, *Without Forgetting the Imam. Lebanese Shi'ism in an American Community*, Detroit: Wayne State University Press, 1997.

3   Personal interview with Hasan al-Qazwini, United States, September 2007. For more details on the life of Hasan al-Qazwini, see his book: Imam Hasan Qazwini, *American Crescent. A Muslim Cleric on the Power of his Faith, the Struggle against Prejudice, and the Future of Islam in America*, New York: Random House, 2007.

practices of the religious institution, by contrast with the political movements which, for their part, were caught in the domestification process. Indeed, what distinguishes the transnationalization process that began in the
1990s from the previous period was its use, besides the traditional interpersonal networks, of the new means of communication as well as the de-
territorialization of financial assets. These privileged tools of globalization
were essential since the enlargement and densification of the transnational
networks occurred at a time of increased pressure on the clerical institution
by the two states that, for different reasons, tried to subjugate it: Ba'thist
Iraq and Islamic Iran. In Iraq, the failed uprising of the southern Shia and
northern Kurdish regions in 1991 pushed the regime to further suppress
any form of dissent; in Iran, the regime strove to impose the religious legitimacy of Ali Khamene'i on the recalcitrant scholars of Qom. As in the
1970s, the dissident clerics of Iraq and Iran resorted to the transnational
space to circumvent the pressure of the state but, unlike previously, they
did not inevitably consider exile as the best option. What is remarkable is
that both the networks of the Najafi *marja'iyya* and of the Shiraziyyin succeeded in developing while their religious authority of reference remained
in the territory of the authoritarian states. It was as if the place of residence
did not matter, as if one could, as Abu al-Qasem al-Khu'i, 'Ali al-Sistani
and Mohammed al-Shirazi did, live clustered in a house in Najaf or Qom
under the pressure of a hostile regime and simultaneously be in touch with
one's followers around the world and manage one's financial assets. How
did this occur?

The question of money is always a difficult one to broach with informants.
This makes it difficult to understand precisely how money and financial assets are managed. Information gleaned among the Shiraziyyin tends to show
that a way to shield finances from state control was to decentralize the collection of religious alms. This is of course not to mention the multiple bank
accounts opened in the West or in the Gulf countries. In general, money was
not conveyed from the peripheries to the centre as used to be the case before.
It was rather spent, in the name of the *marja'iyya*, to finance domestic institutions and projects. This explains why in Najaf itself, the *marja'iyya* gave all
the signs of great material indigence at the time of the 2003 regime change:
its strength resided in its occupation of a highly symbolic territory and its
articulation to a dense transnational network, not in its domestic financial
power. An interesting phenomenon to follow now that the authoritarian
pressure has ended in Iraq, will be the capacity of the *marja'iyya* to revert
the flux of money. Will it be able to repatriate some of its assets to finance
its physical restoration in Iraq? Will it be able to attract money that used to

be spent for domestic projects? Seen from the Gulf, where Shias continue to represent a huge financial power as compared with other Shia zones of the world, one already notices a significant mobilization for the rebuilding of the religious institutions in Iraq. Shia societies and individuals organize in order to convey money to Iraq to build or restore mosques and *huseiniyya*, to fund an orphanage or to support the families of the so-called "martyrs", the victims of the ancient regime's repression. Kuwaiti Shias were still the wealthiest and hence the most generous, and some were abducted in south Iraq in 2003 while on a mission for a Shirazi charitable society, and were released in exchange for a high ransom. The Shiraziyyin, and in particular Mohammed Taqi al-Mudarrisi who returned to Karbala only a few weeks after the fall of Saddam Husein, relies a lot on his networks in the Gulf to try to impose himself as the city's main *marja'*, in the notable absence of his uncle Sadiq al-Shirazi, the younger brother of Mohammed al-Shirazi and his successor as a *marja'*. At the time of writing, the latter was not envisaging a return to Karbala in the near future. This was again revealing of the actual configuration favoured by globalization. During the meeting we had, he clearly explained that, despite the pressure of the Iranian regime, Qom was the most suitable place to administer his worldwide activities. First, as the main place of religious education, it was here that he could best be in touch with the flow of students and teachers. Second, it offered the stability and basic infrastructure that Iraq did not provide.[4]

Another aspect of the capacity of the clerical networks to espouse the logic of globalization to bypass the authoritarian state is their massive investment in the media. As mentioned previously, today every *marja'* and, by the way, any ambitious cleric, has his own Internet site. This permits them to stay in touch with their followers in the most remote corners of the world. While Arabic and Persian remain the main languages of communication together with an increasing importance given to English, all the web sites have pages in many other languages. 'Ali al-Sistani has one central web site (www.sistani.com) that includes pages in Arabic, Persian, English, Urdu, Turkish and French. The pages provide general information about Shia doctrine and give details about the activity of the *marja'*: the institutions that his office is supervising around the world, his main *fatwa* and a whole section where followers can ask him questions about the licit and illicit in concrete situations. The *marja'* himself does not answer directly. The answers are given by a committee comprising scholars with a keen knowledge of 'Ali al-Sistani's rulings. In case of doubt, they can refer directly to the *marja'*. In addition to the central web site, there are some

---

4   Personal interview, Iran, July 2005.

thirty-two other sites to which links are provided from the central one. These are tied to various institutions acting in the name of 'Ali al-Sistani around the world. The content of the sites varies but one generally finds the same basic services: beyond giving accounts of the institutions' activities and providing general information on Shiism, they give biographical details about the *marja'* and offer free downloads of several of his publications translated into a wide range of different languages.

To our knowledge however, and according to many Shia informants from various backgrounds, the Shiraziyyin are the masters of the modern means of communication. They themselves underline that they were the first to resort to Internet when they opened their first Internet site in Sayyida Zaynab in 1997. Their fiercest detractors agree that they remain unbeatable on that ground. They of course interpret it as a sign of their trickiness: as they do not have many followers, they compensate by an all out media campaign that gives them a disproportionate weight as compared to their real audience. There are two main web sites in the Shirazi network: www.s-alshirazi.com, run from an office in Qom a few steps from the house of Sadiq al-Shirazi; and www.alshirazi.com run from the Hawza Zaynabiyya in Sayyida Zaynab. The main language of both is Arabic. The Qom site has pages and links to sites in thirteen languages: Arabic, Persian, English, French, Russian, Bengali, Swahili, Urdu, Azeri, Turkish, Kurdish, Tamil and Indonesian. It is dedicated more particularly to Sadiq al-Shirazi while the Syrian site is more specialized in accounting for the life and thought of Mohammed al-Shirazi. According to the Qom office, there are eighty-two web sites related to the Shirazi network in around fifteen countries.[5] Like the web sites of other *marja'*, those of the Shirazi network provide general information on Shiism as well as "questions and answers" sections. Significantly, the tone of the sites is often much more militant than the site of 'Ali al-Sistani. In 2002 for example, the English web site (www.shirazi. org.uk) managed from the United Kingdom offered pictures, which had disappeared at the time of writing, of the funeral of Mohammed al-Shirazi and of the seizure of his corpse by the hatchet men of the Iranian regime, openly accusing the Iranian regime of having assassinated the *marja'*.[6] In 2006, the Urdu web site (www.almizan.com.pk), managed from Pakistan, showed photos of victims of the sectarian violence perpetrated by some Sunni Islamic groups against the Shias. On the various sites, the section

5   Personal interview, Iran, July 2005.

6   A the time of writing, the pictures and the entire file in English on Mohammed al-Shirazi's funeral could be found at the following link: www.real-islam.org.uk/section4/shaheed/report.htm

dedicated to the actions and deeds of Sadiq al-Shirazi and the other members of the al-Shirazi family is however much more substantial than on 'Ali al-Sistani's site. The al-Shirazi want to show that they are everywhere and do not ration their time in serving the cause of Islam. Contrary to 'Ali al-Sistani, who refuses to be photographed and even less filmed and, therefore, of whom there are only a handful of pictures available, the Shirazi sites provide dozens of pictures of the al-Shirazi in various situations. The following episode will suffice to illustrate the al-Shirazi's peculiar management of their public relations. I met Sadiq al-Shirazi during a stay in Qom in the summer 2005. Before we began our conversation, a photographer came to take pictures of us and immortalize the event. The pictures were released on the web site www.s-alshirazi.com a few days later, with a short article signalling to the Internet surfer that the *marja'* had had a visit from a French researcher. While no details were given on the meeting, it was clear that my visit was taken as a way to suggest that the fact that Sadiq al-Shirazi aroused the interest of a French researcher was a sign of the magnitude of his influence. A few months later when I arrived in Dubai to pursue my fieldwork, I met Sadiq al-Shirazi's official representative in the emirate, a young Iraqi from Karbala. He recognized my face at first glance because he had seen the pictures of my meeting with Sadiq al-Shirazi on the Internet, showing how the site had become an important tool of communication between the *marja'* and his representatives.

Another means of communication that the Shia religious authorities have begun to invest in is television. Here again, the Shiraziyyin have been precursors. In 2005, they established the first TV channel emanating from a *marja'*, al-Anwar (the Lights). The project had been formulated by Mohammed al-Shirazi himself a few years before his death. He had explained to his entourage that he wished to establish what he called a *"marja'i* TV channel", whose conformity to the Islamic ethic would be guaranteed by its direct supervision by the *marja'*. The project was realized only a few years later thanks to generous funding by several Kuwaiti Shia businessmen, as well as the active involvement of Gulf followers of Mohammed al-Shirazi, especially Saudis. This explains why, while the channel is broadcast through the Nile Sat network in Egypt, its offices are based in Kuwait. In 2006, Murtadha al-Shirazi, the son of Mohammed al-Shirazi, left his residency in Washington to take the role of general supervisor of al-Anwar, showing the importance that the family gave to the project. At the time of writing, the executive head of the office was Sh. 'Abd al-Redha Ma'ash, an Iraqi cleric from the al-Ma'ash Arab family of Karbala, to which the al-Shirazi are linked by marriage (*cf.* chapter 3). He more particularly supervised a small committee of clerics who watched each programme destined to be run on the channel to verify its conformity to Islamic tenets: the passages showing non-veiled women were cut, as well as the programmes accompanied by music. Al-Anwar was indeed probably the only TV channel where there was no music. The programmes were accompanied by chanted religious po-ems of the sort that are droned out during Shia religious rituals. The com-mittee also watched carefully to make sure that the narrators spoke correct Arabic, the language exclusively used by the channel. As for the content, it tried to alternate between religious programmes, cultural reports and more entertaining programmes. One found interviews with or conferences by re-ligious scholars – most of whom were well-known figures from the Shirazi school of thought – broadcasts of Friday sermons, reports on sacred places or the life stories of famous religious figures. The channel also purchased many reports from Western channels. The aim here was to enhance the general knowledge of the audience about a wide range of subjects such as new technologies or the geography of mountainous regions. There were also games like the "Golden Answer" (al-Jawab al-Dhahabi). In one of the broadcasts run in November 2005, the presenter walked around the streets of Kadhimiyya, a Shia suburb of Baghdad, and asked passers-by questions about religion like the date of Imam 'Ali's death, the Quranic verse that contains all the letters of the alphabet, etc. The winners were offered a mo-bile phone by MTC (Mobile Telecommunications Company). One can surmise that the fact that MTC was a Kuwaiti mobile phone company operating in Iraq since 2004, where it seeks to win over the market, was not just fortuitous for a channel mainly financed by Kuwaiti businessmen.

Depoliticization as a Condition of Transnationalization

The new wave of transnationalization that occurred in the 1990s did not entail an upsurge of transnational political activities. In other words, while the marja'iyya grew in terms of geographic expansion and effectivity, politics was not included in the domain of exercise of its authority. This means two things. On the one hand, the networks of the marja'iyya did not produce new transnational political movements. On the other hand, the marja'iyya consciously avoided articulating a particular political message or ideology. This explains why the biggest transnational network remains that of the Najafi marja'iyya, headed by 'Ali al-Sistani at the time of writing. While Najaf succeeded in regaining credibility within Iraqi society when, in the late 1950s, it decided to modernize its language and its structure in order to present itself as an alternative to the secular political movements, the repression quickly made it return to an apolitical stance that actually guaranteed its survival under the Baʿth regime. Outside of Iraq, the depoliticization helped consolidate its reputation as the counter-model to the Islamic Republic of Iran and Ruhollah Khomeini. It was the moderate face of the Shia religious institution resisting the radical politicization of the clerical class.

In a move that is only contradictory in appearance, the consolidation of the Najafi *marjaʿiyya* by its conscious retreat from politics attracted to it many political leaders of great stature in the Gulf. In February 2002, on the occasion of the celebration of ʿAshura, and only two months after the death of Mohammed al-Shirazi, Hasan al-Saffar, the head of the Reform Movement in Saudi Arabia, announced publicly and solemnly that he recognized ʿAli al-Sistani as the most learned of the *marjaʿ* and had hence decided to emulate him. Considering the bitter relations between the Shiraziyyin and the Najafi establishment, the move did not go unnoticed. This was especially so since, among the Shias, the choice of a *marjaʿ* is most often considered as a personal matter that need not be made public. Statements of allegiance to this or that *marjaʿ* are not very frequent. When I asked him directly why he made this choice, Hasan al-Saffar did not hide behind religious doctrine. Of course, he stressed that he had reached the personal conclusion that ʿAli al-Sistani was the most learned of the *mujtahid*, but he also explained that his now long political experience allowed him "to make his own choices without being guided by a *marjaʿ*."[7] In other words, he did not choose ʿAli al-Sistani because he saw in him a political guide as Mohammed al-Shirazi was for him in many respects, but because, precisely, ʿAli al-Sistani never articulated a specific political doctrine he would wish to impose on his followers. Choosing the head of Najaf was the last step towards political independence because he was the most neutral religious reference he could choose. He could be sure that ʿAli al-Sistani would never try to meddle in the way he conducted his relations with the Saudi regime.

Such a choice had other, very practical, advantages. First it would reassure the Saudi authorities that he had definitively turned the page of the revolution. Second, it would facilitate his integration into the religious mainstream. For someone who had the ambition of speaking to the Saudi rulers in the name of the whole Shia community, it was indeed imperative to make people forget that he had been the main Saudi relay of the highly contested *marjaʿiyya* of Mohammed al-Shirazi.

Another important political leader in the Gulf who emulates ʿAli al-Sistani is ʿAli Salman, the head of al-Wifaq in Bahrain. Significantly, ʿAli

---

7   Personal interview, Saudi Arabia, September 2004.

Salman does not make a fuss about it. Unlike Hasan al-Saffar, he did not feel compelled to announce publicly who was his *marja'* since his personal achievements gave him an incontestable political legitimacy, that did not need to be reinforced by the allegiance to a particular *marja'*. Many activists of al-Wifaq do not know which *marja'* he follows and, besides, do not attach importance to it. It is only when I asked him directly that he answered that he had followed Abu al-Qasem al-Khu'i and, since the death of the latter, had not quite made a definitive choice but tended to rely on the rulings of 'Ali al-Sistani.[8] Here again, the choice is significant for this political leader who never relied on an external source of authority to justify his political positioning. It is therefore on a purely individual basis that does not spill over into the public sphere that he relies on a *marja'* known for avoiding interference in the political choices of his followers. As for Hasan al-Saffar, 'Ali al-Sistani is a convenient reference to claim, because of his neutrality. As such, emulating 'Ali al-Sistani does not mean anything specific politically.

The trend towards depoliticization is further confirmed with the Shiraziyyin. At the time Mohammed al-Shirazi was living, he had already progressively retreated from politics. Under the pressure of the Iranian regime, he contented himself with working to enhance his religious following and abstained from publicly expressing his divergent opinions about Iranian policy. The only political issue about which he went on openly manifesting his point of view was Iraq, but this was in the form of a general condemnation of the Ba'thist regime and not the recommendation of a precise policy towards it. The tension that arose between Mohammed al-Shirazi and his nephews Mohammed Taqi and Hadi al-Mudarrisi was another manifestation of the progressive political disengagement of the former. When the al-Mudarrisi brothers took their independence by continuing to espouse the policy of exportation of the revolution despite their uncle's disengagement with the Islamic regime, Mohammed al-Shirazi took on the mantle of the enactor of big general principles – non-violence and the *shurat al-fuqaha* – and did not engage in any form of concrete action in order to make his views prevail: he neither involved himself in Iranian factional competition for power, nor tried to create a new political movement. A logical consequence of this withdrawal from the political arena was that, contrary to what happened in the 1970s, no structured political organization was created in the new countries where Mohammed al-Shirazi's *marja'iyya* gained followers in the 1990s, including in the countries with an overwhelming Shia majority like Azerbaijan. In this country where Mohammed al-Shirazi

---

8   Personal interview, Bahrain, October 2002.

succeeded in attracting an embryonic following in the 1990s and founded a *hawza* in 1992, the Shiraziyyin have not pursued a specific political agenda to date and remain content with religious and charitable activities.[9]

The retreat from politics was confirmed after the death of Mohammed al-Shirazi when his brother Sadiq took up his succession. Lacking the personal charisma of his elder brother, he was even more careful than Mohammed al-Shirazi not to meddle in political affairs. When he did, it was exclusively about Iraq and moreover through an opinion that followed the consensus, that is in reality the opinion of 'Ali al-Sistani. He hence supported participation in the 2005 elections as well as the establishment of a single electoral list for the Shias. Some of his followers even described him as a "*hasani*", by contradistinction with his brother whom they depicted as a "*huseini*". *Hasani* refers to the second Imam, Hasan, who preferred to sign a pact with the caliphs in order to protect the Shias from repression. *Huseini* refers to the third Imam, Husein, who on the contrary adopted an uncompromising stance towards the oppressors and preferred to rise against them at the price of his life. The second and third Imams hence provide two different models of relation to temporal political powers that indeed well correspond to the respective positions of the two brothers. Their followers often say that Mohammed al-Shirazi's tendency to "not remain silent" and "speak frankly" was certainly admirable in absolute terms but caused him many problems that, at the end of the day, hampered the enlargement of his audience. The depoliticization of the Shirazi *marja'iyya* is therefore not considered as a sign of decline but of maturity and, moreover, as an unavoidable condition for pursuing expansion.

THE PROFESSIONALIZATION OF POLITICS

The retreat of the *marja'iyya* from the political arena has been felt within the ranks of the Shia movements through the growing activation of a potential fault line that had been there from the start: that between the lay and the clerical cadres.

The Effendis: Profile of a Political Actor

In Iraq and in the Gulf countries, "*effendi*" is a standard word by which the activists of the Shia Islamic movements designate the lay cadres in contrast to the clerics. Initially a Turkish word that passed into Arabic, the meaning of "*effendi*" has evolved from the Ottoman to the contemporary

---

9   Personal interview with Sh. Jawid Mohammadov, the main representative of the Shiraziyyin in Azerbaijan, Syria, February 2005.

period, but still points to the idea of people acculturated to the Western way of thought. During the late Ottoman period in the Arab world, and contrary to the Turkish usage, *effendi* was an honorific title referring to the Westernized lay urban literati, in particular by opposition to the religious professionals.[10] Most of the *effendis* were trained in the nascent modern school system modelled on the Western one. They were the product of the combination of Ottoman tradition and Western knowledge, wearing the tarbush, the typical Ottoman hat, above a dark suit and tie, and often affecting Western manners. The current use of the word *"effendi"* by the Shia activists is in many respects perfectly in line with the Ottoman use. It refers to people often displaying a Westernized outlook while at the same time articulating a discourse about the importance for Shias of preserving their own particular religious identity. Their profile is similar to that described by Houchang Chehabi under the concept of "religious modernists" in his analysis of the Liberation Movement of Iran, a movement founded by religious laymen, most of them educated in scientific domains and eager to reconcile religious values with rapid socio-economic changes – the so-called "modernization".[11]

In the Gulf monarchies, the vast majority of the *effendis* come from what they themselves describe as "traditional" families. Some had a grandfather or grand-uncle wearing the turban, but they are not the majority. All describe their parents as very committed to the obligations of Islam such as prayer, fasting and participation in the popular rituals but say that, while they sometimes were themselves very committed to the preservation of Islamic values, they had a rather negative opinion about the religious scholars. A Bahraini activist of the Islamic Front for the Liberation of Bahrain even once explained blatantly that he considered scholars as "opium sellers taking no interest in the class struggle within society."[12] Despite the fact that his family was particularly religious, even counting one well-known cleric among his forefathers, he chose to embrace the Arab nationalist and Marxist doctrines and became for a while an active member of the Front for the Liberation of the Eastern Arabian Peninsula (*al-Jabha li Tahrir Sharq al-Jazira al-'Arabiyya*), a group inspired by the Ba'thist version of Arab nationalism that, like many such other movements in the Middle

---

10   Bernard Lewis, "Efendi", in *Encyclopedia of Islam and the Muslim World*, Leiden: Brill, 1963.

11   Houchang E. Chehabi, *Iranian Politics and Religious Modernism. The Liberation Movement of Iran under the Shah and Khomeini*, London: I. B. Tauris, 1990, pp. 26-9.

12   Personal interview, Bahrain, August 2002.

East, shifted to Marxism after the Six Day War of June 1967. It was only after the Islamic revolution that he changed his views and came to think that religion could be a more powerful force of change than the secular ideologies, that "an old man like Khomeini could make a revolution and provoke a political change affecting the whole region and say no to the Americans". His encounter with Hadi al-Mudarrisi, shortly before the latter was expelled from Bahrain, confirmed his view, pushing him to become an active member of the IFLB.

While it was by no means always pushed to such an extreme, anti-clericalism was a recurrent element of the way the *effendis* presented their worldview before their involvement in the religious movements. They saw the clerics as an ossified body unconnected with the rapid socio-economic changes of Middle Eastern societies because too preoccupied with formal religious problems pertaining to worship or the physiology of women. Their primary bedside reading was Ali Shariati, the Iranian lay religious intellectual who promoted a return to a correct interpretation of Shiism unvarnished by the gloss of the scholars, in which Shias would find a solution to all the concrete problems posed by modernization. Ali Shariati himself was known for being wary of the clerical class overall, and many clerics considered his interpretation of Islam as a reprehensible deviation.[13] Significantly, what the *effendis* retained from the ideas and way of life of Ruhollah Khomeini or Mohammed al-Shirazi was precisely that the two men were in rupture with their status group, that they effected a revolution within the clerical class as much as they strove to overthrow the political order. Yet, even after they rallied to the revolutionary clerics, the *effendis* remained rebuffed by the clerical career and very few of them embraced it. Few undertook training in the framework of the *hawza*. Their religious education was the product of self-teaching, of the regular frequentation of circles of reflection around this or that cleric and of short-term training courses. They often assert that they are self-taught in religion and, far from considering this as a disadvantage, they are proud to say that this gives them freedom of thought and that, anyway, they are "much more learned than many who studied at the *hawza*", as a Bahraini once put it. Most of the *effendis* pursued careers as engineers in domains as various as electronics, telecommunications, computers and, of course, the various specializations needed in the oil industry. Very few engaged in a social science syllabus.

---

13   Cf. Yann Richard, "Contemporary Shi'i Thought", in Nikki R. Keddie, *Modern Iran. Roots and Results of Revolution*, New Haven: Yale University Press, updated edition 2006 (first edition 2003), p. 207.

Many of the *effendis* completed their education in the United Kingdom or the United States, where they resided for more or less prolonged periods of time ranging from a few months to a few years. Typically, especially in Bahrain and Saudi Arabia, they were recruited after high school by a British or American company, the oil companies of course but, in the case of Bahrain, other companies like Cable and Wireless, which became BATELCO (Bahrain Telecommunications Company) in the 1980s. The company sent them abroad to perfect their education. There, they were further exposed to the Western way of life but, very often, were also socialized within the diasporic communities of Shia students from Iran and the Arab world, mainly Lebanese and Iraqis. The latter had set up various student associations that constituted an important avenue for the political socialization of Shia students while abroad. This was, for example, the experience of Ja'far al-Shayeb, a cadre of the Organization for the Islamic Revolution in the Arabian Peninsula who played a leading role in the organization of the Saudi and Gulf Shia students in the United States in the 1980s.

Often educated in the West before their political engagement, the *effendis* also often opted to spend their exile period in the West. The case of the Islamic Bahrain Freedom Movement is particularly telling in this respect. The *effendis* of al-Da'wa who founded it chose to establish in London (*cf.* chapter 7). The same is true of the *effendis* of the Islamic Front for the Liberation of Bahrain and the Organization for the Islamic Revolution in the Arabian Peninsula. In the direct aftermath of the Islamic revolution, Iran appeared as the obvious choice for many of them. But few stayed in Iran on a permanent basis and rather used the country as a base to travel to other countries to meet with their fellow citizens and establish contacts with international NGOs. In the 1990s when relations between the Shiraziyyin and the Iranian pragmatics seriously deteriorated, the clerics relocated to Syria but the *effendis* opted for Western countries like Denmark, Sweden, Spain, the United Kingdom, the United States or Australia. The choice was often made because these countries offered easier access to political exile status, with the financial facilities that often went with it, in particular in the countries of northern Europe. Unlike the clerics, who could rely on the financial support of the *marja'iyya* to sustain their living while abroad, the *effendis* had to rely on themselves. This was particularly so in the 1990s after the pragmatic turn of Iranian foreign policy, which entailed a sometimes dramatic shrinking of the finances of the various movements. The choice of a Western country was also explained by the wish to complete one's professional education: a diploma from a Western university had a higher value than one from a Middle Eastern one, be it in terms of the quality of the education provided or in terms of social status in the home society. Finally, settling in the West was also a matter of the kind of political strategy envisioned by the *effendis*, who thought it essential to gain at least a measure of international recognition for the legitimacy of their struggle.

The Effendis and the Transnational Space

Because of their cultural and professional profile, and the consequent geographical places of their exile, the *effendis* have a relationship of their own to the transnational space that is not that of the clerics. This has had a determining influence on their experience of the domestification process and, conversely, on their relations with the clerics. This particular relationship to the transnational space is mainly to be expressed in the way the *effendis*, by contrast with the clerics, have lived the structuring political experience of exile and, conversely, the way they have experienced their return home. Societies often show suspicion when confronted with the return of migrants in general and political exiles in particular.[14] Those who remained at times of hardship often consider those who left as having chosen the easiest way out. Hence the returnees have the feeling that they are required to pay a kind of price for return. In conversation with young Shia Islamic activists who had not been exiled, a recurrent idea about the exiled *effendis* was that they had become too westernized and had somehow forgotten their roots. The *effendis* themselves felt they had come back to a somehow backward society by the standards they had known in the West. Feeling they had played a key role in the resistance against oppressive regimes, the *effendis* however discovered that, at home, others who had never left claimed this same kind of legitimacy but with much more credibility in the eyes of the population. In brief, the *effendis* thought they would come back as heroes but actually received a rather cold reception. Beyond the fact that, after so many years of absence, they found themselves in an unfamiliar environment they had difficulties even recognizing, many had difficulties becoming inserted in the new networks of influence of all sorts. To this one should add economic problems linked to the difficulty of finding employment, in particular for those who left as students. Those who had a civil service job were given it back as part of the amnesty agreements, but many had to fight hard to have the deal actually implemented. As a consequence, they found themselves dependent on their families for survival and this was a source of tension.

The way the clerics recounted their return home is totally different to the *effendis*. The huge gathering at the airport to welcome 'Isa Qasem is one

---

14   Dufoix (2002), pp. 291-4.

example of this. While an *effendi* is asked to prove that he is worthy to play a role in a society from which he was absent for a long period of time, a cleric coming from ten or twenty years spent in Qom returns home with an enhanced legitimacy. His absence is legitimate since it enabled him to complete his religious training. His travel to the centres of religious knowledge has permitted him to progress within the transnational religious hierarchy and, since hosting a high-ranking religious scholar is a source of pride for society at large, the population feels that his hierarchical advancement is reflected on itself. The cleric might have gone mainly to escape repression but no matter: what many in society judge as an easy way out for the *effendis* is compensated, for the clerics, by religious prestige. In other words, it is more legitimate, in the eyes of the society, to leave for religious than for political reasons. This is due to the existence of old forms of religiously legitimate voyage for the *'ulama*. Travelling to Najaf or Qom to study is a particular variant of travel seeking for knowledge (*talab al-'ilm*), an old concept found in the Traditions of the Prophet Mohammed which "reminds the believer that the search for knowledge is intimately tied to the physical act of travel".[15] For those who leave their country for the sake of religious knowledge, travelling has traditionally been considered as a meritorious activity. The difficulty that *effendis* face in reinserting themselves back in the social fabric as compared to the clerics show that, no doubt, this ancient representation still holds true for contemporary Muslim societies.

One should add that, because transnationalization is an old habit for the clerical class, they know better how to manage it concretely than the *effendis* for whom it was a way out of a political impasse and not a natural way of life. Upon their return, the clerics who left for political reasons but took the occasion to complete their religious training have been reintegrated in the domestic clerical networks connected to the *marja'iyya*. As with any religious student, they were entitled to a position in society by virtue of their sojourn at the centre of the Shia world. Here we find another example of how the transnational organization of the Shia clergy based on this Islamic concept of travel seeking for knowledge has helped political exiles to overcome what has been a difficult ordeal for the laymen.

---

15   Sam I. Gellens, "The Search for Knowledge in Medieval Muslim Societies: A Comparative Approach", in Dale F. Eickelman and James Piscatori (eds), *Muslim Travellers. Pilgrimage, Migration and the Religious Imagination*, Berkeley: University of California Press, 1990, p. 53.

The Effendis' Relationship to Religious Authority

What the *effendis* probably resent the most about the inequitable way they and the clerics were received by the locals on their return home is, in their eyes, the often unjustified political power entrusted to the clerics. Indeed, politics and political achievement are central elements of what the *effendis* wish to be their social identity and positioning. They see themselves as political professionals entrusted with a specific knowledge that renders them more able than others, in particular the clerics, to exercise political responsibilities of all sorts. This knowledge is, in their eyes, the product of long experience of day-to-day practice of political negotiation and decision-making and, moreover, of their extensive travels around the world that have opened up them to new, more modern, ways to do politics. By articulating this language about politics as a specific social practice they actually contribute to questioning the clerics' political role.

The example of al-Da'wa in Iraq has already shown that, since its inception, the *effendis* and the clerics disagreed over the source of leadership within the party. While the clerics claimed that they, as representatives of the *marja'iyya*, should have the last word, the *effendis* promoted the idea that decision-making should fall into the hands of the formal leadership of the party, designated following internal elections. The logical result was the *de facto* scission between the *effendis* and the clerics, that resulted in the total disappearance of the clerical element from Iraqi al-Da'wa at the time of writing (*cf.* chapter 6). In this sense, Iraqi al-Da'wa had achieved its secularization.[16] Splits between the *effendis* and the clerics did not occur in the Gulf where the various currents and movements stemming from al-Da'wa, be they faithful to the initial line or followers of the Imam's Line, still retain a strong clerical component. However, the tension between the two types of actor is an important line of structuration, and of potential fracture, within the movements.

Bahrain is particularly symptomatic in this respect and can be taken as a case study. This is so for at least two reasons. First, it is the only of the three countries under scrutiny where, after 2001, the Shia movements have not only been able to organize formally but have also established clear formal procedures to designate their leadership. The leadership has a strong legitimacy in the eyes of the grassroots activists because it is elected by them during general assemblies. Moreover, referendums are conducted among

---

16   The secularization through the withdrawal of the clerics is also a feature of the Amal party in Lebanon. I develop this in more details in Laurence Louër, *Chiisme et politique au Moyen-Orient. Iran, Irak, Liban, monarchies du Golfe*, Paris: Autrement, 2008, p. 120.

the activists to take major decisions, for example the decision to boycott the 2002 elections. If both al-Wifaq and the Islamic Action Society self-define as committed to the principle of Islamic law (*shari'a*), there is no explicit reference, in their statutes, to a source of religious authority outside of the internal procedures of decision making.[17] The practice of internal democracy in Bahrain stands in contrast with the Kuwaiti situation. In the emirate, with the possible exception of the Arab nationalists, the political movements in general and the Shia groups in particular, are not parties of masses but parties of cadres. Their capacity to influence the political arena depends first and foremost on the personal social capital of their general secretaries and a handful of other prominent members. The Islamic National Alliance is a typical case. Its general secretary, the cleric Husein al-Ma'tuk, has much less social capital than the *effendi* 'Adnan 'Abd al-Samad who, despite the fact that he has been regularly elected to the Parliament, holds no formal role in the movement. From this follows that the decision making process within the movement is often obscure, resulting from negotiations *in camera* between its cadres.

A second reason why Bahrain can be taken as a case study is that it is, with Saudi Arabia, a country where the clerics have played a leading political role that far outstripped that of the *effendis*. This is due to the socio-historic configuration outlined previously (*cf.* chapter 1 and 2). In Bahrain and Saudi Arabia, the clerical class was constituted early in history and has long had great social power of his own. In Kuwait by contrast, while the Islamic revolution entailed a sudden interest in the professional religious career among young Kuwaiti Shias, the latter were never able, as a group, to match the social power of the lay notables. While religious language has become the main register of political legitimacy among Kuwaiti Shias, the clerics, as a group, did not succeed in imposing themselves as the main source of authority in the political domain. They often complain bitterly that they have difficulties earning a decent living as religious men because people do not feel enough respect for them. Therefore, it is not uncommon to meet *'ulama* who combine their religious occupation with another professional activity. They are civil servants during the day and put on their turban in the evening. Some even end up dropping the religious career.

In the context of domination exercised by the clerics in the political realm, Bahraini *effendis* strove to find a place of their own and this is how they came to embody, within the Shia Islamic movements, a force counter-balancing the clerics' influence. For that, they have mobilized conceptions

---

17   The statutes of al-Wifaq are available on the movement's web site: www.alwefaq. org.

centred on the idea of the necessary autonomy of politics, that is most expressed in their deep commitment to the principal of internal democracy as the only legitimate way to appoint the party leadership. For them, the religious legitimacy of the party is fundamental but it stems from the ideas it promotes, which must fit Islamic law, and from the personal religious dedication of its activists. In other words, religious legitimacy is disconnected from clerical rule. They do not, in principal, oppose political ruling by the clerics but, in their eyes, the status of cleric is a contingent element in the choice of the leader as compared with his personal achievements as an activist. In other words, it may happen that the best leader is also a cleric but there should be not automatic rule in this respect. What the *effendis* consider dangerous for internal democracy is what they perceive as the privileged relationship between the clerics and the masses. The *effendis* often present the masses as ignorant people who "revere the turban" and slavishly imitate the clerics to the point of being totally brainwashed. An *effendi* from the Islamic Action Society once said blatantly: "we must take the young men out of the *ma'tam* and shield them from the influence of the religious men".[18]

Significantly, similar convictions were expressed in Saudi Arabia after the government announced the handling of municipal elections for spring 2005. The *effendis* who had ambitions to be candidates often expressed fear that they could not match the weight of the clerics, that people would *in fine* not vote for political competence but for religious charisma. The problem was finally overcome because the clerics decided not to compete in the elections and left the field to the *effendis*. A reason for that was that the municipal elections left little opportunity to articulate national political issues, as the mandate of the winners would be very limited in scope. Reduced to technical administration, it would leave little space to set out general political debates. This was clearly the position of Hasan al-Saffar, who refused to be candidate because he considered that municipal councils were not the place for a cleric. However, he envisaged competing if there was an election of the Consultative Council because that would offer him an arena to further publicize his ideas on the changes needed inside the kingdom.[19]

The *effendis* dread the clerics' hold over the masses because it gives the clerics an instrument to bypass the formal leadership of the party. In Bahrain, this specific criticism is regularly levelled against 'Isa Qasem. The patriarch of al-Da'wa returned to Bahrain in 2001 in the framework of the

18   Personal interview, Bahrain, August 2002.
19   Personal interview, Saudi Arabia, September 2004.

general détente, after ten years spent in Qom teaching and perfecting his own religious education. Upon his return, he refused to take any formal responsibilities in al-Wifaq. However, the common wisdom of the Bahraini Shia activists is that 'Ali Salman, the formal head of al-Wifaq who happens to be a cleric, is a puppet obeying the orders of 'Isa Qasem, his former teacher and superior in the clerical hierarchy. In other words, the independence of 'Ali Salman as the formally elected leader of al-Wifaq is believed to be limited by his obligation, as a cleric who has not reached the level of independent reasoning (*ijtihad*), to submit his decisions to the sanction of a higher ranking scholar. Because its leadership is considered subservient to an external religious authority, al-Wifaq is considered as lacking the transparency necessary for the normal exercise of internal democracy. Moreover, the *effendis* considered 'Isa Qasem's refusal formally to join the ranks of al-Wifaq as a way of avoiding submitting his opinions to internal democratic debate so that he can retain the final decision without paying the price for it. All the more so since he does not make his preferences known publicly and is content with conducting informal private talks during which he informs a small circle of people of his opinion. At the end of the day, one never knows what the exact position of 'Isa Qasem is so that speculations about what he thinks are an important part of the activists' daily routine.

Significantly, defiance against the clerics and questioning their political authority transcends the boundaries of political identities. Indeed, the discourse about political autonomy is also articulated by the *effendis* who follow the Imam's Line and hence believe in the absolute validity of the *wilayat al-faqih*, a doctrine based on the idea of the clerics' intrinsic right to political rule. It therefore clearly appears as a general trend that has little do to with the ideological options. It is more the result of an "effect of position" (*effet de position*) in the sense of Pierre Bourdieu when he analyzes the logics of what he calls the "fields", that is the relatively autonomous arenas constituted around a specific social activity – politics, religion, intellectual thinking, judiciary, etc. – and governed by specific rules. He shows that ideologies and ideas proper to the various actors whose actions structure the field are a function of their position towards each other.[20] In the concrete case under scrutiny, the *effendis*' effort to define the conditions for the autonomy of politics in the framework of a religiously oriented political

---

20   Pierre Bourdieu developed his concept of "field" (*champ*) in various articles dealing with religion, culture, judiciary and other social activities. For an overview of his theory on the "political field", see Pierre Bourdieu, *Propos sur le champ politique*, Lyon: Presses Universitaires de Lyon, 2000.

ideology is a logical result of them being less endowed than the clerics with religious legitimacy. Contrary to the clerics, the *effendis* are professionals of concrete political negotiation who work in the short term in order to exercise power, not religious preachers working for the long term Islamization of societies. The clerics can fail politically and return to their religious profession. They can indefinitely postpone concrete political achievements by concentrating on all-out Islamization on the long term. The *effendis*, because they are political professionals, have no alternative but to succeed in their political enterprise.

RELIGIOUS AUTHORITY AND POLITICAL DECISION: TWO CASE STUDIES IN BAHRAIN

In Bahrain, the debates over participation in the 2002 and 2006 elections were a particularly fruitful occasion to appreciate the scope of the political actors' autonomy towards religious authority, both domestic and transnational.

Participate or Boycott. Who Decides?

In February 2002 when the Bahraini King enacted the new constitution that caused the anger of the opposition, al-Wifaq took time to decide which strategy to adopt. In the first place, the party resigned itself to playing by the rules of the game imposed by the regime. The leadership, both the *effendis* and the clerics, was convinced that one should not endanger the reconciliation with the regime and risking returning to the old years of repression. Democracy was important, but one could be content, as a beginning, with mere détente. Hence al-Wifaq decided to participate in the municipal elections of May 2002. While it won all the municipal councils in the Shia populated areas including Manama the capital, the low turnout rate, which hardly reached 47 per cent, indicated that the population deemed these elections were not worth being taken seriously and, hence, disapproved of the compromisie chosen by al-Wifaq. It is in this context that the debate about the opportunity to boycott the October legislative ballot was engaged.

Within al-Wifaq, the younger activists, most of whom had participated in the 1990s uprising and had been imprisoned, were unwilling to close their eyes in the face of what they called this "cosmetic (*suri*) reform". They had already accepted, for the sake of reconciliation, that those who had tortured them during the uprising would not be tried. They were unwilling to accept the idea that they had suffered for nothing. The walls of the Shia villages were covered with slogans saying: "this is not the parliament we asked for". The situation was all the more difficult to bear for the young men in that they were among those hardest hit by the economic crisis, being either unemployed or working for mediocre wages in the private sector. In their view, corruption within the government was responsible for their poor economic situation. In brief, there was a real danger of witnessing the formation of a chasm between the opposition's cadres who still favoured compromise and their base, leaving the floor to more radical elements ready for escalation. Hence, the 2002 boycott decision was more about trying to prevent the schism between al-Wifaq cadres and the grassroots of the movement.[21]

The decision to boycott was announced about a month and a half before the first round, during a meeting held jointly by four political societies: the two Shia societies plus two liberal societies with religiously mixed membership. When 'Ali Salman entered the room dressed up in his turban to take his seat on the stage alongside the general secretaries of the other societies, he was welcomed by a group of young men dressed in jeans and tee-shirts, raising their fist while chanting the following slogan: "we are with you 'ulama" (ma'akum 'ulama). I asked the young man sitting next to me why his comrades articulated this slogan in this particular circumstance. He was an activist of al-Wifaq in his twenties, well known for having been alongside 'Ali Salman during the episode of the marathon that sparked the 1990s uprising, which earned him a year and a half of prison. He was a follower of Ali Khamene'i and therefore a partisan of the Imam's Line. His answer to my question was that, in Shia Islam, the clerics were considered as the supreme source of authority because they were the representatives of the Imam. Therefore, what these young men did was no more than swearing allegiance to the clerics as the legitimate decision-makers inside al-Wifaq. In his view, this should not surprise someone like me who knew a lot about Shia doctrine.

It was only a few weeks afterwards when I had the occasion to meet this young man again to do an in-depth biographical interview, that I realized that the slogan of allegiance to the 'ulama should be put in perspective. At a point during the interview, we broached the issue of the role of 'Isa Qasem in al-Wifaq and his attitude during the boycott campaign. Actually, he had abstained from making any public declaration about the legislative elections and the issue of the boycott. However, many activists held the view that he was in favour of participation but was keeping his opinion to

---

21   For further details on this issue, see Louër (2003).

himself. Here is what the young activist answered when I asked him what his reaction would be, as a partisan of the boycott, had 'Isa Qasem expressly said he wished Bahrainis to participate:

"My personal conviction is that I do not trust this regime. OK? So, even if Sh. 'Isa Qasem or Sh. 'Ali Salman had said to participate, I would have boycotted. Because basically I don't trust this regime. This is the first point. The second point is that I trust the leaders. It's not that I follow them and that, because I hesitate between participation and the boycott, I do what they do. No. This is not the way it is. For me, what matters is that I know them and that, knowing them, I know they are people who act for our own good. They are active and can obtain things for us. They have more political experience in Bahrain than I do. So when I hesitate on a particular point – at least this is what I do in general – I ask them questions."[22]

What this young man said is that, on concrete political matters, the opinion of a high ranking scholar like 'Isa Qasem is worth that of a young man who has no religious education, provided he has political experience. He thinks a cleric should not be granted a say in concrete political matters merely on the basis of his status as a religious scholar. The role of the *'ulama* in a political party like al-Wifaq and their legitimacy as leaders, for example in the case of 'Ali Salman, stems from their political experience and the trust they have been able to gain among the population. In other words, they are judged on the basis of pure political criteria such as experience and trust, just like any lay cadre of the movement. What we see here is really a pledge in favour of the separation between politics, conceived as a concrete practice of decision making, and religion.

What another young activist of al-Wifaq explained will further help us to analyse the kind of legitimacy al-Wifaq leaders are entrusted with. A follower of the Imam's Line, he answered the question of what his attitude would have been had his *marja'* enjoined Bahrainis to participate in the elections:

"You have to distinguish between two things. The religious scholar (*faqih*) understands the Quran. He understands the deep things that are in it that I do not understand myself. He says what is forbidden (*haram*) and allowed (*halal*). Singing, for example, is forbidden. These are religious things. In your question, there are two points. On the one hand, there is the opinion of, for example S. Fadlallah, on the events in Bahrain that, for example, would lead him to say that participating is better than boycotting. This is the opinion (*ra'y*) of S. Fadlallah and it is not a duty for me to follow him in that respect because this is something that is out of the realm of Quran and religion. In matters of religion, there are things that I don't know and this is the reason why I must follow a *marja'*. In matters of politics, if people don't know a lot, they must follow those who know. Somebody who doesn't know how to

---

22   Personal interview, Bahrain, October 2002.

make a key, for example, he goes to see one who knows. Me, in matters of religion, I am not specialized. But I have opinions on certain political issues. The *marja'* has an opinion, and I have mine. That's all."[23]

When asked about his reaction had 'Isa Qasem, who has an intimate knowledge of Bahraini political stakes and whom he previously said he respected very much, enjoined him to participate, he answered this:

"He did not release an order that would oblige me to follow his view, a *fatwa* saying that one should participate on pain of doing someting forbidden religiously (*haram*). In general, in these kinds of circumstances, scholars give a mere opinion (*ra'y*) but people take it as a *fatwa*. They have the feeling that it is a *fatwa*. But in reality, this is not a *fatwa*. So that even if Sh. 'Ali Salman tells me that it is better to act from within the Parliament and not boycott, I would say to him that, no, I don't agree."

The answer of this young man was better argued than that of the first because he gave religious arguments to substantiate his views. What he said is that a *marja'* can legitimately issue *fatwa*, that is, strictly speaking, religiously compelling rulings, only in religious matters. The realm of religion includes matters that we would actually consider as political like the modality of government or the legality, religiously speaking, of Muslims participating in an electoral process in a non-Islamic state. But these rulings on political matters are of an absolute nature and do not relate to any concrete situation. They are disembodied. It is the emulator that, afterwards, exercises his own reasoning to evaluate whether, in the concrete situation in which he stands, the ruling of his *marja'* applies or not. That is to say that the emulators actually benefit from considerable room for manoeuvre if one considers the practical implications of following a particular *marja'*. One should add that these implications are even more reduced considering the situation of the present "market of the *marja'iyya*", so to speak. Because of the relative proliferation of the *marja'*, the believers have a wide range of choices and can choose the *marja'* whose rulings best suit their own opinions. This reminds us of a fundamental aspect of the concrete exercise of Shia religious authority: it is not unilateral. The emulated is highly dependant on the emulator so that, in many respects, he actually follows his followers rather than the contrary.[24] In brief, the evolution of religious

---

23   Personal interview, Bahrain, October 2002.

24   This dependence of the *marja'* upon their followers is the object of an old debate among the Shia clerical class. Hence for Sh. Mortaza Motahhari, a leading ideologist of the Islamic revolution in Iran, the practical impossibility for the *marja'* of exercising unilateral influence on the laity was the main argument in favour of the absorption of the religious institution by the state, the coercive

doctrines articulated within the clerical institution follows the evolution of the lay society's own representations.

Tensions between the Domestic and the Transnational

In 2006 when Bahrainis were called back to the ballot boxes to elect a new parliament, the terms of the debate were strikingly similar to those of 2002. Faced with the government's numerous attempts at curbing political freedoms, al-Wifaq was again faced with a difficult decision. This time however, the leadership decided to launch an early campaign in favour of participation. Its main argument was that the four years spent outside Parliament had brought no concrete gains and that one should try another way, that is to influence the institutions from within. As early as March 2006, again following a vote by the party's activists, al-Wifaq hence announced it would compete in the elections. However, many cadres felt that while the party's base had been convinced by their arguments this time, the Shia population remained dubious about the utility of electing people to an assembly with no effective power. They had serious doubts about their capacity to convince the Bahraini Shia population to participate. They had moreover to counter the aggressive propaganda in favour of the boycott carried out by the splinter group al-Haqq (*cf.* chapter 7). It is in this context that some cadres of al-Wifaq reached the conclusion that getting the support of 'Ali al-Sistani would be useful to substantiate their position. The idea was not only to obtain a communiqué from the *marja'* enjoining Bahrainis to participate but, more broadly, to create a process of emulation between the Bahraini and Iraqi situations that would lead Bahrainis to identify their situation with that of Iraq, where Shias went in large numbers to the polls in December 2005.

In the initial step, the Islamic Council of the *'Ulama* (*al-Majlis al-Islami al-'Ulama'i*) served as the main mediator with the office of 'Ali al-Sistani in Iraq. The Council was created in 2004 by a group of Shia clerics headed by 'Isa Qasem in order to reassess the independence of the Shia clerical class in the face of the attempts by the government to place them under its control. At the time of writing, the Council included many influential clerics from the opposition, most notably 'Isa Qasem, the president, and 'Abdallah al-Ghurayfi, the vice-president. However, it excluded other important figures, for example the clerics from the Shirazi current, as well as Sh. Husein al-

power of which would guarantee the clerics independence from the misconceptions of the laity. *Cf.* Mortaza Motahhari, "The Fundamental Problem in the Clerical Establishment" with an introduction by Hamid Dabashi, in Walbridge (2001), pp. 161-82.

Najati, the main representative (*wakil mutlaq*) of 'Ali al-Sistani in Bahrain. The notable absence of the latter explains why, in order to contact 'Ali al-Sistani, the Council passed through the mediation of a foremost member of the al-Ghurayfi family in Iraq and a relative of 'Abdallah al-Ghurayfi, S. Mohammed Redha al-Ghurayfi. The latter was the prayer leader of the Imam 'Ali mosque in Najaf and a close acquaintance of 'Ali al-Sistani and his entourage. According to Bahraini informants, Mohammed Redha al-Ghurayfi did not speak directly to 'Ali al-Sistani but to his eldest son and main assistant, S. Mohammed Redha al-Sistani. It is of course impossible to know the exact content of their conversation but, for the purpose of this analysis, a more important thing to know is what was reported about the conversation by al-Wifaq leadership. During a political meeting held in September, 'Ali Salman declared publicly that 'Ali al-Sistani was in favour of the participation and this is hence what al-Wifaq wrote on several of its leaflets. While none of the leaders of al-Wifaq dared to say that they had received a *fatwa* from 'Ali al-Sistani, the average Bahraini was nonetheless convinced that the *marja'* had actually issued one in which he compelled his emulators to vote.

At this stage of the analysis, one should be aware that the decision by al-Wifaq to seek the support of 'Ali al-Sistani was taken well after the activists' vote in favour of participation. This means that what 'Ali al-Sistani said or, more accurately, what people made him say, came *a posteriori* to give additional legitimacy to a decision that had already been made. Therefore, it should not be analysed as part of the internal decision-making process of al-Wifaq. What the leadership of al-Wifaq hoped to accomplish was to influence the general Shia public and not its activists. This is logical if one keeps in mind the strong conviction expressed by the activists in the above-mentioned interviews collected in 2002 that, in concrete political matters, the individual has a total freedom of choice in relation to his *marja'*. This, by the way, was the analysis made by the activists of al-Haqq who were infuriated by the way al-Wifaq manipulated the ignorance of the average Shia concerning the modality of the exercise of religious authority. For them, making the opinion of 'Ali al-Sistani public was a way to influence ignorant people who think that the doctrine of the *marja'iyya* means that they have to revere the clerics as if their judgement was as infallible as that of the Imams. Hasan Mshaima, the head of al-Haqq and typical of the *effendi* profile drawn above, went as far as saying that the Shias were on the verge of committing the same mistakes as the Christians by giving too much authority to the clerics.[25]

---

25 Personal interview, Bahrain, December 2006.

It is in the context of this growing polemic that the main representative of 'Ali al-Sistani in Bahrain, Husein al-Najati, felt compelled to clarify the situation for reasons pertaining both to the restoration of his own authority and the spelling out of the proper way to understand the words of the *marja'*. Husein al-Najati was ignored during all the debates about participation and, moreover, was totally bypassed by the Islamic Council of the *'Ulama*. There is a simple reason for this: he was perceived by 'Isa Qasem as a rival. Husein al-Najati appeared on the Bahraini religious scene only recently. From a Bahraini family of Iranian stock, he came back to Bahrain in 2004 after more than twenty years spent in Najaf and Qom. There, he became a close associate of 'Ali al-Sistani, in whose Qom office he worked. His advanced religious training allowed him to bear the title of *ayatollah*, that is someone who claims the status of independent interpreter of religious law (*mujtahid*), something 'Isa Qasem never did even if many of his supporters consider he would be entitled to do so. The subsequent story is typical of what has already been described when analyzing the diffusion of al-Da'wa to Kuwait. Because he had long been absent from Bahrain, Husein al-Najati was almost unknown when he came back. Moreover, because he was a Bahraini of Iranian descent, he was not part of the core of the religious local class constituted by the Bahrani clerics. Hence, when he came back to Bahrain, he established himself in Muharraq among the 'Ajam. Despite his marginality however, Husein al-Najati immediately attained considerable local visibility thanks to his status as 'Ali al-Sistani's main representative. He established a big *hawza* in Muharraq. He also opened the first female *hawza* of Bahrain, headed by a fervent follower of the Imam's Line. Without changing her personal convictions, she decided to put her dynamism at the service of this enterprise not only because she was convinced of the utility of this move but because of the personal respect she felt for Husein al-Najati as a religious scholar.

Clearly, the rise of Husein al-Najati indicates that Najaf is still the most prominent centre of religious power in the Shia world. However, contrary to the 1970s, its agents do not use their social power to intervene in political affairs. Hence, while Husein al-Najati succeeded in establishing himself as a key religious figure, he had refrained from expressing political opinions. His intervention in the debate about participation was the first time he broke through his traditional reserve. When I met him to speak about the so-called "*fatwa*" of 'Ali al-Sistani, he was clearly infuriated by the way the words of the *marja'* had been shamelessly used to achieve political purposes, at the price of a total distortion of the facts and of the initial intention.[26] According to him, 'Ali al-Sistani answered to the solicitation of al-Wifaq in the framework of a private telephone conversation between his son, Mohammed Redha al-Sistani, and a Bahraini of al-Wifaq's sphere whose name he did not mention. This conversation was not intended to be made public, precisely by fear of the inaccurate interpretation 'Ali al-Sistani's words could suffer. Moreover, he agreed with the analysis by al-Haqq that whatever 'Ali al-Sistani had said, this should not be taken as a religious commandment but simply as non-binding personal advice.

In brief, Husein al-Najati was caught unawares and this is what pushed him to release a communiqué in late October 2006, hardly a month before the first election round, in which he recounted his own telephone conversation with Mohammed Redha al-Sistani about the elections to come in Bahrain. Like the Islamic Council of the *'Ulama* therefore, Husein al-Najati was unable to obtain a written statement from 'Ali al-Sistani. Neither did he get to speak directly to the *marja'*. This shows two things. First, in many cases, the word of the *marja'* is mediated by his entourage and therefore can be subjected to transformations and interpretations while conveyed to the followers. This is true of 'Ali al-Sistani as of the other *marja'*. The second thing is that 'Ali al-Sistani did not want to be directly involved in the process and to give his advice a formal character. Being aware of the traditional paranoia of the Sunni rulers – especially the Bahrainis – about the transnational allegiances of their Shia citizens, he did not want to be accused of meddling in the internal affairs of a state of which he was not a citizen. He was also probably well aware that even his most devoted emulators risked considering his intervention as overstepping the scope of his competence. In such circumstances, what they expected from him was to remain silent or at least not give his opinion a public character. This is at least what can be drawn from the communiqué by Husein al-Najati.

The communiqué was very clear concerning the opinion of 'Ali al-Sistani about the issue of participation or boycott of the elections: "His Excellency S. 'Ali al-Sistani considers that participation is most appropriate (*aslah*)". The *marja'*, he immediately clarified, had given detailed reasons to substantiate his "advice" (*nasiha*) but he did not wish them to be publicized. He nonetheless agreed to make known that he considered the boycott could be useful provided it would be total. Considering that the conditions were not met for a complete boycott, participation would be more useful, even though the competence of the Bahraini parliament did not match that of the Iraqi one. Husein al-Najati followed by specifying that 'Ali al-Sistani was well aware that some Bahraini political leaders favoured the boycott,

---

26   Personal interview, Bahrain, December 2006.

and that he respected their point of view. He carried on with a sentence highlighted in red explaining the scope of the words of 'Ali al-Sistani: "the point of view of His Excellency the Sayyid is not a *fatwa*, not a religiously legal ruling (*hukm shar'i*) and not a religiously legal duty (*ujub shar'i*). It is an objective assessment (*tashkhis mawdu'i*) and anybody has the right to make his own assessment even if this leads him to boycott."

The conception of the exercise of supreme religious authority given here is the very same as that expressed by the activists of al-Wifaq in 2002. This is interesting since it shows that their discourse is not isolated but reflects a widely shared conception according to which, in concrete political matters, the *marja'* is entitled to give an opinion but not a religiously binding ruling. Since this opinion is based on a personal assessment of a particular situation and not on the exegesis of the religious sources, it can be legitimately challenged by anybody.

Another interesting argument given by the communiqué in order to give 'Ali al-Sistani's advice its full scope, is that the best qualified people to assess a situation are those who know it closely: "his Excellency the Sayyid is well aware that those who live close to a situation, who are mixed up in it day and night, are aware of things others do not know. The one who is present knows more than the one who is absent. For, contrary to the opinion of some, who suspect that he meddles in the affairs of others, his Excellency the Sayyid, by giving this advice, does not intend to impose his view on anybody. He merely clarified what was the most appropriate thing to do in response to demands made by some believers who think he has great experience and knowledge in these kinds of affairs." Actually, the argument that one should be involved only in the affairs one knows from within had already been expressed by Hasan al-Saffar when articulating his conception of nation and nationality in 1996 (*cf.* chapter 7). It was also what Sadiq al-Shirazi explained to me when, in the presence of his main Bahraini representative, I asked him why his political communiqués only concerned Iraq and not the Gulf countries, where his many followers were also suffering from great difficulties. Wasn't his role to denounce the wrongdoings against the Shias in Bahrain or Saudi Arabia? He answered that his local representatives were the most able to assess the situation because they lived it on a daily basis. He therefore preferred to let them have freedom in these matters. Moreover, he said, people do not expect from the *marja'* to give inappropriate advice on their political affairs.[27] Once again, this shows that the conception articulated by 'Ali al-Sistani is not his own but is widely accepted as the consensual opinion on the role of the transnational *marja'*

27   Personal interview, Iran, July 2005.

in domestic politics, even among those, like Sadiq al-Shirazi, who are the representatives of a rather interventionist school of thought.

In Husein al-Najati's communiqué, the lines following the account of 'Ali al-Sistani's position are dedicated to explaining the position of Husein al-Najati himself on the elections. They offer a clear illustration of the tensions that can arise when a *marja'* ventures to give his opinion on a concrete political issue. Husein al-Najati begins by reminding that, in response to false allegations in the Bahraini media saying that he was in favour of participation, his office had released a communiqué in September 2005, in which he made clear that he did not wish to pronounce officially on this issue. The communiqué is quoted. Without clearly unveiling Husein al-Najati's point of view, it is rather ambiguous and suggests that he actually did not favour participation at the time: "the past and recent political events, more particularly the failure of the present parliament, the constitution and the unfair apportionment of the electoral constituencies, do not encourage participation. The final communiqué on this question will be released in due time." The communiqué on 'Ali al-Sistani's advice was the occasion for Husein al-Najati to release his final decision. But it remained highly ambiguous: "today, not only is the reality not better, it is even worse, as shown by the Bandar report which revealed a secret and dangerous project to remove a particular religious group from all sensitive positions. In various domains, there are widespread acts of political discrimination on a religious basis, as for example the practice of political naturalization."[28] He then highlighted in red: "however, despite all this, his Excellency Sh. Husein al-Najati considers that there is absolutely no advantage (*maslaha*) in contravening the words of his Excellency S. al-Sistani. He is the highest *marja'* for the followers of the Family of the Prophet and it is therefore appropriate for everybody to do what his Excellency the Sayyid said and to respect his word. However, one should note that this is neither a religiously legal obligation (*taklif shar'i*), nor a religious duty (*wajib dini*). His Excellency Sh. Husein al-Najati considers that to make this a religious obligation (*hashr dini*) is incorrect and this is also the point of view of his Excellency S. al-Sistani. This would lead to great damage, the least of which would be to make people believe that those who do not participate must be condemned and that there would be a religiously legal condemnation against them. This would mean leading people in a direction that is absolutely not accepted by the sacred religious law."

---

28   *Cf.* Chapter 7 on the issue of the massive naturalization of Sunnis in Bahrain, which the Shias consider as a means to alter the political equilibrium.

What can we conclude from the personal advice of Husein al-Najati? People from his entourage affirmed what the letter of the text only suggested: he was in favour of the boycott. This is another reason why he was infuriated by the initiative of al-Wifaq to solicit 'Ali al-Sistani's advice. Not only did the *'ulama* supporting the party, first and foremost 'Isa Qasem, bypass him and distort the real nature of 'Ali al-Sistani's declarations. They furthermore forced him to take a public position that contradicted his personal conviction. He might have wished to remain silent or he might have chosen to express his support to the partisans of the boycott publicly. Be that as it may, he had no choice than to be subject to the opinion the *marja'* while clarifying that this was a matter of respect and not of religious obligation. What should be read behind the word "respect" (*ihtiram*) is the expression of the unstable balance of power between the *marja'* and his representative. In the particular case of 'Ali al-Sistani and Husein al-Najati, the latter is more dependant on the former than the opposite because, having been absent for so many years from Bahrain, he has little social power of his own in domestic society and has gained quick ascendancy thanks to his proximity with the *marja'*. Therefore, even if religious doctrine allowed him to disregard the opinion of 'Ali al-Sistani, this would have put him in a practically difficult position as it risked jeopardizing his status as the main representative of the *marja'iyya* in Bahrain. To put it bluntly, 'Ali al-Sistani could have fired him and chosen someone else to represent him. And candidates are not lacking. One could imagine another scenario where the local representative would have held enough social power independent from his link to the *marja'iyya*. Would the local representative then have dared to publicly challenge the opinion of the *marja'*? It is doubtful since while the representatives retain their autonomy of judgement in such matters, they do not enjoy the total feeling of freedom that the laity have. As part of the clerical class, they are tied to the *marja'iyya* by a hierarchical link and a tacit obligation to respect the suzerainty of the *marja'*. What a domestically stronger representative could have done is to foresee that his rivals would try to get through to the *marja'* and to publicize his own position earlier by a communiqué. He would have then put the *marja'* in the position of not being able to publicly disavow his representative and hence not responding to the solicitation by al-Wifaq.

The Triumph of Traditional Conceptions of Religious Authority

The final conclusion that can be drawn from the phenomena and events analyzed in this chapter is that, beyond all the doctrinal polemics about the role of the *'ulama* in political affairs, there is a marked tendency, among Shia Islamic activists of all persuasions, to embrace the traditional conceptions of religious authority according to which the clerics' authority does not include the temporal powers devolved upon the Imams. Hence the general affirmation, by these same activists and the scholars in general, that Islam does not admit the separation of religion from politics should be put in perspective. What is meant here is that politics is a teleological practice, oriented by what must be its final objective: the compliance of the political institutions and the overall social order with the religious norms, of which the *marja'* are the ultimate guarantors. The political interventions of the *marja'* are deemed legitimate as far as they are confined to reminders of this intrinsic teleological aspect of politics. But the concrete ways of achieving this final end of politics remain outside of the domain of competence of the *marja'* and of religious authority in general. The inevitable day-to-day adjustments and compromises that one needs to make in order to progress on the difficult road to the ideal Islamic society are the affair of the political professionals and specialists. This distance between the teological and the practical dimension of politics, and more precisely the fact that the inevitablility of this distance is recognized by both the activists and the religious institution, is the moving force of the political movements' secularization.

The fact that even the activists who claim to follow the Imam's Line and hence accept the validity of the *wilayat al-faqih* doctrine – government by the *mujtahid* – agree about the necessary autonomy of concrete political decision making shows that it is the object of a broad consensus beyond the harsh quarrels between the pro- and anti-Iranian currents. This means that, at the end of the day, the dispute over the doctrine of *wilayat al-faqih* is first and foremost the symbolic expression of a competition for religious and political power. It is one of the major fault lines that defines the outlines of competing networks and political identities within the Shia Islamic circles but is by no means a concept useful to describe the concrete modality of exercise of religious authority in the political domain. This is another argument in favour of the idea that Iran cannot exert any sort of unconditioned influence on decision making within the Shia Islamic movements which refer to its model. Recognizing Ali Khamene'i as the leader of the Muslims worldwide does not equate to granting him a say in one's autonomous capacity of decision.[29]

---

29   This is even the case with the Hezbollah in Lebanon, where the modality of the intervention of Ali Khamene'i is actually very similar to that of 'Ali al-Sistani in the 2006 Bahraini elections. They are *a posteriori* validations of autonomous internal decision making. I analyze this in further detail in Louër (2008), p 128.

CONCLUSION

The history of the Shia Islamic movements, whether in the Gulf or in the Middle East overall, is intimately tied to that of the clerical institution. The birth of these movements in Iraq was one manifestation of the *marja'iyya*'s endeavour at reconquering the ground it had lost in Iraqi society. By the same token, their transnationalization was a modality of the lengthy centralization process of religious supreme authority in the city of Najaf. As for their transnational ideology, it was an expression of the old cosmopolitan ethos of the clerical class. In brief, the Shia Islamic movements were the result of the resilience of pre-modern social forms in the contemporary world. This is what makes their specificity as compared with what is becoming known as the "new transnationalism", born from globalization and the new opportunities it engendered. Indeed, to understand the Shia transnational political practices, there is no need to refer to the concept of globalization, which is only relevant when one looks at the redeployment of the clerical networks from the 1990s on.

What this study of the Shia Islamic movements has shown is paradoxical if one is to give credence to a certain type of literature on globalization and transnationalism, which underlines the weakening of the nation states' capacity to define the rules of the game in an increasing range of domains, be it economy, security, politics, culture, etc. The evolution of the Shia Islamic movements since the 1990s displays a different and more complex reality. What is the domestification process, indeed, if not the manifestation of the formidable powers of the states in shaping the rules of the political game? This is even more noteworthy since the states in question, the Gulf monarchies, have often been deemed "weak" by observers, mostly because they are rather young entities consolidated by the long protectorate of foreign powers on which they still largely depend for their external and even internal security. It remains that these states largely penetrate the societies under their control. At the centre of the political arena, they have *in fine* succeeded in imposing their frames of reference on movements still endowed with a coherent alternative vision of the political order.

The capacity of these putative weak states to put the Shia movements into their orbit *a fortiori* tells us a lot about the necessity of not excluding the state from the analysis of transnational political practices. Actually, states have appeared at every stage of the history of the Shia movements in the Gulf. The latter's transnationalization was accelerated by the repression of the religious seminaries by the Ba'thist regime. By the same token, they dropped their transnational pledge to revolution in large part because of the pragmatic turn of Iranian foreign policy. Finally, their domestification resulted from the new policies of the Gulf monarchical regimes after the geopolitical upheaval brought about by the 1991 Gulf War and the 2003 war in Iraq. In brief, the states gave the impetus to the main historical threads that forced the Shia movements to adapt their strategies, agenda and even identity. But if there is no doubt that the progressive mutation of these movements is a deeply historical process, hence contingent and possibly reversible, is it not also revealing of more intrinsic dynamics, something that has to do with the very nature of politics as a concrete practice?

In his essay *In search of Politics* where, among other things, he tries to analyze the consequences of globalization on politics, Zygmunt Bauman reminds us that one always does politics somewhere: "politics stays [...] territorial and national [...] physical, geographical space remains the home of politics".[1] He goes on to say that globalization implies "the progressive separation of power from politics".[2] In the context of globalization, capital, information and, I would add, activist networks, are no longer embedded in particular loci but are used in order to exercise power within a concrete society that, as a political entity, is most of the time bounded by the frontiers of the nation-state. From this it results that any genuine political enterprise is framed by its relation to the state, whatever its agenda: destroy this state, conquer it or integrate into it. This is also one of the major conclusions reached by Sydney Tarrow in his analysis of the new transnational activism and of what he called "rooted cosmopolitans", that is transnational activists who mobilize resources both domestic and international, at both domestic and international levels but who favour the domestic scene.[3] In brief, what he described is very similar to what this research has shown,

---

1   Zygmunt Bauman, *In Search of Politics*, Cambridge: Polity Press, 1999, p. 120.

2   *Ibid.*

3   Tarrow (2005), pp. 42-3.

that is, the unavoidable attraction of the political movements and activists towards the domestic space.

When we turn specifically to the transnational Islamic networks, one finds a similar trend of domestification among the Sunni movements. In his analysis of "globalized Islam", Olivier Roy showed that the latter have become nationalist. Like their Shia counterparts, they do not wish to abolish the inter-state system and rather seek to insert within it, by conquering the state or, more often, by playing the domestic political game of which the state defines the rules.[4] He also showed that this compromising attitude with their environment on the part of the political movements is paralleled by the development of a deterritorialized Islamic fundamentalism for which the implementation of the Islamic ethic is disconnected from the conquest of the state and for which the ideal Islamic community is not embedded in any concrete locus. Transnational terrorism and jihadism are the radical forms of this trend. Violence here does not serve a political project but a broad civilizational fight with no specific territory. When transnational jihadists join forces with local Islamic movements, the latter always end up subjugating them to their domestic agenda. In brief, here again, if religion can be transnational including in its most violent manifestations, politics is domestic.

The social conditions from which Sunni transnational radicalism was born also affect the Shia, in particular the failure of the revolutionary project and the co-optation of the movements that carried it, the existence of dense transnational inter-personal networks and migration to the West that creates a disconnection with the societies of origin. Yet one has not witnessed the development of any form of genuine Shia transnational radicalism. In particular, there has been to date no equivalent, for the Shias, of the Afghan jihad against the Soviets undertaken by the transnational Sunni fighters in the 1980s, which played a central role in the structuration of Sunni transnational radicalism. In this respect, it is remarkable that while post-Saddam Husein Iraq has attracted thousands of Sunni jihadists eager to fight the Americans and their putative Shia allies, no Shia transnational jihad developed there, neither against the Americans, nor against the Sunnis. As shown, Muqtada al-Sadr does not emulate anybody outside of Iraq and in particular in the Gulf. His fight is perceived as domestic, concerning only the Iraqis. If Gulf Shias contribute financially to the restoration of the Shia religious institutions in Iraq, none of them thinks of joining the ranks of the Shia militias. In the matter of Shia radicalism, what we

---

4   Olivier Roy, *Globalized Islam. The Search for a New Ummah*, London: Hurst/ New York: Columbia University Press, 2004, chapter 2, pp. 58-99.

see from time to time is occasional traditional terrorist acts, sponsored by Iran as a state with specific national interests. In other words, when Iran supports terrorism, it is not with the prospect of supporting a disembodied general civilizational fight but in order to reinforce itself within the inter-state system to negotiate from a power position on this or that particular issue. Hence Shia violence is never disconnected from domestic political stakes and from a concrete political project. This is because the Shia Islamic movements are intrinsically political and, as shown in this book, are at ease with this identity.

One can venture a hypothesis to explain why Shia Islamic activism has not degenerated into transnational radicalism. In the Sunni world, reli-gious authority is diffuse. The clerical establishment exists but, contrary to its Shia counterpart, suffers from an essential problem of legitimacy mainly due to the absence of a solid doctrinal base justifying its existence and to its accommodation with authoritarian regimes. Hence the clerics have difficulties guaranteeing their monopoly over religious authority, which is all the time called into question by outsiders. Anti-clericalism also exists in the Shia world but it never succeeded in really challenging the cleri-cal hierarchy's monopoly over religious authority for mainstream devotees. Moreover, its remarkable capacity of adaptation to globalization has put the *marja'iyya* in a position of strength to supervise the religious transna-tional space, hence leaving little space for autonomous entrepreneurs of religious authority of the type of Osama Bin Laden. This resilience of tra-ditional clerical authority has occurred at the price of the containment of authority within a relatively restrained conception of what religion is, not including legitimate intervention in concrete political affairs. But this is not really a loss for the clerical establishment. The reinforcement of the bound-ary between religion and politics is indeed protecting their legitimacy since they are not splashed by the necessary compromises made by the political professionals who have "dirty hands" – to quote Jean-Paul Sartre.

For all of that, does it mean that one must totally rule out the possibil-ity of the emergence of a Shia version of transnational radicalism? Since those phenomena are essentially historical in nature and not determined by intrinsic characteristics, it is not impossible. Considering the Shia move-ments' deep anchorage in the domestic arenas, such development could be the result of the failure of the current strategy of integration. As with the Sunni movements, the rapprochement of the mainstream with the au-thoritarian rulers could lead to the radicalization of growing segments of the activists. Seeing the impossibility of any genuine equalization between Shias and Sunnis through the institutional means of conflict regulation, they could well express their anger on other grounds than their countries of origin and, in particular, engage in anti-Sunni violence. But this is only one scenario, which is not more probable than that of a radicalization finding its expression within the domestic sphere, in the form of another uprising in Bahrain for example, or terrorism targeting the regime in Saudi Arabia. In this latter scenario, very likely in Bahrain in the short term and possible in the medium or long term in Saudi Arabia, Iran could again play a role. This is so in particular if its relations with the United States and their Arab allies in the Gulf severely deteriorate, making Iran feel that it needs to show its nuisance capacity. But for all of that, one needs to repeat that Iranian involvement will be tactical in nature, based on its perceived direct national interest and the necessity for the Shia radicals to be financially and logistically supported by a foreign power, be it Iran or any other state. In these matters indeed, ideology and religion are of little importance. In no way should the possible Iranian influence on the Shia communities and movements outside of its borders be analyzed as a modality of the exercise of religious authority.

BIBLIOGRAPHY

al-'Abdallah, Hamed, "'Azz al-Din Salim. The Assasination of a Thinker" (in Arabic), *al-'Asr*, n° 35, August 2004.

Abdul-Jabar, Faleh, (ed.), *Ayatollahs, Sufis and Ideologues. State, Religion and Social Movements in Iraq*, London: Saqi Books, 2002.

—— "The Genesis and Development of *Marja'ism* versus the State", in Faleh Abdul-Jabar (ed), *Ayatollahs, Sufis and Ideologues. State, Religion and Social Movements in Iraq*, London: Saqi Books, 2002.

—— *The Shi'ite Movement in Iraq*, London: Saqi Books, 2003.

Abu Hakima, Ahmad Mustafa, *The Modern History of Kuwait 1750-1965*, London: Luzac and Company Limited, 1983.

—— *History of Eastern Arabia 1750-1800. The Rise and Development of Bahrain and Kuwait*, Beirut: Khayats, 1965.

Adelkhah, Fariba, Jean-François Bayart and Olivier Roy, *Thermidor en Iran*, Paris: Complexe, 1993.

Afrasiabi, K. L., *After Khomeini. New Directions in Iran's Foreign Policy*, Boulder: Westview Press, 1994.

Allen, Calvin H. Jr., "The Indian Merchant Community of Masqat", *Bulletin of the School of Oriental and African Studies*, vol. 44, n° 1, 1981.

Allouche, Adel, *The Origins and Development of the Ottoman-Safavid Conflict (906-962/1500-1555)*, Berlin: Klaus Schwarz, 1983.

Aloysius, G., *Nationalism without a Nation in India*, Oxford University Press, 1998.

Amanat, Abbas, "In Between the Madrasa and the Marketplace: The Designation of Clerical Leadership in Modern Shi'ism", in Said A. Arjomand, *Authority and Political Culture in Shi'ism*, Albany: State University of New York Press, 1988.

Anonymous, *The Good Tree. The al-Shirazi Family: Its History, its Thought and its Fight* (in Arabic), Beirut: Dar al-'Ulum, no date.

Arjomand, Said Amir, "A Victory for the Pragmatists: The Islamic Fundamentalist Reaction in Iran", in James Piscatori (ed), *Islamic Fundamentalisms and the Gulf Crisis*, The American Academy of Arts and Sciences, 1991.

—— *The Turban for the Crown. The Islamic Revolution in Iran*, Oxford: Oxford University Press, 1988.

—— *The Shadow of God and the Hidden Imam. Religion, Political Order, and Societal Change in Shi'ite Iran from the Beginning to 1890*, Chicago: The University of Chicago Press, 1984.

Ayubi, Nazih N., *Over-Stating the Arab State. Politics and Society in the Middle East*, London: I. B. Tauris, 1995.

Aziz, T. M., "The Role of Muhammed Baqir al-Sadr in Shi'i Political Activism in Iraq from 1958 to 1980", *International Journal of Middle East Studies*, vol. 25, n° 2, May 1993.

Bahry, Louay, "The Socioeconomic Foundations of the Shiite Opposition in Bahrain", *Mediterranean Quarterly*, vol. 11, n° 3, summer 2000.

—— "The Opposition in Bahrain: A Bellwether for the Gulf?", *Middle East Policy*, vol. 5, n° 2, May 1997.

Bakhash, Shaul, *The Reign of the Ayatollahs. Iran and the Islamic Revolution*, London: I.B. Tauris, 1985.

Barth, Fredrik (ed.), *Ethnic Groups and Boundaries. The Social Organization of Culture Difference*, Boston: Little, Brown and Company, 1969.

Bauman, Zygmunt, *In Search of Politics*, Cambridge: Polity Press, 1999.

Beblawi, Hazem, "The Rentier State in the Arab World", in Hazem Beblawi and Giacomo Luciani (eds), *The Rentier State*, London: Croom Helm, 1987.

Beck, Ulrich, *What Is Globalization?*, Cambridge: Polity, 2000.

Beling, Willard A., "Recent Developments in Labor Relations in Bahrayn", *The Middle East Journal*, vol. 13, n° 2, 1959.

Bell, John Bowyer, "Contemporary Revolutionary Organizations", in Robert O. Keohane and Joseph S. Nye Jr (eds), *Transnational Relations and World Politics*, Cambridge, Massachusetts: Harvard University Press, 1972.

Bill, James, "Resurgent Islam in the Persian Gulf", *Foreign Affairs*, vol. 63, n° 1, 1985, pp. 108-27.

—— "Islam, Politics and Shi'ism in the Gulf ", *Middle East Insight*, n° 3, 1980.

Bourdieu, Pierre, *Propos sur le champ politique*, Lyon: Presses Universitaires de Lyon, 2000

——*Le métier de sociologue*, Paris: Mouton, 1973 (second revised edition).

Buchta, Wilfried, *Who Rules Iran? The Structure of Power in the Islamic Republic*, The Washington Institute for Near East Policy and the Konrad Adenauer Stiftung, 2000.

Byman, Daniel L. and Jerrold D. Green, "The Enigma of Political Stability in the Persian Gulf Monarchies", in Barry Rubin (ed.), *Crisis in the Contemporary Persian Gulf*, London: Frank Cass, 2002.

Calder, Norman, "Accommodation and Revolution in Imami Shi'i Jusrisprudence : Khumayni and the Classical Tradition", *Middle Eastern Studies*, 18/1, January 1982.

Cave Brown, Antony, *Oil, God and Gold. The Story of Aramco and the Saudi Kings*, Boston: Houghton Mifflin, 1999.

Champion, Daryl, *The Paradoxical Kingdom. Saudi Arabia and the Momentum of Reform*, London: Hurst, 2003.

Chehabi, Houchang E., *Iranian Politics and Religious Modernism. The Liberation Movement of Iran under the Shah and Khomeini*, London: I. B. Tauris, 1990.

Cohen, Samy, *The Resilience of the State. Democracy and the Challenges of Globalization*, London: Hurst, 2006.

Cole, Juan R. I., *Sacred Space and Holy War: The Politics, Culture and History of Shi'ite Islam*, London: I. B. Tauris, 2002.

—— "Shaykh Ahmad al-Ahsa'i on the Sources of Religious Authority", in Linda S. Walbridge (ed.), *The Most Learned of the Shi'a. The Institution of the Marja' Taqlid*, Oxford: Oxford University Press, 2001.

—— and Nikki R. Keddie (eds), *Shi'ism and Social Protest*, New Haven: Yale University Press, 1986.

—— "Shi'i Clerics in Iraq and Iran, 1722-1780: The Akhbari-Usuli Conflict Reconsidered", *Iranian Studies*, vol. 18, n° 1, Winter 1985.

Cleveland, William L., *The Making of an Arab Nationalist: Ottomanism and Arabism in the Life and Thought of Sati' al-Husri*, Princeton, New Jersey: Princeton University Press, 1971.

Crystal, Jill, *Kuwait. The Transformation of an Oil State*, Boulder, Colorado: Oxford University Press, 1992.

—— *Oil and Politics in the Gulf: Rulers and Merchants in Kuwait and Qatar*, Cambridge: Cambridge University Press, 1990.

Dazi-Héni, Fatiha, *Monarchies et sociétés d'Arabie. Le temps des confrontations*, Paris: Presses de Sciences Po, 2006.

—— "Hospitalité et politique. La *diwaniyya* au Koweït", *Maghreb-Machrek*, vol. 142, n° 1, 1994.

Dekmejian, R. Hrair, "The Rise of Political Islamism in Saudi Arabia", *The Middle East Journal*, vol. 48, n° 4, Autumn 1994.

Dufoix, Stéphane, *Politiques d'exil*, Paris: PUF, 2002.

Dunn, Michael, "When the Imam Comes: Iran Exports its Revolution", *Defense and Foreign Affairs*, July-August 1987, vol. 15.

Duriez, Bruno, François Mabille and Kathy Rousselet (eds), *Les ONG confessionnelles. Religions et action internationale*, Paris: L'Harmattan, 2007.

Ende, Werner, "The Nakhawila, A Shiite Community in Medina. Past and Present", *Die Welt des Islams*, vol. 37, n° 3, 1997.

—— "The Flagellations of Muharram and the Shi'ite 'Ulama", *Der Islam*, vol. 55, n° 1, 1978.

al-Fahad, Abdulaziz H., "The 'Imama vs. the 'Iqal: Hadari-Bedouin Conflict and the Formation of the Saudi State", in Madawi Al-Rasheed and Robert Vitalis (eds), *Counter-Narratives. History, Contemporary Society and Politics in Saudi Arabia and Yemen*, New York: Palgrave, 2004.

Fakhro, Munira A., "The Uprising in Bahrain: An Assessment", in Lawrence G. Potter and Gary Sick (eds), *The Persian Gulf at the Millennium: Essays in Politics, Economy, Security and Religion*, New York: St Martin's Press, 1997.

Fandy, Mamoun, *Saudi Arabia and the Politics of Dissent*, London: Macmillan, 1999.

Fisher, Michael M. J., *Iran. From Religious Dispute to Revolution*, Madison Wisconsin: The University of Wisconsin Press, 1980.

Fuccaro, Nelida, "Mapping the Transnational Community. Persians and the Space of the City in Bahrain, *c.* 1869-1937", in Madawi al-Rasheed (ed.), *Transnational Connections and the Arab Gulf*, London: Routledge, 2005.

Fuller, Graham E. and Rend Rahim Francke, *The Arab Shi'a. The Forgotten Muslims*, New York: Palgrave, 2001.

Fürtig, Henner, *Iran's Rivalry with Saudi Arabia between the Gulf Wars*, London: Ithaca Press, 2002.

Gause, Gregory III, "Revolutionary Fevers and Regional Contagion: Domestic Structures and the 'Export' of Revolution in the Middle East", *Journal of South Asian and Middle Eastern Studies*, vol. 14, n° 3, 1991.

Gellens, Sam I., "The Search for Knowledge in Medieval Muslim Societies: A Comparative Approach", in Dale F. Eickelman and James Piscatori (eds), *Muslim Travellers. Pilgrimage, Migration and the Religious Imagination*, Berkeley: University of California Press, 1990.

Ghabra, Shafeeq N., "Balancing State and Society: The Islamic Movement in Kuwait", *Middle East Policy*, vol. 5, n° 2, May 1997.

—— "Voluntary Associations in Kuwait: The Foundation of a New System?", *The Middle East Journal*, vol. 45, n° 2, Spring 1991.

Ghods, M. Reza, "Government and Society in Iran, 1926-34", *Middle Eastern Studies*, vol. 27, n° 2, April 1992.

de Goeje, Michael Johan, *Mémoire sur les Carmathes du Bahrain et les Fatimides*, Onasbrück : Biblio Verlag, 1978.

Goffman, Erving, *Stigma. Notes on the Management of Spoiled Identity*, New York: Touchstone Book, 1986.

Goldberg, Jacob, "Saudi Arabia's Desert Storm and Winter Sandstorm", in Gad Barzilai, Aharon Klieman and Gil Shidlo (eds), *The Gulf Crisis and its Global Aftermath*, London: Routledge, 1993.

—— "The Shi'i Minority in Saudi Arabia", in Juan R. I. Cole and Nikki R. Keddie (eds), *Shi'ism and Social Protest*, New Haven: Yale University Press, 1986.

Halm, Heinz, *The Shiites. A Short History*, Princeton: Markus Wiener Publishers, 2007.

al-Hasan, Hamza, *The Shiites in the Arab Kingdom of Saudi Arabia. Vol. I: The Turkish Period 1871-1913*, and *Vol. II: The Saudi Period 1913-1991* (in Arabic), Mu'assasat al-Baqi' li Ihya al-Turath, 1993.

Hairi, Abdul-Hadi, *Shi'ism and Constitutionalism in Iran. A Study of the Role Played by the Persian Residents of Iraq in Iranian Politics*, Leiden: Brill, 1977.

Heard-Bey, Frauke, *From Trucial States to United Arab Emirates*, Dubai: Motivate Publishing, 2004.

Hegghammer, Thomas and Stéphane Lacroix, "Rejectionist Islamism in Saudi Arabia: The Story of Juhayman al-'Utaybi Revisited", *International Journal of Middle Eastern Studies*, vol. 39, n° 1, 2007.

Herb, Michael, Kuwait Politics Data Base on the web site of Georgia State University: www2.gsu.edu/~polmfh/database/database.htm.

Hicks, Neil and Ghanim al-Najjar, "The Utility of Tradition: Civil Society in Kuwait", in Augustus Richard Norton (ed.), *Civil Society in the Middle East*, Leiden: Brill, 1995.

Holes, Clive, "Dialect and National Identity. The Cultural Politics of Self-Representation in Bahraini *Musalsalat*", in Paul Dresch and James Piscatori (eds), *Monarchies and Nations. Globalization and Identity in the Arab States of the Gulf*, London: I. B. Tauris, 2005.

—— *Dialect, Culture and Society in Eastern Arabia, vol. 1 Glossary*, Leiden: Brill, 2001.

Hourani, Albert, "Ottoman Reform and the Politics of Notables" in William Polk and Richard L. Chambers (eds), *Beginnings of Modernization in the Middle East. The Nineteenth Century*, Chicago: The University of Chicago Press, 1968.

Ibrahim, Fouad, *The Shi'is of Saudi Arabia*, London: Saqi Books, 2006.

International Crisis Group (ICG), *The Shiite Question in Saudi Arabia*, Middle East Report n° 45, 19 September 2005

—— *Can Saudi Arabia Reform Itself?*, Middle East Report n° 28, 14 July 2004.

Ioannides, Chris P., "The PLO and the Islamic Revolution in Iran", Augustus Richard Norton and Martin H. Greenberg (eds), *The International Relations of the Palestine Liberation Organization*, Carbondale and Edwardsville: Southern Illinois University Press, 1989.

Ismael, Jacqueline S., *Kuwait. Social Change in Historical Perspective*, New

York: Syracuse University Press, 1982.

Jaffrelot, Christophe (ed.), *Pakistan. Nationalism without a Nation?*, New Delhi: Manohar, 2002.

Jamal, 'Abd al-Muhsin Yusuf, *A Survey of the History of Shias in Kuwait from the Birth of Kuwait to Independence* (in Arabic), Kuwait: Dar al-Naba' lil-Nashr wa al-Tawzi', 2006.

al-Jamri, Mansur, "Prospect of a Moderate Islamic Discourse. The case of Bahrain", www.vob.org/english/information-db/mesa.htm

al-Jib, Fawziyya, *The Portuguese Power in Bahrain (1521-1602)* (in Arabic), Beirut: Al-Mu'assasa al-'Arabiyya lil-Dirasat wa al-Nashr, 2003.

Jones, Toby Craig, "Rebellion on the Saudi Periphery: Modernity, Marginalization, and the Shi'a Uprising of 1979", *International Journal of Middle East Studies*, n° 38, May 2006.

—— "The Iraq Effect in Saudi Arabia", *Middle East Report* n° 237, winter 2005.

al-Katib, Ahmed, *The Shia Marja'iyya and the Prospects for its Development. Imam Mohammed al-Shirazi as an Example* (in Arabic), Beirut: Arab Scientific Publishers, 2002.

Katz, Elihu, "Theorizing Diffusion: Tarde and Sorokin Revisited", *Annals of the American Academy of Political and Social Sciences*, vol. 566, November 1999.

Katzman, Kenneth, *The Warriors of Islam. Iran's Revolutionary Guard*, Boulder, Colorado: Westview Press, 1993.

Kazemi Moussavi, Ahmad, "The Institutionalization of the Marja'-i Taqlid in the Nineteenth Century Shi'ite Community", *The Muslim World*, vol. 83, n° 3-4, July-October 1994.

—— "The Establishment of the Position of Marja'iyyat-i Taqlid in the Twelver-Shi'i Community", *Iranian Studies*, vol. 28, n° 1, 1985.

Kechichian, Joseph A., *Succession in Saudi Arabia*, New York: Palgrave, 2001.

Keddie, Nikki R., *An Islamic Response to Imperialism: Political and Religious Writings of Sayyid Jamal al-Din al-Afghani*, Berkeley: University of California Press, 1968.

Kepel, Gilles, *The War for Muslim Minds. Islam and the West*, Cambridge, Massachusetts: The Belknap Press of Harvard University Press, 2004.

Khalaf, Abdulhadi, "What the Gulf Ruling Families Do when they Rule", *Orient*, vol. 44, n° 3, 2003.

—— "Contentious Politics in Bahrain. From Ethnic to National and Vice Versa", The Fourth Nordic Conference on Middle Eastern Studies: The Middle East in a Globalizing World, Oslo, 13-16 August 1998, www.hf.uib.no/smi/pao/khalaf.html

Khalaji, Mehdi, *The Last Marja. Sistani and the End of the Traditional Religious*

Authority in Shiism, The Washington Institute for Near East Policy, Policy Focus n° 59, September 2006.

Khaldi, Mansur Hajji Isma'il, "Mohammed Mahdi al-Qazwini. A Forgotten Figure of Kuwaiti History" (in Arabic), *al-Qabas* (Kuwait), 7 December 2006.

al-Khaldi, Sami Naser, *The Islamic Parties in Kuwait. The Shias, the Muslim Brotherhood, the Salafis* (in Arabic), Kuwait, Dar al-Naba' li al-Nashra wa al-Tawzi', 1999.

Al-Khalifa, May Mohammed, *From the Surroundings of Kufa to Bahrain. The Carmathian, from an Idea to a State* (in Arabic), Beirut, Al-Mu'assasa al-'Arabiyya li al-Dirasat wa al-Nashr, 1999.

Khalil, Samir, *Republic of Fear*, Berkeley, University of California Press, 1989.

Khosrokhavar, Farhad and Olivier Roy, *Comment sortir d'une révolution religieuse*, Paris: Seuil, 1999.

Khuri, Fuad I., *Tribe and State in Bahrain*, Chicago: Chicago University Press, 1980.

Kohlberg, Etan, "Aspects of Akhbari Thought in the Seventeenth and Eighteenth Centuries", in Nehemia Levtzion and John O. Voll (eds), *Eighteenth Century Renewal and Reform in Islam*, Syracuse, New York: Syracuse University Press, 1987.

Kostiner, Joseph, "Shi'i Unrest in the Gulf", in Martin Kramer (ed.), *Shi'ism, Resistance and Revolution*, Colorado, Westview Press, 1987.

Kramer, Martin (ed), *Shi'ism, Resistance and Revolution*, Boulder: Westview Press, 1987.

—— "The Structure of Shiite Terrorism", in Anat Kurz (ed.), *Contemporary Trends in World Terrorism*, New York: Praeger, 1987.

al-Kurani, 'Ali, *Hezbollah's Approach to Islamic Action* (in Arabic), Beirut: Al-Dar al-Islamiyya, 1406 A.H. (1985).

Lacroix, Stéphane, "Between Islamists and Liberals; Saudi Arabia's New "Islamo-Liberal" Reformists", *The Middle East Journal*, vol. 58, n° 3, Summer 2004.

Lambton, Ann K. S., "The Tobacco Regie: Prelude to Revolution I", *Studia Islamica*, n° 22, 1965.

—— "The Tobacco Regie: Prelude to Revolution II", *Studia Islamica*, n° 23, 1965.

—— "A Reconsideration of the Position of Marja' al-Taqlid and the Religious Institution", *Studia Islamica*, n° 20, 1964.

Lawson, Fred H., "Repertoires of Contention in Contemporary Bahrain", in Quintan Wiktorowicz (ed.), *Islamic Activism: A Social Movement Theory Approach*, Bloomington: Indiana University Press, 2004.

—— *Bahrain. The Modernization of Autocracy*, Boulder, Colorado: Westview

Press, 1989.

Lewis, Bernard, "Efendi", in *Encyclopedia of Islam and the Muslim World*, Leiden: Brill, 1963.

Lipsky, Georges Arthur (ed.), *Saudi Arabia. Its People, its Society, its Culture*, New Haven, Connecticut: HRAF Press, 1959.

Litvak, Meir, *Shi'i Scholars of Nineteenth-Century Iraq. The 'Ulama' of Najaf and Karbala'*, Cambridge: Cambridge University Press, 1998.

Longva, Anh Nga, "Nationalism in Pre-Modern Guise: The Discourse on *Hadhar* and *Badu* in Kuwait", *International Journal of Middle East Studies*, n° 38, 2006.

—— "Citizenship in the Gulf States: Conceptualization and Practice", in Nils Butenschon, Uri Davis and Manuel Hassassian (eds), *Citizenship and the State in the Middle East. Approaches and Applications*, Syracuse, New York: Syracuse University Press, 2000.

Louër, Laurence, *Chiisme et politique au Moyen-Orient. Iran, Irak, Liban, monarchies du Golfe*, Paris: Autrement, 2008.

—— "The Political Impact of Labor Migration in Bahrain", *City and Society*, vol. 20, n° 1, 2008.

—— "Les aléas du compromis des élites au Bahreïn", *Maghreb-Machrek*, n° 177, 2003.

——"Démocratisation des régimes dynastiques: le modèle bahreïnien en question", in Rémy Leveau et Frédéric Charillon (eds), *Monarchies du Golfe. Les micro-Etats de la péninsule arabique*, Paris: La Documentation Française, 2005.

Luizard, Pierre-Jean, *La formation de l'Irak contemporain. Le rôle politique des ulémas chiites à la fin de la domination ottomane et au moment de la création de l'Etat irakien*, Paris: CNRS, 1991.

Mabro, Robert (ed.), *The 1986 Oil Price Crisis: Economic Effects and Policy Responses*, Oxford: Oxford University Press, 1988.

MacAdam, Doug and Dieter Rucht, "The Cross-National Diffusion of Movement Ideas", *Annals of the American Academy of Political and Social Sciences*, vol. 528, July 1993.

Madelung, Wilfred, "Authority in Twelver Shiism in the Absence of the Imam" in George Makdisi (ed.), *La notion d'autorité au Moyen-Age: Islam, Byzance, Occident*, Paris: Colloques Internationaux de La Napoule, 1982.

al-Mahfuz, Mohammed, *Political Reform and National Union. How To Build a Nation in order to Live Together* (in Arabic), Casablanca: Al-Markaz al-Thaqafi al-'Arabi, 2004.

—— *Islam and the Challenge of Democracy. To Give a New Energy to the Political and Civic Life* (in Arabic), Casablanca: Al-Markaz al-Thaqafi al-'Arabi, 2002 .

Mallat, Chibli, *The Renewal of Islamic Law. Muhammed Baqir as-Sadr, Najaf and the Shi'i International*, Cambridge: Cambridge University Press, 1993.

Mandaville, Jon, "The Ottoman Province of al-Hasa in the Sixteenth and Seventeenth Centuries", *Journal of the American Oriental Society*, vol. 90, n° 3, 1970.

Marschall, Christin, *Iran's Persian Gulf Policy. From Khomeini to Khatami*, London: Routledge Curzon, 2003.

al-Mdayris, Falah 'Abdallah, *The Political Movements and Groups in Bahrain 1938-2002* (in Arabic), Beirut: Dar al-Kanuz al-Adabiyya, 2004.

—— *The Shia Movement in Kuwait* (in Arabic), Kuwait: Qurtas, 1999.

Menashri, David, *Iran. A Decade of War and Revolution*, New York: Holmes & Meier, 1990.

Ménoret, Pascal, "Le cheikh, l'électeur et le SMS. Logiques électorales et mobilisation islamique en Arabie Saoudite", *Transcontinentales*, n° 1. *Réformes et « Grand Moyen-Orient »*, 2005 (http://pascal-menoret.over-blog.com)

Mervin, Sabrina, "Sayyida Zaynab: banlieue de Damas ou nouvelle ville sainte chiite?" *Cahiers d'études sur la méditerranée et le monde turco-iranien (CE-MOTI)*, n° 22, July-December 1996.

—— "Les autorités religieuses dans le chiisme duodécimain contemporain", *Archives des sciences sociales des religions*, n° 125, January-March 2004.

—— *Un réformisme chiite. Ulémas et lettrés du Gabal 'Amil (actuel Liban-Sud) de la fin de l'Empire ottoman à l'indépendance du Liban*, Paris: Karthala, 2000.

Momen, Moojan, An *Introduction to Shi'i Islam. The History and Doctrine of Twelver Shi'ism*, New Haven, Yale University Press, 1985.

Moslem, Mehdi, *Factional Politics in Post-Khomeini Iran*, Syracuse, New York: Syracuse University Press, 2002.

Moss Helms, Christine, *The Cohesion of Saudi Arabia: Evolution of Political Identity*, London: Croom Helm, 1981.

Motahhari, Mortaza, "The Fundamental Problem in the Clerical Establishment" with an introduction by Hamid Dabashi, in Linda S. Walbridge (ed.), *The Most Learned of the Shi'a. The Institution of the Marja' Taqlid*, Oxford: Oxford University Press, 2001.

Mottahedeh, Roy P., "Shi'ite Political Thought and the Destiny of the Iranian Revolution", in Jamal S. al-Suwaidi (ed.), *Iran and the Gulf. A Search for Stability*, Abu Dhabi: The Emirates Center for Strategic Studies and Research, 1996.

Nadjmabadi, Shahnaz R., "Travellers between 'The World' and 'The Desert': Labour Migration from Iran to the Arab Countries of the Persian Gulf", unpublished paper presented at the Bellagio Conference on Transnational Migration in the Gulf, June 2005.

al-Najjar, Ghanem, *Introduction to the Political Development of Kuwait* (in Arabic), Kuwait: Qurtas, 2000 (first edition in 1985).

Nakash, Yitzhak, *Reaching for Power. The Shi'a in the Modern Arab World*, Princeton, New Jersey: Princeton University Press, 2006.

—— *The Shi'is of Iraq*, Princeton, New Jersey: Princeton University Press, 2003 (second paperback edition, first hardcover edition in 1994).

Nakhleh, Mohammed 'Urabi, *The Political History of al-Hasa (1818-1913)* (in Arabic), Kuwait: Dhat al-Salasil, 1980.

Nasr, Vali, *The Shia Revival. How Conflicts within Islam Will Shape the Future*, New York: Norton, 2006.

Newman, Andrew J., "The Nature of the Akhbari-Usuli Conflict in Late Safawid Iran, Part 1: 'Abdallah al-Samahiji's '*Munyat al-Mumarisin*'", *Bulletin of the School of Oriental and African Studies*, vol. 55, n° 1, 1992.

—— "The Nature of the Akhbari-Usuli Conflict in Late Safawid Iran, Part 2: The Conflict Reassessed", *Bulletin of the School of Oriental and African Studies*, vol. 55, n° 2, 1992.

Niethammer, Katja, *Voices in Parliament, Debates in Majalis, and Banners on the Streets. Avenues of Political Participation in Bahrain*, EUI Working Papers RSCAS n° 2006/27, The European University Institute, Robert Schuman Centre for Advanced Studies, Mediterranean Programme Series, Florence, 2006 (www.iue.it/RSCAS/WP-Texts/06_27.pdf).

Okruhlik, Gwenn, "Networks of Dissent: Islamism and Reform in Saudi Arabia", *Social Sciences Research Council*, www.ssrc.org/sept11/essays/okruhlik.htm, p. 3 (published in *Current History*, vol. 100, n° 651, January 2002).

Onley, James, "Transnational Merchants in the Nineteenth Century Gulf. The Case of the Safar Family", in Madawi al-Rasheed (ed.), *Transnational Connections and the Arab Gulf*, London: Routledge, 2005.

Peters, Ralph, "Blood Borders. How a Better Middle East Would Look", *Armed Forces Journal*, June 2006 (www.armedforcesjournal.com/2006/06/1833899).

Peterson, J. E., "Oman's Diverse Society: Northern Oman", *The Middle East Journal*, vol. 58, n° 1, winter 2004.

—— "Bahrain: The 1994-1999 Uprising", *Arabian Peninsula Background Note*, n° APBN-002, published on www.JEPeterson.net, January 2004.

—— "Bahrain's First Steps towards Reform under Amir Hamad", *Asian Affairs*, vol. 33, n° 2, June 2002.

Piscatori, James P., *Islam in a World of Nation-States*, Cambridge: Cambridge University Press, 1986.

Popovic, Alexandre, *La révolte des esclaves en Iraq au IIIème/IXème siècle*, Paris: Geuthner, 1976 (translated into English by Léon King, *The Revolt of the African Slaves in Iraq in the 3rd/9th Century*, Princeton, New Jersey: Markus Wiener Publishers, 1999).

Rajaee, Farhang, *Islamic Values and Worldview. Khomeini on Man, the State and International Politics*, Lanham: University Press of America, 1983.

Ramazani, R. K., "Iran's Foreign Policy: Both North and South", *The Middle East Journal*, vol. 46, n° 3, Summer 1992.

—— "Shi'ism in the Persian Gulf", in Juan R. I. Cole and Nikki R. Keddie (eds), *Shi'ism and Social Protest*, New Haven: Yale University Press, 1986.

Ranstorp, Magnus, *Hizb'allah in Lebanon. The Politics of the Western Hostage Crisis*, London: MacMillan, 1997.

al-Rasheed, Madawi (ed.), *Transnational Connections and the Arab Gulf*, London: Routledge, 2005.

——*A History of Saudi Arabia*, Cambridge, Cambridge University Press, 2002.

—— "The Shi'a of Saudi Arabia: A Minority in Search of Cultural Authenticity", *British Journal of Middle Eastern Studies*, vol. 25, n° 1, May 1998.

——"God, the King and the Nation: Political Rhetoric in Saudi Arabia in the 1990s", *The Middle East Journal*, vol. 50, n° 3, Summer 1996.

—— "Saudi Arabia's Islamist Opposition", *Current History*, vol. 95, n° 597, 1996.

al-Rashid, Khaled, "Political, Economic and Demographic Aspects and Roots. The Road to Separatism in the Arab Kingdom of Saudi Arabia" (in Arabic), *Saudi Affairs*, n° 18, July 2004.

Ra'uf, 'Adel, *Iraq without Leadership. Lecture of the Crisis of the Shia Religious Leadership in Iraq* (in Arabic), Damascus: Al-Markaz al-'Iraqi li al-I'lam wa al-Dirasat, 2003.

—— *Islamic Action in Iraq. Between Marja'iyya and Parties. A Review over Half a Century (1950-2000)* (in Arabic), Damascus: Iraqi Centre for Information and Research, 2000.

—— *Mohammed Mohammed Sadiq al-Sadr, the Popular Marja'. His Project of Change and Facts about his Assassination*, (in Arabic) Damascus: Al-Markaz al-'Iraqi li al-I'lam wa al-Dirasat, 1999.

Richard, Yann, "Contemporary Shi'i Thought", in Nikki R. Keddie, *Modern Iran. Roots and Results of Revolution*, New Haven, Connecticut: Yale University Press, updated edition 2006 (first edition 2003).

Rosenthal, Franz, "The Stranger in Medieval Islam", in *Arabica*, vol. 44, n° 1, 1997.

Roy, Olivier, *Globalized Islam. The Search for a New Ummah*, London: Hurst/ New York: Columbia University Press, 2004.

—— "The Crisis of Religious Legitimacy in Iran", *The Middle East Journal*, vol. 53, n° 2, spring 1999.

Rubin, Michael, *Into the Shadows. Radical Vigilantes in Khatami's Iran*, The Washington Institute for Near East Policy, 2001.

Rugh, William, "Emergence of a New Middle Class in Saudi Arabia", *Middle East Journal*, vol. 27, n° 1, 1973.

al-Ruhaimi, Abdul-Halim, "The Da'wa Islamic Party: Origins, Actors and Ideology", in Faleh Abdul-Jabar (ed.), *Ayatollahs, Sufis and Ideologues. State, Religion and Social Movements in Iraq*, London: Saqi Books, 2002.

Rumaihi, Mohammed Ghanem, *Bahrain. Social and Political Change since the First World War*, London: Bowker, 1976.

Sa'ada, Yousef Ja'far, *The Political Force in the Hasa Fortress and its Role in the Events of the Gulf* (in Arabic), Kuwait: Matabi' al-Majmu'a al-Duwaliyya, 1997.

al-Saba', Wissam, *The Story of Political Islam in Bahrain* (in Arabic), in *al-Watan* (Bahrain) 2005-2006 (series of articles).

al-Saffar, Hasan, *Nation and Nationality. Rights and Duties* (in Arabic), Beirut: Dar al-Safwa, 1996.

Sankari, Jamal, *Fadlallah. The Making of a Radical Shi'ite Leader*, London: Saqi Books, 2005.

Sajedi, Amir, "Iran's Relations with Kuwait", *Strategic Analysis*, vol. 16, n° 7, 1993.

Salameh, Ghassane, "Political Power and the Saudi State", *Merip Report*, n° 91, October 1980.

Salih, Kamal Osman, "The 1938 Kuwait Legislative Council", *Middle Eastern Studies*, vol. 28, n° 1, January 1992.

—— "Kuwait's Parliamentary Elections: 1963-1985: An Appraisal", *Journal of South Asian and Middle Eastern Studies*, vol. 16, n° 2, Winter 1992.

al-Salihi Al-Shahid al-Thalith, 'Abd al-Husein, "The al-Shirazi and the History of the Great *Marja'iyya*" (in Arabic), *Al-Naba'*, n° 69, ninth year, Dhu al-Qa'da 1423/January 2003.

Saudi National Security Assessment Project (SNSAP), *A Shia Crescent and the Shia Revival: Myths and Realities*, Riyadh, 27 September 2006, Phase A Iran Project, Nawaf Obaid managing director.

Schain, Yossi, *The Frontier of Loyalty. Political Exiles in the Age of the Nation-State*, Ann Arbor: The University of Michigan Press, 2005.

Seccombe, Ian J. and Richard. I. Lawless, *Work Camps and Company Towns: Settlement Patterns and the Gulf Oil Industry*, Durham: University of Durham, 1987.

—— "Foreign Worker Dependence in the Gulf, and the International Oil Compagnies: 1910-50", *International Migration Review*, vol. 20, n° 3,

Autumn 1986.

al-Shamlan, Saif Marzuq, *About the History of Kuwait* (in Arabic), Cairo: Matba' Nahdat Misr, 1959.

al-Shirazi, Mohammed, *How and Why Was I Expelled from Iraq?* (in Arabic), Beirut: Mu'assasat al-Mujtaba lil-Tahqiq wa al-Nashr, 2002/1422.

Simmel, Georg, *The Sociology of Georg Simmel*, translated, edited and with an introduction by Kurt H. Wolff, Glencoe, Illinois: The Free Press, 1950.

Smith, Anthony D., "The 'Golden Age' and National Renewal", in Geoffrey A. Hosking and George Schöpflin (eds), *Myths and Nationhood*, London: Hurst, 1997.

Smith, Simon C., *Kuwait, 1950-1965. Britain, the al-Sabah, and Oil*, Oxford: The British Academy/Oxford University Press, 1999.

Steinberg, Guido, "The Shiites in the Eastern Province of Saudi Arabia (al-Ahsa), 1913-1953", in Rainer Bruner and Werner Ende (eds), *The Twelver Shia in Modern Times. Religious Culture and Political History*, Köln: Brill, 2001.

Stewart, Devin, "The Genesis of the Akhbari Revival", in Michel Mazzaoui (ed), *Safavid Iran and Her Neighbors*, Salt Lake City: The University of Utah Press, 2003.

Tarrow, Sidney, *The New Transnational Activism*, Cambridge: Cambridge University Press, 2005.

—— and Doug McAdam, "Scale Shift in Transnational Contention", in Donatella della Porta and Sidney Tarrow (eds), *Transnational Protest and Global Activism*, Lanham: Rowman & Littlefield Publishers, 2005.

Taylor, Charles and Amy Gutmann, *Multiculturalism. The Politics of Recognition*, Princeton, New Jersey: Princeton University Press, 1994.

Teitelbaum, Joshua, *Holier than Thou. Saudi Arabia Islamic Opposition*, Washington Institute for Near East Policy, Washington: 2000.

—— "Saudi Arabia's Shi'i Opposition: Background and Analysis", The Washington Institute for Near East Policy, Policy Watch n° 225, 14 November 1996.

Tétreault, Mary Ann, *Stories of Democracy. Politics and Society in Contemporary Kuwait*, New York: University of Columbia Press, 2000.

Touraine, Alain, *Production de la société*, Paris: Biblio, 1993 (first edition Seuil 1973).

Tucker, Ernest S., *Nadir Shah's Quest for Legitimacy in Post-Safavid Iran*, Gainesville: University Press of Florida, 2006.

Valéri, Marc, *Les chiites d'Oman entre visibilité socioéconomique et quête de reconnaissance*, unpublished research paper, 2006.

Vassiliev, Alexei, *The History of Saudi Arabia*, London: Saqi Books, 2000.

Vertovec, Steven, "Fostering Cosmopolitanism: A Conceptual Survey and a Media Experiment in Berlin", Oxford: Economic and Social Research Council, Transnational Communities Programme, Working Paper WPTC-2K-06 (www.transcomm.ox.ac.uk).

Veyne, Paul, *Bread and Circuses. Historical Sociology and Political Pluralism*, Penguin Books, 1990 (translation from *Le pain et le cirque*, Paris: Seuil, 1976).

Vidal, F. S., *The Oasis of al-Hasa*, Dhahran: ARAMCO, 1955.

Vitalis, Robert, *America's Kingdom. Mythmaking on the Saudi Oil Frontier*, Stanford, California: Stanford University Press, 2007.

Walbridge, Linda S. (ed), *The Most Learned of the Shi'a. The Institution of the Marja' Taqlid*, Oxford: Oxford University Press, 2001.

—— "The Counterreformation. Becoming a *Marja'* in the Modern World", in Linda S. Walbridge (ed.), *The Most Learned of the Shi'a. The Institution of the Marja' al-Taqlid*, Oxford: Oxford University Press, 2001.

Walzer, Michael, *The Revolution of the Saints. A Study in the Origins of Radical Politics*, London: Weidenfield and Nicolson, 1965.

Weber, Max, *Economy and Society. An Outline of Interpretative Sociology*, edited by Guenther Roth and Claus Wittich, New York, Bedminster Press, 1968.

Wieviorka, Michel, *The Making of Terrorism* (translated by David Gordon White), Chicago: The University of Chicago Press, 1988.

Wiley, Joyce, N. *The Islamic Movement of Iraqi Shi'as*, Boulder, Colorado, Lynne Rienner Publishers, 1992.

Winckler, Onn, *Arab Political Demography. Volume 1: Population Growth and Natalist Policies*, Brighton: Portland, 2005.

Wright, Robin, *Sacred Rage. The Wrath of Militant Islam*, New York: Simon and Schuster, 1985.

Yamani, Mai, *Cradle of Islam: The Hijaz and the Quest for an Arabian Identity*, London: I. B. Tauris, 2004.

INDEX

11 September 2001, 31, 243, 245

'Abd al-'Aziz ibn Sa'ud, 22

'Abd al-Nasser, Jamal, nasserism, 2, 39, 43, 44

'Abd al-Samad, 'Adnan, 136-8, 204, 208, 217, 229, 251, 254, 282

'Abdallah (Crown Prince and King of Saudi Arabia), 231, 246-7, 250

'Abdallah II (King of Jordan), 4, 243-4

'Akri (al-), 'Abd al-Nabi, 11

'Akri (al-), Mohammed, 159

'Alawi (al-), 127-9, 133, 140, 142-3

'Alawi (al-), Ja'far, 129, 160, 214-5

'Alawi (al-), Kadhem, 128-9

'Alawi (al-), Mahmud, 127-8

'Alawi (al-), Mohammed, 128-9, 133, 160, 186

'Alawi (al-), Musa, 143

'Alawi, 'Alawiyyin, 196-7

'Ali (al-), Jamil, 160

'Arafat, Yasir, 182

'Aref, 'Abd al-Rahman, 86

'Aref, 'Abd al-Salam, 86

'Asfur (al-), 104, 133

'Ashur, Saleh, 120-1, 123, 125, 217, 229, 251, 254

'Ashura, 6, 23, 25, 38, 94, 96, 128, 143, 148, 160-3, 166, 207-8, 212, 215-6, 251, 273

'Awda (al-), Salman, 230, 247

Abadan, 181

Abu Dhabi, 119

Afsharid, 71

Ahmadinejad, Mahmud, 212, 245

Ahsa'i (al-), Ahmed, 17, 49

Ahvaz, 189

Akhbari, Akhbarism, 18-20, 70, 104, 110-1

Akraf (al-), Husein, 208

Albright, Madeleine, 256

Amal, 175, 205, 281

Amal Islamiyya, 175

American, United States, 31-2, 34, 40-1, 43, 61, 124, 163, 173, 175, 181, 183-4, 194, 196, 204, 211, 230, 235, 243, 245-6, 261-2, 266-7, 277-8, 299, 301

Ancient Bahrain, 12-6, 23-4, 26-32, 46, 241

Ansari (al-), Ibrahim, 205, 207, 210

Ansari, Murtadha, 76-7, 79-80, 90, 152

Anwar (al-), 271-2

Arab nationalism, Arab nationalist, 38-9, 55, 60, 63-4, 67, 82, 86, 101, 105, 107, 127, 134-5, 169, 239, 276, 282

ARAMCO (Arabian American Oil Company), 40-4, 162-3, 249

Asefi (al-), Mohammed Mahdi, 115-8, 200, 206

Asir, 22

316